GLIMPSES OF OLD BOMBAY AND WESTERN INDIA

GLIMPSES OF OLD BOMBAY AND WESTERN INDIA

JAMES DOUGLAS, J. P.

GYAN

Published by

Gyan Publishing House
5, Ansari Road
Daryaganj, New Delhi-110002
Phone: 011-47034999, 9811692060
E-mail: books@gyanbooks.com

Distribution Network
gyanbooks.com
India, USA, Canada, UK, Australia, France

ISBN: 978-81-212-8708-1 (PB)
First Published, 1900

2nd Impression 2023

Printed at: Gyan Press, Delhi.

GLIMPSES OF OLD BOMBAY AND WESTERN INDIA
Author: James Douglas

GLIMPSES OF OLD BOMBAY

AND

WESTERN INDIA.

GLIMPSES OF OLD BOMBAY AND WESTERN INDIA

WITH OTHER PAPERS

BY

JAMES DOUGLAS, J.P.

FELLOW OF THE UNIVERSITY, AND LATE SHERIFF OF BOMBAY

URBS PRIMA IN INDIS

LONDON

SAMPSON LOW, MARSTON AND COMPANY

LIMITED

St. Dunstan's House

FETTER LANE, FLEET STREET, E.C.

1900

Dedicated,

BY PERMISSION,

TO

THE RIGHT HONOURABLE THE EARL

AND

THE COUNTESS OF ELGIN.

PREFACE.

By the kindness of the proprietors of the *Calcutta Review*, *Pioneer*, *Times of India*, and the *Bombay Gazette*, the papers of which this volume consists are now published, after revision, in a collected form. They are mostly on Bombay and Western India, as were the two volumes under that title published in 1893. Humanly speaking, this is the last stone I shall heave on to the cairn of Old Bombay. Now that all the parts of the contribution are brought together, they appear to me to form a crude and heterogeneous mass, whilst their defects are accentuated. But the labour of research and preparation has been one of love, a delightful pastime for many years in the intervals of a busy life; and my hope is that the investigations I have made will encourage a young and rising generation to follow up this attractive study, while the minds of others may be refreshed by stories of the olden time.

To the many friends (and their name is legion) who have assisted me in various ways I tender my warmest thanks.

To the native and the European, but chiefly to the latter, Bombay is a city of temporary habitation. Men and women come here and go away, and the place that knew them knows them no more. There is little of the continuity of tradition from father to son. Take the plague, for example. No one by tradition knows anything about it—contrasting with the knowledge upon the subject in Venice, or Genoa, or in Edinburgh.

With such a fluctuating population, here to-day, there to-morrow, there is little pride of place. The removal of ancient landmarks and monuments cannot always be avoided; yet there are doubtless many things that we inherit from past ages which ought to be sacredly guarded, but are often thoughtlessly destroyed. It is not the plague only which drives the tourist away from Bombay—it is also the want of objects of interest, and the difficulty of seeing such as exist. You will now seek in vain, for example, for the bungalow, "Surrey Cottage," which was the home of Arthur Wellesley when he resided in Bombay. Where is the room (and it probably exists) in which Jonathan Duncan died? Child's grave was here, but it is as unknown as is General Aungier's at Surat. Jacquemont's tomb is now a cenotaph, for his bones were given many years ago to the French nation. The Yoni, or Stone of Regeneration, through which Sivaji wormed himself, has disappeared. He will be very clever who could make out the site of "Belvedere," Eliza Draper's abode at Mazagon. For the disappearance or demolition of every one of these objects of interest there are, no doubt, most just and sufficient reasons.

Everybody knows that Government House at Parell is now a plague hospital. The Cooperage is doomed, and it seems but yesterday that the children of the Duke and Duchess of Connaught were gambolling on its greensward. The birth-place of Kipling, and that of Farrar, Dean of Canterbury, are levelled with the earth. The old Court House, which resounded with the eloquence of Mackintosh, is the dining-room of a hotel. The Oriental Bank, whose financial voice was once as lusty as that of the East India Company, is now a boot and shoe shop. I am sure if Dr. Wilson were to revisit us he would have great difficulty in recognising his old bungalow, "The Cliff." Parell has one memorable room, that in which the Prince of Wales slept, on the wall of which, by loving command of the Queen, was hung, during his sojourn here, a portrait of the Princess of Wales. There need be no difficulty in identifying it. These instances are illustrations of the changes going on in Bombay, and show how much need we have of the written record, and the necessity also of keeping a sharp outlook upon such relics as we possess.

To add to our objects of interest has been my aim, and I have repeatedly called the attention of the powers that be to the duty of their preservation, and a movement in that direction was never more needed than at present. Already the ploughshare of the Improvement Trust is driving deeply through the material framework of Bombay, and the men who have put their hand to the plough will not look back, for the genius of Sanitary Reform is inexorable, and brooks neither delay nor obstruction. A Burns' Cottage at Alloway Kirk, or even a Holy House of Loretto, is not of much consequence when men are dying by thousands. You must clear the ground for the living, and let the dead look after themselves.

I suppose ELEPHANTA and KANHERI are Bombay acquisitions. They are first-class antiquities, for they were constructed before Columbus discovered America. They are not now in danger, and may safely be left to the caretaker, though it was once proposed that the former should be converted into a ball-room and drinking-shop.

We have still the CATHEDRAL. Its preservation to our time is merely the result of an accident; for, had it not been built within the walls, it would inevitably have gone by the board, like the first Roman Catholic Cathedral and the first Temple of Mombadevi. Let no new edifice ever supplant the venerable building, which is hallowed by time and sacred associations.

BOMBAY CASTLE requires to be popularised; but you need not give up its secrets to the Russians. To the public purview it maintains a feeble existence. Ask a European or native resident. He knows it not—has never seen it; and probably not one in a thousand who passes through the city has even heard of it, or knows of its existence, except that the name appears in the heading of the Government *Gazette*. Something ought to be done to make the Hall of Audience (where so many early Governors were conspicuous) an object of attraction to the passing traveller, as well as to our citizens, native and European.

Stone and lime, however, are not everything. There are some men whose reputations are impervious to the touch of time, and do not need monuments to commemorate the deeds that have made them worthy of the memory of mankind. They rest on an imperishable basis. The "three mighty men," for example, who made Western India a kind of soldiers' playground in their youth, until Divine Providence transferred them to a more exalted arena, in which they changed the destinies of the world, need neither brick nor mortar to keep their memory green—

> "No sculptur'd marble here, nor pompous lay."

We need scarcely say that Bombay holds the record of their earliest years as one of her most cherished possessions. That record is engraven with a pen of iron in the Book of History, and can never be disturbed. The names of CLIVE and NELSON and WELLINGTON are emblazoned on Bombay's shield of arms for evermore.

Equally imperishable are the beauties with which Nature herself has bestowed upon the place of our habitation. The cincture of her embattled walls is gone; but a new City of Palaces has taken its place, and the sea, the sky, and the everlasting hills will be a joy and a rejoicing to many generations yet unborn.

J. D.

BOMBAY, *September 28th*, 1899.

CONTENTS.

III.

ROADS BY SEA AND LAND.

IV.

CLUBS.

V.

BIOGRAPHICAL.

VI.

HISTORICAL.

GLIMPSES OF OLD BOMBAY

AND

WESTERN INDIA.

I.

SOCIAL.

(1.) BOMBAY DOMESTIC ANNALS, A.D. 1800–1810.

Three important events—Extent of Bombay at the beginning of the century —Spasmodic charity—Noted friendships formed in Bombay—Public spirit—The Bombay Fencibles—Merchants—Amusements—Storm of November, 1799—Crimes and offences—Mackintosh's address to a Grand Jury—Obituary.

"FOR a century and a half Bombay has been of little importance to the Company. Till very lately did the establishment and all its interests appear with those in other parts of the Company's territories, and a settlement on the coast of Africa could scarcely have been a subject of less consideration."

This was written in 1825. In 1780 Sion and Sewree were our two frontier posts of dominion in Western India. The three great events which made Bombay what it is, are the Treaty of Bassein, the Annexation of the Dekhan, and the opening of the Suez Canal. The first destroyed the Mahratta confederacy, the second gave us the Bombay Presidency nearly as it exists, and the third made Bombay the gateway of India. When night closed in, on December 31st, 1802, on the tents of Sir Barry Close at Soopara, as the last rays of the setting sun gilded the pinnacles of the Bassein Cathedral and a cold mist swept up the Creek, enveloping everything in its ample folds, I dare say he scarcely realised what he had done on that fatiguing day of betel-nut, pan-supari and rose-water. The Treaty of Bassein was the thin end of the wedge, which split asunder an immense fabric of misgovernment and imposture.

Here is a list of our proud possessions in 1799, taken from Government notice and emanating from Bombay Castle:—"L. Cockran to be Judge and Magistrate of the Islands of Salsette, Caranja, Hog and Elephanta, with revenue jurisdiction over the Island of Bombay and its ancient dependencies of Colaba, Old Woman's, Cross and Butcher's Island."

To-day this reads like a caricature. Think of Cross Islet with its gibbet, and Butcher's Island with its Lazaretto, furnishing a revenue to the Government of Bombay! Judge and Magistrate of Elephanta seems strange in these latter days. However, this notification shows the small kernel out of which grew the tree which now overshadows the Konkan plain, the Dekhan plateau, and some of the rich province of Guzerat.

One has only to look at the English journals which devoted themselves to Asia in the early part of the century to see how small a space, compared with Bengal, or even with Madras, Bombay occupied. Take the year 1810 for example; the promotions in the Civil, Military and Naval Departments for Bengal and Madras occupy nine and twelve closely-printed columns respectively of an octavo Report. Bombay is satisfied with one! Madras was then *urbs prima*. The "obscure corner," so described in Mackintosh's Diary, was no figure of speech It was an understood thing. A record of 1805 tells us that Bombay "could muster only three old musty chariots, Mr. Collet's equipages, and half a dozen Parsee buggies." You may fancy, then, Bombay, in the first decade, a place of 150,000 inhabitants, with a few English residents, some of whom were very rich, for Bombay was then strong in the resources of money. On October 7th, 1810, I find the following:—"At a meeting of the Bobbery Hunt on Sunday last" (you see, the better the day, the better the deed) "the subscription for the orphan children of that most respected and lamented officer, Major Carter, was introduced, when, with a liberality that reflects the highest honour on the members of that society, and which is, indeed, above all praise, upwards of Rs. 10,000 were contributed."

In 1802, when a sailor-boy had his leg taken off by a shark in the harbour, £280 was immediately raised for his behoof. Such things could not happen here in 1892. Spasmodic outbursts of charity arrest attention, but it is well to remember, if we can trust the lists made up in the present year, that not one of our charitable or philanthropic institutions existed in those days; so, when a case of clamant misery came before the Nabobs, there was more chance of turning on the tap of special beneficence than in our so-called degenerate days, when the good deeds of a few individuals have expanded into the benevolence of many. Charity nowadays filters in many unseen channels, and does not need Bobbery Hunts or the jaws of a shark to quicken its pulsations. This leads us to speak of friendship—not the colourless thing we sometimes hear of, but such fast friendship as stands men in good stead and lasts for life; the friendship, for example, of Wellington and Malcolm, made up in India about this time, or of Mountstuart Elphinstone and the Stracheys, also of this date; and of an earlier period, of John Hunter and James Forbes of the *Oriental Memoirs*. I dare say the reader recollects their introduction (1766), when, on Forbes (*ætat.* 17) entering the dining-room in Bombay, Hunter, leaving his midday meal, took the bashful youth by the hand and (wonderful expression) "did not let it go for forty years." Forbes is very minute as to the details of this visit. It made a deep impression on him; and well it might, for to Hunter he owed his post at Broach, where he made most of his money. He tells of his host becoming Chairman of the East India Company and buying an estate in Hertfordshire, but gives no other clue to his name. We have often wondered who he was. The following note, however, for the modern reader, solves the mystery.

"December 6th, 1802.—Died at Bath, John Hunter. He made a princely fortune in Bombay. Became Director of E. I. Co., purchased estate of Gubbins in Hertfordshire, devoted to agriculture, and received a gold medal from the Horticultural Society for his plantation of oaks. Age between eighty and ninety."

It is impossible to deny the public spirit of the men of Bombay at this period. A subscription, for example, was opened for the Patriotic Fund, which Jonathan Duncan headed with Rs. 25,000 and General Stewart with Rs. 35,000; and £35,000 sterling was at once sent home to assist in carrying on the war. As Napoleon was in Egypt, and the fear and dread of him on all men (Arthur Wellesley excepted), something here may be set down to the motive of self-preservation. It was public spirit, all the same. Two of the most costly monuments in Bombay belong to this period, those of the Marquis Wellesley and Lord Cornwallis. Neither of these two men, I suppose, was ever in Bombay. It gave a substantial contribution to the statue of William Pitt in London; and the battered hulk of the *St. Fiorenzo* was no sooner signalled from Malabar Point than a subscription was opened to commemorate, by a monument in the church, the heroic death of Hardinge, who fell in the moment of victory. The subscription amounted to £2,000 to commemorate an action off Cape Comorin, a thousand miles away. The first statue ever erected to Robert Burns owes its existence to the same noble spirit.* The movement for the Pitt and Burns statues is destitute of every atom of human selfishness or local pride. But everything at this period, in these parts, was done on a magnificent scale. The gold vase presented to Arthur Wellesley by the officers in the army of the Dekhan cost 2,000 guineas.

However, at this critical time men were willing to act as well as to pay. No laggard or half-hearted feeling animated the volunteers of these days. The Bombay Fencibles were commanded by the Governor himself, and in March, 1799, a vast concourse assembled to see the presentation of colours and listen to the speech of Mrs. Rivett which accompanied it—given with all that lady's "accustomed gracefulness and ease." Mrs. Rivett was a lady of great beauty. Including the Mahim Division of the Portuguese Militia, there must have been 1,000 volunteers in Bombay.

The Bombay merchants, though few in number—I mean, of course, the English merchants—were, as I have said before, mostly

* It is in the Edinburgh National Gallery.

very rich, and no wonder. It was their good fortune to be in the place before it was exploited. Their trade was not only large for the time (indeed for any time), but very lucrative. I call an export *ad valorem* of ten millions sterling of our money in two and a half years, from 1806 to 1808, to China alone, a big trade; and I say that it was a rich trade when I see that their merchants admitted to Sir Edward Pellew, in 1806, that his convoy to China had saved the Bombay underwriters £316,000! What a chance for an Income-tax Commissioner! I say, moreover, that they were an enterprising body of men, when I see that, in spite of great disasters (eleven of their ships were lost in eighteen months on its shores), they continued to prosecute a large trade with the Red Sea. Exchange was 2*s.* 6*d.*, or eight rupees to the pound sterling, and that they were cautious, I gather from Mr. Remington's expression about mines. "Mines," he says, "into which gold and silver are being thrown, instead of being dug out."

And they had their amusements. The Bombay Theatre, on the margin of the Green (not far from the *Times of India* office, 1892), dated from 1770 and was the oldest in India, so we are told. The players were amateurs, and the purpose was charity as well as amusement. Gaiety culminated in 1804, with Arthur Wellesley, after his splendid victories. General Bellasis gave a dinner to him in the Theatre, and Colonel Lechmere and the officers of the Fencibles a magnificent fête in the same place. Dinner at seven. Illuminations all over the Green, far and wide. The Governor gave a grand ball at Parell, when that sheet of water, to which succeeding generations of wearied dancers have repaired to recruit their exhausted energies, became a fairy scene of gorgeous fireworks, which blazed away, far into the night and early morning, over the faces of fair women and brave men. The Duke, though a man of few words, was not callous to these ovations. It was the first blast of that mighty trumpet of praise which, in successive bursts, was to sound over him for the next fifty years. "The approbation of this Settlement is a distinction which will afford a permanent source of gratification to my mind, and I receive with a high sense of respect the honour conveyed to me by your address." And much more to the same effect.

Here is an amusement that has not been seen in our day in Bombay. The date is January, 1800, when a great number of gentlemen and some ladies attended on a Saturday at the Riding School, to witness the baiting of a horse, a wild boar, and some buffaloes by a leopard. The first object of attack was a dummy man, which leopardus tore to pieces in a twinkling. He then essayed the wild hog, for which he soon showed a Muslim aversion, and "backed," with his tail between his legs, which did not suit the spectators, who goaded him into fury by squibs and crackers until the brute, becoming exasperated by its tormentors, suddenly, by one tremendous leap, alighted on the edge of a high bamboo palisade which divided the spectators from the arena. You may well believe that, as he hung in mid-air, there was a great consternation. The account says that "each waived all ceremony in the order of his going, to establish his own right of precedence." The riding-master, who happened to have a loaded pistol in his hand, was equal to the occasion, and shot the leopard dead on his perch, his body falling with a thud into the enclosure, while the crowd flew helter-skelter.

The staple of amusement in these days was, no doubt, balls, dinners, reviews, and launches. The driving of the silver nail when the keel was laid down was always a big day. When, on May 4th, a ship of 1,250 tons, the *Bombay*, was launched, and christened, by Sir Edward Pellew, with a bottle of good English porter, the affair drew the principal people of the Settlement. But some more expensive liquor, was, no doubt, used at the launch, in 1810, of the *Minden*, of seventy-four guns. That was an event of which Bombay was very proud, according to the *Chronicle*: "Bombay has the singular credit of being the first place out of the British dominions at which a British seventy-four was ever built." The Duncan Dock was completed on June 23rd, 1810; and it is a singular fact that the *Minden's* keel was laid down while the dock was being constructed, the two works going on simultaneously.

Then as to reviews. On June 4th, 1801, the old King's birthday, still sacred at Eton, the 74th Regiment marched past the Governor, their war-worn colours, which they had carried for fourteen years in Asia, on many a battle-field, waving in the breeze.

The night of November 4th, 1799, was one long remembered. A storm blew with terrific violence, and, when day broke, a spectacle of appalling ruin was revealed. The shore from the bunder-head to Mazagon, far as the eye could reach, was piled with wrecks. Under Hornby's Battery, round the Castle sea face, as far as Fort George, were great heaps so completely dashed to splinters that not a trace could be discovered of any individual ship. The *Resolution*, ship of war, went to pieces under the Castle walls, and more than 100 craft and 500 lives were lost.

In 1802 a young man of the name of Maw arrived by the *Scalesby Castle*, and immediately raised an action against Learmonth, the commander, for the hard treatment he had experienced during "Neptune's rites" on crossing the Line, having been soused, and shaved with dirty water, and otherwise tumbled about by the officers and sailors. The captain was fined Rs. 400. Fines like this soon put an end to the custom.

On August 12th, 1799, Government ordered that no European should travel without a passport. But, with or without a pass, four officers, in 1800, crossed over the harbour to Panwell, and proceeded to Chowk, twelve miles. Here a surprise met them. At a turn of the road they beheld six headless men suspended by the legs from a tree—dacoits, suspected of waylaying treasure from Poona. The Peishwa's amuldar had settled the matter by cutting off their heads! Without mentioning Matheran, they note that it was "a beautiful country of hill and dale."

Another adventurous individual made his way, the same year, to "Carachee." There he found a population of 10,000, mostly in mud huts, and a fort garrisoned by twenty men, "conspicuous by their poverty and insolence." Think of this, ye Sindians, driving to-day to Clifton, and of the other fact, illustrative of the insecurity of life and property in these dry and sandy regions, "even the shepherd tending his flock is accoutred with his gun, scimitar, shield and dirk."

On January 1st, 1800, Colonel Dow obtained leave to proceed to Europe "overland," which meant in those days *via* Bagdad, as Colonel Hartley had done in 1781, taking a year to make the journey.

We now come to crimes and offences. I confess to a shudder as I read the following:—

Bombay, April 23rd, 1799.

"This day, Ismail Shaikh, Borah, was convicted of stealing different articles of property of James Morley, Esq., part of which was found in the prisoner's possession. Guilty. Death. On May 9th he was executed, pursuant to the sentence." He had been engaged in another robbery; but forty shillings constituted a capital offence. Short shrift in those days was given to the condemned.

On May 10th, 1804, Mulharow was sentenced to be executed on the 14th instant, and hung in chains.

On May 11th, 1804, Heerjevan was sentenced to a like punishment.

On no site could the gruesome spectacle be so widely and conspicuously exhibited as on Cross Island.

The pillory and whipping were much in vogue.

October 15th, 1804, James Pennico, three months' imprisonment for theft, and to be whipped once from the Apollo to the Bazaar Gate.

1804.—A woman imprisoned for five years for perjury, during which period she is to stand once every year, on the 1st day of the October Sessions, in the pillory, to be placed in front of the Court House, with labels on her breast and back explanatory of her crime.

1806.—A man who stole a watch was sentenced to two years' work in the Bombay Docks; and another to stand in the pillory before his own shop in the bazaar.

In 1806 a profound sensation was created by a rumour that an attempt, which was frustrated, had been made to murder Sir James Mackintosh. It was quite true. Two young lieutenants, who were prisoners, came into court with apparently a writing desk, ostensibly for the purpose of holding papers which they might wish to use in court. The box was taken from them and found to contain four pistols loaded with slugs. There seems to have been little doubt that they came into court with intent to kill Mackintosh and afterwards commit suicide. It must have been an event in one's life to hear Mackintosh rise to "the height of his great argument." "If that murderous project had been executed, I would have been the first British Magistrate who ever stained with his blood the bench on which he sat to administer justice. When I accepted the office of Minister of Justice, I knew that I ought to despise unpopularity and slander—and even death itself. Thank God, I do despise them." The young men were sentenced to twelve months in Bombay gaol. All this exhibits the prevailing feeling *at the time*, and we now see that all parties were under unnecessary alarm, for a letter exists, written by Mackintosh to Cauty, one of the prisoners, many years after, when he was high up in the army, exculpating him from an attempt to assassinate him. The letter is dated November 6th, 1824.

Next in importance was the trial of the conspirators to murder George Cumming Osborne, of the Treasury, in the year 1810. He had been Private Secretary to the Governor and afterwards Secretary in the Foreign and Political Department. Three native servants of the Treasury—rich men—were placed in the dock and sentenced to five years' imprisonment, to be annually exposed in the pillory, to be twice whipped in the bazaar, and each to pay Rs. 10,000, and to be further imprisoned until the said fine was paid. This is a typical case of what occurs when law and justice begin to force their way upon a reluctant people. A solitary Englishman of position was found foolish enough to compromise the English name, for Charles Joseph Briscoe, Esq., was found guilty of accepting a bribe to prevent the trial of these wretches, and, after a trial of three days, was sentenced to twelve months' imprisonment in Bombay gaol. The case, so complicated, gave Mackintosh a great deal of trouble, and he had no one to consult. Briscoe was high in the employment of Government—in what position I know not—was an officer of the Bombay Volunteers—was made an Alderman in 1803, an office which carried magisterial powers; and it is a significant fact that the clerk and the cash-keeper of the police were tried for the same offence. The Grand Jury paid a high compliment to the Recorder for his ability in unravelling the widespread ramifications of the conspiracy, and the powerful enginery which had been set in motion to prevent the trial and defeat the ends of justice.

On May 4th, 1801, the news that Mitchell had been killed by Bellasis in a duel came upon Bombay like a thunderclap. Arthur Forbes Mitchell was a young man of great promise, and only twenty-two years of age. When nineteen, he was in Malabar, in a post of much responsibility, which he managed with credit to himself and signal benefit to his employers, and at the time of his death was a member of the Civil Service and a partner of Forbes & Co., and his death was greatly deplored. Bellasis was a lieutenant, and was tried by a jury of naval men—chiefly captains and others. Tried and convicted of manslaughter, George Bridges Bellasis was sentenced to be transported to Eastern Australia for a period of fourteen years. He received the medal for Seringapatam in 1799.—(*Dict. Nat. Biog.*) His *second*, Captain Charles Byne, was sentenced for seven years. Bellasis received a free pardon on June 4th, 1802—the King's birthday—at Sydney, when he and Mrs. Bellasis (she was a Miss King, one of seven sisters renowned for their beauty) returned immediately to India. He rose to the chief command of Artillery in the Peishwa's dominions.

Of vulgar robberies and attacks on the person, there was a plentiful crop in this decade. George Osborne, coming home from dinner, was attacked by twelve men, and he owed his safety to his personal courage. The Surat mail was robbed on the Parell Road by a gang of men. As Captain Henderson was returning from dinner in his palanquin, with six bearers, and a mussaul carrying a light, two privates stopped him and presented a bayonet to his breast. They searched him and found he had no money, and left him with, "D—n the old fellow, as he has no money, it's not worth while taking his life!" One of them was caught and transported for life. Another gentleman was stopped in his carriage by a number of persons with long poles and swords. He aimed a blow at one of them, shouted to his coachman to "drive on," and so escaped. On October 14th, 1798, a stranger, happening to be in the Colaba Light House, observed that a peaceable dinghy was being attacked off the harbour by five Mahratta gallivats throwing in shot, burning her to the water edge, when she blew up, leaving her crew the choice of the flames or a watery grave.

Such were the occasional scenes in these days. During the most of this decade Mackintosh was Recorder, which was Chief Justice and Judge rolled into one. In 1807, the Company's counsel and Counsel for the Crown were altered to the new style of "Advocate-General." Stewart Moncrieff Threipland in this decade carried all before him. He was, in Bombay, what, nearly about the same time, Robert Cutlar Fergusson, of Craigdarroch and Orroland, was in Calcutta.* But Threipland, with all his eloquence, was a mere hewer of wood and drawer of water compared with Mackintosh. The fashion of this world passeth away, and so has the fashion of these Advocates-General vanished, who were great, no doubt, in their time, convincing, and sometimes converting, both Judge and Jury. Strange to say, in these dim and misty records, where everything is antiquated, you will never read anything old-fashioned in Mackintosh. His eloquence is like gold, and does not become dim or tarnished by the lapse of time; and neither moth nor rust doth corrupt that imperishable armour of his which is ever burnished. It is all fresh as of yesterday. He concludes his address to the Grand Jury in August, 1803, with this peroration:—

"I am persuaded that your feelings entirely accord with mine, being convinced that, both as jurors and private gentlemen, you will always consider yourselves as interested, in this remote region of the earth, in the honour of that beloved country, which I trust becomes more dear to you, as I am sure it does to me, during every new moment of absence; that, in your intercourse with each other, as well as with the natives of India, you will keep unspotted the ancient character of the British nation, renowned in every age, and in no age more than in the present, for valour, for justice, for humanity and generosity; for every virtue that supports, as well as for every talent and accomplishment which adorns, human society."

Brave words these, spoken in "this remote region of the earth," as good and cogent now, when Peshawur, and not

---

* 1768–1838.—Twenty years in Calcutta. In 1799, in London, found guilty of riot and attempted rescue, and imprisoned for one year. In 1826 M.P. for Stewartry of Kirkcudbright.—*Dict. Nat. Biog.*

Tanna, is the outpost of British dominion, as good when Wellesley broke the Bonsla's ranks at Assaye, as when Roberts became Lord of Kandahar. Such is the prerogative of genius, that it overleaps the barriers of time and appropriates the homage of successive generations. Words like these, often spoken to a few merchants in the old dingy Court House of Bombay, burst the bonds of Apollo Street and become the property of civilisation. He found Bombay, as he says himself, "a desert"; but, all unconscious of the fact, he made it blossom as the rose. A silent revolution was going on in this decade, much of which was due, no doubt, to Mackintosh.

Some of the following obituary and other notices have more than a local interest :—

May, 1800.—Stephen Whitehill, senior Merchant.

1800.—Nana Farnavese, at Poona.

March, 1800.—Jeremiah Hawkins, drowned, while bathing, between Bombay and Coloba.

1800.—At Cuddalore, Andrew Kerr, "The old Commodore." Kept his coffin; used it as liquor and gram chest.

1st November, 1801.—Brigadier General Carnac dies at Mangalore, age 84. "The friend and associate of Clive."

"16th July, 1802.—At Bombay, James Carnac, formerly Member of Council. Buried with military honours. Long respected and beloved. All the principal gentlemen of the settlement attended his funeral."

1803.—During the famine, in the village at the top of the Ghauts (Khandala ?), 100 dead bodies were seen lying, some of them at the door of their own houses.

Colonel Joseph Boden, Quarter Master (founder of Boden Professorship), retires 1807.

11th February, 1808.—General Bellasis, in Bombay.

We observe that Daniel Draper, relict of Eliza, was alive in 1803, and that his address was St. James's Street, London.

Also note a birth announced in Vaux's tomb, near Surat. It is roomy enough to live in, but a birth in a tomb is unique, at all events in prose. In Scott's *Lady of the Lake* we have Brian—

"Bred
Between the living and the dead."

(2.) BOMBAY DOMESTIC ANNALS, 1810-1893.

Church and Kirk—Religious and philanthropic enterprise—Marriages, births and deaths—Bungalows—Malabar Hill—Mazagon residences—Corygaum—"The Fighting Doctor"—Education—Theatre and other amusements—Merchants—Exports, exchange, etc.—Globe-trotters—An East Indiaman—Press—Lawyers and High Court—William Erskine—Glimpses in 1823—Hormasjee Bomanjee—Pindarries and robbers—Gauls—Hill-stations—Colaba—Overland, and mails—Archæology—Asiatic So iety—The "upper ten"—Longevity.

ON June 19th, 1715, Cobbe preached a sermon in furtherance of building a church in Bombay, which fired the zeal of the community. After the sermon he waited on Governor Aislabie, and here is Dr. Cobbe's own account of the interview :—

"Well, Doctor, you have been very zealous for the church this morning."

"Please, your Honour, there was occasion enough for it, and I hope without offence."

"Well, then, if we must have a church, we will have a church. Do you see and get a book made, and see what everyone will contribute towards it, and I will give first."

The Governor subscribed Rs. 1,000, leaving a blank for the Company's subscription, which was afterwards filled in with Rs. 10,000. The church was erected and opened in 1718. Very little change was made in its internal economy, and the pews and seats remained unaltered for a hundred years. In 1818, exactly a century after the church had been opened for the first time, the pews were altered, and new chairs set down. Being entirely re-seated, the interior presented quite a different aspect, was much more comfortable for the worshippers, and more seemly for a house of God, inasmuch as some invidious distinctions between the well-to-do and common people had been abolished. On Christmas day, 1818, it was re-opened with considerable *éclat*, when Archdeacon Barnes preached a splendid sermon. It was announced that Divine service would be held at 10 A.M. and 4 P.M. every Sunday.

The Kirk.

St. Andrew's Scotch Kirk, near the Apollo Gate, was opened for public worship on April 25th, 1819. The Rev. James Clow preached a sermon, and his text, taken from Nehemiah, was—

"And we will not forsake the house of our God."

The Church as a body was in existence some years before this, and its beginning was in this wise. A small advertisement, in the most conspicuous part of the paper, appeared in the *Bombay Courier*:—

"Card.

"Divine Service, according to the forms of the Church of Scotland, will be performed next Lord's Day in the Mess Room of the King's Barracks at 10 A.M. Government House, November 15th, 1815.

"James Clow."

Mr. Clow, no doubt, was a guest of the Governor. Here, then, in the barracks, for two Sundays, Divine Service was holden. But the place was found too noisy and otherwise unsuitable. After this the church services were held in the Court House, where, on week-days, the Criminal Sessions took place, now (1893) the dining-room of the Great Western Hotel. There was to be no excuse for want of psalm books, for Baxter and Co. advertise that they had received a supply—

"In Metre:

Translated and diligently compared with

The Original Text.

More plain, smooth and agreeable to the text than any heretofore allowed by the authority of the General Assembly of the Kirk of Scotland, and appointed to be sung in congregations and families.

Printed by Authority."

Between 1815 and 1819 the congregation had not been idle, for I read that on February 4th, 1816, after Divine Service, the following gentlemen were ordained elders of the Scotch Church:—John Stewart, Hugh Stewart, John Taylor, M.D., and William Erskine. Erskine was Sir James Mackintosh's son-in-law; now, or shortly after, Master in Equity, and known in future years as the author of the *Life of Baber* and other works.

There had been great difficulties about a spire. The "powers that be" (Sir Evan Nepean, Governor, 1812 to 1819) objected to a spire. The matter had to go to the India House, and two years elapsed before authority was obtained to erect one. These were the days before the Queen worshipped in Crathie Kirk. At length the spire was finished. It was a great boon to the master-mariner, for it competed with the tall brab trees on the Castle bastion as a guide into Bombay harbour. The spire, like most Scotchmen in their early years, had a hard time of it, and in its upbuilding was a type of the progress of religious liberty, which, after getting many hard blows and knocks, still points the way to heaven. One night, in the year 1826, it was shivered to pieces by lightning, and so its troubles were not yet over. Its enemies, of course, said that its promoters were punished for their audacity. The promoters treated the matter as a secondary consideration, compared with previous obstructions. Like Ajax, they could defy the lightning, but they dared not defy the India House. The Kirk's motto is *nec tamen consumebatur*; so they built another spire, which remains to this day, unscathed by man or the violence of the elements.

Mr. Clow's portrait still hangs in the vestry. About thirty years ago the native servants were beginning to hold it in such veneration as to do pooja to it, a proceeding, of course, most abhorrent to the feelings of the then padre—Cook or Macpherson. A white sheet was hung over the portrait, which exorcised the evil spirit, and put an end to the worship of the dead.

I read that in 1852 an organ was in use in the Bombay Kirk.* The Calcutta Scotch Kirk had one so far back as 1818 —*Lux ex Oriente*, of which Scotland has tardily availed itself.

The apotheosis of Englishmen by natives of India is a curious subject. We all remember Nicolseyn and his saints. I am certain the natives will be doing pooja to Sir Albert

---

* April 10th, 1852, £500 raised for organ, which was in due course sent out from England.—*St. Andrew's Session Minutes.*

Sassoon's equestrian statue of the Prince of Wales in another generation. Look at that statue almost any time of the day you like, and you will see a group gazing at it. They are much exercised to understand why the Queen's statue is white (marble) and the Prince's black (bronze)!

I notice that Colonel Wallace's tomb at Siroor was, as early as 1818, decked with flowers. In 1840, when Nesbit was there, they were praying to his ghost, and the worship may still exist.

There is the very fine monument, in the Elphinstone Circle, to Cornwallis. Go when you will, you will see flowers placed on the open book, or garlands on the figures. This is not a new custom. In 1825 it was thought by the natives to be a place of religious worship, and they called it *Chota Dewal*. Government tried to stop this, and issued some vernacular notices that it was a mistake. But it was of no use, for when these feelings take possession of the natives they are not easily eradicated.

Religious and Philanthropic Enterprise.

The arrival of Dr. Duff and Dr. Wilson in the next decade —1820–30—gave an immense stimulus to missionary enterprise; but the spirit was not dead, nor did it even slumber in this period, as the ample pages in the magazines devoted to missionary effort testify. In 1815 a branch of the Bible Society was started in Bombay. That Society had been founded in London in the year in which Napoleon had appeared on the war-path, and, now that his empire had been shattered to pieces, broke ground beyond the extremest limit of his conquests. In the same year also appeared the Bombay Society for the Education of the Poor. These two Societies, in 1815, are the only representatives of more than 100 educational and benevolent institutions which now (1892) crowd fifty-eight pages of our *Bombay Directory*.

I have always understood that James Farish (Dr. Wilson was unwearied in his praises of him) was a man who, amid good and bad report, and in these troublous times of grim warfare, kept alive the spirit of religion, and, by a consistent life, vindicated its claims to the attention of mankind. His name has almost faded into oblivion; but it is worth remembering that, though he had acted as Governor, he did not disdain to keep a Sunday School in the Town Hall. He retired in 1841.

MARRIAGES.

As a rule, births, marriages, and deaths have been announced in this sequence. Occasionally "christenings" and "baptisms" are, in the period under notice, substituted for the first, and "interments" for the last; but these vagaries speedily disappear, and we do not meet with them much after 1818. One jungle-wallah takes exception to the priority of "births," and adds to his announcement of a son and heir the unequivocal word "legitimate." In 1822 an obituary notice closes with, "An amiable and beautiful young lady, aged twenty." And of a marriage it adds, "The bridegroom will come to £10,000 a year"; and of the bride, "A beautiful and accomplished lady." Anything *outré* seems to be put in to attract the *insouciant* reader. The following belongs to *fin de siècle*—the eighteenth century: "At Tranquebar, H. Meyer, Esq., aged sixty-four, to Miss Casina Couperas, a very accomplished young lady of sixteen, after a courtship of five years."

BIRTHS.

For nearly the first half of the nineteenth century the announcement of births was in this wise:—

"The *lady* of John Smith, Esq., of a son."

There was, however, a social boundary line, and below it all announcements were—

"The *wife* of John Smith, of a son,"

or Mrs. John Smith, of a son. One fine day however in "the fifties" the whole Anglo-Saxon world changed its mind on this subject. "Wife" drove out "lady," and ever since has been paramount in all birth notices. In this Presidency, about the first example of the change was on September 14th, 1840. "At Poona, the wife of the Rev. George Candy of twins—a son and a daughter." Henceforth the custom ran like wild fire. "Lady" was ousted by "wife," as the term "gentlemen" is now by "the men" of fashionable society. The "men" in our young days in the Highlands were the "unco guid."

Dr. Wilson, who was a model of correctness in everything he printed, thus announces his own marriage:—

"August 12th, 1828.—Comely Bank, Edinburgh: Rev. John Wilson, Missionary* to Bombay, to Margaret, daughter of the Rev. K. Bayne, Greenock."

DEATHS.

When the rich man died he had always a special paragraph to himself, *i.e.*, Nisbet of "Nisbet Lane" repute, and on August 14th, 1841, Dr. Milne is thus signalised. "One of the oldest and richest inhabitants of India; a misanthrope; wrote in the *Gazette* articles against missionaries and against Government." This came, no doubt, from the opposition paper.

BUNGALOWS.

To speak of the names of the Bombay bungalows of this period is like raising the dead. "Westfield," "Lowji Castle," "The Beehive," and "Apollo House" still assert their existence under the same names in the end of the nineteenth century, as they did at the beginning of it. "Belvidere," "Tarala," "Non Parell," "Randle Lodge," "Ridgway Cottage," "Huntly Lodge," "Somerville Lodge," "Prospect Lodge" have disappeared.† I imagine I have seen the "Hermitage," "Storm Hall" and "The Mount," which sheltered the Persian Ambassador. "The Retreat" I have seen on the map. But where were "Belmont," "Belleville," "Breach House," and above all, "The Parsonage"? Did it abut on our Cathedral? Or was it that tall house overlooking Sonapore Churchyard, which was called by the sailors, Padre Burrough's compound, and no wonder, from the fact, which he stated in 1818, that he had been Resident Chaplain in Bombay forty-two years!

---

* On the dedication of the fund which now constitutes the "Wilson Philological Lecture," in the getting up of which I had a small hand, he insisted more on the word "Missionary" being on the inscription than the much coveted F.R.S.

† "Randle Lodge" was on Breach Candy, the "Beehive" and "Tankerville" are still visible. In "The Parsonage" are now (1894) the offices of Mr. Roughton, the solicitor.

In 1820 assistance was advertised to be given to cholera patients at "Malabar Point Bungalow." "Parell" was of course Government House, and it still stands (1892), like a ghost in a garden of many memories. Will it be converted into a cotton mill? (1898, converted into a plague hospital.)

MALABAR HILL.

Except the Governor's bungalow, nowadays at Malabar Point, the impression seems to be that there were no bungalows for European residents on Malabar Hill till about 1840. This must apply to the west side, as we meet with an advertisement headed Malabar Hill, under date of December 4th, 1816, of a house on the *east* side for sale, which had been built eight years previously, say in 1808. The compound contained 3,345 square yards, and the auctioneer describes it as a "beautiful country residence." It belonged to the deceased General James Douglas, with whom the writer regrets he cannot claim kindred, or otherwise score himself heir to the owner of the cognomen. We mention these particulars so that future antiquarians may be able to identify the plot, and mark down the spot where the Douglas first broke ground in this bosky wilderness. Possibly it may be the "Wilderness" itself, a bungalow of storied renown, which, by its honourable host in "the sixties," was often filled with the youth and beauty of Bombay in those days when Fitzgerald, the gay Governor, led off the ball.

MAZAGON RESIDENCES.

The first birth recorded on Malabar Hill is on January 18th, 1837:

> "At 'The Craig,'* Malabar Hill, the lady of Charles Ducat, M.D., of a son."

Then follows:

> "14th October, 1842, at Malabar Hill, the lady of J. P. Larkins, Esqre., of a daughter."

---

* Dr. Smyttan gifted his Malabar Hill bungalow to Dr. Wilson. Dr. S. retired December 28th, 1833. Dr. Wilson called his bungalow "The Cliff," and was said to have been offered a very large sum of money for it during the mania. "Craig" may have been altered to "The Cliff."

Sir Robert Grant, the Governor, died at Dapoorie, near Poona, on July 9th, 1838, of apoplexy. The cause of his death was reported to be that he rode out in very heavy rain during the monsoon. On October 11th, Lady Grant was confined of a daughter, born after the death of the father, at Malabar Point. In 1837 several of our merchant princes, such as Harry George Gordon, lived at Mazagon; he became Chairman of the first Oriental Bank. At Mazagon also, in 1840, lived John Skinner, first Chairman of the Chamber of Commerce, and subsequently partner to Jardine, Skinner & Co. In 1840–42, Robert Wigram Crawford's bungalow was the "Wilderness."

CORYGAUM.

In the heroic defence of Corygaum, where 500 kept at bay 25,000 men, Dr. Wyllie, a Scotchman, did some good work—I mean, "threw physic to the dogs," and, sword in hand, cut up the enemy hip and thigh. How he earned his guerdon on that immortal day was often told in after years, by camp fire on Dekhan hill, or in the grey metropolis of his native land. It earned him the sobriquet of "The Fighting Doctor." The emergency was there, and he, like Wilson, another assistant surgeon, who saved the life of the Duke of Cambridge in the Crimea, was equal to the occasion; but unlike Wilson he carried his honours with a steady head. Wyllie's valour was not a myth. It is written that he acted "a most distinguished part at Corygaum," and the document is signed "F. F. Staunton, the hero of Corygaum. Seroor, 25th January, 1818." Dr. Wyllie belonged to the Madras Artillery, and a story illustrative of his *bonhomie*, was told to me in 1869 by General Stretton, then one of the oldest officers of the Indian Army. It belongs, I think, to 1824, the Cholera year, when, within a very short time, the Chief Secretary to Government of Madras, a Judge, and the President of the Medical Board, were all cut off suddenly by the fell disease.

"THE FIGHTING DOCTOR."

Scene: Artillery Mess, Madras.—During dinner, a note is handed to Dr. Wyllie, who rises abruptly, begging to be excused.

Commanding officer to the Doctor, in a low voice, as he is taking his departure: "I hope, Doctor, there is nothing wrong?" "Naething pertikler. Mrs. Smith has a wee touch of *coalara morebus.* We'll gae her a peel, and she'll sure be a' richt the morn."

This, no doubt, to put the party off the scent, as it was announced next morning that Mrs. S. had been safely delivered of a son! Next evening, as the dinner party were unfolding their table napkins, the Colonel, with a twinkle in his eye and full of humour, reconnoitred the sapient son of Esculapius thus, in the Doctor's accent: "Any more cases of *coalara morebus*, Dr. Wyllie?"

EDUCATION.

The following advertisement, dated February 18th, 1811, and signed John Forbes, we give, because it illustrates three things: (1st) that Bombay did not confine its benefactions to local schemes (the subscriptions to this one already amounted to Rs. 7,224); (2nd) that the Forbeses had already produced a strong Aberdonian feeling of clanship in the island; (3rd) that the schoolmaster was abroad:—

> "Aberdeen Society, for the benefit of children of deceased clergymen of the professors in the University of Scotland."

Some of the confusion here may be owing to the printer's devil. Charles Forbes's speeches in the India House, and his Bombay letters, are models of perspicuous English. Manockjee Cursetjee, who must have been at school about this time, had a fair education, which enabled him to hold forth to kings, and even to the Pope. I asked him about his teacher. His reply that he was a Mr. Mackay in Mr. Joliffe's school, near St. Thomas's Church, though of date 1822, shows that there was good education in Bombay about this period.

DINNERS AND ENTERTAINMENTS.

I am sure the men of this period were able to eat and drink more than we do, or could do with impunity. Take Malcolm for example, in October, 1811. On the 12th, there was a dinner to Mackintosh in the theatre; on the 16th a dinner to Charles Forbes; and on the 19th, a dinner to Rickards, a civilian of twenty-six years standing. Malcolm presided at the two last, and was the Jupiter Tonans of all three. Here were three great public entertainments in eight days, speeding the parting guests from our island. Could any man among us do this nowadays with impunity? I trow not.

During this decade there were many big dinners. Malcolm was a better diner-out than Elphinstone. There was a Commemoration dinner at Poona (of the Battle of Kirkee) in November, 1818. I should like to have seen Elphinstone on that occasion rise to propose "The immortal memory of Burns," and hear him add the words, "Success to his offspring," for a son of Burns was there, and sung one of his father's blythest lays. There is a Madras notification of February, 1811, that, Mr. William Nicol Burns * having produced requisite certificates of his appointment to be a cadet on this establishment, the Government in Council is pleased to admit him in that capacity, and promote him to the rank of an ensign, the date of commission to be settled hereafter. Was this the man, born in 1791, "the wee rumble gumption urchin of mine whom I named Willie Nicol, after a certain friend of mine," or was it he who stood of most interest, a man of pale face and grey hairs, at the Burns festival—Colonel James Glencairn Burns? Both these appointments were due, in the first instance, to the Marchioness of Hastings.

Sometimes a round of amusements lasted from daylight to dusk, or even far into midnight, and yet people carried their drink with surprising discretion. The strongest of our latter-day good livers, I imagine, would think twice before gulping down all the good things contained in this invitation to the *élite*, for Saturday March 9th, 1811:—

"PIC NIC.

"Meets at gunfire this morning on the Byculla Course, where the hounds will throw off a numerous field, and great sport is expected; afterwards Bobbery Hunting, &c., until breakfast, which has been ordered for fifty at the stand at nine; the party will then proceed to Lowji Castle, where various Hindustanee gymnastics, wrestlings, pigeon shooting, juggling and tumbling will be exhibited till four o'clock, when a dinner, in the best English style, will be served up for the same number as at breakfast. The sports of the day to conclude with music, fireworks, &c."

---

* 1828, Deputy Assistant Commissary General, Madras Army.

The men of this decade (1810–20) were a sober and righteous race; but they were men. At a great entertainment given to General Abercrombie, son of the hero of Alexandria, on May 25th, 1811, to celebrate his conquest of Mauritius, it is recorded (and you will please remember the date, for there are no hotter nights in Bombay than in the end of May):—

"After supper the dancing again commenced and continued to a late hour, nor did the brilliancy of the scene lose any effect, until the rising sun began to eclipse the minor artificial illuminations of the night."

Ten years later on, May 2nd, 1821, the first general meeting of the Bombay Highland Society, established for the cultivation of Caledonian proclivities, took place at Parell, under the discreetest of men, Mountstuart Elphinstone, on which the *Courier* remarks: "Various other excellent songs were sung, but latterly the recollection of our friend was not quite so clear as in the early part of the evening to detail particulars." Nothing now remains of this august Celtic corporation (it died out about 1840) but a black-faced sheep's-head mull, or Highland snuff-box, silver and cairngorm mounted.

The entertainment given to Sir John Keane by Sir Jamsetjee Jejeebhoy was the first occasion on which Parsee ladies appeared in public. Sir Jamsetjee left the room, and his temporary absence caused a feeling of suspense among the guests. Then the door suddenly opened, and Sir Jamsetjee made his appearance with his wife leaning on his arm, followed by his sons and their wives and his daughters. This was about 1841.

THEATRE, AND OTHER AMUSEMENTS.

During the cold seasons of these eventful years (1810–20), the theatre was in evidence, the actors being all amateurs. Many of the play-bills lie before us. Some of the pieces were—*The Road to Ruin*, *The Heir-at-Law*, *Old Mother Goose*, and *The Wheel of Fortune*; and on one occasion, we observe, the whole is to conclude with a recitation of the celebrated poem of *Glenfinlas*, a piece which, at the moment, we cannot recall to memory. All these fancies were bodied forth in the old theatre; but in 1818, after our great successes in Europe.

and the Dekhan, a brand-new theatre was constructed: "Doors open at 4, performances to begin at 7 precisely. Tickets for box and pit, Rs. 8"; and we observe (1811) no tickets were to be issued for the gallery. Doubtless a select audience, and the proceeds for some charitable object.

Gentlemen, unless actors, were on no account to enter the green-room, or go behind the scenes, and all gentlemen without ladies were earnestly entreated to make their way to the pit, leaving the boxes to the ladies and the gentlemen who escorted them.

1820–40.—In August, 1828, we read: "The Bombay Theatre is now a desert"; and the writer attributes its decay to "the march of morality, the want of money, the growing love of early hours, fashion, and the progress of fastidiousness." July 11th, 1829.—"The Bombay Theatre is now consigned to such ignoble purposes as the reception of Gogo cotton and gunny bags; once fertile in good performers, as in the age of the Brooks, the Bellasis, the Stanleys, and the Bells." 1831.—Arrangements to open the Bombay Theatre, which has been long suspended. March 13th, 1834.—Theatre half filled. "We may now sing a requiem over the drama in this Presidency." July, 1835.—Bombay Theatre offered for sale. "After Mr. Newnham left last year there was no hope for it." John Peter Grant was also a steady supporter of the drama, both in Bombay and Calcutta. October, 1835.—Theatre sold to Jamsetjee Jejeebhoy for Rs. 50,000. 1837.—"Theatrical displays are scarce worth attending." July 24th, 1840.—A petition, signed by 425 inhabitants, for a new theatre in Bombay. These notices sufficiently disclose the state of the theatre in Bombay, and its decadence for a dozen years.

From some observations we gather that the Native Theatre was not extinct, and what was called the "Legitimate Hindoo Drama" in Poona, in Sir Philip Woodhouse's time (1872–7), flourished unabashed in its travesties of the English, until it was suspended by authority. The following refers to something similar, satirising our noble selves. The time is 1830–40; scene, the Mofussil Court House. We merely give a *petit morceau* before the curtain fell. As the case proceeds, and the time approaches for the midday meal, the butler comes in and announces to the Judge, "Tiffin tyar hi." This, of course, he does with joined hands and obsequious deportment. The Judge immediately stops the case, and is proceeding to leave the Court-room, when he is accosted by the officers of the Court with, "Pray, your lordship, what shall we do with the prisoner?"

Judex exit, with "D—n his eyes, hang him!"

Bombay and Poona (1820–30) were not without other amusements. In connection with the revival of cricket in 1825, we read:—

"There will be tents for the ladies, and as the cricketers are all to be dressed in an appropriate uniform, we anticipate one of the most gay and animated scenes that has ever graced our island.

"We feel infinite pleasure in announcing amusements which tend to counteract the effects of this enervating climate, by raising the spirits from apathy, and the physical powers from that feminine indolence which is generally rewarded by premature old age, skin hanging in drapery, and muscles reduced to pack thread."

This same year, on October 28th, there was a very big dance in Poona in honour of Sir Charles Colville, Commander of the Forces, and 200 were present on the eve of his departure. There was a suite of tents, and his great battles were blazoned in letters of light—San Domingo, Martinique, Egypt, Badajos, Salamanca, Vittoria, Nive Nivelle, Waterloo. There were country dances, quadrilles, succeeded by waltzes and Spanish dances till 12. Then followed supper; then they danced till dawn, when the morning gun was the signal for departure.

Races.

The Bombay Races and Hunt were in this decade (1810 to 1820) in the full flush of prosperity. They took place in February; began with daylight, and ended in a big breakfast, which, most probably, before it was ended, annexed itself to a tiffin. The races of 1819 are a fair sample. Mr. Remington's Cup was presented to the victor by Lady Grant Keir. The

Forbes Stakes, £100—which are still (1892) run for—were won by Mr. Warden's Arab horse Dapoorie, beating Guzerat and Hotspur. The Ladies' Purse, Rs. 400, with five gold mohurs each, was run for by Clan Alpine, Speculation, and Greybeard.

4th day.—The Malet Stakes.

5th day.—The Batchelors' Purse, Rs. 400, with five gold mohurs each.

6th day.—The Gold Turf Cup, value 100 guineas, given by the Turf Club in 1802, and now in possession of Mr. De Vitre.

In 1816, for the purpose of attracting the fair sex, the Bombay Races were held no longer in the morning, but in the afternoon, a custom from which there has been, we believe, no departure.

The period of 1820–30 was an era of decline for both hunt and races. On February 1st, 1828, it is noted: "Bombay Races are not remarkable enough to be recorded." The following wail had appeared in the *Bombay Gazette* in 1827:—

> "'Twas in the olden time our Bombay Races
> Commenced at daylight, spite of fog and dew.
>
> *   *   *   *   *
>
> The 'Bobbery Hunt's Delight' or 'Garry Owen'
> Was sure to set the nimble feet agoing.
> All's over—early rising—breakfast—all;
> Yet what mementos do the names recall
> Of spirits—blotted from the things that be,
> Gone like the 'Bobbery Hunt' and 'Sans Souci,'
> For though the Bobbery, when in search of game,
> Were terrors to old crones and yelping pyes,
> Convivial friendship will preserve their name
> As those who bade the brightest fires arise.
> And but once more to hear their bugle strain
> Bombay might rouse thee to be gay again."

This spirited piece was headed "Lost Gaiety of Bombay."

In 1815 Poona seemed more vigorous, and received from England eight couple of hounds in the highest condition, with four couple of whelps produced on the voyage. Calcutta, up to 1840, held their races in the morning. The hunt there also involved a start at 4 A.M., and for this reason seldom more than fifteen gentlemen responded; and the ladies, at both hunt and races, were very few.

Merchants.

On May 20th, 1818, appeared the following advertisement in the *Bombay Gazette*:—

"Messrs. Ritchie, Steuart & Co. have the honour to announce this establishment as a Mercantile House, the partners of their firm being—
James Finlay and Co., Glasgow,
H. J. and R. Barton, Manchester,
Mr. James Ritchie, and
Mr. John Robert Steuart."

This rivulet of type represents the fountain-head of a great firm which had much to do in moulding the destinies of Bombay during the next fifty years. Harry George Gordon, a partner in this firm, was in 1838 voted first Chairman of the Chamber of Commerce; while another, Michael Scott, was the wizard of 1864. Both these men had great talents, and the pale and classic features of the latter, with hair black as the raven's wing, will live in the memories of all who have seen him, and live in local history also, as the most conspicuous character of these enterprising and anxious and exciting times. Panmure Gordon, writer and London financier (1892), is a son of the first, while Dr. Scott, the well-known author of *Tom Cringle's Log*, and *The Cruise of the "Midge,"* was the father of the second.

On April 9th, 1831, died on board the *Upton Castle*, off the Cape of Good Hope, John Ritchie, Esq., thirty-five, of Messrs. Ritchie, Finlay and Co.

March 4th, 1842, died at Castle Tower, E. Argyllshire, Kirkman Finlay, Esq., late M.P. and Lord Provost of Glasgow, founder of the firm.

Great Indian Firms.

The following were the leading Indian firms in London on February 18th, 1828:—

Messrs. Bazett, Colvin, Crawford and Co.
" Cockerell, Trail and Co.
" Fletcher, Alexander and Co.
" Farlie, Bonham and Co.
" Palmers, McKillop and Co.
" Inglis, Forbes and Co.
" Rickards, Mackintosh and Co.
" Finlay, Hodgson and Co.

Messrs. Maclauch'an, Macintyre and Co.
" Zachary Macaulay and Babington.*
" Small, Colquhoun and Co.
" R. Scott, Fairlie and Co.
" Gregson, Melville and Knight.
" Hunter and Co.

* No doubt the origin of the prenomen Thomas Babington Macaulay.

Exports.

The Bombay exports, in the three years ending 1815, amounted *ad valorem* to forty-five crores. With the advent of machinery, England now exported, instead of importing, cotton goods, which leads a merchant to exclaim in 1819, "Who could have imagined, fifty years since, that Manchester and Glasgow would send muslins to Bengal?" The tide had completely turned. One can scarcely imagine the horror with which people contemplated the spectacle of an East Indiaman loading coals for the East. And as for freights, one groan must suffice. In the year 1814, Liverpool despatched only one ship to the East Indies—that ship was of 512 tons.

1817—"Freights have fallen from £8 to £6 per ton, which can never pay even the expenses of the voyage." What would have been thought of 15*s.* per ton? However, throughout most of this decade exchange was 2*s.* 6*d.* and 2*s.* 8*d.*

Exchange.

The reason of such a high exchange in India at this time is not far to seek. The whole Peninsula was swarming in 1819 with armed men. War and tumult filled every corner of it. In such times there is no need to ask where money goes; it simply disappears.

The English Government were in great want of the sinews of war in India, for I think I am within the bounds of truth when I say that the army of the Dekhan, with its subsidiary forces, numbered 100,000 men. Those men required to be clothed and fed, and the money somehow had to be found. Given time, the resources of England are always equal to any emergency, and bullion came out, and exchange dropped and dropped until, in 1824, it reached 1*s.* 8*d.* In 1816 it had been 2*s.* 8*d.* When the rupee reached its lowest depth of degradation I cannot find a single groan. There were certainly no petitions, no meetings, no letters in the newspapers or journals. The situation was accepted, and men made the best of it.

A nephew who had gone home recounted to his uncle the great improvements in Bombay. "I don't want to hear of your improvements; give me back 2*s.* 8*d.* and ten per cent.!" was the reply.

1817—Six months' sight or twelve months' date Bills on London, 2*s.* 6*d.* to 2*s* 8*d.* per sicca-rupee.

1823—November 10th, six months' sight Bills, 1*s.* 8*d.*

1824—April 5th	ditto	1*s.* 10*d.* to 1*s.* 10½*d.*
„ June 19th	„	1*s.* 8*d.*
1825—July 2nd	„	1*s.* 10*d.*
1826—January 11th	„	1*s.* 11*d.*

Council Bills.

1843—January.—The Chamber of Commerce, Bombay, "complains of evils and grievances to which trade is subjected by the extraordinary fluctuations and uncertainty in the rates of exchange caused by the mode in which the Court of Directors at present provide themselves with the funds required for the home charges. Prays that the exchange operations between the two countries may be placed on a sound and proper footing, and be conducted on some fixed, just and well understood principles."

In May, 1837,	Sterling	Bills were	...	2*s.* 3*d.*
In July	„	„	„	...	1*s.* 9½*d.*
In Sept.	„	„	„	...	1*s.* 9*d.*

Indian Wheat.

I dare say, in these days, the export of wheat to England was deemed by most men chimerical. Lord Dalhousie gets the credit of having been the first to point out the advantages of an Indian wheat supply for England. But in September, 1818, H. T. Colebrooke, President of the Asiatic Society, Calcutta, anticipated him by nearly forty years. Here are his words:—

"That India is capable of supplying wheat, and that the difference of the usual prices there and in England is amply sufficient to defray the charges of importation, and leave an adequate profit, has elsewhere been intimated."

Not until early in "the fifties," however, was anything done, when three cargoes of wheat found their way to London, to the infinite regret and loss of those who had the doing of it. I am within the bounds of truth when I say that it took the importers *years* to get quit of it. There is an Italian proverb, "He that deals in corn shall die on straw." The importers nearly realised the truth of it. It was in the face of such difficulties that attempts were made to open the wheat trade.

Globe Trotters.

Part of this decade was very awkward for globe trotters. In April, 1818, Government issued a notice that passports were necessary for all Europeans, and any vagrants of this race found prowling about were to be taken to the nearest English official; and if I remember right, a reward was offered for their apprehension.

The war correspondent also was at a discount. Archibald Forbes would have been a voice crying in this Dekhan wilderness; for the Bombay papers, by a Government notice, dated December 25th, 1819, inform them that during the Mahratta war, every article must be submitted to Government before publication. All which regulations were, no doubt, just and proper at the time.*

An East Indiaman.

The commander of an East Indiaman was, of course, king of his castle: a great man and not to be trifled with. Sometimes an overbearing manner degenerated into sheer brutality. In 1818 a ship arrived in Bombay having a passenger on board who had been in irons, and had been deprived of his servant, for a period of twenty-one days! He had hummed and whistled (it was a low whistle) in the presence of the captain on the quarter-deck, and he continued to do so after he had been told to desist. The captain threatened him with imprisonment,

* Bombay was sometimes near enough to the seat of war. In January, 1818, the firing of the guns was distinctly heard at the taking of Kurnalla (Funnel Hill).

and he, the whistler, a young lieutenant in the army, told the captain that if he put him in irons he would lose his ship. All this, no doubt, was very exasperating to the captain, but could not justify such savage procedure. So the jury in Bombay, before whom the case was tried, gave the captain their sense of his conduct by fining him in Rs. 5,000. Exchange was then 2*s.* 7*d.*

PRESS.

The *Gazette* and *Courier*, established about 1790, the latter by Mr. William Ashburner of the Civil Service, continued to be weekly papers for about forty years. Both then merged into bi-weeklies, and the *Gazette* in its daily form "died about seven years ago" (1843). The *Star*, the *World*, the *Herald*, and *U. S. Gazette* were short-lived papers. The *Courier* and *Gazette* were in shape something like the size of the (1892) *Overland Times* and *Gazette*, with not a twelfth part of the printed matter. In 1820 both the *Gazette* and *Courier* were flourishing.

On December 30th, 1821, at Poona, died Adolphus Pope, late Sheriff of Bombay, and editor of the *Bombay Gazette*. In 1822 the Indian Press was much hampered by inland postage. A notice published in England states that the Post Office in India will not deliver a newspaper at any distance under half a rupee, or 1*s.* 3*d.*

1825.—The *Bombay Courier* published on Saturdays, the *Gazette* on Wednesdays, the *Weekly Gleaner* on Sundays. Only native paper, *Samachar Chandrika*, weekly. There were three dailies in Calcutta, the *John Bull*, *Scotsman in the East*, and *Hurkaru*.

Bombay Civil Servants were not seldom proprietors of papers. Colonel M. Stanhope, at the East Indian House, March 21st, 1827, stated that, though Mr. Fair was the nominal owner of the *Bombay Gazette*, Mr. Francis Warden, Chief Secretary, was the real proprietor, maugre the threat of the Chief Justice, September 16th, 1826: "I will punish the editor and proprietor both with fine and imprisonment." As late as 1841 the proprietors of the *Bombay Courier* were Humphrey Francis Boaden, Jamsetjee Jejeebhoy, Henry

Fawcett, and Robert Wigram Crawford; and of the *Times*—Messrs. Skinner, Gordon, Stewart, Dawson, Cardwell, Richmond, Mackie, and Russell, all well-known partners of leading firms in Bombay.

A writer in 1840 tells us of a catastrophe which took place in these unwholesome days. Three journalists died in as many months—Mr. Rousseau, sub-editor of the *Courier*, of cholera; Mr. Callum, editor and proprietor of the *Gazette*, of cholera, aged twenty-nine; Mr. Brennan, editor of the *Times* and Secretary of the Chamber of Commerce, of apoplexy, thirty-six. The *Bombay Iris*, a weekly paper for Government servants, had a short life. Dr. Wilson's *Oriental Christian Spectator*, a monthly, begun in 1827, lasted until 1856, and comprehends twenty-seven volumes.

Occasionally there were trials for libel. In June, 1833, Mr. R. X. Murphy, editor of the *Gazette*, challenged Colonel Vans Kennedy. The Colonel refused to accept the gage of battle, whereupon the editor, in his paper, denounced him to the public and the army as a slanderer and a coward. Murphy was sentenced to pay Rs. 500. The same year Captain Morley sued R. C. Money and Dr. Wilson for some printed matter in the *Spectator*, anent a tomb at Ahmednagar which had been raised to a native mistress and converted into a Hindoo temple, and obtained damages, Rs. 350.

Lawyers.

No men were more widely known in legal circles than Henry Forrester Constable and John Henry Stephenson. The former was Solicitor to the Company, Captain of the Bombay Fencibles, had been twenty-eight years in Bombay, died in 1802 at the age of forty-two, and was buried with military honours. Stephenson held the same office, and died in 1816 at Bussorah, aged thirty-eight. On his monument, in the Cathedral, may be found these halting lines:—

"Bombay admired, bewails thy short career,
And o'er thy ashes sheds a grateful tear:
What nobler monument can marble yield,
What brighter trophies deck the blazon'd shield."

In September, 1834, died James Morley. He had been a barrister in Bombay for fifty years.

High Court and Sir Edward West.

It was a great day for Bombay when the Supreme Court of Judicature was substituted for the Recorder's Court.

On the 8th day of May, 1823, at a few minutes past 10 A.M., the new Charter of Justice was read and proclaimed, after which Sir Edward West took his seat as Chief Justice. On the publication of the Charter, a royal salute of twenty-one guns was fired, and, upon the Chief Justice being sworn in, seventeen guns. The echoes had scarcely died away when an event came upon Bombay like a thunderclap. The Chief Justice dismissed William Erskine from his office of Master in Equity and Clerk of the Small Cause Court. He next suspended five barristers, including the Advocate-General (August, 1823), and thirdly, but not lastly, he deported Fair, the editor of the *Gazette*. The fire did not burn low in these times.

William Erskine.

Erskine did not kill himself, as James Outram's brother did under a somewhat similar charge. He died peaceably at Bonn, in 1851. The Advocate-General did not kill himself, though a Solicitor took his place; and editors have nine lives, and never suffer death from any amount of persecution. I cannot imagine a case, though all these men are now in their graves, that is calculated to awaken deeper sympathy than that of Erskine. Any man, wounded in the tenderest part, and the object of unfounded suspicion, may be as true a martyr as ever died by stake or faggot. The flames are not material, but they burn nevertheless. Erskine's case was that of a sick man whose subordinates in his absence, allowed the affairs of his department to drift into confusion, and startle the auditor with a balance on the wrong side. When under examination, Erskine replied to the charge that "these irregularities were totally unknown to him, and that he had never knowingly derived any profit from them." That might have been sufficient; but he might have as well appealed to the winds.

Erskine's probity was undoubted; but it was in vain that he had served under six Recorders, that he had been asked by the Royal Asiatic Society to sit for his portrait; that he was Mackintosh's son-in-law, that he was an elder in the kirk.* The enemy blasphemed, and the Judge was inexorable. The enemy wrote that "Mr. Erskine's robberies on the public exceeded Rs. 2,000 monthly." "Erskine is condemned by implication, if not in express terms, of being guilty of fraud, oppression, extortion, and corruption"; and the Judge refused to allow him to quit the country unless he found two securities for Rs. 50,000 each, and his own personal bond for Rs. 100,000. Here was the sequence. Sir Edward West bestowed the office of Master in Equity on his nephew, and we are not surprised to read that, when he retired in 1829, "he left his own arena of exertion unregretted by a mortal." But Erskine was like his native heather, which, though burned to the ground in one season, springs up the next.

GLIMPSES IN 1823.

We get a glimpse of the state of Bombay in 1823 from a Calcutta visitor. The people were less cringing and subservient than they were in Bengal. The climate was preferable. A great paucity of punkahs even in the best houses. A dirtier town than Calcutta; and he adds: "The olfactory horrors of the Bombay bazaars may possibly be equalled—they can be exceeded in no part of the world."

Wages, four palanquin bearers, Re. 1 per diem; table servant, Rs. 10 to Rs. 16 per mensem; ayah, Rs. 12. House rent, half the Calcutta rate. A family mansion obtainable at Rs. 200 per mensem. Saw one of very large size that let at Rs. 300. "Parell," the country house of the Governor, can only be equalled in the bad taste of its architecture by his residence in the Fort. "Also a pair of tigers guarding the gate of an elegant villa (Jugganath Sunkersett's) in Gorgaum," still to be seen (1892). Parties not so agreeable as in Calcutta. In Calcutta you call on people; here you must wait until you are called on.

* Resigned, 1820.—*St. Andrew's Session Minutes.*

In Bombay every article of European produce and manufacture is double the price of Calcutta. Fish delicious, bread excellent; good water is scarcer than good wine. Here we "see oursels as ithers see us." We will now hear what Bombay has to say of itself.

In the same year (1823) a Bombay man speaks more hopefully: "Owing to some big fires, Government wish the cotton bales removed from Bombay Green, and have appropriated a portion of the Esplanade near the Apollo Pier for the purpose." And here follows a glowing anticipation of the Elphinstone Circle, built 1864–65: "The great square of the Fort, which we hope on some future day to see surrounded with buildings worthy the good taste and public spirit of the people." This was the vision when the Town Hall had just risen above its foundation. The Town Hall took fifteen years in building, and was finished in 1834, costing five lakhs.

The year 1826 opens with great changes and substantial progress. "Population has increased as if Cadmus had sewn 'dragon's teeth,' mercantile houses have multiplied, charities have been founded, public tanks have been enlarged so as to afford a constant supply of water, the ways have been elegantly lighted, the Esplanade has been levelled and cleared, roads have been made and edifices have arisen, designed with architectural taste and executed with masonic skill, and the Governor is congratulated on opening a sally-port through the ramparts, which has been so useful to the inhabitants of the Fort in getting water both by day and night, and by repairing old wells and making new ones in every part of the island."

Hormasjee Bomanjee.

Hormasjee Bomanjee, the most prominent native citizen of Bombay during the first quarter of this century, died on the morning of March 8th, 1826, in the sixtieth year of his age. He was for more than thirty years associated with Forbes and Company. He left three sons and two daughters. He was the youngest brother of builder Jamsetjee Bomanjee and of the celebrated merchant Pestonjee Bomanjee, head of the Wadia family. He was succeeded in his *station* by his nephew Nowrojee

Jamsetjee, head of the Parsee Punchayat, the respected head builder in the naval yard. When the news reached England, it was said "he died worth two millions." Though this was a great exaggeration, the family held a strong position, and dispensed festivity at Lowji Castle from early times. So shortly before his death as August 3rd, 1825, Hormasjee Bomanjee gave a splendid entertainment at Lowji Castle which was long remembered by the European inhabitants. His son Ardaseer upheld the position and dignity of the family far into the eighties. He too was of dignified deportment.

PINDARRIES.

The Pindarries were a never-failing source of anxiety at this time. The *Bombay Courier* of January 4th, 1817, announces that communication from Siroor to Poona, and from Poona to Panwell, is unsafe without a guard; and no wonder, for reports came in on February 22nd, that a body had appeared before Desgaum, after having plundered Mhar, and that 700 of them were seen in the neighbourhood of Panwell, and made tracks in a northerly direction. Here follows how they harassed our soldiers:—

> "On December 27th, 1816, the Native cavalry, under Major Lushington, marched from 1 A.M. to 6 P.M., seventy miles after Pindarries, killed a. d wounded seven to eight hundred, and then by easy stages made their way to Ahmednagar. Captain Drake was killed by a spear wound."

1816. The Bombay Marine Battalion was raised.

1817. The Poona Horse was raised. Siroor became their *locale,* and a pleasant habitation it is.

ROBBERS.

One of the roads referred to by the writer on Bombay was the beach road to Sewree, which was finished in 1825. The Colaba Causeway was projected, but was still a work of the future; what need there was of lighting the streets is apparent from the number of robberies. In 1827 the robbers actually entered the house of the Chief Justice after he had publicly denounced their depredations. And in the same year Mrs. Sparrow, wife of a member of Council, when returning from church in her carriage, was attacked by a mounted Armenian, who seized the horse's reins and shot away the coachman's ear. About that time a gentleman was deterred from buying the "Wilderness" because it was so remote, and exposed to the attacks of robbers. The island was infested that year with a number of audacious villains with swords, who hacked at whoever came in their way, sahib or servant. Numbers of palanquins were stopped on the Parell Road in 1826 and their occupants plundered. The same year, while attempting to enter the house of the Commander-in-Chief, a sentry, loading his musket, had a stone thrown at him to his hurt.

In addition to the insecurity of property, there were three great plagues. There was the plague of beggars, the lame, the halt and the blind, and the armless flourishing their stumps. There was the plague of pariah dogs infesting every street in the Fort, and every lane and road on the island, endangering the lives of those on horseback. There was the plague of hamuls, that rascal multitude who carried on the business of locomotion, bearing and overbearing, insolent as the buggy-wallahs in the sixties, and levying blackmail, and sometimes black death, on whoever entered their dirty and infection-carrying palanquins. It was in vain that the Grand Jury proclaimed the ill-regulated condition of the palanquins and those who plied for hire. The latter were masters of the situation. If they struck there was an end of all juries and dinner parties. The only owners of palkies are now (1893) the solicitors. And there was the plague of irate judges.

Fancy, at such a time, men's minds being exercised with the problem—Who was entitled to the affix of "Esquire"? Whether the servant of a Knight or of Magister was the greater? It was left to the genius of Lord Clare (1834) to solve this knotty question, and a Minute of Council was issued that the following gentlemen should be addressed as "Esquire":—

Jugganath Sunkersett.
Jamsetjee Jejeebhoy.
Dadabhai Pestonjee.
Dhakjee Dadajee.
Bomanjee Hurmasjee.
Framjee Cowasjee.
Nowrojee Jamsetjee.
Cursetjee Cowasjee.
Cursetjee Ardaseer Dady.
Mohammed Ali Rogay.
Cursetjee Rustomjee.
Mohammed Ibrahim Macha.
Hormasjee Bhicajee Chinoy.

This is a leaf from the Golden Book of Bombay which some of our golden youth (1893) may be pleased to look at.

From these troubles and tomfooleries relief came to Bombay from an unexpected quarter. As early as May 20th, 1826, Mahableshwur had been pointed out as a suitable hill station, and on January 24th, 1829, a Parsee opened a shop there. So the lieges found that the best way to make the most of Bombay was to get out of it, and recline their wasted minds and bodies on the Mahableshwur Hills.

GAOLS.

During the first two decades of this century the gaols were worth looking after. Some local Howard was abroad, for in 1821 the Grand Jury of Bombay told the Judge that the prisoners for minor offences ought to be separated from those of deeper dye.

In 1823 one debtor had been in gaol nine years, and if the creditor made an allowance the debtor might be detained all his life. All kinds of prisoners were mixed, for minor and heinous crimes, those convicted, as well as those waiting their trial. In 1827 an Englishman died in the Calcutta gaol who had been in prison for debt for nine years, and on August 7th, 1827, died at the great gaol of Calcutta, Mrs. Mary Moore, wife of Mr. Robert Moore, who had been imprisoned for debt for upwards of twelve years. The number of executions had very much decreased compared with old times. Mackintosh tells us that in Bombay, from May, 1736, to May, 1763, there were 141 capital convictions and 47 executions; from May, 1804, to May, 1811, there were 109 capital convictions and no executions. A man executed on July 20th, 1811, was the first European executed for twenty-five years in Bombay.

HILL STATIONS.

The settlement on this hill widened the horizon and expanded the ideas of that generation enormously. There had been watering-places where people went for change of air in the hot season. But Bankote and Gorabunder (the Hippocoura of Ptolemy ?) are quite as hot as Bombay.

Vizrabhai, the Lady of the Thunderbolt, with its hot springs, once quite fashionable, was, on the discovery of the new hill station, at once relegated to the natives, whose rèsort it has been ever since. It has not a few military memories, and its neighbourhood was once well ploughed up by field artillery. Here are a few lines redolent of feeling, albeit destitute of poetic fire, culled from an old album, and dated 1786, on Vizrabhai:—

"Hail, sacred spring, salubrious fountain—hail!
Not far removed is that illustrious spot
Where, dearly bought, the gallant *Hartley* gained
Increased renown; where, with a faithful few,
He bore the onset of a numerous foe,
Whose chief, unlike his dastard kindred, showed
The path to glory, and pursued the way.
And there the generous *Goddard* pressed with speed
(His fresh earned laurels blooming on his brow)
To share his partner's toils."

Matheran was not yet dragged from its obscurity, but a gleam of light flashes on its darkness in 1822. Colonel Delamain writes: "Very rich scenery. In every direction noble mountains. To the north, Mathé Ram, bearing at first view a stupendous square fort on the top; but it is natural. It was, however, fortified." This last is a hard nut for the topographer to crack.

COLABA.

In 1826 we read that "Colaba is becoming celebrated for unaffected and social intercourse, that scarcely a week passes without some particular manifestation of it."

The suspicions that it was unhealthy in the years which followed, took tangible shape in 1840, when it was announced, to the dismay of all concerned, that Colaba, having been pronounced by the medical authorities a most unhealthy station for European troops, is to be forthwith abandoned as a military station. And in 1841 a Medical Board found that a deadly malaria was caused by the mangrove trees on the western shore and the sea washing thereon twice in twenty-four hours. Colaba would have soon justified its name of "Old Woman's

Island," had not the two Napiers, Charles and Robert, stepped in successively to avert this disaster. The spade and the hatchet were the remedies.

Bombay itself must have been bad, if we can believe the *Gazette* of June 4th, 1841: "Calcutta is bad enough, Madras worse; but, with six times the native inhabitants, Madras is a Belgravia Square compared with Bombay."

Though the Colaba Causeway, connecting it with Bombay, was projected as far back as 1820, it was not actually commenced till 1835.

Overland.

On July 12th, 1823, the first steamship, the *Diana*, was launched at Kidderpore, and had a splendid trial trip—"velocity perfectly astonishing." On January 22, 1825, the steamship *Enterprize* was launched in England to run to India. On November 24th, 1824, £10,000 was voted by the merchants of Calcutta to the first person who would navigate a steamship to India. On August 16th, 1825, the *Enterprize*, of 500 tons, and containing twenty cabins, leaves Falmouth for Calcutta. On 30th July, 1828, Mr. Thomas Waghorn, of the Pilot Service in Calcutta, proposes to bring out the mails to Calcutta in seventy days, *via the Cape*. On the same day Mr. G. A. Prinsep states that a letter might be carried from Calcutta to Cosseir in twenty-nine days, and thence to London in twenty-five days. On March 12th, 1829, the *Bengal Chronicle* styles Waghorn, "This intelligent, active, and enterprising individual." November 15th, 1829, first steamship to start from Bombay to Suez. Waghorn's services in opening up the Overland route are matter of history. Not until this was secured was Bombay called "the rising Presidency."

Government advertise the fare Rs. 1,200, independent of the table. Servants, European, Rs. 150; natives, Rs. 75. The total expenditure of each traveller from Bombay to London was £300, which included the Rs. 1,200 passage money by the *Hugh Lindsay*, from Bombay to Cosseir. We learn incidentally that in Calcutta, in 1822, Rs. 800 sicca were paid for a second-class passage home by sailing vessel. A single letter, Rs. 2-6, double, Rs. 5, for postage.

Mails.

1825.—The Madras mail to Calcutta, by land, was done in 10 days 17¾ hours.

1826.—From Bombay to Calcutta, an express mail was done in 11½ days.

Archæology.

A great deal has been written on the wanton acts of the Portuguese in destroying the sculptures of Elephanta. We have not been blameless in this matter ourselves. Hector Macneil, writing from Bombay (*Archæologia*, Vol. VIII.) in 1783, boldly charges "those heroes who grace our fleets and armies in India," with the spoliation. I dare say it was the fashion of the day, witness James Forbes and the Gate of Diamonds at Dubhoi. There is ample evidence of the truth of Macneil's assertion. In *Archæologia*, Vol. VII., 1785, there are three magnificent plates of heads brought by Sir Ashton Lever from Elephanta, and, that there may be no doubt regarding the extent of the plunder, the same journal adds:—"The Society are possessed of a drawing of another group of figures from the same quarter by Captain Allen of His Majesty's ship *Cumberland*." So late as 1840 a correspondent of the *Asiatic Journal* writes, that he saw persons in Elephanta break off pieces of the statues to sell to visitors. In the *Bombay Gazette* of 1822 there is the following notice of what the writer saw in the Canara Caves in Salsette, some part of which, but not much, may still be visible: "We observed very distinctly the vestiges of fresco painting, representing, in simple colours of red and blue, single figures of the Hindoo deities." Charles Bonne (Governor, 1724–31) notices also the red and blue paint on the statues at Canara (*Archæologia*).

Asiatic Society.

In 1829 the Royal Asiatic Society removed their library and museum to the north rooms of the Town Hall, which they have since occupied. In 1832 several meetings were held to put an end to scribbling on the books of the library. *Colonel Welsh's Memoirs* seems to have been well annotated.

Under June 10th, 1833, we read: "Manockjee Cursetjee, a Parsee of some distinction, was proposed as a member. The President supported his pretensions, and proposed that all natives who sit on Grand Juries should be eligible. Dr. Wilson objected, because it would give a preference over their countrymen of the highest literary attainments to those whose only literature was their acquaintance with the English language. The ballot showed fourteen black balls against him. In 1836, however, Manockjee was elected a non-resident member, and on January 29th, 1840, was elected the first native member of the Bombay Royal Asiatic Society. Since that time there has been a gradual accession of natives, who are now a preponderating element in all the meetings of the Society.

And the Asiatic library was not to be despised. In 1839 Principal Mill of Calcutta said to Dr. Wilson, "There is nothing like this on the banks of the Ganges." At the beginning of 1810 it consisted of 2,000 volumes, and the Society had an income of £400 to be devoted annually to the purchase of books. The library was housed in Medows Street, and the meetings of the Society were at this period held in the theatre. No books were issued the last week of the year, when all books were ordered to be returned, and a searching examination was made as to their condition. Sir James Mackintosh advertises three times for people to return his own books. Bombay, then as now, was in no hurry to return borrowed books.

There were some dungeons of learning, like Vans Kennedy, its Secretary, in the Asiatic; but after Mackintosh left, Elphinstone held up the blazing torch, which illuminated his sphere of action with the light of day. Contributions came in from many quarters. Rich discoursed on Babylonian bricks; and another son-in-law of Mackintosh, to wit William Erskine, discussed Elephanta; and Frank, the ill-starred brother of James Outram, produced a new theory of perpetual motion; and Malcolm, like Saul among the prophets, when he did manage to attend its meeting, stood head and shoulders above all the people at the meetings in this decade (1810–20). The natives were conspicuous by their absence; but it is pleasing to record that no long time elapsed before they took their part, both as hearers and as speakers, in the proceedings of this learned Society.

The Upper Ten.

Hormasjee, Jamsetjee Jejeebhoy, Cursetjee and Jehangier Ardaseer, Davidass Hurjeevandass and Cajee Golam Hossein were conspicuous natives in 1823.

This year the Grand Jury consisted of the following names:—

Benjamin Norton.	J. Fawcett.	W. C. Bruce.
W. Mainwaring.	E. Elliott.	William Peel.
William Nicol.	F. Bourchier.	J Forbes.
J. Saunders.	W. T. Graham.	T. Riddock.
D. Seton.	T. Crawford.	A. Mackintosh.
A. Inglis.	S. D. Beaty.	P. H. Hadow.

This is the earliest appearance I can find of the founder of the great firm of William Nicol and Co., which was almost an institution in Bombay for fifty years.* He lived to a great age, and, though a little man in size, was in his time one of the biggest merchants in Bombay. His portrait, as an old man, is in possession of the Parsee lady, Bhai Motlibhai.

A meeting of the Asiatic Society in August, 1823, at which the Hon. M. Elphinstone presided, consisted of the Archdeacon, Messrs. Wedderburn, Farish, Henderson, Lieutenant-Colonel H. Blair Gordon, Kemball, Norris, Macleod, Captain Bruce, Dr. Sproule, Norton, Fawcett, D. Malcolm, Elliott, Hadow, Waddington, Ogilvie, Prinsep, J. R. Stuart, Brydon, Ritchie, Arbuthnot, Bruce, and the Secretary, General Vans Kennedy.

Longevity.

There were two patriarchs of Bombay who disappeared in this decade. In 1815 died General Kenneth Macpherson who had fought for Prince Charles at Culloden. His home was near Sion, on the Tanna road, and everybody knew and respected him. On May 9th, 1818, died George Dick. He had come out as a writer in 1759, and had never been out

---

* William Nicol was nominated an elder in St. Andrew's Church, July 28th, 1822.—*St. Andrew's Session Minutes.*

of Bombay, except on an occasional trip to Bancoot, for nearly sixty years. He died in Byculla, and his name may be seen in the list of the Governors of Bombay in 1795. He was universally respected, and there is a tablet to his memory in the Cathedral. May 15th, 1834, at Madras, died General Sir Andrew McDowall, K.C.B. He had been fifty-one years in the country without going home. At his funeral, fifteen men of the 63rd Regiment fainted, having walked four miles in the hottest time of the day, leaving their barracks at 4 P.M., of whom one sergeant and two corporals died, and were buried next day.

Charles Crommelin, Governor of Bombay, 1760–67, "served the Company thirty-five years, returned to England in 1757, suffered greatly in trade, returned to India in 1772 as a free merchant, and now (1777) resides at Canton." He had joined the Company in 1732. James Forbes saw him at Goa in 1784, when he was acting British Consul.

Can this be the same man whose tomb in the Presidency graveyard at Kasimbazar, Moorshedabad, is described by Mr. Beveridge, in the *Calcutta Review*, July, 1892? The inscription—"C. Crommelin, eighty-one. December 25th, 1788"—seems to indicate that he may have wandered there at last. *Requiescat in pace.*

(3.) BOMBAY, SOCIAL AND CONVIVIAL, DURING THE PAST HUNDRED YEARS.*

MAILS.

ONE of the greatest elements of social happiness in this country consists in the regularity and speed with which we receive our home letters and news from the old country. In olden times the mails were slow and very irregular. For example, the news of the death of the Princess Charlotte, which took place on November 6th, 1817, was only known in Bombay on February 28th, 1818, and the death of George III., which took place on

---

* A lecture delivered at the Sassoon Institute on February 6th, 1895, with additions.

January 29th, 1820, was not announced here until May 23rd. On March 1st, 1823, there had been no arrivals from Europe for a month. An editor in 1824 thus consoles himself on January 24th of that year: "We have been obligingly favoured with the loan of papers for July and the beginning of August, 1823." When in this year it was asserted that steam would bring letters in one-fourth of the time then taken, the statement was looked upon as an idle dream. On January 10th, 1827, the latest London dates were June 8th, 1826. Malcolm left on December 1st, 1830, in the *Hugh Lindsay* steamer for Cosseir, which seems to have been the beginning of our steam navigation. In 1831 Lord Clare, our Governor, was six months in reaching Bombay, *via* the Red Sea. He was detained at Jeddah two months for want of coals. This year there was a mail made up, *via* Bussorah.* It was limited in space, but the agents politely offered to take two letters from each merchant at Rs. 20 each. It cost the man in charge his life, for Mr. Taylor was murdered in Mesopotamia, but the letters were delivered in London all right. In 1837 the *Berenice* steamer returned after being four days out. Starting again she returned a second time, after seventeen days, without reaching Aden. This explains a picture in the Delhi Sketch Book of a man in a tub propelling it with a tea-kettle, with the heading "Bery Nice." Steamers were not in favour at this period.

Our land locomotion in these days was mostly done in palanquins, not only in town but to every region in the Mofussil. The charge to Calcutta, I understand, was Rs. 800. Andrew Hay, who, in 1841, came out in the same steamer as Sir Charles Napier, was said to have been the last person who travelled from Bombay to Calcutta in a palanquin.

In 1839 first-class fare, Overland route, Bombay to London, was £111. Waghorn's postage for a single letter under one ounce was Re. 1, or 2*s.* 3*d.* In 1840 the mail closed in Bombay for England at 11 A.M.; letters received until 1 P.M., Re. 1

* Postage Monthly Mail by Bussorah.—Bombay Castle, Dec. 7th, 1797. First dispatch January 1st, 1798, one letter weighing quarter of a rupee, Rs. 10; one letter weighing half a rupee, Rs. 15; one letter weighing one rupee, Rs. 20. This would cost £12,600 per annum, or £1,000 each mail.—*John Taylor's Travels*, 1799.

extra. In 1841 the steamer generally took three hours from the time she was signalled until she was anchored, and three hours more were required to sort the letters. The transport of the mails before this throughout India was generally done by dâk-runners, who ran three *koss*, or six miles, with the mail bags, and had often to cross swollen rivers. In 1810 the mail to the north was robbed by a gang of persons on Parell Road. From 1816 to 1821 the Calcutta dâk to Bombay, 1,300 miles, took eighteen and a half days, which was reduced in 1824 to twelve days seven and a half hours, and this was thought extraordinarily quick. The arrival of the Calcutta mail was always a source of general interest, for, from the condition in which the letters arrived, was judged what the weather was in the interior. Absolutely, this was all people then had in place of our elaborate daily telegraphic weather reports. The correspondence with Calcutta was limited. In 1826 the mail was lost between Calcutta and Nagpore. It consisted of only forty-five letters. In 1833 the Surat *dâk-tapal* was drowned, and in 1850 a *mail gharry* in Salsette was bowled over by a tiger, and nobody was hurt. And on one occasion, before 1843, her Majesty's mails were lost in a buggalow eighty miles from Aden, but were recovered, though much saturated. In 1853 the postage on a daily paper for a moderate distance in India was Rs. 50 per annum. In 1859 first-class fare, Southampton to London, was reduced from £95 to £85. People who came in the vans or omnibuses from Cairo to Suez in the "fifties" did not soon forget it. They were well horsed, but the road was a caution—mounds of sand and gravel. We had a bi-monthly mail in 1845. In 1860, July 6th, fortnightly mails commenced. In 1868, March 23rd, "we are now hourly expecting our first weekly mail."

Carriages.

We will now speak of carriages. The Governor had a carriage, at an early time, say, in Grose's period, 1760, but bullock *gharries* were quite fashionable in the end of last century, and Mr. Vaupell of the High Court, until he died in 1852, used to delight in driving a pair of fast-trotting oxen from Bandora to the Fort daily. In Qui Hi's last journey to

Padre Burrough's Godown (1814), the tattered and lugubrious hearse is depicted as drawn by oxen. But carriages soon began to prevail. In 1821 Mr. Mitchell advertises that he will not do any business in coach-building except for ready-money, so the demand had exceeded the supply on credit. In 1824 Mr. Lewis Collett advertises that he will continue the coach-making business of Mr. John Mitchell, and soon Collett's equipages were in the language of the day "all the go."

For business locomotion the *palky* was everywhere, but the last specimen in Bombay will soon, like the sedan chairs of our great-grandmothers, be relegated to the museum of antiquities. I am sure the Esplanade was never so crowded with fashionable equipages as it was in the season of 1865. It was a perfect carnival. Steamers were then coming with sometimes a million sterling of bar silver, an instalment of the eighty millions of profits which were said to have been made by Bombay traders during the American cotton famine, and the display of wealth did not seem out of proportion to the means of that period of exaltation. These were the days when bungalows were wanted at Rs. 500, and Altamont was let at Rs. 1,000 a month. It would be impossible in a sketch like this to chronicle even the names that were borne by the vehicles of this century, and which prevailed at different periods. In the few years which succeeded 1818 we read of chariots, Bengal-built dennets, coaches, barouches, shigrampos, curricles, buggies, tilburys, sociables, landaulets, britzskas and clarences. The last man who used the word "clarence" in Bombay must have been Norman Macleod, who asked his host—it was after tiffin—if his "clarence" was ready. This was, no doubt, a Glasgow archaism or slip of the tongue and relic of William IV.'s days. The rise, progress and extinction of hack buggies would need a history by itself. They were fearful instruments of torture, and for more than one generation at least the drivers had the credit of being thieves and pick-pockets. As you sat next the driver, and were jolted against him, there cannot be a doubt that he disseminated dirt, disease and vermin. For the victoria we are indebted in a great measure to Sir Frank Souter and Mr. Weber. Mr. Vincent, then the head of our police, took a most distinguished part in this crusade against the detestable buggy, which ceased to exist about 1881. Several attempts were made by Mr. Weber to introduce the hansom, which were unsuccessful, and this vehicle, we think, does not now exist in Bombay. The tramway, which has been such an inestimable blessing to us all, began about 1874. The bicycle, here as elsewhere, looks as if it would carry everything before it.

DINNERS AND BALLS.

We come now to speak of dinners, and we only notice such as are distinguished by some special incident. On November 5th, 1818, Mr. Elphinstone gave a dinner to commemorate the Battle of Kirkee. Twenty-nine toasts were given, with appropriate tunes after each toast, and his health was drunk with nine times nine! We have no such functions nowadays. At a dinner on November 29th, 1821, at Government House, Apollo Street, in honour of Sir John Malcolm, 200 sat down. This dinner was noticeable in this, that the chairman in his speech observed (jocularly we will suppose) that a considerable degree of apprehension was felt by their female friends that the zeal which the bumpers would derive from the toasts of the evening would render a great majority of the company unfit to appear in their presence that evening. The chairman's fears seem to have been groundless, for 350 danced till daylight in a pavilion specially erected for the purpose on the Esplanade. The dances in these days were quadrilles, country dances and waltzes. Spanish dances are also mentioned. Occasionally there were masked balls. At another noticeable dinner, which took place at Poona on December 9th, 1826, Sir Lionel Smith in a speech made a delicate allusion to Mr. Elphinstone's remaining on the bachelor list. He said he had been requested by the ladies who had honoured the banquet by their presence to say something for them. "We all know that they are always fluent, generally eloquent, always persuasive. Some of them may perhaps wonder and regret that Mr. Elphinstone has never yet quartered their silken chains in his honourable escutcheon." There was a dinner given by Jamsetjee Jejeebhoy (he was not knighted until 1842) to Lord Clare, Sir Herbert Compton, Sir John Keane and Sir Charles Malcolm. This dinner was on January 29th, 1835, and was signalised by the drawing-room being thrown open to the ladies of the Jejeebhoy family, and was the first instance of Parsee ladies mingling freely in European society. It was Lady Frere who first opened Government House to native ladies (1862–67). On March 5th, 1835, there was a ball and supper to Lord Clare, in the Town Hall, being the first occasion the building was used for this purpose, and the first time on which Chantrey's statue of Mountstuart Elphinstone was displayed to the public, and which of course was a subject of universal admiration.

Two of the most important dinners ever given in Bombay were that to Sir James Outram in 1842, and the Byculla Club Dinner to Sir Bartle Frere in 1867. No higher types of military or civil excellence can be cited in Bombay history. Their statues, like those of two brothers, stand in line on that most conspicuous site, the Thames Embankment. Lovely, and sometimes misconstrued in their lives, in death they have not been divided. The ball given by Sir Albert Sassoon to Lord Northbrook at Sans Souci in 1873 was the most gorgeous and brilliant ever given in Bombay, and it will never be forgotten by anyone who took part in that magnificent entertainment. For conviviality and national enthusiasm the St. Andrew's and Highland Society's Dinners "bear the gree" over all others. The annual ball at Parell, in February, 1872, in Sir Seymour FitzGerald's time, did not take place. While the ladies were at their toilet, and the men ordering their carriages, a wild cry rose in the streets that Lord Mayo had been assassinated. It was too true. Many drove up to the gates of Parell, found them closed, and were stunned by the notice posted on the pillars. There was a dinner given in August, 1824, to John Jukes, a great billiard player. Thirty-five sat down, and in 1859 a native entertainment took place, at which 200 European ladies and gentlemen danced until daylight. The gentleman in whose honour it was given, is in good health, and is now (1894) in Bombay. But what can we say more of Bombay festivities? The Duke said he was feasted into Bombay and feasted out of it. General Ulysses Grant said that we had killed him with kindness and done everything except *bury* him. The Prince of Wales said it was the dream of his life.

SCHOOLS.

With regard to schools, in 1818 Mrs. Hunt advertises a boarding-school for twenty young ladies; Rs. 25 per mensem. English (grammatically), writing and arithmetic, plain needlework, embroidery in silk, in landscape, fruits, and flowers. Lessons in forte-piano. Rs. 20 to boarders only. Drawing, Rs. 10. Dancing, Rs. 10. And in 1821 Mr. Joliffe, from Breach House, calls attention to his tuition in music and dancing, which he terms "the superficial branches of education." A young lady's accomplishments in those days are described by a Bombay poetaster:—

> "She excels on the harp, works patterns with skill,
> Writes a lady-like hand, can waltz and quadrille;
> In temper she is amiable, perhaps to a fault,
> Drinks sparing of wine and abominates malt."

There are some bitter wails from the Mofussil, showing that Bombay was not the dull place we are apt to imagine in 1830:—

> "Caro amico, dwelling in Bombay,
> Resort of all that's beautiful and gay;
> Where routs and balls, with dinners, fêtes and tea,
> Dispel that fiend the ladies call Ennui;
> Where grief, if grief should come, changes her style
> And turns to joy on lovely B——t's smile:
> Listen while I, a banish'd man, deplore
> My hopeless fate and rail at Bassadore."

For the harder sex there was no want of the means of education. Listen to this in 1821:—

"Boyer and Joliffe beg to state to their friends and the public that the individual whom they have selected to attend their establishment, in the capacity of Drawing Master, is Mr. Constantine Augusto, a person who is well versed in the doctrine of angles of animo-anatomic proportion, is peculiarly correct in landscape, chaste colouring, and perspective. Young gentry who are not, therefore, receiving instruction at the mathematics school and may wish to benefit by Mr. Augusto's abilities, may be accommodated by sending their commands to the Masters of that establishment."

In 1831 Mr. Bennett's Day School, No. 6, Rampart Row: reading, writing and arithmetic, Rs. 5 per month; English, German and book-keeping, Rs. 7 per month. In 1837 Mr. Boswell's School is highly commended. We rather think Mr. Vurjivundas Madhowdas, the head of the Hindoo community (1894), was a pupil of Mr. Boswell's, as Mr. Manockjee Cursetjee, familiarly called the "Byron of the East," was of Mr. Bennett. Education in England you see is not a *sine qua non.* Mr. Telang, late Judge of the High Court, was the flower and fruit of a later period, that of the Elphinstone College, and had never been in Europe. James Thomason, the founder of Roorki, had to content himself with Calcutta upbringing until he was 10, like Robert Grant, who became Governor of Bombay, and spent his early years in the boarding-school of the Rev. Mr. Brown of the same city.

Manners, etc.

Every man early in the century, as you may see from their portraits, had a clean-shaven face until you come down to Sir Charles Napier in 1843, "the bearded vision of Sind." Malcolm wore a queue until he was thirty, when he abandoned it for ever. This was in 1799. Events and cycles repeat themselves, for shaven faces, from Lord Rosebery downwards and upwards, if you like, are now the fashion. A Persian asked Malcolm early in the century if it were true our cavalry wore moustaches, and if they were likely again to be popular. "Perhaps they might," said Sir John. The Bombay officer must have been grandiose in chapeaux in 1820. Here is something on headgear: "For sale, superfine cocked hats, Waterloo shape, trimmed to the Prince Regent's order, for infantry, cavalry or staff officers, bound with black figured lace, embroidered with silver and cord star loops, rich cockades, and very rich bullion tassels, feathers and Saxon plumes complete, Rs. 75 to Rs. 95." "At Homes" were fashionable in Bombay in 1824. In 1852 the Hope Hall Hotel advertise per mensem, for gentlemen, Rs. 135; lady and gentleman, Rs. 250. Not much change this from recent rates.

This is how the lieges are to walk. February 22nd, 1823. Bombay Castle.—1. Every person in walking, riding or driving on the road must keep the left-hand side of the road, that is the side of the road that is on his left hand. 2. A person overtaking, and walking, riding, or driving past another on the road must keep the person or carriage he passes on the left hand. 3. Any person violating these rules is liable to the penalties and damages occasioned by the infraction of them.

Published by the order of the
Honourable Governor in Council,
WILLIAM NEWNHAM, Chief Secretary.

To what minutiae extended our legislation in those days. Some of the following articles, I believe, were of better quality than they are to-day. In 1820 you have Hodgson's Pale Ale, and in 1836 Tennant's and Allsopp's. In 1821 Madeira was Rs. 14 per dozen; in 1826 Manilla cheroots were Rs. 5 per 100, and whisky Rs. 18 to Rs. 40 per dozen. As to oatmeal, Stoqueler says there was porridge at Malcolm's Public Breakfasts. Was it "No porridge, no promotion?" We hope not. In 1826 hot-water plates, soda-water, Glo'ster cheese, Loch Fyne herrings were on sale. Notices of births, marriages and deaths were charged Rs. 2 for each insertion. In 1854 wages were: coachman, Rs. 12 to 20; horsekeeper, Rs. 6 to 8; butler, Rs. 12 to 15; cook, Rs. 8 to 15; table boy, Rs. 6 to 10; hamal, Rs. 7 to 9; mussaul, Rs. 7; dhobie, Rs. 8 to 10; derzy, Rs. 6 to 14; sweeper, Rs. 4 to 6; bheestie, Rs. 5 to 8; mallie, Rs. 7 to 9; coolie, Rs. 4 to 5; palanquin (4 hamals) 3 miles, 8 annas; whole day, Rs. 1; shigram in 1857, Rs. 3 per day, same as for half an hour.

CLUBS AND SOCIETIES.

The following are the dates approximate of Clubs and Societies, &c.:—

Bombay Theatre built	1776	India Naval Club	1850
Sans Souci Club founded	1785	Poona Gymkhana	1853
Bombay Turf Club about	1800	Bombay Golf Club	1856
Bapre Hunt	1800	Bombay Gymkhana	1860
Highland Society	1821	Poona Club of Western India	1865
Mason Lodge	1825	Bombay Yacht Club, mentioned	1849
Byculla Club	1833		

A Character.

An Armenian, until within the last dozen years, used to stand at the corner of Forbes Street; would not take coppers, or allow himself to be photographed, was said to have been a ship-master, wrecked, and lost his mind. John Fleming, C.S.I., told me he saw him standing on the pier when he arrived in Bombay in 1849. He had generally three hats, terai fashion, on his head. He left about Rs. 8,000.

Changes.

A few items will show how much the Bombay of the present differs from that of the past. In 1800 black coats were the exception at funerals. In 1811, when rich men went home, they scattered rupees from their palanquins on their way to the bunder-head. We have seen nothing of this custom in our generation. Back Bay Sands was used by the natives as a place for burial, and you could scarcely ride along without unearthing a human skull. Toleration was at a discount, and about 1817 the East India Co. refused the Scotch a steeple on their church. Colaba and Sonapore burying-grounds were not consecrated till 1820. In 1823 the Mahomedan burying-ground, which you pass every day on your way to Malabar Hill, was nearly washed away by the monsoon waves of the sea. In 1827 Bombay was overrun at nights by armed burglars. A body of thirty dacoits came down Dady's Road, Malabar Hill, and attacked the police, who killed one of them. In 1835 Colaba Ferry (for the Causeway was still unfinished) was so badly lighted that passengers were in danger of being drowned. In 1849 Colaba church was thatched with palm leaves, and people were told to bring their chairs with them. In 1854 Sir William Yardley rebuked a juror for indecorousness in his dress, he having come in a kind of shooting-coat. In 1856 young men smoking at the bandstand were threatened with the police. They waited until it was dark before "lighting up," but people said the nuisance was all the same. In 1861 carriages and pairs had the first right to enter the portico of Byculla church, the one-horse buggy was told to "pass on."

The church authorities, no doubt, had nothing to do with this weakness.

THE FIRST ——

The first dentist in Bombay was a lady—Clara Rainitz, from Cairo and Constantinople: "Professes to clean the teeth and plug them up, extracts, and fixes new ones." In the same advertisement her husband professes to paint the interior of houses! This was in 1822. Before 1850 Dr. Hugh Miller, an eminent dentist, had established himself in Rampart Row. He left £10,000 to the Bombay Medical Mission. The first attempt at the relief of the poor was in 1831, the groundwork of the District Benevolent Society. The first house lighted with gas was that of Ardaseer Cursetjee, son of Cursetjee Rustomjee, Mazagon, in 1833. Poets broke into rapture when the first ice-ship arrived from Boston in 1836, and the coolies who carried it on shore said it scalded their backs. The first artificial ice came about 1877. The first exhibition of electric light was before Lord and Lady Falkland, in the Town Hall, in 1847. When the gas-lamps were first lighted on the streets several natives felt the pillars to discover if they were warm, and crowds collected to take their turn to climb up the lamp-posts to discover how the light was made. The first weaving company started about 1854. The first telegram was sent to England early in 1865. I did all I could to expedite it, but it hung fire ten days in Constantinople.

SMOKING, ETC.

In regard to smoking, a remark made to me in 1850 by one who had been in Egypt in 1801, and in Bombay in 1817, crops up. "In my young days," said he, "young men did not wear shooting-coats or smoke cigars." My earliest notice of cigar smoking in India is of Madras in 1829. "Some are to be seen lolling in their buggies and enjoying their evening drive on the beach, puffing away with the greatest *nonchalance* possible, while others on horseback or palanquin are to be seen amusing themselves in a similar way." From the acerbity of a Bombay paper in the following paragraph it would seem that smoking in public had not made much progress down to 1856, the date of this Bombay blast against tobacco. "Several young men light their cheroots as soon as the dark of evening is sufficient to prevent a full recognition of their persons and veil their impertinence.. The police ought to extinguish this nuisance at the bandstand." In Calcutta, smoking at the bandstand was not allowed. In Bombay I cannot remember European cigarettes much before 1870. The native *beedies* are, no doubt, of unknown antiquity, and may be the origin of our cigarettes.

One of the greatest factors of social enjoyment is exercise of the body, and this includes boating, riding, walking, and everything of an athletic nature. The man who walks or rides, or makes daily use of his muscles, is, *cæteris paribus*, a better companion than he who neglects his physical responsibilities. The name Gymkhana—I mean the word and club itself—is familiar to you. It originated in Poona in 1853, and came into use in Bombay a few years afterwards. In this land of so many Nimrods, both past and present, it would be an impertinence to ask what is the use of bodily exercise. It has passed into a proverb that a good shikarry makes a good soldier. The man who climbs the Dekhani Hills or rides over the Versova Sands is doing, at all events, some part of his duty, in that he is preserving the tabernacle which God has given him, fitting himself for the business of life, and doing what will tend to make him better able to fulfil his obligations to himself and to his fellow-men.

MERCHANTS.

Anyone who thinks the merchants of Bombay, in the first half of the nineteenth century, had an easy time of it is very much mistaken. If business was less exacting, life itself was more in hazard than it is now. Take one or two instances. In 1801 Arthur Mitchell, a partner of Forbes and Co., was killed in a duel. In 1820 Theodore Forbes, another partner, died at sea. In 1828 George Forbes, of Forbes and Co., died, aged twenty-eight; and on the Christmas holidays of 1828 John Forbes was killed by a fall from a ruined church wall in Salsette. In 1830 died James Forbes. Or take the case of Robert Edward Stephenson, of Remington, Crawford and Co., a most gifted and lovable man, whether in his business or the social circle. Some time ago I read a good many of his letters with very great pleasure. He and a Dr. Armstrong meditated going home, doing Egypt and Greece on their way—with many men the dream of their life. In February, 1819, they left Bombay in great spirits, by buggalow no doubt, the only method then of voyaging to the Red Sea. They saw all they wanted of Egypt and made their way to Greece. By this time it was August, the hottest month of the year. On the 6th of that month Armstrong fevered, and laid him down to die in the marshes of Albania. Stephenson, wearied with watching his friend, managed, through Thessaly, to reach Corfu, where he died on August 28th, 1819. *Risque de la guerre* no doubt. But how different in this age of Cook's Tours.

All was not plain sailing in those days, neither is there a royal road to fortune. You have only to read the Hon. John Jardine's story of some members of the Bombay Civil Service to discover that, even in a worldly point of view, when they managed to survive, many of our merchants had not a triumphant career. Many a monument of fame and fortune was no doubt carved out during these hundred years. But sometimes it was the reverse. Who does not recollect, in 1866, when the gains and losses were reckoned up, the fortunes could be counted on the fingers of one hand, while the dead and wounded literally strewed the field of battle? It is very easy to be wise after the event. But there were two men—one dead, one alive—who had the prescience to discover the breakers ahead in which so many were engulfed. Richard Cobden, on February 6th, 1865, sat down at Midhurst and wrote to a friend in Bombay: "My advice to you is to make as much as you can, professionally, during the saturnalia of rising prices, but not to take a part in any speculation, or to invest a farthing in any shares or joint-stock undertakings, or to commit yourself to unpaid-up shares of any kind. I am old enough to have been a witness of the panic of 1825, and of all the crises that have followed, and depend upon it the present state of speculative excitement will be followed by its revulsion as sure as the headache succeeds the debauch. (Signed) Richard Cobden." The recipient added: "All that he can say is that he wishes he had taken the above advice."

Another man, then young and undistinguished, wrote a series of trenchant letters signed "Q." in the *Bombay Gazette*, exposing the fallacies upon which the whole fabric of speculation was built, the financial imposture and Bombay mania of 1865. That man has now a statue in our island, and his name is Thomas Blaney. John Smith, of the "Old Financial," lived with credit to himself through that wild time, now Commissioner of Bankruptcy in London, and I am glad to see that his great experience has been availed of in his appointment by the Board of Trade as member of the Commission for rectifying the evils and abuses which have crept into the promotion and constitution of public companies, which we all know are manifold. Her gracious Majesty has just made him (1895) a Companion of the Bath.

Fifty Years Ago.

Fifty years ago Bombay was a very different place from what we see to-day. With some exceptions it was a city unpaved, unlighted, undrained, unventilated. There was no gas, no tramways, no hotels worthy of the name. Hospitality then did duty for hotels. No water from Vehar—only wells. We had only monthly mails, the Tanna Railway was still unopened. A steamer was a rare sight, and Bombay Harbour from Malabar Hill appeared a forest of masts. Fifty years ago Government had just swooped down on the Bunder gang and sentenced them to transportation. They had worked at their nefarious business for twenty-five years, at a profit of £60,000 annually. Malabar Hill had only half a dozen bungalows on it, and when the "Wilderness" was offered for sale some of the best buyers were frightened away from purchasing it, so much was it in the region of nocturnal robber kolis and dacoits. Fifty years ago old Napier, with his hooked nose, was making Sind. Manockjee Cursetjee had returned from Europe. Our Governor, Sir George Arthur, had excused himself from attending parties of the natives. Dr. Wilson was at home with Dhunjeebhoy Nowrojee, who is still doing good work among us. David McCulloch was chairman of the Commercial Bank, and William Graham, the philanthropist, was here, his long hair still unwhitened by the snows of years. George Buist edited the *Bombay Times*. Fifty years ago—let us be particular—so late as from 1826 to 1830, the shroffs of this Presidency had their caravans looted and sixty-four persons escorting them killed by Thugs. With returning commercial prosperity, the old Bank of Bombay and the old Oriental Bank were pluming their wings for that flight of credit which suffered no diminution for twenty years, and which in its day was second only to that of the East India Company. It was said that John Stuart, manager of the old Bank of Bombay, discounted bills to the value of £30,000,000 sterling with a loss of only £2,000. Fifty years ago Rudyard Kipling was as yet unborn, but Farrar (Dean of Canterbury) had left the parent nest in the Marine Lines, as Monier Williams had done some years before, the birthplace of these three men, each eminent in his own vocation, having been, we believe, in this city. We had Russian scares fifty years ago. I read in a newspaper of July 9th, 1828: "The Russians are not come yet. It will be time enough to board up your ghee jars and bury your gold mohurs when the croak of the frog ceases to charm away the night and the neighing of the Cossack's horse is heard at your door." And fifty years ago it was gravely propounded that the mangroves round our shores ought to be cultivated, as their existence constituted a standing menace to the boats of a hostile force in any attempt to effect a landing. Fifty years ago Matheran was an untrodden wilderness except by the denizens of the jungle. Colaba, Sion, Bankote and Mahableshwur were the only seaside or hill stations available. Fifty years ago there were many white jackets at dinner parties, and the hubble-bubble was not absent after dinner.

Advantages of Long Residence.

The advantages of living in those old times were that you were not worried by competition, and the telegraphic system, which has made all the world your next door neighbours. Men had more time to think. The factors were fewer in estimating probabilities, and speculation, if it dared a longer period, was not so much disturbed by unforeseen contingencies. There were no Council Bills. Men stayed longer in the country, and there was more time to create fast friendships.

The time men lived in the country enabled them to learn

the languages better, become familiar with the ways of the natives, not being blind to the excellences of the native character. Sir James Rivett Carnac, the Governor, at durbars, and John Fleming at meetings, delivered all their speeches in Hindustani, while Dr. Wilson conned over the Old Testament with David Sassoon in the same language, eked out by snatches of Arabic and Hebrew. All this created a fountain of sociability and well-doing towards Europeans. Witness the delicate and munificent instances of benefactions recorded by Mountstuart Elphinstone in his *History of India*; and in later days we find Cowasjee Jehangier Readymoney dividing Rs. 15,000 among the assistants of a European house, while Premchund Roychund gives a donation of Rs. 50,000 to an Italian Opera Company. We must not forget the late benefaction of Sir William Mackinnon, £10,000 to the employés of Messrs. Mackinnon, Mackenzie & Co., in Bombay and Calcutta, which surpasses, I imagine, any similar bequest ever made in the East.

Disadvantages.

Men who took the bright side of life found, they said, when they went home, that all things continued as they were. Malcolm's aunts were still playing at their old game of whist; the same old fogies were at the club, with their feet on the fender, pouring over the inevitable *Times*; the fields of England were as green as of yore, and the heather of Scotland as purple as in the days of old. But there was an obverse to the medal, the comic aspect of which was in the old Indian uncle asking his nephew, "Is that thing going on yet?" when he saw a crowd making their way to the new Houses of Parliament, and the pathetic aspects of which are delved in deep furrows on many a brow.

Dr. Carter (now deceased), the President of the Bombay Natural History Society of 1857, when he went home, could find scarcely a single friend that he had left in London. The story is full of pathos. "I will go," he said, "and see my old mother, and she will know me." When he reached his home her faculties had fled, and she had not the power of either articulation or recognition. "Vanity of vanities, saith the preacher; all is vanity." The burden, however, of every old Indian is, that the former times were better than these, and we too will go on repeating that there are no days like the days when we were young. Somebody, the other day, re-visited Bombay after an absence of thirty-five years. He found it a manufacturing city, and Malabar Hill under a canopy of smoke. Its sky when he left it was cerulean blue. But he found the men, with their telegrams and weekly mails, abreast of the age, which was not the case when he left its shores in the year 1860.

An Ancient City.

From the first day of 1800 to the last day of 1894 there are some people who have described Bombay as a dull place. The wail crops up at intervals like a weary refrain throughout the century. Sometimes it is a faint querulous minor, then a loud-mouthed diapason, when Bombay is called the "Morgue of India," an "intellectual desert," and all that sort of thing. People will do anything or go anywhere to get out of it. Then the flutter subsides, and the question is asked, "Are *you* here again?" Bombay is something more than a pile of buildings and a million of human beings. Lord Elgin was the first to call it an "Ancient City." But so it now is, hoary with associations, venerable by tradition, sacred as containing the dust of those who are dear to us, proud of her past, and looking boldly with an eagle eye to the future. Never in her history have such shoals of men and women from many lands as in this season cast eye on our city of palm trees. Battered by war, decimated by famine and pestilence, riddled by panics, still her towers gleam bright—

> "Across the dark blue sea."

If Pliny or Strabo were alive again and saw, week after week, the arrival of our mails, sometimes numbering half a million of letters, and the train of wagons laden with bullion and specie, it would make them think less of the glory and might of that dominion—

> "When Rome, the Mistress of the world,
> Of yore her eagle wings unfurled."

CONCLUSION.

Socially we should be nowhere without the Press, which would require a history by itself; and I have been compelled to omit all notice of the teachers of religion and morality—the fountain-head of all social happiness. My standpoint in this lecture has been one of necessity from an English point of view, but I would like to see one of our thoughtful natives doing more than I have even attempted to do, and from his own coign of vantage, and a more intelligent grasp of the subject of social progress, let us see how the changes have affected the social condition of the natives themselves, and how much of solid and substantial advantage the peoples of this country have acquired, instead of what they think or wish to secure. The retrospect, if complete for a hundred years, would, I am persuaded, be a startling one, and none more so than in regard to the security of life and property, which has added so much to the sum total of social enjoyment. While the richest man in Bombay is secure in his person and possessions, the poorest has liberty, the most priceless of all earthly boons, for the gold of Ophir and the topaz of Ethiopia cannot equal it, for by it, in the words of Burns—

> "The poor but honest man
> Is king o' men for a' that."

But I have done. The City of Bombay was built by God's assistance, and her citizens have ever traced their blessings to Divine Providence. *Pax Deo* was engraven on the first coin issued from the Bombay Mint in 1676, and we need not remind you that our last great ovation, in 1894, opened and closed with the sublimest strains of music, being an ascription of praise from all people that dwell on earth to the Almighty Creator, Lord and Father of us all.

(4.) SOME ST. ANDREW'S DINNERS.

"THERE is no mistaking the national attachment that is so strong in the Scottish character. Men return after long absence unchanged in this respect, whilst absent Scotchmen never forget their Scottish home. In all varieties of lands and climates their heart ever turns to the 'Land o' Cakes and Brither Scots.' Scottish festivals are kept with Scottish feeling on 'Greenland's icy mountains' or 'India's coral strand.' I received an amusing account of an ebullition of this patriotic feeling from my late noble friend the Marquis of Lothian, who met with it when travelling in India. He happened to arrive at a station on the eve of St. Andrew's Day, and received an invitation to join a Scottish Dinner Party in commemoration of old Scotland. There was a great deal of Scottish enthusiasm. There were seven sheep-heads (singed) down the table; and Lord Lothian told me that, after dinner, he sang with great applause 'The Laird o' Cockpen.'" *

1825, November 30th.—A small party at Mr. Cresselman's Hotel held a St. Andrew's Dinner. There was haggis and Glenlivet.

1831, November 30th.—The Highland Society held St. Andrew's Dinner in Lowji Castle. Seventy sat down to dinner. Rev. Mr. Laurie, the Scotch Padre, made a fervid speech, Mr. J. Sutherland in the chair. Among those present we observed Major-General Stevenson-Burns, Mr. Newnham, Sir Charles Malcolm, Colonel Pottinger, and Major Hunt. Band—Her Majesty's "Queen's." At a little past seven o'clock the Piper gave "Ae blast baith loud and fierce as ever Piper's drone could blaw." Mr. John Skinner gave "The Land o' Cakes" and "The Immortal Memories of Bruce and Wallace." Then followed "The Memory of Sir Sidney Beckwith." Mr. Farquharson gave "Sir John Peter Grant," and eulogised the

* From the Preface to the twentieth edition of Dean Ramsay's *Reminiscences of Scottish Life and Character*, 1871.

admirable way in which he had filled the vice-chair in 1828. (Band: *The Laird of Rothemurchus*). After which the Pipers played *The Rothiemurchus Rant.* We ought to have stated that the first toast was "The Kirk o' Scotland," after which the band struck up *My Love she's but a Lassie yet.* Then followed "Our Chief the King." Major Dunsterville had composed a song for the occasion which he sang. We give two verses:—

> "'Tis the Whiskey that has made the Southern wight
> To be blethrin thus of a Scottish tune,
> But ye ken the Minister's always right,
> And he thinks I'll make a hopeful loon.
>
> The other day as I the Manse passed by,
> A searching glance he gaed at me,
> Saw in my face sae mickle grace,
> His boon companion he's made me."

Broke up three short hours "ayont the twal." We'll meet again.

1832, November 30th.—At the St. Andrew's Dinner, Sir John Peter Grant proposed "The Memory of Sir James Mackintosh." Here are one or two snatches: "I propose the memory of a man whose society from the earliest days of my life I enjoyed, and whose friendship I had the happiness, etc. In youth he surpassed every one of his time, as much as in the full vigour of his life he surpassed every other man." Sir James had just died, and Sir J. P. Grant added a story of Mackintosh's boyhood. An English stranger, about the year 1780, happened to be wandering in the neighbourhood of Inverness when he met a boy and chatted with him. The youth made a deep impression on him. At a large party the stranger stated he was much struck with the boy's uncommon parts, and wondered who he could be. The host replied, "Oh, it's Jamie Mackintosh: everybody in Inverness-shire kens Jamie."

1834, November 30th.—At the St. Andrew's Dinner in Calcutta, Thomas Babington Macaulay, in proposing the "Civil Service of India," spoke thus: "Elphinstone I have seen, and I have seen him in England in a society widely different to that to which he had been accustomed. I have seen him supporting the dignity of his own character in the crowded streets of London. You seemed at once to be impressed with the idea that you were approaching a great man. It is difficult to describe what I mean, but there are some here, no doubt, will understand me when I say that I never saw any man who carried about him the character of greatness more than he did. It was impossible when you saw him not to think that you spoke to a very great man."

1854, November 28th.—St. Andrew's Dinner held in Masonic Hall, No. 1, Grant's Buildings, W. P. Adam, Private Secretary to the Governor, and afterwards Governor of Madras, took the chair. D. Davidson, Post-master, Cruopier. The Stewards were W. S. Ellis and Dr. Buist, also John Stuart and W. Forsyth Hunter, of the old Bank of Bombay, whom some of us remember. A. G. Frazer, descended from Lovat, was the chief speaker, who, we believe, is still alive.

There was nothing talked about then but the rumour, which was anticipatory of what was to take place in the following generation, that Lord Harris was to be the next Governor of Bombay. The papers stated he was then Governor of Trinidad, adding, "He is the grandson of the Hero of Seringapatam." It was at this dinner that Dr. Ross, an Ayrshire man, gave an impromptu verse of Burns, which we at the moment do not recollect in his poems: it could never apply to any kirk in Bombay:—

"As cauld a wind as ever blew,
A cauld kirk and in't but few,
As cauld a minister's ever spak—
Ye'se a' be het or I come back!"

1856, December 1st.—A St. Andrew's and Golf Dinner took place in the Masonic Hall, Grant's Buildings. The leading Golfers of that time were A. Robertson, C.S., P. H. Dunn, W. F. Hunter, Dr. Buist, J. M. Erskine, T. P. Riach, J. C. H. Brown, C. J. Kemball, James Blair, John Macfarlane.

Kemball and Blair we believe are hale and fere.

1859, November 30th.—There is no word of a Dinner; but a splendid Ball took place at Ardaseer Nusservanje Davur's at Tardeo. 250 European ladies and gentlemen were present.

It was at this Mansion, on January 25th of the same year, that the celebrated Burns's Centenary Ball took place.

1866, November 30th.—The St. Andrew's Dinner in the Town Hall was the largest ever held—more than 250 being present—the Honourable A. J. Hunter, of Graham and Co., Chairman (still well and hearty), and the Hon. A. Brown, of W. Nicol and Co., Croupier. The hilarity of the evening culminated in James Maclean's speech (still doing good work). In a vein of inimitable raillery (for Scotsmen can stand an immense amount of glorification on these occasions, particularly as the evening advances) he proposed the "Literature of Scotland," his opening sentence being, "The first great Scotsman I will allude to is William Shakespeare"—covering the extravaganza with "One touch of nature makes the whole world kin." This astounding hyperbole brought down the house. In such a heated atmosphere one could imagine anything, even a stony smile playing on the classic features of Elphinstone. He then leaped at a bound over several hundred years, to the next great Scotsman, Lord Byron, "Though half an Englishman, by birth a Scot."

Next morning, in a corner of the *Bombay Saturday Review*, the following *à la* Sir Walter Scott's confession met the eye on the woeful effects of the national beverage:—"The St. Andrew's Dinner has taken all the go out of us. It was not the Haggis, nor the 'Cockie-leckie,' but let us fairly confess, as Mr. Hunter assured us honesty is the best policy—the Whiskey Toddy." It was on this occasion that the Town Hall was first lighted with gas. A nest of unfledged sparrows caught fire in one of "the moons" on the ceiling, and, sad to say, flopped on the table as the guests were sitting down—a gruesome *antipasto* which the makers of the elaborate *menu* had not reckoned on. There are numerous traditions connected with this jovial dinner which we consign to the mists of antiquity, which is their merit.

1867, November 30th.—This dinner was held in the Durbar Room of the Town Hall, and was much more limited than the last—confined to about 100. A. D. Grant, Chairman; Hamilton Maxwell, Croupier. But two conspicuous men were there—Dr. Norman Macleod and Lord Napier of Magdala. Macleod deprecated the half-hesitating style of praising the Scotch. "I will make no deductions," he said emphatically, "from the assertion that Scotsmen and Scotswomen are the finest men and women in the world. This is the first article of your belief, and the second article is like unto the first—*Go and get all Englishmen to believe it.*" As it was a Saturday evening, Dr. Macleod would not accept the invitation unless the gas was turned off at twelve. I can verify that the croupier put us in total darkness at that hour, leaving us to grope our way out as best we could.

1872, November 30th.—I rather think Mackintosh Balfour was chairman of this dinner in the Town Hall. He did his duty well. I asked John Connon how he managed to make such an excellent speech. "By walking up and down the verandah for half an hour before I delivered it." Allen, of the *Pioneer*, was a perfect torrent of after-dinner eloquence. His subject was "The Press," and he did not weary us with the commonplace of the subject—the Press is "a mighty engine" and all that sort of thing. The Commander-in-Chief spoke of the defenceless state of Bombay and the desideratum. There happened to be a Masonic Dinner on the same evening, and the Admiral on his way home—Hewitt, I think—looked in. There were immediately loud calls for him to return thanks for the Navy. He did so in a most amusing speech, the gist of which was that we need be in no concern as long as he was there with his ships—never mind the Army, *sotto voce*—and concluded that we might rest perfectly satisfied of our security. "While I am outside I will see to it that you are all right." This was vastly fine, and we were pleased with a rattle, tickled with a straw.

1879, November 30th.—The dinner at Altamont was a big affair, Mr. Mowatt, Chairman—Magnus Mowatt. Cameron, the war correspondent, sat next me. He sang some Jacobite songs, and the plaintive strain of "When the King comes ower the water" still lingers like a melancholy refrain on the ear. Wordsworth, the Principal and son of the poet, was good. He had never been in Scotland, but from the hills of Cumberland he had once "a glimpse of the Promised Land." Everything he touched, on "The Literature of Scotland," was true and eloquent, though a little long. There was a story, most probably an invention, that a huge cauldron was steaming away during the small hours, out of which ladlefuls were swept as continuously as if from the goblets round a Persian wheel, that the cauldron suffered no diminution, that the thirst of the applicants was insatiable, and that someone scattered the byke in the words of the old song—

> "Drink thy nicht and day's desire!
> Get up this precious hour, or, faith,
> I'll fling your whiskey i' the fire!"

We merely mention the last great dinner of 1886, at which Lord Rosebery and many other notables were present. It was so recent it must live in the memories of all, and requires at present no recapitulation. We never recollect a time in which some festive occasion was more needed. For a long drawn monotone, like the swell of the Indian Ocean, we will back Bombay at present against the world. There have been similar periods in the old times before us, but never, we make bold to say, from the same causes. Such a time was in 1804—the days of wig and queue—when Bombay seemed to burst away from the clouds of misfortune which had enveloped her, and when we expended our festive energies on Arthur Wellesley. And such a time was 1866, "an ill year to reckon frae," as the Scots said of Flodden, but which furnished the largest Bombay St. Andrew's Dinner on record.

Of course, Malcolm was the Jupiter Tonans at all meetings of Scotchmen in Bombay before his big fight with John Peter Grant.

"The former times were better than these," said James Taylor to me in '66, speaking of the St. Andrew's Dinners of the "fifties." "*These*," said he, tossing to me a printed report, in his broadest vernacular, "were the kind of speeches we had then—Seton Karr and Henry Lacon Anderson."

One word more. The reader of this book need not jump to the conclusion that the Scots are not a sober people. An English Bardolph of the sixteenth century, sitting opposite to George Buchanan, ventured to tackle him with the question, "What is the difference between a Scot and a sot?" "Feel the breadth of the table," was the reply. And a Scotsman of the eighteenth century, while Burns was yet alive, Hector

Macneil, wrote these lines, which he may have thought out in the jungles of Salsette or the halls of Elephanta, for he was here in 1787—

"Robbie Burns in mony a ditty
  Loudly sings in whiskey's praise:
Sweet the sang! The mair's the pity
  E'er on it he wared sic lays.

O' a' the ills poor Caledonia
  E'er yet preed or e'er will taste,
Brew'd in Hell's Black Pandemonia,
  Whiskey's ill will skaith her maist." *

(5.) A BOMBAY HOTEL FIFTY YEARS AGO.

Hope Hall Family Hotel.

"The proprietor of the above establishment has spared neither expense nor trouble to deserve the distinguished patronage with which he has been honoured, and the continuance of which he most respectfully solicits.

"The house is situated in Mazagon, on one of the most agreeable, healthy, and fashionable spots of the island, and contains apartments particularly well adapted for families. Every room has a bathing place, etc., attached to it, and there is a number of single and double pole tents, with very desirable accommodation for single gentlemen. A bungalow containing a billiard table is set apart for smoking, which is not allowed in the house.

"The meals, consisting of breakfast, tiffin, and dinner, besides coffee and tea, are served Table d'Hôte or separately, as may be desired.

"For passengers by the Overland route, boats are kept ready to take them on shore as soon as the steamer is anchored. An agent of the establishment will take care and bring to the hotel the luggage, which every passenger is requested to point out to him. Arrived on shore an omnibus and private carriages belonging to the establishment will bring the ladies and gentlemen to the Hotel.

---

* *Scotland's Skaith: or Will and Jean.* Published Edin., 1795, ran through five editions of 500 each in seven weeks, and fourteen editions in twelve months.

"The proprietor, importing most of the articles of luxury, including beer, wine, and liquors, from England and France direct, is enabled to offer the best choice at reasonable rates.

"There are conveyances of all kinds in the establishment to be had at a moment's notice.

TERMS OF BOARDING.

"Board and lodging for a person occupying one room and taking meals at Table d'Hôte:—

Per month	Rs. 130
Fortnight	„ 75
Day	„ 6

Children and European servants, Rs. 2 per diem.

J. M. SCHULHOF.

"The proprietor begs most respectfully to draw the attention of messes, families, etc., to his stock of claret, champagne, and other foreign wines and liquors imported by him, which he offers at very low rates if taken from his godown.

"N.B.—Board and lodging for a gentleman or lady in their own rooms:—

Per day	Rs. 7
Fortnight	„ 85
Month	„ 160

REDUCED CHARGES OF BOARD AND LODGING FOR FAMILIES.

		Old Charge.	New Charge.
Lady and Gentleman, Table d'Hôte,	per month . . .	Rs. 260	220
Do.	Fortnight . . .	„ 150	110
Do.	Private, per month	„ 320	260
Do.	Fortnight . . .	„ 170	150

CARRIAGE.

1 horse conveyance, per month . .	Rs. 150	100
Do. do. Fortnight .	„ 75	60
2 horse conveyance, per month . .	„ 300	200
Do. do. Fortnight .	„ 150	110"

This is a most important document. No question has been more discussed than the cost of living in Bombay, and whether it has increased or diminished during the past half-century. But something has to be said on the other side, for exchange overshadows European life in India, and makes the life of many scarce worth living out here.

Hotel expenses mean rent, taxes, servants' wages, lights, and other items of bed and board. Readers of the document will form their own conclusions. Of course, in addition to the items we have named, there are many luxuries we have added which have become necessaries; but confining oneself to strictly hotel expenditure, the conclusion seems to me irresistible that there is no difference whatever between the year 1845 and 1895. The value of the rupee, *quoad* all other things, from gold down to coolies' wages, is quite another story. Leaving economists to pursue the subject, we gather from this announcement that smokers were less liberally dealt with than at present, and that the word "bath-room" had not as yet found a place in the hotel owner's dictionary.

(6.) BOMBAY HOTEL SCRAPS.

"Better a bush to sleep under in one's own country than a palace in a foreign land."—*Meer Roostum, Ameer of Sind, at Sassoor in the Dekhun.* 1844.

"There is nothing which has yet been contrived by man by which so much happiness has been produced as a good tavern or inn."—*Dr. Johnson.* 1776.

FROM these pessimist notions let us turn to the following Bombay advertisement of 1845. We give it with its bad spelling, grammar and punctuation :—

"BRITISH HOTEL, BOMBAY.

"For the accomadation of Families and Gentlemen. These specious premises are desirably situate in the Fort, and wethin five minutes walk of the Banks of Dock Yard, Custom House and principal House of Agency.

"Wines and liquors of the best description. Tiffins and Dinners sent out on short notice.—T. BLACKWELL, Proprietor."

In 1799 the Races Banquet was held at the Bombay Hotel.

On May 9th, 1800, we find a number of gentlemen dined at Maclean's Hotel to commemorate the capture of Seringapatam.

On August 15th, 1818, Duncan Cameron appears as sole proprietor of the Bombay Hotel and Tavern. This was the resort for many years of the celebrated Sans Souci Club, which entertained Sir Arthur Wellesley. Cameron is immortalised in the page and picture of *Qui Hi.*

In 1820 there must have been a number of hostelries of sorts from the following notice:—

October. "The Bombay Tavern *par excellence.* The mighty Tavern of the East. In the Fish and Vegetable Bazaar are The Country Tavern, The Duke of Wellington, The Lord Nelson, The Bootful of Mischief, The Chinaman's Tavern.

'Pay To-day and Trust To-morrow.'"

This is akin to the Italian shopkeeper who, during a commercial crisis, stuck every morning in his shop-window, "Credito Domani." When to-morrow came the same notice was exhibited.

September, 1826. The Elphinstone Arms shut up.

November, 1835. The Albion Hotel. R. T. Hart.

December 14th, 1837. Victoria Hotel opened, 15, Apollo Street.

December 31st, 1837. Hope Hall opened, Mazagon.

August 24th, 1839. A Bombay Hotel Company started to supply the want of a good hotel.

Boarding-house Advertised.

March 30th, 1842. It is remarked "there is no Hotel in Bombay at present," hence a Joint Stock Hotel and Boarding House Company is started with a capital of 2 lakhs.

November 26th. The British Hotel and Boarding House, Apollo St., Mrs. Blackwell, announced.

December 10th. The big dinner given to Outram advertised to take place in this hotel.

1850. A single man may live most comfortably on £100 a year.—*Dr. Moses' Sketches.* 1851.

1850, June 1st. Benson's Hotel, Rampart Row, opened.

1852, June 21st. Sailors' Home, Sanatoriums and Hotels filthy.

1853, May 16th. Hope Hall Hotel. Annie Blackwell.

1854, September 10th. John Manuel de Souza, Matheran, starts a Bakery and can receive and lodge two gentlemen. This is the smallest hotel on record.

1856, February 26th. Good entertainment for gentlemen and parties visiting this delightful station. Matheran Hotel, B. Basteon.

January, 1857. The *Bombay Quarterly Review* says:— "A broker introduced at a festive dinner at the Family Hotel, the Theodore Hook of the Fort Community, extracts a yellow handkerchief from his white jacket and sings. Considered a wonderful and inimitable being."

1358, March 4th. All liquor shops to be closed on Sundays between 10 A.M. and 1.30 P.M. and from 5 to 8 evening.

1859, April 1st. There is a goodly show of hotels. One paper says:—"If people must stand on their dignity there is The Hope Hall; if convenience is preferred above fashion there is The British and the English Hotel in the Fort."

1859, July 16th. Adelphi Hotel, names of residents published.

December 16th. The Clarendon Family Hotel.

August 12th. Smith's Oriental Hotel, Mazagon, each person Rs. 3, or Rs. 60 per mensem.

1861. Kaka and Mendoza's Hotel at Matheran well patronised.

1864, August 30th. Watson, for an Esplanade Hotel, bought from Government at auction a lot of ground at Rs. 110 per square yard. Competitor the Bombay Club.

(7.) SOME CATHEDRAL MONUMENTS.

PERHAPS the earliest inscription in the compound of the Cathedral is that over the remains of the wife of Rawson Hart Boddam, Governor of Bombay, 1784–1788. She died in 1762. The last time a grave was opened in the compound was to receive the body of the Rev. Charles Green, M.A., on August 15th, 1861. On January 9th, 1882, a grave was excavated for the deeply-lamented Lady Fergusson, near Bishop Carr's cenotaph in the Cathedral itself, but she sleeps in Sewree. The grave was six feet deep. The contents thrown out were simply sea-sand, as on the esplanade, warranting the belief that very few persons were buried in the church enclosure, and a glance at the monuments on the walls confirms this opinion, for they are mostly cenotaphs of people who died elsewhere on land or sea.

Probably not more than three or four dozen people were ever buried within the church (and mostly in vaults) from first to last. For example, Admiral John Watson—who was brought in mortally wounded from the siege of Tanna on December 21st, 1774—I am almost certain, is buried in Sonapore, though his monument is here. For every burial within a church in India the fee to the chaplain was Rs. 600 (1833). You may be sure when Hart Boddam's wife was not allowed a resting-place under the church roof in 1762, and Andrew Nisbet, perhaps the wealthiest man in Bombay at his death (1790), lies in the compound, that admission was a matter of extreme difficulty. Besides, there was no necessity for filling the temples of the living with the bodies of the dead. As soon as Mendham's burying-ground was swept away, Sonapore was opened in 1763, and probably during the interregnum the two ladies we have named found a last resting-place, "welcome guests," as the poet hath it, during the transition period when tombs were being trundled down by the score, and everything outside was a hurly-burly of confusion.

The dust also of Elizabeth Rivett-Carnac, the young and the beautiful, is twice vouched for, though she died at Broach. Her grave lies at the eastern end of the church; the tablets were recently placed over the western porch. This change was an exigency not to be avoided. And here I may be allowed to make my *amende honorable* to the Cathedral authorities with regard to the broken and shattered monuments which had to come down in building the new chancel twenty years ago. They have done everything they could and done it well. They have placed the tablets, built them I should say, into the wall with much care in a room in the Clock Tower, where their beautiful sculpture and epitaphs now look down upon you, suspended between heaven and earth, and undisturbed by the bustle of the outer world.

Mr. Keess, the Cathedral clerk, led the way up rather a rickety stair and showed them to us; but I assure you that if

Hector Cherry, the representative of the impoverished Government of Bombay in the Cotton Loan of 1802, or Alexander Dow, so unmercifully discredited by Burke and Johnson for his History, were now to look into this domicile of their cenotaphs, they would be vastly pleased. If only the deft fingers of some neat-handed Phyllis were brought to bear upon the adornment of this abode, it might become a veritable drawing-room of the dead, like that in Cairo, where Indian shawls, Persian carpets, and the sepulchres of Mahomed Ali and his son Ibrahim are the only furniture. Dow's grave was lately discovered in Bengal, so this is only "an empty honorary tomb." Between the upper and lower *alto-relievo* sculpture, the vacant space where the epitaph had been stares you in the face, for it has disappeared. I dare say the man did not want any more. With Burns—

> "Go to your sculptur'd tombs, ye Great,
> In a' the tinsel trash o' state!"

But the words "History of Hindustan," graven with a pen of iron on the book which rests on Clio's knee, is a sufficient memorial. Not he who runs may read the inscription now, but he who climbs high and cranes his neck at the requisite altitude:—

[*East Wall.*]

In Memory of
KATHERINE KIRKPATRICK,*
Obit 27th January 1766,
Æt. 22.

> Image of truth! In mind by few surpassed,
> In Beauty's mould, by Nature chastely cast;
> That here thy relics long reposed in earth
> Have slept without a tribute to thy worth,
> Arraign not conjugal nor filial Love,
> For pledged by each the sacred shrine will prove
> That memory, clinging to a consort's heart,
> Tho' late, pays homage to thy mortal part,
> And with thy image graven on his soul
> Wafts many a sigh to India from the Pole:
> That thy own sons asserting Nature's claim
> Join to commemorate a mother's name,
> And hallowing with their tears the votive stone,
> Record her virtues and attest their own.

---

* Her husband was Colonel James Kirkpatrick, of the Madras Army.—*Calcutta Review*, April, 1899.

A very fine monument, representing in high relief a beautiful female form in the attitude of devotion. This is a tomb worth looking at, for here lies all that remains of Katherine Kirkpatrick, the mother of him who concluded that treaty with the Nizam which crushed the power and influence of France in the Dekhan. This was James Achilles Kirkpatrick, whose talents extorted the admiration of the Duke of Wellington, and who has further claims on our interest from the fact that his daughter Katherine (you see she bore the honoured name) was the adored of one of the greatest writers in the English language. The name is here inscribed in marble, less durable I ween than the Kitty Kirkpatrick of Carlyle's *Reminiscences*, or the Blumine of *Sartor Resartus*. When this tomb was erected is all conjecture. William,* the elder brother of Achilles, when Resident at Hyderabad, was driven by sickness to Bombay in 1797, and here, thirty-one years after their mother's death. the two brothers *and* their father, who no doubt was the writer of the inscription (then living at Holydale in Kent), may have joined hands across the seas in placing this memorial of affection over the grave of wife and mother. Don't you think the words "conjugal," "filial," and "sons" establish this conclusion? Carlyle himself could have written no epitaph in poetry more tender and appropriate. It remains here only to note that Katherine Kirkpatrick, whose young life ended so briefly in Bombay, was a daughter of Alexander Munro, and that her husband survived her fifty-four years, dying at Holydale in 1818, eighty-nine years of age, his grand-daughter "Kitty," as Mrs. Phillips, surviving to 1889, eighty-seven years of age, which are good examples of Anglo-Indian longevity. Everything on this tablet is good and the sculpture exquisite.

---

* His daughter was the mother of Charles Buller, see *Cornhill Magazine*, September, 1897. William Kirkpatrick married. at Calcutta, September 26th, 1788, Miss Maria Seaton Rawson, and left four daughters: Clementina, married Admiral Sir John Louis, Baronet; Barbara, Charles Buller, M.P.; Julia, Edward Strachey, father of the present Sir Ed. Strachey, Baronet. W. K. died August 22nd, 1812, aged fifty-eight.—*Dict. Nat. Biog.*

[*No.* 11, *South Wall.*]

To the Memory of
Admiral
Sir F. L. MAITLAND, K.C.B., F.M.R.G.,
and Commander-in-Chief
Of Her M. Naval Forces
In the East Indies.

Departed this Life
Nov. 30, 1839.

This monument is erected by the officers of the Indian
Navy,
As a token of respect and esteem for the memory of this
distinguished officer,
Particularly to mark their sense of the kind and considerate conduct
uniformly shown by him to their Corps
During his Command and Service with them
In 1838–39.

[*No.* 3, *Centre Aisle*]
[*Over Grave.*]

Here lie the remains
of
Rear-Admiral MAITLAND, K.C.B.,
Naval Commander in the East Indies,
Who died on November 30th, 1839.
Aged 62 years.

He commanded the *Bellerophon* when Napoleon surrendered his sword and person, all which may be found in the history of the times. I read that at this period Bonaparte felt the heat very much, and when it was over seventy degrees became very uncomfortable. I conclude that he could not have stood a hot weather campaign in India, or even a march like Sir Henry Daly's. Lady Maitland died at Lindores, in Fifeshire, in 1865. The house, a small one, is most beautifully situated on a rising ground, the green sloping banks of which, dotted with laurels, run down to a lake well stocked with perch. There is a table in the house made from the timber of the *Bellerophon*, and when I was at Lindores someone pointed out a pane of glass in the schoolroom on which young Maitland had scribbled his name with a diamond, a name afterwards "writ large" on the history of 1815-16. I saw a letter in 1893 in the *Standard*, from an officer of the Navy, who had been at the funeral, and he attributed Maitland's death to the climate. I am not surprised at this, nay more, can believe that the statement is perfectly true, for the more I look into the history of Bombay during the first half of this century the more I am convinced that the chances of prolonged existence in it were exceedingly small, and if any man lived to the age of threescore and ten it was only by a kind of miracle. 1829, with its material, comes more ready to my hand than 1839, but that decade shows little progress compared with the times nearer our own, when the two Crawfords—the one on land, the other on water—for did not the one give us our markets and the other Vehar?—when Hewlett extinguished many sinks of filth, and Blaney poured oceans of fresh water among us. I think there is nothing more appalling than the mortality among our countrymen and women which these tablets declare. Why, confining ourselves to the Judges from 1828 to 1830, four of them died within twenty-seven months, and two of these held the office of Chief Justice. From 1828 to 1834 there died two Advocates-General. Nor did the wives fare better. Lady Awdry and Lady Dewar in 1834, and Lady Perry in 1841; and look at their ages. The greatest age attained by any of these individuals was Sir Edward West, 45. Sir William Dewar, Chief Justice, died at 33! and the children died like flies. Verily, in 1894 we have something to be thankful for. Two monsoons do not now measure the life of man. Something has been added to the term of existence. Pure water and sanitary reform are priceless blessings, the importance of which it is impossible to exaggerate.

A pessimist poet of Bombay in 1829 contributed these lines to a local journal, and considering the date and the black funeral pall which hangs over it, I do not wonder at the spirit which they manifest. It is a wild cry of delight of some Bombay youth all alive and about to quit its moribund shores:—

> "Adieu, Bombay! May I forget the ever-
> Pestiferous hole, all other pests excelling
> In dust, mosquitoes, pariah dogs, and liver:
> Not Milton's limbo would be worse to dwell in.

Life in that Island is scarce worth the living—
  A sheer existence without one emotion
Save from the Physic dying 'Pills' are giving,
  Themselves more fit to quaff the patient's potion.
And Rampart Row, our Fort's great New Bond Street,
  No more down thee I'll drive—a Bombay blade,
Cravatted, stayed—my Rosinante fleet,
  Or glide along the peopled Esplanade."

This may not be poetry, but we can understand the sense of it in 1829.

Here are the ages and dates of decease of the respective Judges and Law Officers we have referred to :—

Sir Edward West, 45	1828
Sir Charles Harcourt Chambers, 39 * . . .	1828
Sir William Seymour, 35.	1829
Sir James Dewar, 33	1830
Richard Orlando Bridgman, Advocate-General, 30	1828
Graves Chamney Irvine, Advocate-General, 42.	1832

[*No. 2 North Transept.*]

Beneath this stone
are deposited
The remains of
EMMA,
Wife of William Newnham, Esq.,
and
Daughter of the late
Nathaniel Newnham, Esq.,
of Barn-Rocks, in the
County of Sussex,
Obit 29th July, 1823, Æt. 24.

William Newnham was a Bombay civilian of great distinction, and for twenty years Secretary to Government. You can scarcely take up a Bombay paper, for the first quarter of this century, without finding his name in it. Newnham stands first in the social scale. Governors were but birds of passage—he was a fixture, a man who was the life and soul of every move-

* Nephew of Sir Robert Chambers, Chief Justice of Calcutta.

ment that contributed to the happiness of the community. One day he gives two hundred guineas for a cup to be run for at the races. The next he becomes security for the debts of the Bombay Theatre, which, I think, totalled up to Rs. 30,000: the Government took his place afterwards, but that does not affect the intention. Another day he founds the Byculla Club. His picture still hangs there to remind us of his busy life. On his retirement on December 29th, 1834, after twenty-nine years' service, a big ball was given to him by the European inhabitants at Lowjee Castle. He lived at Belvidere, kept up the sparkling traditions of that hospitable mansion, and at his leisure could see from his verandah the finest view to be had of Bombay, which you will find verified by Dr. James Campbell in the Bombay Administration Report, 1893–94.

[*No. 5 Porch, North Wall.*]

In Memory of

GEORGE DICK,

Who died on the 9th May, 1818, aged 78 years,
Entering early in life into the employment of
the Hon. the East India Company,
His talents raised him to the office of
Accountant and Director of the Company's Bank, and,
By a series of subsequent promotions, to the honourable
post of Governor of Bombay.
During the long and eventful period of his services he
Discharged the duties of his several stations with
Fidelity to his employers and honour to himself.
This Tablet
was erected, in commemoration of
His distinguished virtues,
By an affectionate son.

George Dick was Governor of Bombay exactly one hundred years ago, in succession to Sir Robert Abercrombie, son of the hero of Alexandria. At his death he was the oldest civil servant of the Company, having come out in 1759. His friends advised him to go home—he preferred Byculla, and was never out of Bombay except on one occasion when he made a trip to Bankote. He had uninterrupted good health until a few days before his death.

Dick at home, no doubt, was accounted a "nobody." He was *somebody*, however, throughout the length and breadth of our island in 1794.

Another Governor, Crommelin, had elected to live in the country, and died at Moorshedabad at the age of eighty-one.

Sir William David Evans, made Recorder of Bombay, took up his appointment in 1820, and in little more than fifteen months after his arrival died, December 5th, 1821, in his 55th year.—*Dict. Nat. Biog.*

[*No. 15, South Wall.*]

Sacred
To the memory of
JAMES WALES, Gent,
A native of Peterhead, Aberdeenshire,
Who died in Nov. 1795,
Aged 48 years.

Also
To the memory of Margaret, his wife,
Daughter of William Wallace,
Annie Taylor, his wife, of Dundee,
Who died in May, 1795,
Aged 36 years.

Also
Of Angelica, their Infant Daughter,
Born at Colaba,
Who died in Dec., 1795,
Aged 7 months.
This Tablet is erected by Susan,
The eldest of
Four surviving daughters,
In grateful and affectionate
Remembrance of her parents.

The lady who erected this monument to her father, James Wales, the painter, was the progenitrix of all the Malets, for Susan here mentioned became the wife of Sir Edward Warre Malet. Mr. Hugh Poyntz Malet, the discoverer of Matheran, one of her sons (born 1808), writes us, under date June 8th, 1893, that Susan Wales was born July 30th, 1779, married September 17th, 1799, and died December 21st, 1868. His authorities are unimpeachable—the insurance office, the Bible at Willing, and tablet in Newton Tavoy Church, Wiltshire.

Everybody at Matheran knows Malet's spring and has drunk thereof, and this statement is like unto it, clear, perennial, and incontestable.

I conclude by expressing my warmest thanks to the Venerable Archdeacon Goldwyer-Lewis for a copy of the inscriptions in the Cathedral. Without it this paper could not have been written.

(8.) SOME BOMBAY STATUES AND PORTRAITS.

"OCTOBER 10th, 1812.—The new Town Hall to be built is intended, among other purposes, for the reception of the statues of the Marquess Cornwallis, Mr. Pitt and any future monuments of British Art which public gratitude may bring to Bombay": and again—

"1816.—For the reception of the statues of the late Marquis Cornwallis, Mr. Pitt, and the Marquis of Wellesley, which have cost nearly £20,000 sterling raised by the contribution of individuals. These, as they have hitherto done, are likely to remain in an obscure warehouse, unless we can rear a suitable edifice for the reception of such splendid and exemplary testimonies of public respect and gratitude to the services and to the virtues of the most eminent statesmen of our country."

Bombay Government Letter of 22nd February, 1817.

Bombay Gazetteer, Vol. XXVI.

Of Mr. Pitt's statue we know nothing, and have no further record about it. We have the following notice under date of 1854:—"The statue of the Marquess of Wellesley was suffered to be neglected for years after its arrival in the warehouse of Messrs. Forbes and Co., and it was with the greatest difficulty, and only through the influence and liberal contributions of Sir Charles Forbes that money was raised to put it in its place." Cornwallis's and Wellesley's statues are now (1895) in the Elphinstone Circle.

March 23rd, 1821.—This day the foundation of a monument was laid at Corygaum to commemorate the battle fought at that place.

May 13th, 1821.—Subscription being raised in Bombay for the National Monument in Edinburgh. The *raison d'être* may be new to many of our readers. "To record the Victories in Europe and in Asia in which Scotsmen were engaged, and to provide a Temple for the Worship of God." This taken evidently from the home appeal to the public. I have never heard in Edinburgh the last-named purpose even hinted at.

January 26th, 1822.—Subscriptions solicited for a statue in Edinburgh of Robert Burns; amount now £373 12*s*. This I believe was the first statue raised of Robert Burns. It was started in Bombay, and this fact is recorded on its pedestal. The statue is now in the Royal Institution of Edinburgh.

August 2nd, 1823.—William Erskine to sit for his portrait for the Royal Asiatic Society, where it may now (1895) be seen.

"August 16th.—Sir James Mackintosh's portrait, which was voted to him twelve years since, has not yet reached Bombay." Nor has it yet, and I believe there is neither marble nor canvas in the Asiatic Rooms to represent this distinguished man. I see the question is asked on April 4th, 1841 :—"Why is there not a picture or bust of Mackintosh in Bombay?" The same question may be asked in 1895.

1824, August 31st.—The Marquis Cornwallis's statue, sent out some years ago to be erected in the centre of the Green, cost £5,000. The figures right and left are those of Wisdom and Integrity. October 14th.—Statue now being put up. No sooner erected than the natives adjourn to it as a place of worship. Government, by printed placards in the vernacular, tried to explain and dissuade. Worship, I believe, still continues in a mitigated form at this statue.

1825, September 3rd.—Preparations are commenced on the triangular piece of ground on the Esplanade, opposite the Church Gate, for the purpose of erecting the statue of the Marquis of Wellesley.

1830, October 27th.—Statue of Sir John Malcolm proposed.

1833, April 31st.—Subscriptions solicited for Sir Walter Scott's monument in Edinburgh.

1833, December 3rd.—Sir John Peter Grant's portrait arrived. Sir Herbert Compton, the Chief Justice, would not allow it to be put up in the High Court. When Sir Charles

Sargent was Chief Justice in 1892 it was hung in the most conspicuous place facing the Judge in the highest criminal court of Bombay.

1836, September 20th.—Malcolm's statue arrived. December 27th.—Put up in Town Hall. Everybody pleased.

1839, October 26th.—Statue of Sir Charles Forbes extensively subscribed for, now amounting to £3,000.

1841, March 24th.—Statue of Marquis Cornwallis to be removed to Town Hall. This was not done, and I observe on June 9th of this year, at the beginning of the monsoon, a scaffolding was put round the statue of Wellesley on the Esplanade to protect it from the weather. This statue must have been removed to its present site some time thereafter.

1854.—The bust of Sir James Carnac, which was subscribed for in 1841 and arrived in 1846, lay three years forgotten in its packing-box under one of the Town Hall stairs, and was only discovered by accident. This is something of a piece with Bentinck's statue, which was detained in pawn in Calcutta in the year 1841.

(9.) THE GARRISON OF BOMBAY, 1845.

THE Garrison of Bombay within the walls, in the year 1845, consisted of about 3,500 men, as follows:—

2nd Battalion Foot Artillery.

A wing H. M. 22nd Regiment.

The 9th Regiment Native Light Infantry.

The 10th Regiment Native Infantry, and the Marine Battalion.

The fortifications of Bombay, we are assured, required a garrison of 8,000 men to man them sufficiently.

The Governor of Bombay commanded these troops, the Town Major was his representative in the Fort, and the Commander-in-Chief could not exercise any direct control over the troops in garrison. First there was the Commandant of the garrison, then the Town Major, then the Adjutant of the day, who was not to quit his lines during his tour of duty. Then there were Adjutants of Corps, who were either to attend at the Town Major's office at 12 o'clock daily, or direct their Sergeant-Major to do so. Recruits were victualled three days by the Commissariat gratuitously after their arrival. The line turned out without arms whenever the General commanding-in-chief came along the front of the rank. On such occasions tents of the quarter-guards were struck, the camp colours planted in line with the sergeants' pikes and tents, the drums piled up behind the colours, and the line dressed by the standards or colours of the regiment. Such were some of the honours paid by the troops according to the Bombay Garrison Regulations of 1845. The fortifications of Bombay, fifty years ago, mounted 1,100 guns, and yet in 1850 this was considered insufficient, and we need not say they required minute and daily inspection. Even with every precaution, there were sometimes lamentable accidents and offences. On June 9th, 1820, when George IV. was proclaimed in the Place of Arms, near the Main Guard, at 5 P.M., at the close, a weather-chest on Hornby's Battery exploded, killing six Europeans and two lascars. On February 22nd, 1831, an English private was hanged for shooting the sentry at Church Gate. The Commandant of Artillery had exclusive charge of the guns on the fortifications and the bastions, and was subject to the orders of the Governor alone. With the latter rested solely the allotment and distribution of public quarters in the garrison and Colaba. The garrison was quartered within the walls, and the walls had three gates, guarded by sentinels. These were the Apollo, Church, and Bazaar Gates. There was a fourth gate, the land entrance (a water-gate also on the sea face) to Bombay Castle, which was the Balla-Killa, a fort within a fort. The bastions were named after such magnates as Granby, Nelson, Moore, or Hornby; Fort George after George III. But the names graven on stone with a pen of iron have passed away, and are to be found in the more enduring book of History.

During the period that Bombay dwelt within stone walls there were fewer complaints than one would have expected. The irksomeness arising from a sense of confinement was inevitable. "Oh, that I had the wings of a dove!" The streets were narrow, which tempered in some degree the glare; but the dust! For, so far as we can see, they were never done hammering, widening gates, making sallyports, repairing breaches, and the noise must sometimes have been sickening. And the unexpected would often happen. In May, 1851, the moat, 2¾ miles in length, was dry from end to end, an incident which had never occurred before in the memory of the oldest inhabitant. The drying up of that ditch must have made it a fine hotbed of zymotic diseases.

The Governor, as far as we can see, though he had a giant's power, did not use it as a giant. He did not worry the colonists; did not, like him of Gibraltar, as tradition avers, assert his right to have the first selection of the fish exposed in the market, and hang a butler who presumed to make a purchase before his Excellency's table wants were supplied! And Governor Yale of Madras (we are sorry to say an American—the founder of Yale College) hanged his English groom, as mentioned in a previous article, for leaving his service without notice, at least so it is averred. But the reminiscences of Bombay's Governors are mostly of a kindly nature. When a fire took place, the great Elphinstone was at once on the spot, working with his hands like an ordinary mortal, animating and encouraging everybody in extinguishing the conflagration. During the French scare somebody roused Duncan in Apollo Street, in the grey of the morning, and announced to him that the French Fleet was sighted. I tell you he was not long in getting into his Commander-in-Chief's uniform, hurrying across the Green, and through the Castle gates in a twinkling. "But where are my men?" It was a false alarm—some English ships hove in sight. He only laughed. Nobody knows what became of his money. The tradition in Arbroath, his native place, was that Leatham Grange was purchased for him, and when he died, in 1811, the Provost of that town came into possession. This estate was sold in 1869 for £120,000. What boots it?

> "Duncan is in his grave;
> After life's fitful fever he sleeps well;
> Malice domestic, foreign levy, nothing
> Can touch him further."

Yet, it was in these old Castle walls that a Governor was wont to hob-nob after dinner with the skipper of an East Indiaman, pass the bottle of arrack, and drink the King's health. "Slow poison this," said the skipper in a jocular way. "It must be slow," replied his host, "for I have drunk it for forty years!"

At all the gates in 1845 there was a close inspection by the sentries of articles going out or coming in, and the officers in charge examined every package suspected of containing arms or ammunition. No hay, straw, pitch, tar, rosin, dammar, turpentine, varnish, painting oils, gunpowder, bamboos or bamboo mats, tattas, cadjans, dried cocoanuts or arrack, copperas, toddy or country liquor were allowed to come in through the gates. Liquor was allowed *exit* without demur. A considerable source of irritation arose from the following notice, and the grievance was ventilated in the newspapers as falling heavily on the natives, though, so far as we can see, it applied also to Europeans. "No open umbrellas or *summer-heads* allowed to pass through the gates." This was felt as an infliction by the natives, as a lowering of their position, and evidently there must have been some irritation, and even tussles between passengers and sentries, for it is added, "but the sentinels were not to use their musket or bayonet in enforcing an order with which some people may have been unacquainted."

The highest authority on this subject at present in Bombay is inclined to the opinion that this order was to guard against the concealment of illicit materials which could not be seen by the guard overhead. The reader will remember that it was in such a chamber, over the gate, that David wept over Absalom. Summer-heads are supposed to be discs on poles, such as are still carried at Roman Catholic funerals. In how short a time a word in Bombay in familiar use becomes archaic we may learn from "summer-heads." In the year 1845 it was part of a public notice stuck up on the gates of Bombay to be known and read of all men. Fifty years thereafter it has dropped and is as dead as a door-nail. Like Eliza Draper's "conjee cap" (starched) it has become obsolete and has ceased to exist. The rapid fluctuations of our English population, so unlike that of Europe or even of America, explain, what otherwise would be unintelligible, that a word in current use in 1845 should, in 1895, find scarcely one person in Bombay who knows the meaning of it.

Church Gate and Bazaar Gate were in 1845 open all day and night. By an order of July 5th, 1832, Church Gate had been closed during Divine service, as there had been many complaints of its interruption by processions and beating of tom-toms. Apollo Gate was opened at gunfire and closed at 10 P.M. Gunfire was a long-established custom. On April 11th, 1760, was heard for the first time the morning and evening gun, which for more than a century has shaken the rickety rafters of Bombay, from Apollo to Bazaar Gate. No European non-commissioned officer or soldier was permitted to go out of Church Gate without a pass, and no coolie or other porter with loads of baggage to go in or come out; but hamals and coolies, bringing water into the Fort, were permitted to pass till 9 A.M. Many of the best houses in the Bazaar had deep wells of fairly good water within their tenements, which still (1895) exist, but an abundant supply was available for those who had it not from the wells which had been dug outside the walls on the Esplanade, and during a severe drought in Mountstuart Elphinstone's time he had two sallyports constructed to afford additional means of ingress to water-carriers during the water famine.

The ramparts and bastions of Bombay were a favourite promenade of the lieges at sundown, where there was a good breeze and a fine view of the harbour. People arriving by sea at this hour could see the promenaders taking their constitutional. The Castle Gate had a number of restrictions. It was opened at sunrise and daybreak. The same gates (1895) have been there for 200 years, and are a veritable antique. All persons within the Castle were forbidden smoking under the severest penalties. No fire or light allowed to pass except in a lanthorn. The fire-engine house was opposite to the monument on the Bombay Green. Persons entering the Laboratory are to take off their arms and spurs, and are to have no iron in the soles of their boots or shoes. The money room in the Castle was never to be opened but in the presence of the Sub-Treasurer or his assistant. On entering the Treasury many years ago we went with shoeless feet, as you do in the Mosque of Omar in Jerusalem, or that of Sultan Hassan in Cairo. The fortifications were always jealously guarded from the inspection of the curious, particularly foreigners. I have read somewhere that Niebuhr, the father of the historian, was either cautioned or arrested while making sketches, and now, even if you were Chairman of the Corporation, you could not gain admission without an order from the Inspector of Ordnance, to which restrictions we all say Amen.

Natives on horseback were not to pass through Church Gate, except at a moderate pace. No hackery, or carriage without springs, to enter in or go out by it, also carts of burden, except bullock carts laden with meat for the use of the army or navy. No led horse to pass. The reason of this last prohibition is quite unknown to us. The Apollo Gate was locked at 12 P.M., but to be opened for ladies' or gentlemen's carriages after this hour. No soldier to go out without a pass. No filth to be carried out of this gate.

Bazaar Gate.—Hallalcores with their carts to pass through this gate only, covered hackeries with women are not to be inspected or molested. Dressed provisions, fish, and mutton for private use to pass unexamined. Beef not allowed to pass through. This last no doubt in deference to the natives. Covered hackeries ostensibly for women, one would suppose, would be a favoured method of smuggling. Persons to be apprehended who wash in the town ditch; also idle natives found in the works, and people who dry clothes on the palisade or buildings. No person to swim in the ditch; and no person to fish in it without permission. Such were some of the restrictions imposed by the authorities on passengers and goods at the three great gateways of Bombay. We may here note that when dining outside the Fort, you had only to ask the password for the night to secure your admission at any hour.

The demolition of the walls and fortifications of Bombay (1862-4) was a question that was settled by the public long before the East India Company took it in hand. As early as May 1855 the public had fully made up its mind on the matter. "Down with them into the Ditch, say we"; and querulously, on April 1859, "We suppose there is no probability of the Fort walls being thrown into the Ditch to admit fresh air and expansion." On August 10th, 1861, a memorial to Government is spoken of to demolish the ramparts, and it is added, "We shall perish if we do not get it." Sir W. R. Mansfield, the Commander-in-Chief, was convinced of their inutility, and has left in a Minute, dated January 18th, 1862, his opinions thereon: "That the Town or Fort of Bombay was, a hundred years ago, somewhat in the same case as Genoa and Venice at the era of the Italian Republics. The State was in the town itself, and in the safety of the town the preservation of the State was consequently involved. The Island of Bombay, instead of being an isolated town exposed to piracy and other dangers, with no field army from which to call for help, was now an enormous and growing commercial capital of a large and flourishing province, studded with the stations of an army, a considerable portion of which was immediately available by railway." He thought that the conclusion was inevitable, that while the Government could not be too careful of the harbour defences, all anxiety was removed as to any possible danger that could come from the interior. His conviction was that the position of the Fort was either untenable or one which should not be held. He accordingly recommended the razing of the ramparts (*Bombay Gazetteer*, Vol. XXVI.).

These are words of weight, and must have told where they were needed most. The Company certainly required information, for as late as December 7th, 1859, we read that "new fortifications are to be commenced immediately at a cost of twenty lakhs!." It is now more than thirty years since these fortifications were dismantled, and the time is fast approaching when it will be difficult to meet with a man or woman who will be able to say, "I have lived within the walls of Bombay," or "I remember well the rumble of my carriage crossing the drawbridge." To hear that rumble again you must go to Toulon, or some other fortified city, and enter by diligence. It is difficult to realise the change that has been effected by the demolition of the walls; for all our palatial buildings and gardens, now in their glory, could not have been constructed unless this great measure had been carried out. India may be the "Land of Regrets," but I never heard a regret at the disappearance of the walls of Bombay.

About the time the walls were beginning to be demolished an event took place which made men reflect. You remember the Trent affair of 1861, and how near we were being involved in war with America. We were naturally very uneasy about our defences at that time—not these old walls; nothing of the kind. They had been pronounced mere buckram and pasteboard, in the light of modern armaments. So great was the anxiety on the subject, that a meeting of the Chamber of Commerce was called (January 15th, 1862), and eloquent speeches were made by Mr. Cassels and Mr. Fleming. Our aggregate annual commerce, they said, was then forty millions sterling, with a shipping capacity of 770,000 tons, and a bombardment was possible. Yet in that numerously attended meeting there was not one man who bewailed the loss of our fortifications; and, please remember, at the date of that meeting the last of our artillery had been already trundled off to the Dekhan—in fact we had scarcely guns or gunners wherewith to fire a salute. Like a strong wrestler we had cast off our superfluous clothing, that cincture of moat and curtain, scarp and counterscarp, which encumbered our action and impeded our growth and very existence. That meeting called on Government for harbour and naval defences—a cry which should never cease as long as we have life and property to defend. Woe to them that are at ease in Zion. The Duke of Connaught was not one of those. The subject was much in his heart. If we cannot take care of such a valuable property as the City, Docks, and Harbour of Bombay, we are scarcely worthy of their ownership, and do not deserve to be the custodians of the lives of 800,000 human beings.

There was no part within the walls of Bombay so jealously guarded by its citizens as the Green. Who first gave it that name we know not; but all honour be to the man who first called the unoccupied space by a word of such hallowed associations, redolent of Merry England, and memories of home, Maypole, and "Christ's Kirk on the Green." Often, indeed, it belied its name: a swamp, and mother of dead dogs in the monsoon, and of living ones in the hot season; "a free coup" for all rubbish; a yard filled with cotton bales; the Place of Arms where sovereigns were proclaimed, troops reviewed, dead men's chattels bought and sold, but the Bombay Green all the same; the counterpart of that unenclosed common of every village at home, overshadowed by its church, of which no power on earth could deprive the people; the People's Park, native and European equally proud of such a heritage. It came in with the English, and will exist until the last Englishman is exhibited in an iron cage to the delectation of the residuary legatees! Did anyone ever attempt the invasion of the sacred soil? An attempt was made during Lord Falkland's administration (1852), and not until a monster petition to the Directors had been despatched to every man of influence at home who knew anything about Bombay was the scheme of building on the Green abandoned.

It was the same spirit—I mean the greed of converting everything into money—that at an earlier period (1840) dictated the proposal to sell the Malabar Point bungalows, which was only, we believe, averted by the decision of the supreme Government. And akin to this, we read (1850) of a serious proposal to let the Elephanta Caves as a tavern and ball-room! I want to know, in passing, by whose authority the old tamarind tree at the foot of the Siri Road, at the Wood Wharf, Chowpatty, to which patimars for ages were moored, has been recently destroyed.

A writer on the Bombay Green in 1850 with a prophetic instinct makes the shrewd guess: "Shall we ever see fond lovers there, sitting under the shade of umbrageous trees?" I suppose that it is quite unnecessary to remind the present generation that our Elphinstone Circle is the nucleus of what was once the Bombay Green. The gardens there now in all their splendour can answer that question. Arthur Crawford, in 1869, stuck a few trees there into the vacant space, from which has arisen a fairy scene which now surpasses the wildest dreams of his imagination.

(10.) BOMBAY 1857.—A FORGOTTEN CHAPTER.

As the months rolled on people were divided on the question, Was there, or was there not, disaffection in Bombay? At length Forjett answered the question. He had been to Parell, and obtained ample powers from the Governor. "Do as you will, Forjett; I know you will do nothing wrong," was his answer on opening his eyes after a momentary cogitation. Fortified by such an authority, Forjett was not slow in using his powers. It was then, and not till then, that he told a meeting of Mahomedans that every guilty man would be steadily dealt with, undeterred by the trammels of law, and strung up before his own door. We all know how, with Major Barrow and Edgington, of the police, he went on Saturday evening, October 3rd, to the house of Gunga Pursad, in Sonapore, and again to the same place on Wednesday, the 7th idem, and unearthed the conspiracy; how Drill-Havaldar Syed Hoosein, of the Marine Battalion, and Private Mandul Guddrea, 10th Regiment Native Infantry, were arrested, tried for sedition by courtmartial on the 13th, and found guilty; how the conviction was confirmed on the 14th, and they were sentenced to death; and how, on the Esplanade, the site of our polo-ground (1894), on the following day, October 15th, at ten minutes past 5 P.M., they were blown away from the guns. Captain Bolton gave the signal to be "ready," and then in a loud tone ordered the gunners to "fire," when the wretched men were launched into eternity; a gruesome sight. No man or boy forgot it, for it haunted the spectator in his dreams ever afterwards.

Every section of our community, in this season of sorrow and prodigious calamities, bowed their faces to the earth before the great God of heaven and earth. In the day of adversity we are told to "consider." So the Lord Bishop sets the 14th of August as a day of humiliation in view of the dreadful judgment with which God is visiting this land. Many also repaired to St. Andrew's Kirk, and Dr. Wilson summoned the members of every branch of the Nonconformist churches to daily meetings in Ambroli. In the fire-temples there was no uncertain sound. One thousand Hindus, headed by Vurjivundas Madhowdas, Nurotamdas, and Jugganath Sunkersett, met for prayer on October 6th, at the Temple of Shree Mombadevi. Two men only visited Mahableshwur this season. People were chary about moving through the districts, where many of the relatives of the men who were executed at Satara resided. The season of 1856 had been the most brilliant on record. But gaiety was now out of place when so many of our brothers and sisters were in affliction. In this time of wild and conflicting rumours, to the honour of Bombay it did not lose its head. Only once did a tremor fall on part of our community. At Colaba, on August 3rd, many Europeans took to the ships in the harbour, leaving their goods and chattels, as they thought, to be looted or burned in their absence. No doubt, some Gunga Pursad business had reached them in exaggerated form. And on Saturday, August 8th, the *Berenice* arrived in our harbour with the residents of Rutnagherry, who had come off in a hurry, and were no sooner here than they wished to be "back again." You need not ask if the military authorities were on the alert. On August 10th the Moulvie of Satara was brought down from Poona by the police, and, with eight accomplices, was made a close prisoner on board the *Akbar*. The population of Satara and Ahmednagar were disarmed before August 24th. At Kolhapur, on August 19th, eight men were blown away from the muzzle of the guns, seven "shot to death," and two hanged. At Satara, on September 8th, eighteen mutineers were executed. At Karachi, on September 14th, seven mutineers were hanged, and three blown away from the guns. At Ahmedabad, on October 26th, ten were hanged, three shot, and five blown away. Poona was somewhat alarmed. Two guns were stationed, during Divine service, a few hundred yards from St. Mary's Church, artillerymen ready horsed. This was on August 24th. There had been treasonable placards to murder all Europeans, and offering Rs. 5,000 for the Governor's head. They were signed by Nana Sahib Peishwa, now reported to be marching to the throne of Poona. Bombay, you may depend upon it, at this time was not idle. There was a proposal to start a regiment of cavalry, consisting of two hundred European gentlemen volunteers. All furlough was stopped except on medical certificate. A garrison order prohibited the use of razors. The Governor's body-guard was disarmed; they quietly surrendered their sabres, carbines, and pistols. This is noted on August 24th. Colt's revolvers were supplied to 192 of the police on August 13th by Colonel, familiarly known as "Tommy" Tapp. The European sailors from the harbour were quite willing to aid the rich natives in defending their lives and property, principally as night watchmen. The consumption of spirits was large, and they had, as they long remembered, a jolly time of it. At Karachi, no one was allowed to go abroad after ten at night. It was then the Press was shackled, judiciously enough, as I suppose, though John Connon inveighed against the "Gagging Act." There was an editor's room at the Secretariat, where you could learn what you were, or were not, to publish. Every now and again there were arrivals dropping in from the beleaguered districts.

August 15th.—At Poona a few ladies arrived from Sholapore—fifteen more expected.

August 20th.—Forty to fifty distressed ladies expected from Karachi, or the population of Satara and Ahmednagar would be disarmed, or the Divali would cause a stampede among Europeans and a cessation of business.

But internal affairs were not neglected. Buist proposes to cover the main drain. Forjett advocates gas to light the city. The buggies are condemned as the most disgraceful conveyances in the civilised world. Wilson opens an orphanage at Mazagon. Arthur Malet and the Byculla Club dine the officers of the 33rd Regiment. A meeting is called by the Sheriff, in the Town Hall, to express admiration for Sir Henry Havelock. Henry Carter founds a Natural History Society. Framji Nusserwanji Patel gives a catalogue to the Asiatic Library. Henry Austin Layard, of Nineveh, is among us. The Bible Society is represented by Major Mylne, and Dr. George Birdwood is balloted a Member of the Royal Asiatic Society, all which we must put to the credit of 1857. Even the amenities of the town were discussed. For it is an extraordinary incident, and shows what faith men had in the future, when they busied themselves with the best means of making beautiful the suburbs of Bombay. When treasonable placards bespattered the walls in Poona, and when one would suppose a great fear and dread had fallen on all men we read (*Bombay Times*, September 16th): "For thirty years successive Governors have ineffectually endeavoured to have the open road across the Esplanade planted with an avenue of trees, to afford shelter to the Natives during the heat, and to the European, pleasure of the eye." Come what will the European had determined to shelter the native. He may pray in Cathedral, or St. Andrew's, or Ambroli, but Trust in God and Do the Right is his motto. His cheek may be pale, but no terror shall affright him, not even the violence of frenzy or fanaticism can divert him one hair's breadth from the path of duty. There is a world of philosophy in this sentence, "shelter to the Natives," uttered, not in the calm which followed the storm, but when we were in the vortex with the wind and waves of revolt all around us. It is straws like this which tell us how the wind blew in Bombay on September 16th, 1857.

You may ask what became of business all this time, and how were the merchants occupied? And it will come upon you as a surprise that cotton exports were never exceeded by those of 1857 until the American War. Never before this date had they bulked so large. The exports of cotton were 680,000 bales. The panic which followed the confiscation of Nana Sahib's investment in Government Paper, sending it down to eighty, soon subsided. The Mutiny expenses were over twenty-eight crores. Has anyone complained of the money he lent to Government? If property at any moment decreased in value, it was merely the delusion of a day. Somebody tells a story that when the barbarians were thundering at the gates of Rome a plot of land which lay outside them was put up to auction, and knocked down at as good a price as could have been obtained before the enemy was heard of. Here is an incident that may be cited in the same breath. On the self-same day in which the men were blown away from the guns people were calm enough to discuss the question of a gold currency for India. A letter, several columns in length, appeared in the Bombay papers, signed Goldmore, which traversed the effect of the Californian gold discoveries. These were the days when sovereigns could be purchased at a few annas over ten rupees. Gold was then the debased metal, and now silver is of no account, and we are all fighting our way through the paroxysm. The Chairman of the Chamber of Commerce, this year, was John Fleming, and he lived at Love Grove, at the end of the Vellard, one of the ablest men who have ever filled the chair. He is only twenty-six. A fine-looking man, and of a leonine countenance, destined to play an important part, during the next twenty years, in the commercial drama of Bombay. William E. Frere, a much respected man, and brother of Bartle, lives at Altamont. In December of this year the Rev. Philip Anderson dies at his house, and Frere smooths his dying bed, for he is a good Samaritan. Few men have left sweeter memories behind them in Bombay than William Frere. Anderson died a young man; he was only forty-two. He left behind him a book on Western India, which, so far as it goes, is unrivalled, and its accuracy has never been impeached. The bulk of it appeared in the *Bombay Gazette* in 1854, and in the *Bombay Quarterly Review*, which was started in 1855, in January, and of which, I think, he was the first editor. If Anderson had lived there cannot be a single doubt that he was the man to have written the history of Bombay from first to last. The rest of us have been merely scraping on the surface. Anderson came out in 1842. Stationed in Surat 1847, he came to Colaba 1849.

On October 19th the *Bombay Gazette* congratulates Forjett, and later on the natives presented him with plate to the value of 1,250 guineas. No other man can claim the guerdon of 1857 with Forjett. He was well seconded, not only by Europeans, from the Governor downwards, but by many natives, of whose names there are no memorials in bronze or marble or in the records of the city. The city itself is their memorial. The bread we eat and the water we drink we owe to them. To them also we owe security of life and property, for had they been against us there would have been only chaos and confusion—for a time. It was a proud announcement which Lord Elphinstone made on leaving our shores on May 9th, 1860: "The native inhabitants of Bombay, not one of whom was implicated in treasonable designs." We accept the dictum without modification or reservation of any kind, impugn it whoso list. Lord Elphinstone was a truthful man, and knew about what he spoke, or he would never have uttered the statement. There are few cities that can say, after the lapse of two hundred years, that no son of theirs has suffered death for his religious or political opinions within its walls.

(11.) BOMBAY STREET NOTES, 1810 TO 1860.

WHOEVER reads these scraps is hereby warned that they have nothing to do with the present time. "'Tis sixty years since" makes all the difference in towns at home or abroad, but even now (1896) our odours are not always of Araby the Blest, though our sanitary salvation has been almost accomplished by the Tansa Water Works.

1808, September 10th.—"In the Parell Road the water ran with a considerable velocity at a depth of four feet."

1819, April 23.—"Cholera considerably increasing." Was not this about the time of its first advent in India?

1820, July 1st.—"Colaba Ferry is a cincture of reeking straw and filth, skirting with pestilence the breach before the Fort. I could put up with the rocking of a passage boat, if it were possible to avoid that devil of a road, bumping you over a rugged mass of rocks from one island to another." Burns, the poet, in a letter of 1786 speaks of the "hallalcores of the human race." They were much wanted in Bombay in 1820.

1820, July.—We have this speculation, "that he should not wonder even if the whole of Back Bay should fill up and become as dry in time as the Esplanade; what an accession to our territory, Mr. Editor, this would be—with suitable residences in Henry and Kennery for invalids." A pleasant forecast of what the Back Bay scheme of '65 aimed at doing, and did add a small slice, and which is no doubt being added to gradually by the silting up of sand during the last thirty years.

1821, June 9th.—"A heavy death-roll from cholera."

1822, November 6.—"I hope on my next visit to Bombay to find that the Flats, a large portion of Bombay, have been drained and brought under cultivation." Yes, the main drain, under Sir Robert Grant's administration (1835-38), must surely have done some good, though itself the *cloaca maxima* and greatest nuisance of the century. The Flats are (1896) in a fair way of reclamation for building sites and gardens, and probably in some future age may become the site of a New Town. August 22nd.—"Panwell, the very acme of mud and filth."

1823, July 5th.—"The Green is a space of ground which we hope some day to see surrounded by buildings worthy of the good taste and public spirit of the people." Realised to the letter in the Elphinstone Circle of 40 years afterwards.

1823, August 16th.—"Continued rain and universal sickness." October 11th.—"Rumour that the charcoal used by Europeans consists of wood which had been used by the natives in burning bodies in Bombay." No doubt a *canard.* "Bombay Green to be enclosed by posts and iron chains as an oval."

1824.—"No monsoon. Government Proclamation on October 15th anent economising water in tents and wells. Police peons to be stationed at each well."

1825, January 5th.—"Fort ditch drying up rapidly." August 25th.—"The approach to the Esplanade is vile beyond description, logs of wood and stinking rubbish almost fit to knock you down." December 17th.—"Bombay afflicted with a plague of beggars."

1826, January 7th.—"The monsoon of 1825 was almost a total failure, and it was a year of universal sickness, some of our brightest ornaments having fallen victims." February 11th.—"The Fort, even at 11 A.M., remains in a most filthy state." April 1st.—"Dogs on the Cotton end of the Esplanade and on the sands, pariahs and curs with clipt tails and ears." A kind of Alexandria or Constantinople. April 29th.—"Temporary bungalows on the Esplanade have all got dunghills before them." This would remind Scotsmen of the old song—

"There lay a duck-dub at my daddy's door."

1826, May 16th.—"When the grand depôt of cotton was removed from the Green to the Esplanade its limits were fixed. The passage to Colaba is now obstructed here, there, everywhere." August 5th.—"Esplanade—A huge dunghill covers half the road." October 11th.—"After an absence of fifteen years I am disappointed in Bombay. We then hunted pariahs in the

Black Town on a Sunday; now laws are created for the murder of pariah dogs." November 11th.—"Turn your steps towards Back Bay and be thankful you are of the Kirk of Scotland, and have not to blush at the state of consecrated ground." I gather from this that the conservancy of Sonapore cemetery was then at a low ebb. June 17th.—Trenchant articles in the papers to "fill up the Ditch and throw down the walls. Fortifications once necessary, now useless. Batteries at Colaba would be more effective." Suggestions not fully realised till 1864.

1832, August 4th.—"Back Bay malodorous."

1835, December 26th.—"Fearful stenches in the Native Lines."

1836, August 9th.—"Markets propcsed to be built near Erskine Road."

1837, September 26th.—"Fearful smells at night caused by drying bumaloes on the rocks."

1839, March 19th.—"Government orders six additional wells to be sunk on the Esplanade." July 27th.—"Warden Road greatly obstructed by rubbish." October 12th.—"Bombay has been very properly named the Morgue of India—hope H. E. will infuse a little life into the dead carcass of society." This is social, however, rather than sanitary.

1840, July 22nd.—"Great increase of jungle on the island." August 5th.—"Many bodies found in wells." November 6th.—"Bombay still unlighted; nothing but black, gloomy and melancholy darkness."

1841, February 24th.—"The Fort is now a second Augean stable—heat suffocating." March 24th.—"We are informed that H. E. has directed that the oval space called Bombay Green, in the centre of which the statue of the Marquis Cornwallis now stands, is to be neatly laid out and railed in as a garden. Sir Robert Grant suggested the planting of all the roadsides with trees. Now *un fait accompli*, well and truly done." October 12th.—"The unhealthy position of the Colaba Barracks is now fully demonstrated." All nonsense. The two Napiers put this all to right.

1849, February 16th.—"Our nuisances are the barking o pariah dogs at night. Ferocious dogs attack people at Church

Gate at night." I am afraid they are like the poor, "always with us."

1850, September.—" Rumour that Elephanta is to be turned into a tavern and ball-room." More nonsense. The next fond anticipation has been answered by the custodians (1896) locking the Elphinstone Garden gates at sundown. "Bombay Green—a swamp in monsoon and a receptacle of stones and dust in fine weather. Shall we ever see fond lovers there, sitting under the shade of umbrageous trees"? November.—"Children not burned, but buried in the sands of Back Bay."

1851, May.—"The moat round Bombay, 2¾ miles in length, is now dry from end to end, and was never dry before."

1852, June 18th.—"The Fort is no cleaner nor more savoury than it was in your time" (say 1832).

1852, April 11th.—" A monster petition to the Court of Directors, London, from the inhabitants of Bombay, against any building being erected on Bombay Green. Copy sent to every firm or individual in England who knew Bombay."

1853, November 19th.—"Saw a corpse strung by four cords jostled through the streets to its shallow hole in the sands of Back Bay."

1854.—"Hornby Row is one of the filthiest streets in Bombay." Many letters in the papers on the Main Drain Nuisance. August 19th.—"The Town Hall is now in a very dirty condition; the stairway the resort of idle gamblers and so forth." November.—"Corpses floating in harbour after the Great Storm. Public notice to abstain from fish, as was done in 1827 and '37."

1856, September 9th.—"Vehar works in progress."

1857, October 20th.—"Dr. Buist proposes to cover the main drain." A most earnest and useful man. Who knows if the seeds of his illness and death were not sown in such foul surroundings?

1858, May 15th.—"The sanitary condition of Bombay is a disgrace to us all."

1859, May 17th.—"Ditch fearfully foul."

1860, February 29th.—"From Colaba Church to the light-house the stink might be cut with a knife." May 3rd.—"A

Goanese corpse from the Jejeebhoy Hospital was left at Sonapore Churchyard and eaten by vultures and dogs."

1861, November 23rd.—"Mr. James Gibbs (a most estimable man) moves in Justices' Meeting that, Bombay being in possession of the English for two centuries, coolies and others should not be allowed to go about in a state bordering on absolute nudity." This motion fell to the ground. Some one travestied—

> "Lo, the poor Indian whose untutored mind
> Clothes him before, and leaves him bare behind."

(12.) THE BLACK DEATH.

"Give me the hurricane rather than the pestilence."—*Brougham.*

On August 15th, 1348, which means 25th by our calendar, a strange disease appeared at Bristol. The harvest of that year could not be gathered for rain, and, while it lay rotting in the fields, people were wondering how they would subsist during the coming winter. It looked as if half the population would not be able to find bread. It never occurred to anyone that in a few months half the population would cease to exist. At first people were disposed to laugh at the new importation, and they thought little of it; but by and bye, when a thousand or two fell before it, unconcern gave way to the deepest anxiety or the wildest terror. People fled from it as from a destroying angel. The mysterious visitor which had reached our shores was the most mortal of all epidemics, and was no other than the black death, or Bubonic plague of the Ptolemies and of Justinian, and carried the mind back to the emerods and rats of Gaza and Askelon with the Ark, and the "oxen lowing as they went" on their way to Kirjath-jearim. The disease had never been known in England before it appeared in Bristol in 1348, and it deserves to be noted that it remained domesticated on the soil of England, with slight intermissions, for three hundred years, and never left our shores until it finally took its departure in 1666, since which date, let us thank God, it has never returned.

It reached London on November 1st, 1348; but the news of its approach by ships from the Levant and from across the Channel had long preceded it. As the mighty wave rolled from realm to realm, the tidings came like the portents of a thunderstorm. There had been mutterings from the Caspian, the Bosphorus, and the Adriatic. Cairo, Damascus, and Byzantium were merely the milestones of its onward journey. Boccaccio limned it at Florence; Petrarch spoke of it as a world's wonder; and Laura died of it at Avignon.

It seemed to have come to a head in England when Bradwardine, Archbishop of Canterbury, died of it at Lambeth on August 26th, 1349, one week only after his arrival at Dover, with the fatal botch in the armpits. Long before this, thousands had fled from the various cities of Europe and Asia. The Bosphorus was subsidised by Constantinople, while Naples fled to the slopes of Mount Vesuvius, Rome to the Alban Hills, Florence to the Apennines, London to Epsom or the New Forest, and Edinburgh to the Braid Hills, while, away over the sea, Damascus was making tracks for the Lebanon, and Cairo for the Lybian Desert, and Delhi, under Tughlak, was being shovelled wholesale to Dowlatabad. I stop not to inquire the reason why. Famine was in evidence and plague in India in 1345.

The duration of the Black Death in London was seven to eight months, and in all England fourteen months, the population of the city being then about 200,000. It had the same duration as the plague of 1666, the same curve of increase, maximum intensity, and decrease. The five highest weeks of 1563 were successively in deaths, 1,454, 1,626, 1,372, 1,828 and 1,262; and 1348 resembled it.

At Avignon it was very fierce: sixty-seven Carmelite monks were found dead in one monastery, no one outside having heard that the plague was among them. In the English College the whole of the monks were said to have died of it.

At first science and its students walked up boldly to it. It was belabouring an elephant with a feather. They then pelted it with nostrums. The Black Death would be neither scotched nor killed, and laughed at science and empiricism. The wisest doctors of the age in every country in which it appeared were confounded. How and whence it came, how long it would remain, over what area it would spread—the Black Death was inscrutable. The disease defied investigation and cure. Petrarch tells us, "If you question the philosophers they shrug their shoulders, wrinkle their brows, and lay the finger on the lip"; or, as Lucretius wrote in reference to the plague in Egypt, "The healing art muttered low in voiceless fear." All the medical records of 1348–49, if printed, would not fill one of our daily newspapers. The sovereignty of man lies hid in knowledge. How much do *we* know about it?

Meanwhile Kali, with her necklace of human skulls, secure in her seat, rode on in triumph, conquering and to conquer. You may find her footprints on the mounds of Delhi, as well as in the ruins of Memphis, for it was she who made them both. Everything consumable was to be burned up; and until that came to pass there would be no end to the great tragedy which involved twenty-five millions of human beings.

The disease now among us in 1898 is the same as the Black Death of 1348. It is the same in its causes, its antecedents, and its mortal effects. Its characteristics are mostly the same. Its violence and rapidity are in cases as intense, though its contagiousness is less apparent. The exception of the general immunity of Europeans from attack hitherto has proved a stupendous mercy for us all. But, in its sweep, the plague of 1348 far exceeds our own; for it took a much more extended range, embraced an area wide as the known earth, desolated some of its fairest regions, and swept a moiety of population from the greatest cities of the world. Asia Minor, for example, seems never to have recovered from its desolating effects. The two catastrophes, as far as we know, were the same in their origin. Man, and man alone, was responsible for them both. Man does not make the earthquake, the cyclone, or the thunderbolt; but he makes the pestilence. It is he, and he alone, who allows filth to accumulate, surround and enter his dwelling, soak into the soil, and impregnate it with its deadly poison. This is not "the act of God or the Queen's enemies" (as the old shipping documents express it). Frankenstein creates the monster that destroys him; or as Homer hath it, "We blame the gods for that, of which we ourselves are the authors." We have been seeking for its origin in many places; and as distance lends enchantment to the view, we have gone to Hongkong, to the slopes of the Himalayas, the roof of the world, or the back of the east wind. "It is not in heaven, neither is it beyond the sea, that thou shouldest say, who shall go over the sea for it and bring it to us?" It is verily at your own doors at Mandvie, 1·90 foot above the level of high tide. Volney remarks, "In a crowded population, and under a hot sun and in a soil filled deep with water during several months of every year, the rapid putrefaction of bodies becomes a leaven of plague and other disease." And Creighton, a hundred years thereafter (*Epidemics of Britain*, 891): "Given a soil charged with animal matter, the risk of those living upon it is in proportion to the range of fluctuation of the ground water."

The reader need not be reminded that a considerable portion of Bombay is under the level of high tide, and presents obvious difficulties to the drainage engineer. Add to this the volume of water which is poured in day and night by the Tulsi and Tansa aqueducts, and the fact that there are wide spaces in Bombay where there are more people crammed within the same area than in any city in the world. Each of these plagues was heralded by the same antecedents. You remember the great rain of 1896. It rained day and night consecutively in Bombay for two or three months (eighty-seven inches) almost without intermission. This was in June, July and part of August, followed, of course, by tropical heat. There were people who remarked at the time that such an abnormal rain would be followed by some abnormal disease. Once the word "plague" flashed across the mind it was summarily dismissed as unworthy of suspicion. The plague was discovered here in September, 1896. This great rain had its counterpart in England and in Italy in 1348, where it fell almost without a break from Michaelmas to Candlemas. Then the rats (those awful rats which devoured Sennacherib's bowstrings) in both cases came forth from their holes, half choked, driven to the surface seeking for air, a ghastly premonition, staggering at first as if drunk, and littering the alleys with their dead bodies. Dead rats have ever been an accompaniment of the plague. In ancient Memphis there was a statue of Horus with outstretched arm, on the palm of which was a rat saltant, with this inscription: "Look at me and learn to reverence the gods." There was the same concealment of cases, and when houses were deserted or shut up, robbers went afoot to pillage them. People shut themselves up in country houses, and unwittingly enclosed the enemy also within their gates, or, fleeing for very life, went on board some old hulk; as well get quit of their own shadows. The only highly-paid and fully-employed labourer was the grave-digger, until he also toppled over. Everything that was of use before became suddenly of no account. "All that a man hath will he give for his life"—money, lands, houses, furniture, plate or the costliest jewels. Industry and trade ceased to exist. Debtor and creditor were merely names. Ambition was a rotten virtue; what was the use of economy?

"Let us eat and drink, for to-morrow we die." Yesterday morning a corpse was seen lying on the edge of the Queen's Road, and to-day (March 17th) two others on the same side-way. These were samples—the last remains of a hundred "unknown residents"—nondescripts who now are sowing the earth with their ashes. You understand the reason of what has now ripened itself into a custom. In the darkness of the night, and perhaps when there might be still a glimmer of light, they had been dropped near the burning ghaut. Relatives have, you see, no further trouble and expense. Government cremates, and the surviving tenants are protected from eviction. It is here you see the sacred relations of father and mother, wife and children, brother and sister, which have been established by God and Nature for wise purposes, and everything comprehended in that sacred word "family," cast to the winds, and the bonds which bind society together broken and destroyed. Can a greater evil befall humanity than this?

Buboes in groins and arm-pit have been the concomitants and, in each of these plagues, indications of the disease. There was the same delirium. A man would run across the street and fall down dead. With the dawn of day dozens of dead bodies, nameless and unknown, were found in wells, ashpits, dunghills, sewers and street corners. Many had been abandoned by their relations, and some had committed suicide

And happy was he who at sunset could say with the Emperor, "I haye lived a day."

When the total losses of the first twelve weeks of 1898 were counted up, there had fallen 20,000, and the plague was not stayed. I suppose that few of the great battlefields of history have presented a more formidable list of dead and dying than the city of Bombay in the first three months of 1898. For some days the only traffic observable in the streets was the wood wherewith to burn the dead. In the plague of 1348 it was the dead that menaced the living. Cremation has happily, in part, saved us from this great catastrophe. At first we were curious and anxious, then dull and stupid, now we are callous and indifferent, and the daily mortuary returns of 300 to many people awaken as little interest as the figures in an account-book or multiplication table. In the funerals that pass I observe that the body of the deceased makes very little appearance. The corpse, as a rule, is "unco wee," as the Scotch would say, or bulks but little under the mortcloth; and this leads me to believe that the harvest of death has been reaped among the weak and the wasted, whether from famine or disease. The lowest stratum has been the first attacked—those who were destitute of good food, warm clothing, or good lodging. Those who had none at all have fallen an easy prey to the insatiable devourer. So was it with the Black Death. Its effects on the labouring class are displayed in the preamble of the Statute of Labourers, November 18th, 1350. "Forasmuch as a great part of the people, principally of artisans and labourers, is dead of the late pestilence." In the worst dens and hovels of the disease—and some of them are several stories high—you see to-day houses that have been unroofed to let in the light, dislocated tiles, and rafters dirty and blackened, cleaving the skyline.

"The pestilence that walketh in darkness" is as true to-day as when the words were first uttered three thousand years ago. A gleam of light bursts upon us in this weird and wild time of 1348. The Church was still undivided in these pre-Wycliffe days, and claims an undivided interest from Catholic and Protestant. Whatever may be said of that early Church, the priests of it exhibited a heroic devotion, died at their posts, and have bequeathed a legacy of courage and fidelity to all time coming. In East Anglia alone upwards of 800 parishes lost their parsons from March, 1349, till March, 1350. When Parliament was twice prorogued, when the Assizes were disbanded, when Oxford and Cambridge were closed, the inmates of the great religious houses, unmoved, unshaken, unseduced, unterrified by either infection or contagion, upheld the banner of the cross, and bore it bravely in their high and holy work until they were relentlessly mowed down, and were ushered into their eternal reward. There was surely some gain in this salvage from the immense wreck, over which the black Angel of Death was beating its wings.

From the Archbishop of Canterbury, ensepulchred in marble, down to the meanest acolyte cast out on a dungheap—

> "Their names shall nerve the patriot's hand
> Upraised to save a sinking land,
> And piety will learn to burn
> With holier transports o'er their urn."

(13.) THE WILD BEASTS OF BOMBAY.

1783.—The Governor and most of the gentlemen of Bombay go annually on a party of pleasure to Salsette, to hunt the wild boar and royal tiger, both of which we found here in great plenty.—*Hector Macneill.*

1806, December 17th.—Two gentlemen at 7 A.M. riding towards the bungalows of General Macpherson on the Island of Salsette, near the village of Coorla, two tigers came out of the jungle as if ready to spring, crouched, and were observed to betake themselves to the jungles and hills of Powee, fifty yards in front of the horses.

And in this connection two persons on November 4th were carried off by two tigers from a native village nearly opposite to Powee, near the high road leading from Sion to Tanna. The natives believe the tigers are human beings, and have gold rings in their ears and noses.

One native's body they had sucked all the blood out of it,

otherwise not eaten. They took away a herdsman driving his flock.

1819.—There were in all only three deaths recorded in India of Europeans from snake-bites in the years 1817, 1818 and 1819.

1820, December 23rd.—A large lion killed within eight coss from Ahmedabad.

1822, February 9th.—A tiger on Malabar Hill came down, quenched his thirst at Gowalla Tank, and ran off over the hill between the Hermitage and Prospect Lodge. Prints of its feet were distinctly visible this morning.

1828.—At Colaba Ferry a huge shark was observed in proximity to some bathers.

1830, January 13th.—A large hyena is prowling about Malabar Hill on the western side between Mr. Nicol's residence and Vaucluse, "as good sport as a Mazagon tiger."—*Bombay Gazette.*

1839, June 25th.—Lieutenant Montague, at Colaba, returning from mess, put his foot in a hole, received a slight wound which in twenty-five minutes carried him off. Some jurors thought it was from the bite of a serpent.

1841, September 15th.—A man bitten by a snake on the Esplanade.

1849.—A finback whale driven on shore at Colaba, 60 feet long, 30 to 40 feet round the thickest part. All along the road from the Fort to Colaba was a perfect fair. The stench was felt from the town side of the causeway from where it lay at the back of Colaba Church. Jawbone taken away.—*Gentleman's Gazette.*

1850, Oct. 9th.—A tiger at Bandoop leaped upon the mail-cart and upset it, and the gharry-wallah was little injured. I saw jackals several times in the gardens of the Colaba Observatory in 1844.—*Dr. Buist.* On this Mr. Charles Chambers, F.R.S., observes (1893): "I found a jackal in my bedroom in the Colaba Observatory about fifteen years ago."

A jackal was killed in the new High Court Buildings shortly after they were finished.

1858, March 3rd.—Some officers of the P. and O. steamer *Aden* observed a tiger swimming from Mainland to Mazagon.

A boat was lowered and the crew armed with ship's muskets. When they came up to it the brute was boarding a buggalow, and was being kept off by the lascars by handspikes. It was shot through the head by six balls. Weight, 353 lbs. Length to tip of tail, 8 ft. 9 ins.

1858, May 26th.—A young Portuguese this day shot a tiger at Mahim, and on the 27th inst. brought the carcass to the Chief Magistrate for the reward.

1859.—To-day Mr. Forjett with a fowling-piece shot a tiger within a few hundred yards of the fashionable drive on the Esplanade, and on the beach of Back Bay near Sonapore. Mr. Forjett promised the hide to Dr. Birdwood for the Museum. —*Bombay Gazette.*

Feb. 6th.—On this day, Sunday evening, the wife of Mr. Pratt, uncovenanted assistant in the General Department Secretariat, walking along with her husband in the fields adjoining their residence at Mahim, trod on a snake and died two hours afterwards.—*Bombay Gazette.*

Feb. 15th.—A tiger was seen sloping about the nooks of Kalpadavie, but disappeared.

Nov. 12th.—Dr. Turner, P. and O. service, at his residence, Chinchpoogly, was bitten by a venomous snake on the calf of the leg. His leg swelled to an immense size. A friend of his made an incision, sucked the wound, and he is now recovering.

Nov. 16th.—A cobra, 4 ft. in length, killed in Secretariat compound, Apollo Street.

1860, Oct. 31st.—On Sunday a snake was seen amusing itself round one of the pillars in St. John's Church, Colaba, a few yards from the reading-desk, and not long ago a cobra was found in the organ.—*Times and Standard.*

Dec. 5th.—A hyena shot while devouring a bullock not far from the Byculla Club House.

1861, Nov. 26th.—Hyenas quite common at night, prowling about the Byculla Flats.

1863, Jan. 25th.—Tiger at Mahim, near railway station. Two natives killed by it. Shot.

II.

BANKS AND MERCHANTS.

(1.) THE OLD BANK OF BOMBAY.

THE earliest notice we possess of the origin of this institution is the following:—

Dec. 26th, 1836.

A meeting at the office of John Skinner and Co., to establish a Bank on the same lines as the Bank of Bengal.

Committee:

J. R. Richmond.	A. S. Finlay.
James Wright.	W. Turner.
Colonel Wood.	David Greenhill.
Dadabhai Pestonjee.	M. Brownrigg.
E. C. Morgan.	Captain W. Henderson.

George Ashburner, *Secretary.*

Capital 30 lakhs divided in 3,000 shares.
20 lakhs subscribed.

Meeting agreed to procure a Charter.

Prospectus to be published on December 31st.

To be called
The Bank of Bombay

On January 3rd, 1837, it was announced that nineteen and a half lakhs more were applied for by men of substance than the Directors want. A meeting was called of the new Bank, the notice being signed by Archd. Robertson, Edmond Bibby and Co., John Skinner and Co., D. Greenhill, Ritchie Steuart and Co., Dirom Carter and Co., McGregor Brownrigg and Co., Framjee Cowasjee. On January 20th, A. S. Finlay was appointed officiating Secretary, and on February 2nd the capital of the Bank was fixed at fifty lakhs; the Chairman being Sir Charles Malcolm.

We may glance at some of the promoters. James Wright was a partner in William Nicol and Co., A. S. Finlay in Ritchie Steuart and Co., and J. R. Richmond and M. Brownrigg in Bombay firms which bore their names. Dadabhai Pestonjee deserves more than a passing notice, *he being the first native whose name appears conspicuously in Bombay Banking enterprise,* one of those pioneers who broke away from the crowd, and whose name is deeply indented in the forefront of this great movement. He came of a good stock of the Wadia family. His great-grandfather was that Lowjee who came down from Surat in 1735, the progenitor of all the Wadias, shipbuilders and merchants who have since contributed so much to enhance the importance of our city. His father was Pestonjee Bomonjee, one of those seven righteous men who, in Bombay's hour of need in 1802, came forward as sponsors of the Northern Loan and relieved the Government with their money at one of the most critical periods of its history. Dadabhai was a man of unbounded means, of great credit, of great possessions in land, property, and merchandise. It was said that half of the land around Parell at one time belonged to him, and that his Mazagon estate was enormous. What he inherited and what he made by conquest, as the Scotch lawyers define money made in trade, I know not. All I know is that his country house was Lall Baugh, and, I believe, Tarala (the Sadar Adawlut once occupied by Sir James Mackintosh, and afterwards in our day the property of the Honourable Byramjee Jejeebhoy) belonged to him, and his town house, built by himself, a most substantial edifice, which you may see to this day in Parsee Bazaar Street, the home of the Chamber of Commerce. How he entertained is written in the annals of the time. One line must suffice:—March 5th, 1832. Dadabhai Pestonjee gave at Lall Baugh a ball to the Commander-in-Chief, Sir Colin and Lady Halkett, Members of Council, &c. Mr. Newnham a well-known civilian, gave the toast of Mr. D. Pestonjee.

He was amongst the thirteen of the native population declared by Lord Clare, in 1834, to be entitled to affix to their name the word "Esquire." Happy man! Call no man rich until he's dead. Dadabhai Pestonjee died in 1885, bereft of all his acquisitions by the vicissitudes of fortune. It was said that he once held three-eighths of the entire shares of the Oriental Bank. Dadabhai in his days of prosperity was a fine-looking man, tall and erect. He spoke a little English. Of Framjee Cowasjee we need not speak in Bombay. His is a name which this city will not willingly let die; in fact she has taken every care to prevent such a consummation. The charming story told of Malcolm's visit to him at Powai will live when Powai is forgotten. "I quite forgot to bring you a present; here are my watch and seals; take them if you will as a souvenir." There is a depth of feeling here which neither marble, nor painting, nor words can represent.

As for John Skinner, his career is familiar to our readers, and his services to the Bank, the Chamber, and in prosecution of the Overland route, can never be forgotten. We will follow him if you like to the end, after eighteen years of brilliant work in Bombay. Leaving his brother, C. B. Skinner, in Bombay he set out for Calcutta in December, 1843, and there, in conjunction with David Jardine, founded the firm of Jardine, Skinner and Co., now eminent for fifty years, and there he died on 23rd March, 1844, of cholera, scarcely three months from his departure from Bombay. The Bombay firm was at once dissolved, C. B. Skinner proceeding to Calcutta. He survived his brother well-nigh fifty years.

These digressions have left us little space for the details of the war which the promoters of the Bank had to wage before it was established in 1840. How no one man was its architect; how Ashburner, Finlay, Johnson and John Smith all did duty in succession as honorary secretaries; how Ashburner was sent to London to secure a charter; how the great houses of agency frowned upon it; how the Bank of Bengal, strong in the right of primogeniture (1806), viewed its establishment with hostility and threatened to open in Bombay; how the Bengal Government took the same views and imparted them to the Bombay Government; how our Chamber of Commerce remonstrated; how in February, 1839, the whole body of shareholders, with Harry George Gordon as Chairman, met in Dirom Carter and Co.'s office "to consider Prinsep's extraordinary letter"; how, a year after, a negative from England cast a general gloom over mercantile society; how the feeling was to open, charter or no charter,—are not these things all written in the Bombay Chronicles doomed to oblivion? At one time it seemed, from this advertisement, as if the whole business was to end in smoke:—

"BANK OF BOMBAY.

"The Bank Committee regret to have to announce that the Vice-President of the Council in India has postponed the passing of the Charter Act in consequence of a resolution to revise the list of shareholders and to frame a new one. The Committee can now form no opinion when the Bank will be opened, its establishment being in the hands of the Government and beyond their control. Bombay, 27th January, 1840. By order of the Committee. W. W. CARGILL, Secretary."

But the darkest hour is nearest the morning, and light came from the east—the usual quarter—though murky enough before. 1840, March 11.—Meeting in Town Hall to elect Directors. This means business. On March 20th they advertise for Secretary and Treasurer at Rs. 1,200 per mensem with Rs. 50,000 security. And now on April 1st (*absit omen*) the Bank secured No. 23, Rampart Row, belonging to Jehangier Nusserwanjee Wadia, the same premises, we may add, which have been occupied for the last thirty years by Messrs. Ralli Brothers. The Bank opened on the 15th April, 1840.

(2.) BANK OF WESTERN INDIA.

CAPITAL 50 LAKHS.

Trustees.	Present Directors.
Lieut.-Colonel Stratford Powell.	General T. Vailant, K.H.
Framji Cowasji.	Thomas Robert Richmond.
S. D. Murray.	E. C. Morgan.

Gisborn, Menzies and Co., Rampart Row, will receive applications for shares, and the Bank will commence business as soon as the necessary arrangements can be completed.—Bombay, May 25th, 1842.

THIS is the first Bombay Bank that dealt in European Exchange. Out of it came directly the Oriental Bank.

On June 15th, John Alexander Russell, father of the Hon. Justice Russell (1899), Juggannath Sunkersett, and Jejeebhoy Dadabhoy join the direction.

On June 25th, W. W. Cargill sends in his resignation as

Secretary and Treasurer of the Bank of Bombay, and on July 18th, signs as Managing Director of the Bank of Western India.

On August 5th, in the same year, the Committee consists of A. S. Ayrton, W. Escombe, Captain Unwin, Lieutenant W. S. Suart, E. C. Morgan, T. R. Richmond, and John Alexander Russell.

On October 6th, 1842, the Bank opened for business.

Dr. Robson, Gregor Grant, and Ardaseer Hormusjee do not appear on the board of direction until February 17th, 1844.

We are thus particular in these details as there are claimants outside of this list for the honour of introducing Exchange Banking into Western India. And no doubt, as the years roll on, the tendency will be for legend to displace facts. But all the same, *Litera scripta manet.* Outside of Bombay, the Union Bank of Calcutta (1829) and the Agra Bank, who had their agents, Dirom, Carter and Co., in Bombay (1841), have priority in exchange banking with Europe. We confine ourselves, however, to banks originating in Bombay.

When W. W. Cargill had resigned the post of Secretary and Treasurer of the Bank of Bombay in 1842, to be succeeded by John Stuart, he had already been over two years in that office. The Bank had been successful under his administration, and, as everybody knows, it was equally successful under that of Mr. Stuart during the long tenure of his office. The acquisition of Mr. Cargill, with all his experience, by the promoters of the Bank of Western India was thus a clear gain to it, and it is beyond controversy that he threw his whole soul into it, for he was a man of uncommon energy. A Bank of Western India was projected, or thought of, under this name as far back as August 24th, 1839 (contemporaneous with the appearance of Mr. Cargill in Bombay), by whom we do not know. But, as we have recorded, it only took definite shape on May 25th, 1842.

From a glance at the list of trustees and directors then and afterwards, it will be seen that there were some men of uncommon mark among them. Framjee Cowasjee was there, so there is some truth in the saying that he helped to found three banks in Bombay. Jejeebhoy Dadabhoy, the father of the Honourable Byramjee Jejeebhoy of our day, had been a private banker for years. Juggannath Sunkersett, I believe the son of the chief of the goldsmiths, was a tower of strength. Ardaseer Hormusjee was the son of Hormusjee Bomanjee, of Lowjee Castle, the most prominent native citizen of Bombay during the first quarter of the century, and perhaps at his death (1826) the wealthiest man in the island, and the associate of Sir Charles Forbes. As far back as 1802 Bomanjee was one of the pillars of the earth, when the credit of the British Government in Western India began to tremble. Among Englishmen there was Thomas Robert Richmond, who, along with Skinner and Brownrigg, gave Bombay probably its first reclamation in all that land on which Grant Buildings and other edifices were erected.

There was S. D. Murray, who was chairman of the Chamber of Commerce in 1842–43, and T. R. Richmond, who was chairman of the Chamber in 1840–41. There was John Alexander Russell, of Grey and Co., of whom we are sure there must be many memories in Bombay, and Ayrton also, before he blossomed into one of the members of Mr. Gladstone's first Administration. The Ayrtons had been long about Bombay. His father, Frederick Ayrton (died 1829), had been a Proctor. A. S. Ayrton left Bombay in 1852, was M.P. in 1853, and culminated as the Honourable Acton Smee Ayrton, Parliamentary Secretary to the Treasury, Chief Commissioner of Works, and Judge-Advocate (died 1886).

It will be thus apparent that the men connected with, and at the head of, the Bank of Western India were mostly men of mark—not persons but individuals; and in spite of differences of race, religion, and up-bringing, Cargill was undoubtedly the man who welded them into one homogeneous mass, devoted to one purpose. The Cargills were men of indomitable energy; witness Invercargill in New Zealand, a town of 8,000 inhabitants, founded by his brother.

The Bank of Western India opened in Medows Street, and on April 6th, 1842, removed to No. 7, Rampart Row. Was not this last, now (1895) Thacker and Company's shop, the same building so long occupied by the Oriental Bank, and only vacated when they moved (about 1866) into their fine new offices which were known as the Oriental Bank Buildings? They did the ordinary business of an exchange bank, and published their rules. They drew upon the Union Bank of London, and issued notes. The notes were refused in payment at the Bank of Bombay and also at the Government Treasury. The "Western" retaliated, and refused payment of Bombay Bank notes, and so the war went on. Meanwhile (I speak without book) the bank was a success, and paid a dividend of 7 per cent. In view of opening in Ceylon in April, 1843, they issued 2,000 reserved shares at a premium of 6 per cent. At a time when the Union Bank of Calcutta was in a state of suspended animation, the shares of the Bank of Western India maintained a premium of 25 per cent. on a paid-up capital of Rs. 300 per share.

On 18th September, 1844, Mr. Cargill left Bombay by the overland route for London, leaving Mr. Charles Stuart as acting manager until his return.

This was a famous journey, big with the fate of an immense undertaking. Whether it was the idea of Mr. Cargill or that of others, or that of all the directors combined, it had been gradually dawning upon them that to open in Ceylon, Calcutta, and Hongkong, they must sooner or later obtain a Charter, and that the swaddling clothes made in Rampart Row were all too meagre for a Corporation which was soon to cover a hemisphere with its operations. Their capital, therefore, must be doubled, 100 lakhs instead of 50, and their head office must be in London, the centre of the world's finance, and it was no idle dream. Mr. Cargill was equal to it all. Whoever originated the idea, it was he who carried it out. He came, he saw, he conquered. He obtained at once as chairman a former acting Governor of Bombay, and after constituting his board—court of directors we ought to say—he returned to Bombay, and on his arrival on the 15th June, 1845, issued the following notice. So runs the rede :—

"The Bank of Western India will henceforth be carried on under a new deed of settlement under the name of THE ORIENTAL BANK."

This paper has nothing to do with his after career, but we humbly think that the reader will share our opinion that this journey of William Walter Cargill vindicates his title to have been the founder of the Oriental Bank. At all events we shall hold this opinion until some new light reaches us.

We have little more to add to the above notification, taken from the newspapers. The times were propitious—the men who embarked in this enterprise brooked no opposition—a charter would no doubt be soon forthcoming; so before 1845 was out the magnificent new notes of the Oriental Bank, engraved specially for Bombay, Rs. 5 up to Rs. 1,000, were passing from hand to hand, the finest specimens of the London engraver's art, and everyone of them good for the amount, blazoned with our Town Hall, and a glory of palm trees, with the Royal Standard floating over the bastions of Bombay Castle. "Western India" was henceforth swallowed up in the Oriental, which at once, Minerva-like, had risen fully armed from the head of Jupiter.

(3.) ORIENTAL BANK, 1845.

THE following is the first announcement of the opening of the Bank in Bombay:—

HEAD OFFICE IN LONDON.

COURT OF DIRECTORS.

G. W. Anderson, Esq. . . . . Chairman.
R. H. Kennedy, Esq. . . . . Deputy Chairman.
W. W. Cargill, Esq. . . . . Chief Manager.

CHIEF OFFICE IN INDIA.

BOMBAY.

Board of Directors.

Thomas Robson, Esq., M.D., Chairman.
Jugganuath Sunkersett, Esq. Dadabhoy Rustomjee, Esq.
Ardaseer Hormusjee, Esq. James Boyd, Esq.
Gregor Grant, Esq., C.S. Captain Unwin.
T. R. Richmond, Esq.

Trustees.

Dr. James Burnes. Juggannath Sunkersett, Esq.
K. H. Dadabhoy Rustomjee, Esq.

Charles J. F. Stuart . . . . Managing *ad interim.*
Dugald Bremner . . . . Accountant.
C. G. Ingelow . . . . Deputy Accountant.
Wissanath Balcrustnajee . . . . Cashier.
Dorabjee Hormusjee . . . . Check Office.
Mr. J. Hurst . . . . Transfer Office.

CALCUTTA BRANCH.

Robert Glaspoole Lancaster	Manager.
William Anderson	Accountant.

CEYLON BRANCH (Colombo).

George S. Duff	Manager.
Peter Rankine	Accountant.
J. F. Moir	Agent at Kandy.

CHINA BRANCH.

James Sinclair	Joint Managers, *ad interim*.
James McEwen.	
S. J. D. Campbell	Inspector of Branches.

Holidays—Christmas and Good Friday.

We are here met by a multiplicity of names—G. W. Anderson, Acting Governor of Bombay, 1841–1842. Dadabhoy Rustomjee, China merchant, son of the celebrated Framjee Cowasjee. It seems but yesterday that Ardaseer Hormusjee, of great dignity and much respected, was among us. And Juggannath Sunkersett, foremost man in these early days of banking enterprise, cut off in 1865. Of him Dr. Birdwood (Sir George) then wrote:—"One can hardly believe that he has passed for ever from our midst, and that the elements of his stout frame—unchained by fire—are scattered to every wind of heaven." There were also Duff, now tea planter in Ceylon; Peter Rankine, not unknown in Bombay; Mr. Moir, whose genial face many of us remember, and who piloted his ship discreetly in evil days and evil times, and Anderson, afterwards agent in Calcutta, who added much to the resources of the Bank. There is one name there embedded as if in obscurity, Charles James Stuart, in Bombay managing *ad interim*, who was destined to rise to great eminence as General Manager in London of the Bank, and, we might add, as the wise Dictator of Eastern Finance in "the sixties." How many could have wished that in his superintendence of the whole concern his "sittings could have been declared permanent!" He died about 1876.

(4.) BOMBAY BEFORE JOINT-STOCK BANKING.

HINDOO SHROFFS.

Gunasdass Crustnajee, 1809.	Gunasdass Nursingdass, 1825.
Sheram Dowlatram, 1819.	Jewraz Balloo, 1789.
Chimodass Madodass, 1824.	Gowandass Ragunathdass, 1834.
Latchmandass Sewdass, 1834.	Sownathroy Punnalal, 1829.
Jewram Sewjee, 1809	Bunsilal Abiechand, 1845.
Kesowjee Jadowjee.	Veerjivundass Madowdass.
Hajaremull Narsingdass.	Hattevsing Kessresing & Co.
Goculdass Lilladhur.	Currumchund Premchund.
Damodur Mohunjee.	Hemchund Adicchund.
Jevanjee Najee.	Ruganathdas Goverdhunjee.

Atmaram Bhoocundass.

Here are twenty-one of the conspicuous shroffs of Bombay in 1845, whom we would now call leading men in the great field of Inland Exchange, and the sole conductors of it before the old Bank of Bombay broke ground in the year 1840, and I have given the dates of the establishment of some of them in Bombay. What we mean to say is this, that you might have gone to almost any of them, and if you wished a draft on any place from Peshawur to Travancore you would get it. As a general remark they were perfectly good, as is abundantly proved by the fact that (as we have stated elsewhere) the old Bank of Bombay, during the first seventeen years of its existence, made very little loss by them. Some of them were head offices and some of them were branches. All this means that they were men of undoubted wealth. Some of them rendered important service to the Government here and elsewhere, and we need not remind the reader of the well-timed assistance of Bunsilal to the British Government in the North-West during the days of the Mutiny in 1857. Counting over seventy names I find one-half of them had their places of business in Bazaar Gate Street, a kind of Rialto then, "where merchants most do congregate." This in part answers a very interesting question which arises: How did the world of Bombay fare before the advent of Joint-Stock Banks?

Sir George Birdwood, in his most interesting "Old Records of the India Office," 1891, tells us that in 1671 the East India Company banked with Alderman Edward Backwell of London, and at one time £175,000 of their money lay in his hands.

This was before the Bank of England was thought of. We have seen that in Bombay there were no banking companies, foreign or domestic, until 1840, and until this period, if you substitute a number of firms, English and native, for Backwell, you will answer the question. The Bombay Government itself, in 1806, was quite content when Bruce, Fawcett & Co. became its bankers, and it had no need to be otherwise. Bombay, like Calcutta, Alexandria, or Manilla, did a very large business before the advent of Banking Companies. Here we meet with what seems to us a phase of the question that belongs entirely to India—the Hoondie system, and the establishment of shroffs in correspondence, and which covered India's great towns, as with a network so perfect that not one of them was left out, and working in so complete unison that, in that very year of 1840, our disaster in Afghanistan was known by the Calcutta shroffs some time before the news reached Government.

To have, in vulgar parlance, drawing-posts in each town, by whom the money of a second party could be received and paid away to a third party, seems to us an invention purely Indian and indigenous to the country, and possibly Europe got it from India. The how or the why may be ascertained, but when this custom obtained in India I despair of finding, as I would to find out the origin of caste. Gour, Kanouge, and the successive cities which flourished and fell on the environs of modern Delhi, as I take it, all had their shroffs. The plunder of their piles may have swollen the sacks of Timour and Nadir Shah. You may go back to Ozein and the Christian era, and seek in vain for a time when there were no shroffs in India. There is ample evidence of this banking in India before a single Englishman touched its shores.

There is a story given by Ferishta, under date of 1366, how the King of Gulburga drew a hoondie at sight on the King of Vizianagar, the greatest Hindoo potentate of his time, giving it to a blind musician with the threat of war to the knife if the bill was unpaid. And there is another old-world story of a dervish, who, after entering a town, produced from his wallet a bill drawn by the god Ram, whereat everybody laughed except an oil man, who did the needful, and saved himself from the blasting curses of the dervish. Sivaji's bill also, dishonoured for a time (1675), proves that the bill system, drawer and acceptor, was in vogue centuries ago in India, and the so-called Government Paper of 1678, with Sir John Child's signature, now in the Empire of India Exhibition, is simply a hoondie or promissory note, as we would say, for value received. India, therefore, did not need to go to Venice or Amsterdam for a system of internal banking by which, through means of hoondies, the business of the country was carried on, as it is apparent that this was in vogue before Amsterdam was founded or Venice became Queen of the Adriatic.

Nobody could be at any loss in Bombay in procuring a bill on any town in India. Here is a Bombay shroff's advertisement of 1825:—

"Balcrishna Gopal will buy and sell hoondies on the various towns in India." This is the Alpha and Omega of Indian Exchange. When the Bank of Western India broke ground in Bombay there were half a hundred shroffs in and outside the Fort, more or less engaged in the business of inland exchange. The general reader may have skipped our list at the head of this section, but it will be acceptable to the natives interested in the history of Banking and Exchange. I have selected the most considerable names among the Bombay shroffs of 1845—that is, the vanguard of that year alone—and curiously enough I am indebted for the information to a MS. copy which I believe was the actual list held by the Bank of Western India, and which, by a series of migrations, has come into my hands. The document has an antique flavour about it, and divides the Bombay shroffs into their several races or castes. There are the Futtoporiah and the Gosavey, &c., those having their places of business in the Fort and those at Chinch Bunder. These shroffs were, of course, of different degrees of credit, and some of them had carried on business for more than half a century.

Bullion.

From the earliest ages bullion has been the one thing needful in India, "the sink," as it has been termed, of the precious metals. The cry of the Zamorin of Calicut to Vasco da Gama was, "What I seek from thy country is gold and silver," and it has been the cry almost ever since. Its transmission by land or by sea was a risk, and this trade in bullion was fearfully handicapped by pirates, dacoits, and thugs, who were ever on the watch for buggalow or cafila.

Aungier, before 1676, started an Insurance Fund against loss by robbery, as far, at all events, as Ahmedabad. A great deal of gold in the fifteenth and sixteenth centuries came to India from Darfur and Abyssinia, where, "Afric's sunny fountains roll down their golden sand." The sequins which for ages the women of India have worn in their hair were mostly minted in Cairo; and Aden, in 1503, was a favourite emporium of bullion brokers. The account we have of their bargaining with a shawl over their heads is an exact counterpart of what you may see in the Bombay Goldsmiths' Bazaar, or for that matter out of it. Great experts they were in testing the purity of gold, and their scales were so fine as to turn with a single hair.

Angria's fleet and the Barbary corsairs were pretty well disposed of by the beginning of the nineteenth century, and war risks were covered by insurance. But what about your own flesh and blood, when a man's enemies become those of his own household? One looks for piracy on the high seas, but not at Greenwich or Blackwall. In 1816 Fairly and Co. despatched thirteen chests of dollars (£13,000) to Calcutta, intended for the *Lady Campbell*, lying at Greenwich. They were put into a hoy, which proceeded down the river. Darkness came on. During the night a small craft hailed them and came alongside, apparently with two men only on board, to ask some questions. The sudden drawing aside of a tarpaulin revealed twenty men, who at once scrambled into the hoy, armed with pistols and cutlasses. "Your money or your life!" was the question. They broke into the hold and took seven chests, each containing four bags of 1,000 dollars each. Some of the robbers with their plunder were caught in the Essex marshes. Thinking it was low water, they sank three chests in the sand, meaning to recover them at their leisure. But when the tide went out one of the box ends cropped up, and their purpose was baffled. The robbers were veritable pirates, and were called the "Blackwall Gang."

Parsee Houses.

It may serve to illustrate the position of the mercantile world of 1845 in Bombay if we add a list of the Parsee leading firms which were carrying on business at the advent of Exchange Banking. The names of some of their old-world places of business enhance the interest of the note, and while the reader will recognise the "forbears" of some of our honoured magnates, there are others which have disappeared from this chequered web of history.

Bomanjee and Ardaseer Hormusjee, Old Theatre.
Byramjee Jeejeebhoy, Rampart Row.
Cursetlee Ardaseer Dady, Borah Bazaar Street.
Cursetjee Cowasjee Sons and Co., Grant Buildings, Colaba.
Dadabhoy and Muncherjee Pestonjee, Borah Bazaar Street.
Dadabhoy Rustomjee Banajee, Rampart Row.
Framjee Cowasjee, Apollo Street.
Sir Jamsetjee Jeejebhoy Sons and Co., Gunbow Street.
Jeejeebhoy Dadabhoy Sons and Co., Rampart Row.
Manackjee Nusserwanjee Petit.
Muncherjee and Pestonjee Framjee Cama, Old Theatre.
Nusserwanjee Bomanjee Mody, Old Theatre.
Nowrojee Ardaseer Davur, Old Theatre.
Ruttonjee Edusjee Bottlewalla, Gunbow Street.
Jamsetjee Furdonjee Paruck, Church Gate Street.
Manackjee Limjee Cowasjee.

By way of explanation we only now add that on the completion of Grant Buildings there was a considerable migration of native and half a dozen English houses of business to it (1844), as it was the belief then that it would eventually become the mercantile centre. The site of the Old Theatre was Hormusjee's block in the Elphinstone Circle, next to the Chartered Bank, and Gunbow Street is adjacent and has got an ornamental fountain near it.

(5.) SOME MERCHANTS OF 1845 AND THEIR METHODS OF BUSINESS.

BOMBAY CHAMBER OF COMMERCE.
Established September 22nd, 1836.

LIST OF MEMBERS, DECEMBER 15TH, 1845.
John Smith, Esq., Chairman.
W. S. Grey, Esq., Deputy Chairman.

MANAGING COMMITTEE IN OFFICE TILL AUGUST, 1846.

The Chairman, *ex officio*. The Deputy Chairman, *ex officio*.

MEMBERS:

L. A. Wallace, Esq.	A. Cassels, Esq.
J. Stuart, Esq.	W. S. Brown, Esq.
S. D. Murray, Esq.	Cursetjee Cowasjee, Esq.
W. Graham, Esq.	Ardaseer Cursetjee, Esq.
J. Parsons, Esq.	Dhackjee Dadajee, Esq.

Messrs. Ritchie, Steuart and Co., Treasurers.
T. J. A. Scott, Secretary.

FIRMS COMPOSING THE CHAMBER.

Messrs. Ritchie, Steuart & Co.	Messrs. Leckie & Co.
" William Nicol & Co.	" Cresswell, Rawson & Co.
" Dirom Hunter & Co.	" Lyons, Livingstone & Co.
" Brownrigg & Co.	" W. Elsam & Co.
" W. & T. Edmond & Co.	" Henry, Wooler & Co.
" Martin Murray & Co.	" Peel, Cassels & Co.
" Macvicar, Burn & Co.	" Huschke, Wattenbach & Co.
" Ewart, Lyon & Co.	" Cursetjee Ardaseer & Co.
" Higginson & Cardwell	" Cursetjee Cowasjee & Co.
" Frith & Co.	" Dadabhoy & M. Pestonjee.
" Grey & Co.	" Jeejeebhoy Dadabhoy Sons & Co.
" Campbell, Miller & Co.	Framjee Cowasjee, Esq,
" Wm. & Alexander Graham & Co.	Dadabhoy Rustomjee, Esq.
" Campbell, Dallas & Co.	Juggannath Sunkersett, Esq.
" G. S. King & Co.	Dady Rustomjee, Esq.

JOHN SMITH had accompanied Dr. Wilson (1843–44) in his tour through Egypt and Syria. Andrew Cassels and William Graham, M.P., became members of the Indian Council in London. Several of the native members have already been noticed. In 1842 Dhackjee Dadajee's house was the object of suspicions. His place was overhauled, and though fourteen lakhs of the

Gaekwar's were discovered, the suspicions were altogether unfounded.

The Chamber of Commerce was established under the auspices of Sir Robert Grant. He is known to some people as the writer of some of our best hymns, to others as having given his assistance to the removal of the civil disabilities of the Jews, to others as having helped to make "the main drain," and to all petitioners in these olden days as one of the most dilatory of men, insomuch that when applications went in to Parell, it was never known when a reply would come out, and it was then Parell was nicknamed "Chancery." Slow but sure, whenever he saw that his course was clear, in such great enterprises as the Bank of Bombay, the Overland Route, or the Chamber of Commerce, it was then that he threw into the scale the weight of his great authority. The Tanna and Colaba Causeways are his monuments, besides hundreds of miles of good roads between this and Sholapore. I am under the impression that the Chamber voted a marble cenotaph to his memory in the Byculla Church or elsewhere, and he well deserved it, for a better man never filled the Governor's chair.

Here then is the Commercial Body of Bombay as it stood about 1845. It is noticeable that neither Forbes, nor Remington, nor Sassoon had as yet joined the Chamber—for reasons unknown to us. The reason for their not joining in banking enterprise at the first is obvious enough, and one can sympathise with their caution. No doubt the privileges of "The Four Houses," as they were called—Forbes, Remington, Leckie, and Shotton—were abolished by the charter of 1834, when all Indian firms without exception were put upon the same level, but it is a curious fact that so late as 1841, when a charter was applied for, the "Bank of Asia," a big, ill-starred institution, of which some of the capital was paid up, the East India Company gave as one of their reasons for refusing it that the bank would come into collision with houses dealing in European exchange. Be that as it may, we need not say that, at the time of which we write, Robert Wigram Crawford, of Remington and Co., was one of the most conspicuous men in Bombay (he resided here from 1833 to 1817), and the admiration-enlisted by him here was fully justified afterwards by the brilliant career which awaited him in London, and though his name is not in this list, he appears in 1845 as a Director of the Bank of Bombay, the other two houses and his own contributing in subsequent years a most influential quota to the Board of this long well-managed institution.

We have omitted among those who did not join, the name of Edward Bates,* without which any list of the merchants of Bombay in 1845 would be incomplete.

Only three or four firms are now (1895) in existence under the same style and designation. Nor is this at all wonderful, for I dare say the same observation for the same period would hold good in regard to the commercial history of Melbourne, New York, or London. But we are not here to moralise, for there are many firms in India, the family relations of which have descended to the present generation, and whose business is carried on by scions of those who were masters of the field, or were becoming so fifty years ago.

If you wish continuity and instances of how names perpetuate themselves you must go to Government and the men who do its business, and you will find that the most exalted of our day, Mansfield, Birdwood, and Willoughby, are the names of soldiers and civilians of this Presidency fifty years ago—names now "familiar in our mouths as household words," and which constitute a pleasing link between the present time and the past. At this period the English houses were their own bankers and brokers. The exporters generally made as many bills as the importers required, and the business was done direct without the intervention of a broker. The first exchange broker in Bombay was Nelson Howard. When he came brokerage on bills was a half per cent. But he is not due yet for a year or two.

THE *MODUS OPERANDI* OF EXCHANGE.

As we have indicated, exchange business was carried through by the import houses buying from the export ones, and, generally speaking, as the balance was in favour of India, this

* The eminent firm of Sir Edward Bates & Co. was closed in Bombay in 1898.

was sufficient; when any hiatus presented itself the bills drawn in London on the Indian Treasuries were available—what we now call Council Bills, of which the East India Company had been issuing at fitful times and prices about two millions sterling annually for ten years up to 1843. Any balance unadjusted by bills was left to the ultimate ratio of bullion, which was pitched about between Bombay and London according to the exigencies of trade.

Bombay exports to all places of the known world in 1843–44 *ad valorem* were Rs. 8,29,15,366; imports for the same period Rs. 9,25,46,220.

For ten years the shipments of silver from London to all parts of India annually averaged about 160 lakhs. This may satisfy the curious reader as to the bulk and extent of the Bombay trade fifty years ago, and will enable him to compare such items as exports, imports, bullion, and Council Bills with the gigantic proportions they have now assumed.

The houses of fifty years ago advertised in the newspapers when they had bills for sale, and from the replies took their cue as to their disposal. Forbes and Remington do not appear much in this way. The following are a few advertisements culled at random:—

"Messrs. Prinsep and Co., Agents of Messrs. Palmer and Co., Calcutta, will draw upon Messrs. Cockerell, Trail and Co., 6 mos. at 1*s.* 9½*d.* until further notice.—Bombay, 10th Dec., 1824."

"For sale at the office of William Nicol and Co, Bank of England notes for £50, £20, £10, and £5 at Rs. 11 per £1."

And again,

"Bills on London,
Royal Bank of Scotland, on Thomas Coutts and Co., London, at 30 days' sight, at 1*s.* 10*d.* at Ritchie, Steuart and Co., 1834, Dec. 6."

"McGregor, Brownrigg and Co. offer their 30 days' sight bills on Sir Charles Cockerell, Baronet, at 2*s.*, 1837, Jan. 3."

"Bills on Frederick Huth and Co. at 60 days' sight, and in sets to suit the convenience. Edmond, Bibby and Co., 1837, Dec. 9."

The business of dealing in English Exchange was not confined to English Houses. Here are two advertisements:—

"1828, Aug. 13, £5,000 6 months' Bills on a Letter of Credit from a house in London of the first respectability offered at 1s. 9½*d.*"

"Jehangier and Nowrojee Nusserwanjee.

"1829, Feb. 4, Bills on London, Jehangier and Nowrojee Nusserwanjee have received from Calcutta a sum in Bills of Exchange on London at six months which they will dispose of."

And again,

"Jehangier Nusserwanjee Wadia on Baring Brothers six months for sale, 1837, Jan. 17."

These two names as we shall see have more than a passing interest for us in 1895. They belong to the Wadia family, and were the names of brothers in business as private bankers, and for some time financial brokers to William Nicol and Co. (1824 to 1842). Nowrojee died in 1827; Jehangier died in 1849. Nowrojee left one son, Manockji, who was married to the only daughter of Jehangier. That daughter, widow of Manockji (who died in 1837), still lives among us, venerable and venerated—eighty-three years of age—a veritable lady—*Motlibai*—renowned wherever Bombay is spoken of for her deeds of charity and beneficence. Honour to whom honour is due.

"She has a tear for pity and a hand open as day for melting charity." *

Most people imagine that the ancient merchant or private banker of Bombay before the advent of Joint Stock Banks was not troubled much with the exchange question. This is a great fallacy. Between 1817 and 1823 exchange fell from 2*s.* 8*d.* to 1*s.* 8½*d.*, or over 30 per cent. Dear money in these years was caused by the army of the Dekhan, which consumed an immense sum. This was part of the price we paid for our acquisitions.

Again in 1837, on May 9th, exchange touched 2*s.* 0½*d.*, and on June 15th, or six weeks thereafter, it was 1*s.* 9*d.* I think this beats the record of the last thirty years (1865–95) within a similar space of time. The mercantile circulars call the fall 20 per cent., and I am not going to quarrel with their arithmetic. Bad was the best of it, except for the "Bears," if such existed in these prehistoric times, and quite sufficient to turn men's hair gray in a single night. The Chamber had not been in existence for half a dozen years when they were confronted with the exchange question, and the way in which it was affected by the issue of what we call Council Bills to defray the home charges. So far as any body of men can fix the rate of

* Died May 25th, 1897 (one of her two sons, Nusserwanjee, died three weeks before her), leaving N. M. Wadia, Esq., C.I.E., her remaining son, to inherit her great fortune.

exchange, the East India Company had that power in the disposal of their drafts on India in London and their purchase of bills in India, and the Chamber justly complains that in London, by abrupt leaps and bounds of a halfpenny and even a penny at a time, they raised the rate from 1*s.* 11*d.* in March, 1842, to 2*s.* 1½*d.* in April the same year, being a fluctuation of 10 per cent. On the 30th January, 1843, the Chamber sent a memorial to the Board of Control complaining of the evils and grievances to which trade was subjected by the extraordinary fluctuations and uncertainty in the rate of exchange, caused by the mode in which the Court of Directors at present provide themselves with the funds required for the home charges, and pray that the exchange operations between the two countries may be placed on a sound and proper footing, and be conducted on some fixed, just, and well-understood principles.

I do not think the Company in Bombay sold many bills on London. Men took home their piles in produce, if they managed to escape the clutches of Angria—often in diamonds. We are sorry to say anything against this fine old Company. They actually, in 1821, went so far out of their way as to promise to remit the Robert Burns statue fund from Bombay at 2*s.* 3*d.* I rather, however, fancy that when the bill was obtained the rate in the open market was 2*s.* 3*d.*

No doubt the merchant had compensation in the profit that accrued between the selling and buying rate of bills, and the rates which follow will afford a more pleasant perusal than the shadowy differences of recent times.

	Buying Rate.		Selling Rate.
1826, July 1..	2*s.* 1*d.* to 2*s.* 2*d.*	..	2*s.* ½*d.* to 2*s.* 1*d.*
1828, Jan. 1..	1*s.* 11*d.*	..	1*s.* 10½*d.*
1835, Aug. 1..	2*s.*	..	1*s.* 11*d.*
1836, Jan. 23	2*s.*	..	1*s.* 11*d.*
„ Dec. 31	2*s.* 1*d.*	..	2*s.*
1837, Aug. 19, 30 dys' st.,	1*s.* 9¼*d.*	..	1*s* 9*d.*
1839, May 28, 6 mos.,	2*s.* 1⅜*d.*	..	2*s.* 1½*d.*

The flow of gold and silver into India had not been continuous, and it is observed in 1834, "For the last fifteen years there has been a constant exportation of bullion from India to

England going on." The tide is now turned "and exportation ceased, so we may expect a return of the precious metals."

Unclaimed Deposits.

It is now looked upon as a fable that the Bank of Scotland's fine building in Edinburgh was defrayed from these, and there was a feeling of disappointment, when the old Bank of Bombay was wound up, that there was so small an asset from this contingency. The period of that Bank was pacific and unlike the old times before it. There was a heavy death-roll all through the eighteenth and the first quarter of the nineteenth century. We do not set great store on these windfalls as an item in the balance sheet of private or public banking, but M'Cluer (1795), the Master Mason, whose funds our Administrator-General may know about, and for which nobody can substantiate a claim, bespeaks an increment which may have been somewhat substantial. (*Vide* article *Masonic Legacy.*)

Where the Merchants Lived.

Most of them before this time used to live at Mazagon and the Fort. Now they were scattered over the island—John Smith at Love Grove, James Wright at the Rock, Alexr. Hadden at the Mount, Edward Bates at Chinchpoogly (also Sir Henry Roper, Chief Justice), Robert Strong, Edward Lyon, and Thomas Cardwell at Breach Candy. Two young men, shortly thereafter, David Watson and A. J. Hunter (one became Sheriff and the other Member of Council), had their house in Grant's Buildings, which were new, and a favourite place in those days. There was a rush to Malabar Hill, and the ground could not be cleared fast enough, for as soon as plots were laid out and houses available, tenants were ready. Here are the upper ten, or *avant couriers*, in 1845 of all who have since made this pleasant place their habitation:—

Andrew Cassels, Robert Wigram Crawford, Thomas Lancaster, Vincent Ashfield King, John Parsons, Alexander Remington, Archibald Smart, William Scott, J. E. Maclachlan, Mr. Molyneux, to which may be added two or three men of the legal profession.

The earliest English birth notice on Malabar Hill at hand is the following :—

"On November 12th, 1841, at Malabar Hill, the lady of W. M. Coghlan, Brigade-Major of Artillery, of a son."

Death was busy in 1844 with the merchants of Bombay, and had shorn them of some of their brightest ornaments. He is a tyrant, as we may say in our haste, who has no respect for overland routes or banking enterprise.

John Skinner, on March 23rd, as we have seen, led the way into the silent land, and my record hath it that Malcomson, partner of Forbes and Co., died the very same day at Dhulia, in Khandeish. He seems to have been a most lovable man, of great scientific acquirements; for both Darwin and Hugh Miller lamented his early decease and paid a passing tribute to his genius. His full name was Dr. John Grant Malcomson. He was one of the founders of the Free Church in this city, which in 1843 enlisted such bright and youthful spirits as himself, William Graham, David M'Culloch, and Thomas Lancaster.

On November 22nd, 1844, at Regent's Park, London, died James Ritchie, founder of Ritchie, Steuart and Co. in 1818. William Church, of Brownrigg and Co., left Bombay in September, and, shortly after his return home, died on December 18th; Miller, of Campbell, Miller and Co., died about the same time at the Cape on his way home; and George S. King, of G. S. King and Co., was cut off on his return voyage to India by steamer.

(6.) THE GOOD OLD DAYS IN BOMBAY.

General Rates of Commission and Agency, Bombay, 1845.

On the sale or purchase of goods of all denominations (except as under)	5 per cent.
On purchases of all kinds with the proceeds of goods sold and on which a commission of 5 per cent. has been previously charged	2½ „
On the sale or purchase of ships, houses, and lands.	2½ „
On the sale or purchase of opium	2½ „

On the sale or purchase of diamonds, pearls, and jewellery of all descriptions	2½ per cent.
On the sale or purchase of treasure or bullion exclusive of 1 per cent. on receipt of the proceeds	1 „
On ship's disbursements when no commission has been charged on freight or cargo	2½ „
On effecting insurances	½ „
On settling insurance losses, whether partial or total, also on securing a return of premium, exclusive of commission, on receipt of cash	1 „
On guaranteeing the responsibility of persons to whom goods are sold on the amount of sale	2½ „
On the sale or purchase of cattle	5½ „
On collecting house rent	2½ „
On effecting remittances by bills of exchange (not being the proceeds of goods sold)	1 „
On taking up interest bills from the Company, exclusive of 1 per cent. on remitting	½ „
On sale or purchase of public or private bills of exchange	½ „
On exchanging Company's securities of all descriptions, on investing money therein, and on transferring Government Paper from one constituent to another	½ „
On surrendering or depositing in the Treasury Company's securities of all descriptions	½ „
On procuring money on respondentia or on loan	2 „
On recovery of bonds or bills for absentees overdue at the period of their being placed in the possession of the agent	2 „
On debt when a process at law or by arbitration is necessary 2½ per cent., and if recovered by such means	5 „
On managing the affairs of an estate for an executor or administrator	5 „
On guaranteeing bills, bonds, or debts in general by endorsement or otherwise	½ „
On attending the delivery of contract goods to the company or individuals	1 „

On goods consigned and afterwards withdrawn on invoice cost	2½	per cent.
On bills of exchange returned, noted or protested .	1	„
On receipt or payment (at the option of the agent) of all monies not arising from proceeds of goods on which commission has been previously charged	1	„
In all cases where the debtor side of the account exceeds the credit side, including the balance of interest, commission chargeable on the debtor side at the rate of	1	„
On granting letters of credit	2½	„
On becoming security to Government or public bodies in any case	2½	„
On goods consigned which are disposed of by outcry, or sent to a shop on net proceeds, ...	1½	„
On depositing Government Paper as security for constituents	1	„

MEMORANDUM.

Sales on Europe goods, when made at an advance on invoice cost, the amount to be converted into Bombay currency at the exchange of two shillings per rupee.

These are the rates of commission established by houses of agency in Bombay fifty years ago, and before any of us were on the stage. The list covers a great variety of business, and constitutes for us a Paradise Lost, which, as far as man can judge, will never be "regained." No wonder men made money rapidly in those days. They played their cards with trumps, and, with such a lot of picture cards, were bound to win; though it was not always so. Some evil genius occasionally would come in and spoil the broth. Bankers, merchants, and brokers will no doubt scan the details which most concern them with interest. *Tempora mutantur.*

III.

ROADS BY SEA AND LAND.

(1.) THE MAKERS OF THE RED SEA STEAM NAVIGATION.

MR. J. WESTLAKE has presented me with a little book, gilt edged and bound in green, the perusal of which might embolden the young aspirant to write a history of Overland traffic. Printed and published in Calcutta in 1837, it contains a letter of Dr. Dionysius Lardner, of Cyclopædia fame, addressed to Lord Melbourne, then Prime Minister, on Steam Communication with India by the Red Sea.

That was the year when some halting lines appeared in a Bombay journal.

> "Let us set up three lines instead of one
> Ere the Red Sea line has fairly begun;
> O! weep by the waters of Babylon
> O'er two lakhs spent and still more to pay,
> Besides a few mails that have gone astray."

The £20,000 referred to was the Government grant to defray the cost of the Euphrates expedition—a region which the elder Chesney did so much to elucidate.

PIONEERS.

The earliest proposal for steam navigation by the Red Sea is the following ironical notice which appears in the *Asiatic Journal* for May, 1822:—" A Captain Johnston has suggested a plan for opening an intercourse with India by means of steam vessels, and the details he has furnished respecting it are so specious, and all the obstacles in the way of its success are so admirably disposed of, that it is astonishing the projector has not been deluged with contributions or subscriptions already, and that a steamer is not unloading in the port of Suez." *

Mountstuart Elphinstone in 1823 was the first to make a distinct official proposition for the establishment of steam communication between Bombay and England *viâ* the Red Sea, and in 1826 he renewed the proposal, but the Court were unwilling to act upon the suggestion.

Sir John Malcolm contributed to the cause the weight of his great authority, and in December, 1830, he himself embarked on the *Hugh Lindsay* to Cosseir, this being her second voyage. "A pleasanter voyage," says Sir John, "was never made." Of Sir Robert Grant, Governor 1835–38, the verdict of the Bombay Press on his death was:—"He did very much to promote the Overland route by the Red Sea."

These are conspicuous names, and the honour and glory of the first is not dimmed by the lustre of the second or even by that of the third. They simply followed in the train of their illustrious forerunner. With the furtherance of this great scheme there are many names associated, and these are not lightly to be passed over. Each in his day and sphere did his own work. But all their exertions would have been futile had it not been that they were contemporaneous with the rise of that great man Mohammed Ali, who in peace and in war was the friend and patron of the Overland route through his Egyptian dominions. He overawed the Arabs and made the desert as secure for life and property as the highways of London.

Dr. Wilson's opinion as expressed in the *Oriental Christian Spectator* of 1841, of which he was the editor, on one of the foremost men in this work during "the thirties," is in these terms: "William Taylor Money, partner of Forbes and Co., and afterwards her Majesty's Consul at Venice, was the most prompt and energetic advocate of steam navigation in Bombay." And it redounds to his eternal honour that at a meeting in Calcutta in 1828, where the Cape Route was supported by Commodore Hayes, Captain Johnston, and Waghorn himself,

---

* Low's *Indian Navy*, 1877.

Mr. J. A. Prinsep had the hardihood to state that letters might be conveyed from Calcutta to Cosseir in twenty-nine days, thence to Cairo in two days, and thence to London in twenty-three days, doing the entire distance in fifty-four days. But it was a voice crying in the wilderness.

Meetings in Bombay.

The first meeting in Bombay to promote the Red Sea route was on the 17th April, 1830, shortly after Taylor's arrival. I suppose that the name of Robert Wigram Crawford, M.P. for the City, and Director of the Bank of England, should be a good authority on the question as to whom we owe Red Sea steam communication.* A partner of Remington and Co., Bombay, in 1836, he was in the thick of the fight. He has left it on record that the overland route between India and England was due to the community of Bombay, as represented by the Bombay Steam Committee. On May 8th, 1833, the Sheriff was asked to convene a meeting in the Town Hall for the furtherance of the object. Sir Herbert Compton was in the chair, and among the earliest subscriptions were Compton, Sunkersett, Jejeebhoy, Ali Rogay, Rs. 1,000 each. Ritchie Steuart and Co., Forbes and Co., W. Nicol and Co., Adam, Skinner and Co., Remington and Co., Rs. 1,500 each. This was the sinews of war, and before November, 1833, the Bombay Steam Fund amounted to Rs. 1,30,000.

It was to this Steam Committee that Waghorn made his last appeal. "For myself, as I have devoted the best years of my life to this line of route, I offer my remaining ones at your disposal for providing greater rapidity for letters and comfort for passengers between you and England. I pray you to assist me, and if my conscience does not deceive me I firmly believe you will have just cause to congratulate yourselves as well as yours, &c., Thomas Waghorn, Alexandria, 11th Dec., 1839."

Again on March 16th, 1836, another meeting was convened by the Sheriff, W. C. Bruce, in the Town Hall to consider the

---

* Who that saw him could ever forget him. He stood six feet four inches in his white stocking soles—a wonderful physique.

subject of steam communication with England, which the papers describe as "the burning question of the day."

It was following the meeting of 1836 that in 1838 the overland route was established by a monthly mail from Suez, conducted by the Indian Navy, and, though we now anticipate, Bombay never paused in the work of steam acceleration by the Red Sea. In the year 1853 there were serious delays in the Overland Mails. The London mail of June 8th was delivered in Bombay on July 26th, that of June 24th on August 3rd, that of July 8th on August 25th, the last being forty-eight days in transmission. There is a limit to human forbearance, so a great meeting was called in the Town Hall on September 3rd, 1853. That meeting was a memorable one, and the men who took part in it deserve to have their names recorded as benefactors of their species.

I have no doubt that this meeting had a great deal to do with the withdrawal of the mail service from the Indian Navy and the substitution of the contract in 1855 for monthly mails by the P. and O. Co. from London to Bombay. John Stuart, David M'Culloch, Robert Ryrie, J. Graham, Thomas Lancaster, L. A. Wallace, J. Hadow, Richard Willis, T. S. Cowie, Henry Scott and Nelson Howard sign the requisition. John Smith, of William Nicol and Co., was in the chair. Berkeley, the Engineer, was there, a splendid speaker. Bhau Daji followed, and Dr. Wilson by special invitation, as he was always interested in every question that affected the happiness of the public. Of these men (1895) Messrs. Robert Ryrie, James Graham, J. Hadow, and L. A. Wallace are still surviving. Confining ourselves to the practical demonstration of Red Sea Steam Navigation, we ought never to lose sight of the fact that it was during Malcolm's administration (1828–30) the *Hugh Lindsay* was built, launched, equipped, and despatched to Suez on March 20th, 1830. Here were deeds not words. Waghorn and Taylor did not arrive in Bombay until March 21st, or the day after, and it is a curious circumstance to note that while Waghorn at this time advocated the Cape Route, Taylor was in favour of the Red Sea, and still more strange that Waghorn soon after this should become the undisputed apostle and prominent advocate of the Red Sea, while Taylor was killed by the Arabs this very year of 1830 while conveying an English mail through the deserts of Mesopotamia.

THE "HUGH LINDSAY."

The foundation of steam navigation in the Red Sea was without the shadow of a doubt the *Hugh Lindsay*, the first steamship constructed in Bombay (411 tons). She was named after Captain Hugh Lindsay, a man of great bravery, who forced his way to the Canton Palace. In 1865 she broke her back in the harbour of Bassadore. Her first four voyages to Suez were made from Bombay :—

1830	March 20th.
1830	December 5th.
1832	January 5th.
1833	January 14th.

Her passenger accommodation was taken up months before. Several parties, travelling overland 1,000 miles, were disappointed, though arriving two months prior to the time fixed for her departure. We are particular in these details, for they are the initial letters of all steam-navigation in the Red Sea. These four voyages were the basis of the Resolution of a Committee of the House of Commons in 1834, and finally led to the decision in 1837, which settled once for all the Red Sea route. Captain John H. Wilson, of the Indian Marine, who commanded the *Hugh Lindsay*, made seven voyages in her to Suez. He may be fairly regarded as a rival to Waghorn. "He retired in 1838, but from that time to the day of his death in December, 1875, he never received any acknowledgment, honorary or otherwise, for his great services in promoting steam communication between England and the East."

THE EXPERIMENTAL VOYAGE.

There must be some men alive in Bombay who witnessed the first departure of the *Hugh Lindsay* for Suez on March 20th, 1830. That was an event worthy of being recorded—the sailing of the first steamer (she was launched in 1829), and the first steamer which cleared out of our harbour for Suez. Did she steal away past Kennery as private as pestilence, or was her departure heralded by sound of trumpet, or the roar of great guns dying away among the ghauts, and wakening echoes from Thul to the jagged peaks of Karnala and Bhaumalang? Did the boys, Hindoo or Parsee, scuttle away from Bennett's School, No. 6, Rampart Row, to see the fun?

Sir John Peter Grant, having resigned, was in low spirits at the Hermitage. But John Skinner was at Mazagon, James Wright at Belmont, Mazagon, Harry George Gordon in Nisbet Lane, and John Smith at Love Grove. Surely there would be a gathering at one of these lordly mansions to drink success to the Red Sea Route, amid bumpers of wine. What about the theatre? Did a favourite piece of that time, *Ways and Means, or a Trip to Dover*, foreshadow the multiplied wishes for a new route and the wherewithal to accomplish it?

Did Archdeacon Jeffreys preach a sermon on it? "Those that go down to the sea in ships," with counsels of temperance, to which the ribald sailor replied in such doggerel as this:—

> "Mr. Jeffreys, God bless you,
> We're fain to address you
> In reply to your Temperance Log,
> As we really can't see
> What great harm there can be
> In a moderate potion of grog."

Bombay a Point of Departure.

It is very easy in 1895 to sit down complacently and wonder why anybody could ever doubt that Bombay should be the point of arrival and departure of the Indian Mails. "By virtue of its inherent geographical position, and its nearness to Europe"—and so you settle the question once for all. No doubt Bombay's position on the map is unchangeable, and apparently unassailable. But carry yourself back to 1837 and listen to the voice of India—and India, bear in mind, with no Suez Canal, with running postmen in lieu of railway communication to Calcutta, with no Aden as a coaling station, with steam vessels of 400 tons, such as they were. You may also bear in mind that Moresby's survey of the Red Sea was not completed until 1834, and in that year Captain Wilson, who had made four voyages to Suez in the *Hugh Lindsay*, stated that, during the navigation of such a steamer across the Indian Ocean, the South-West monsoon so operates as—if not to prevent the communication—at least to render it useless.

Calcutta had a waterway on the Ganges for a distance of a thousand miles for the distribution of mails and passengers, while you had not a single river on the western side of India, Napier, "the bearded vision," having not yet put in an appearance on the banks of the Indus. As against this great water highway what had you to show? When your mails and passengers were landed in Bombay you had dawk and palanquin through countries recently acquired, or owning at least a nominal subjection to us. What sort of comfort had you to show to ladies and families travelling to Calcutta by weary stages in the heat and the rains, those two factors which, Dr. Lardner remarks, all the wealth and science of the world are unable to eliminate (almost eliminated now by railway to Calcutta)? Calcutta now was the capital of India, with thrice the *ad valorem* of your commerce. Her merchants were princes. When a commercial typhoon raged (1830–32) five of them succumbed with liabilities amounting to fifteen millions sterling! Everything was on a larger scale in Calcutta. Of 3,500 passengers who came annually to India round the Cape, poor Bombay received 600, instead of 6,000, which every year she now receives with open arms.

The commerce of India, I read, is now worth 200 millions sterling. I am sure it was not half this amount in 1837.

British India's population was then one hundred millions instead of three hundred millions of to-day. And think of the steamers of 1837. Would any shipowner nowadays despatch a steamer of four hundred tons across the Indian Ocean during the violence of the monsoon? And, when all was settled, consider for a moment what your introduction of steam navigation meant. The vested interest of sailing ships was enormous. Not alone Green's line of clippers, but a whole fleet of Indiamen scoured the seas, for a funnel had scarcely been seen as yet on the Indian Ocean. It must be borne in mind also that there was a fierce and a bitter hostility against steamers by all seafaring men. The Indian Marine simply hated them and their passenger proclivities. Captain Wilson was the only one of that service who had the courage to volunteer and take command of the *Hugh Lindsay* in 1830.

I should imagine that Lord Clare's voyage out by the Red Sea in 1836 rather staggered all lovers of that route. His six months' weary journey from London to Bombay, varied by a forced halt of six weeks at Jeddah, waiting for coals from Suez, must have left a bad taste in his mouth. He at all events had enough of the Red Sea, and I do not wonder that his efforts to promote its navigation have been left unrecorded.

Red Sea Route Decided Upon.

We read on May 30th, 1837, that the Red Sea Route once for all was decided on by Government. The Government and the East India Company had taken seven years to make up their mind. The Cape route by steam had many advocates, even Waghorn himself, as we have said, at an early stage of his career. If I remember rightly, £10,000 was offered to whoever should bring the first steamer to Calcutta by the Cape. The *Enterprise*, of 500 tons, came out in 1826, and Government purchased her for £40,000; but she took 115 days. Sailing vessels have done the passage in seventy-seven days from the Lizard to Bombay, and on one occasion in sixty-six days. Then there was the Euphrates Valley route, to test which Government voted £20,000. A Mr. J. W. Taylor, agent for some capitalists in London, and brother of Major Taylor, Resident at Bagdad, left Bombay on May 2nd, 1830, with letters *viâ* Bussorah. The party left Bagdad in September, and, within three marches from Mosul, Taylor and two Englishmen were murdered. This was a deathblow to the Euphrates Valley steam communication.

The plague at Bagdad and consequent quarantine of thirty days in Bombay was a most formidable obstacle to any communication by this route, and it was no sham. The first officer of a ship which attempted entering the harbour about this time without *pratique* was shot dead.

There must be people alive who have spent a quarantine of thirty days in the lazaretto on Butcher's Island.

(2.) WAGHORN.

IT is not easy to estimate the encouragement which the Bombay Steam Committee and the Chamber of Commerce after 1837 gave to Waghorn, when we remember that the Government had pronounced the Red Sea unnavigable, and the East India Company laid documents before Parliament showing that the scheme was impracticable, because coals cost £23 a ton at Suez, and took fifteen months to get there! Waghorn dissipated all these delusions, and rose superior to the frowns even of the Bombay Government. What is harder to bear than opposition is neglect.

> "Give me the avowed, the erect, the manly foe,
> Whom I can face, or else avert the blow."

We have now before us in Dr. Lardner's book the following documents:—

A letter to Lord Melbourne by Dr. Lardner	1836
A Circular published in Calcutta	1836
A Petition to Parliament (signatures, 7,632)	1836
A Memorial to the India Board	1836
A letter to Lord William Bentinck.	1836
A Reply of the Bengal Committee to Major Head, Chairman of the Provincial Committee	1836

In all 124 octavo pages of letterpress. Will it be believed that Waghorn's name or services are not even alluded to? The Calcutta pilot—a prophet, if you will—had no honour in his own country, though his bust now greets the stranger as he enters the Suez Canal. And yet before 1836 he had done some things in this overland business to make him a marked man. He was not unknown in Calcutta; he had been in the pilot service of that city from 1819 to 1824, and for two and a half years had command of the *Matchless* cutter, of Sir John Hayes' squadron, and had become early imbued with an interest in steam communication with England. It was in Calcutta at a public meeting in 1828 that Commodore Hayes gave his warmest support to him, and it was its Steam Committee in 1828 which accredited him to persons of official standing in Madras, Ceylon, Mauritius, the Cape, and St. Helena.

He surely had a title to be heard on the question. I presume it was well enough known in October, 1836, that Lord Ellenborough, the President of the Board of Control (October, 1829), had sent for Waghorn to carry important despatches to Sir John Malcolm and demonstrate the practicability of Red Sea navigation. We all know how he performed that journey, how he darted across a continent without railways to Trieste, from Trieste to Alexandria in a sailing craft, to Rosetta on donkeys, to Cairo on a Nile boat, to Suez on camel back, to Cosseir in an open native boat, and by the same conveyance to Jeddah, a distance of 660 miles from Suez. Many of us can follow him on donkey and dahabiah, and on camel back, but for that voyage in an open boat on the Red Sea we would require Burckhardt, or Burton, or Frere to delineate its miseries. He arrived in the Company's cruiser on March 21st, in four months twenty-one days from London. Such was Red Sea navigation before steam was taken out of the tea-kettle. He had already lectured on the subject in all the leading cities of India and England. It is honestly averred that he lived for three entire years with the Arab tribes between Cairo and Suez. Think of that, you who live at home at ease, and all to save you and your kith and kin from the plunder and cut-throats of the desert.

Government and the Company were not generous with Waghorn. They gave him a pension of £200 a year, I understand, in 1848 (he died in 1850), which was immediately mortgaged by his creditors.* They could scarcely be expected to pay his outlay on dhuramsalas, dahabiahs and never-ending *backsheesh*. I dare say if they had known in 1848 what we know now, they would have paid his debts a dozen times over, which would have been cheap at the money. What we complain of was their hide-bound prejudices in their postal system, as if it was immaculate, and their retention of dirty steamers, such as the *Berenice* and *Zenobia*. Did not a P. and O. steamer make Calcutta from Suez in 1843?

How he should have been ignored by Calcutta in 1836 we

* A sister who had all along cheered him in his labours survived him until 1883. She died in a London workhouse.

can only explain by the fact that the Company and the Post Office, the Gog and Magog of these early times, hated Waghorn and every man who dared to interfere with their established custom or routine, and it was the fashion to do so, though for five years (1832 to 1837) he had the absolute control of the Overland Mails in his hands. One of the strangest things was how the truth gradually dawned upon Waghorn. At first he firmly believed in the Cape route and lectured upon it in Calcutta, where he engaged some of the foremost men there to assist him in making his views public to the communities of Madras, Ceylon, Mauritius, and the Cape. But truth travels slowly. He that believeth shall not make haste. I suppose his own passage down the Red Sea in 1829 led up to his conversion, and Captain Wilson's two voyages in the *Hugh Lindsay* from Bombay to Suez completed it. Henceforth nothing could part him from the Red Sea route, and he threw all the energy and perseverance with which he was so largely endowed into the work of its accomplishment. Waghorn is one of the martyrs of science. Galileo on bended knees and Waghorn knocking at the door of the India House are two pictures that will endure to the last syllable of recorded time. Waghorn holds the key of the Overland route, and though he never saw the Suez Canal, he certainly saw the man who made it; and Lesseps has left on record undying words (Nov. 1883) that it was to Waghorn alone that he was indebted for the great idea.

Yes, you may well look at this man, and go back to Spenser in the days of Drake and Raleigh for his portrait.

> "A silly man in simple weeds forworne
> And soil'd with dust to the long dried way;
>   His sandales were with toilsome travell torne,
> And face all tann'd with scorching sunny ray,
> As he had travell'd many a summer day
>   Through boyling sands of Arabie and Ynd."

Pilot of Calcutta and the Hooghly in the first place, and then pilot of the whole Eastern world of commerce, Waghorn died in poverty at Chatham (1850) in the fiftieth year of his age; Taylor was murdered in Mesopotamia in 1830; Wilson, unrewarded, died in 1875, and I rather think that

Capt. Johnston, R.N., of the *Enterprise*, ended his days as English Postmaster in Alexandria. He died May 5th, 1851.*

"Give him a little earth for charity."

Such was the fate of the pioneers of the Red Sea and Overland steam communication.

Some of the following quotations of 1837 are gropings in the dark, but represent the highest wisdom, or what was considered such at the period, on the all-engrossing theme:—

"A steamship does good duty if she works half her time."

"A steamer against the monsoon would tack like a sailing vessel."

"Passages from Socotra to Bombay to be made under sail only."

"Abundance of good steam coal is obtained in America, which would doubtless be taken as ballast by American vessels."

"Cairo to Suez. The road is hard and smooth; there is no need of a railroad."

"It might be found also that correspondence might be forwarded to Great Britain from Egypt with greater despatch by landing it at Marseilles and sending it by land to Calais." So it was.

"The number of passengers and despatches to and from Bombay being less in a considerable proportion than the other ports of India." This seems to have been so in 1836.

"In seasons when the monsoon is most violent the Bombay steamer might meet at the head of the Maldives."

"The course from Bombay to the Maldives would be quite practicable, as well as the course from the Maldives to Socotra."

"If Bombay is decided on, it would be more convenient to land the passengers and parcels from India for Great Britain at Penzance or even the Scilly Islands than those of Great Britain for all India at Bombay."—*Letter from Bengal Committee to Provincial Committee, Dec. 26th*, 1836.

---

* James Henry Johnston.

(3.) THE FIRST P. AND O. THROUGH THE CANAL FROM BOMBAY.

THIS distinction belongs to the *Nubia*, Captain Wilkinson, which left Bombay about March 9th, 1870. My fellow passenger was the late Andrew Hay, Sheriff of Bombay (1868). We had a sickly voyage up the Red Sea and several deaths took place. The heat was blazing. Steaming slowly, we seemed to be cutting our way through a sea as smooth as plate glass. Several times the ship was turned round to create a draught, for there was not a breath of wind, and we were almost suffocated. We buried two men one morning at 6 A.M. By a mischance the bodies were *not* unfastened from the grating, so at the last moment, when Wilkinson read from the Burial Service, "we commit the bodies of our dear brothers to the deep," down went *the grating* with the two bodies on it, nearly carrying the two quartermasters away with it. But Wilkinson did not flinch or falter; he continued reading the Burial Service to the end, when, lo and behold! some miles away the grating was seen floating on the glassy sea, with the two bodies on it, and the British flag atop. "Stop her!" was thundered out, a boat was lowered, the bodies released, and the recovered paraphernalia brought on board. The *Cathay* was at Suez, and the Commander, if still to the fore, may have forgotten the circumstance, which I remember very well, that he entertained us hospitably on board his ship, with the addition of the Agent and English Consul for many years, the well-known Mr. West. The toast was drunk: "May you never touch the bottom." Great Scott! I could see that it was an anxious moment when we entered the Canal. West accompanied us, told us he had often ridden over the ground we were sailing over; and Wilkinson—care sat on his manly brow—muttered something about skippers taking lessons in Dutch navigation.

It was a new experience for the lascars, trudging along the muddy banks with the hawsers wherewith to tie us up for the night. I am not quite sure that they had not to drive in the piles with which to fasten us while the sun descended and darkness covered the land of Egypt. I dare say Wilkinson would have preferred running with bare poles before the South-West Monsoon, or being tossed like a bucket in the white squall of the Mediterranean. That night all was gloom. Not as now, when the electric light clears up a way in the silence and blackness of midnight, a veritable pillar of fire for many an exodus to many a land of promise, changing these mud heaps on either side—the ugliest things in creation—into a weird phantasmagoria, flashing, dazzling to the eye, a wondrous dream, not of the mingling of two seas, but—

> "Twenty seas if all their sands were pearl."

I need not add that the *Nubia's* trip through the Canal was a complete success. This trip was the beginning of a new era, and I ventured to tell the story to one who was much interested in it. "But what did your fellow passengers think of the Canal?" said Lesseps a few months after this. I answered that one of them said it was the greatest work of utility that had been made since the creation of the world, adding that an American *guessed* he would not call it a *great* work until it paid. "It will pay," said the Baron quietly, which was also Beaconsfield's opinion, and which time has amply justified.

The date of this conversation was, I think, in July, 1870, and the place was "The Wick," Richmond, a bowshot from the "Star and Garter," which everybody knows. There were no houses between them in those days, and its garden ran down to the Thames. This house had a celebrated history. It was once given by the King to Sir Joshua Reynolds, and here Dr. Johnson and Burke also, as I suppose, came to dine or sup. Neither of them predicted the Suez Canal, nor dreamed that in the room where they sat would be congregated a hundred men and women to do honour to the maker of it. There they were, however, soldiers, statesmen, artists, P. and O. directors, some old Egyptians, with a sprinkling of undistinguished others. The place was worthy of the occasion, and the Master of Ceremonies did it every honour. He had been deputed by Lloyds as their representative at the opening of the Canal, was an early friend of Lesseps, when they wandered unknown, and bivouacked on scanty fare under tamarisk or acacia in those days when Mohammed Ali, of venerable beard, rode out on a white ass and administered justice *coram populo* in Okella or Bazaar. But why do we hesitate? The name of Alexander Tod was widely known by a generation of Anglo-Indians at his half-way house in Alexandria. Long ere he became a merchant prince his hospitality was boundless, and flowed in a continuous stream.

Missionary, manager, explorer, diplomat, and subaltern, Sir James Outram, Frere, or Lord Dufferin, were all made happy. If the wheels on the Overland Route at first drove heavily, he was a pioneer who smoothed the path and cheered the spirits of the passing traveller. George Gliddon, American Consul, his father-in-law, was Waghorn's representative in Egypt.

Brevity is the soul of wit and of wisdom also, and Johnson himself would have lauded that speech of four words, in which the master of the household toasted his ancient and honoured friend—"genius and energy personified." I am sure Lesseps never spent a happier day, not even in the Guildhall, when he received the freedom of the City. There he was with his young wife, in the blush of early womanhood. The Empress of the French, when she was still the betrothed, at the Canal inauguration paid her marked attention. "The last time I saw you, you were in tears," said one to her who had not seen her since that great day. He was laughing all the time. It was too true. The Empress had embraced her, and overcome by this act of love and condescension she had burst into a flood of tears.

The host was a Scotsman, and as everybody nowadays, when he arrives at distinction, is anxious to show he has a drop of Scotch blood in his veins, Lesseps in his reply to the toast of his health on this memorable occasion spoke in French nearly as follows:—"I too have some claims to be regarded as a Scotsman. If you read the story of the building of St. Giles's Cathedral in Edinburgh you will see that its architect was *Le Sept*. I claim to be a descendant of him." There was no mention of his ancestor in the *Scots Guard* of Paris in this speech.

Alexander Tod, full of years and honour, died at Walmer in 1893; his friend Lesseps in 1894 disappeared in a cloud, from which his name and fame are destined to emerge.* William Paterson founded the Bank of England, and the Darien scheme is forgotten, and Panama will gradually subside into the same oblivion and be swallowed up in the immortal memory of Lesseps as the maker of the Suez Canal.

(4.) ACROSS INDIA IN A PALKEE.

Places.	Distances.		Expense.				
			Day's Pay.		Rate per Diem.		Total of each stage.
	M.	F.					
Khalapoor	18	5	6	5	24	1	50
Karlee	17	4	4	5	16	1	...
Taligaon	15	1	2	5	3	0	50
Poona...	19	6	2	6	9	3	...
Ooroolee	18	6	4	5	16	1	...
Wurwund	18	4	6	5	24	1	50
Rawungaon	18	7	8	5	32	2	...
Daheej	15	3	10	6	42	0	50
Indapoor	17	5	8	6	39	0	...
Temboornee	13	0	6	6	29	1	...
Arrun...	13	0	4	6	19	2	...
Hewur	13	6	3	6	14	2	50
Lambooty	12	7	2	6	9	3	...
Sholapore	15	5	2	6	9	3	...
Tandoolwaree	14	6	4	6	19	2	...

Nuldroog. The Nawab 3. Dooly Khaus 14-6.

From Bombay to Panwell the voyage is from 3½ to 4½ hours.

One set hamals at Panwell, Rs. 2, 8 and Rs. 13.

NOTE.—The set in this division is calculated for 12 bearers and one masauljee. The set at Tandoolwaree carriers to Nuldroog, to which place the Postmaster at Poona has to post bearers for persons travelling by post by order of Government.

The above is the first section of the old Palkee Road to Calcutta *viá* Hyderabad and Orissa.

Andrew Hay, Sheriff of Bombay (1868), arrived in Bombay in 1841, and was a passenger in the *Berenice*, the same steamer

* A statue of Lesseps is forthwith to be raised on the Canal bank.—*Aug.* 1899.

which brought out Sir Charles Napier, and he often used to relate that he was the last through passenger who went by Dâk Palkee to Calcutta.

In 1870 I rode with Mr. Hay on horseback for several hundred miles, and for a few weeks together, through Syria, and had ample time and opportunity to ask him about this mode of locomotion and as to how he stood the journey, but it did not occur to me to do so, and thus much valuable information was lost. The railway having now superseded this method of travelling—drivén it into secluded districts, and so in a manner relegated it to ancient history—it is now my business to endeavour, by ploughing among dead men's bones, to gather together some particulars about Palkee travelling to Calcutta and elsewhere.

This was the mode which Mountstuart Elphinstone generally adopted in his long journey from Calcutta to Poona in 1801, and which touched up his liver so much that he felt the effects of it during the rest of his life. Heber, in 1824, rode on horse and camel-back a good part of the way, but occasionally adopted this method of travelling in his Mofussil journeys. Though cramped, he found it neither violent nor unpleasant, but he could not sketch in a palanquin or read anything but large print. But we must begin at the beginning. Posting by palkee was an organisation of the East India Company, and was entirely under the control of the Postal Department or the District Collectors, and early in "the forties," or, to be particular, say in 1845,. if you intended proceeding from Bombay to Calcutta by this mode of conveyance you had to put yourself in communication with the head of the Postal Department at least ten days before the date of your intended departure, giving him your destination, with many other particulars (which we will endeavour to relate), such as the exact day and hour of your intended departure from Bombay. You elect, we will suppose, the route by Poona, Hyderabad, Vizagapatam, Masulipatam, and Cuttack. Very well. As there are close upon a hundred halting stations, you will require to state how long you intend halting at each of them, and the names of the stations you intend to halt at, stating whether for sleep or refreshment. You are a "stout" party, this word meaning in those days not corpulent but robust, and intend to do the journey in twenty-two days.* You know what palkee travelling is. You have gone to Love Grove, Worlee, we will suppose, five miles, and have emerged as stiff as a poker. Bear in mind your intended journey is one of 500 hours' duration. If it is in April or May you will journey mostly by night and rest during the day. The reason why the Postmaster requires all these particulars is that the laying down a dâk to Calcutta involves an immense correspondence, and the route covers nearly 1,400 miles. You will please to remember the hamals are in sets, and go only a certain mileage, that they are drawn from their homes, which lie at distances from the halting stations, and that in the Nizam's dominions every hamal starts from Hyderabad, or says he does so, to its remotest boundary, and that you, a traveller, will require to pay these hamals every day their wages from the day they are supposed to leave their homes until they return thereto. You will require changes of linen and clothing, so you are allowed two banghy bardars, who will swing on their shoulders your kit, not more than fifty-six pounds. Brandy goes into narrow compass—you must depend upon beer where you can find it, and you will require to pay through the nose for it in these distant regions, owing to the expense of carriage.

If your period is the rains, be thankful if you escape malaria, or if in the hot weather, sunstroke. It may be your last journey, and the palanquin may become your catafalque; certainly, even in our day the dead body of a traveller has been taken out of a palkee. I have not alluded to the crossing of rivers or the danger of being drowned in a box, or surprised by a tiger. Your bearers drop their burden like lightning, and make tracks for the nearest tree, or bumping against some rock in the dark you are shot out of your tabernacle like a catapult, your venetian along with you; happily for you if you fall among the yielding branches of some bush, scrub or tree; or you are attacked by dacoits who hunt in gangs, plundered and left dead or wounded in the jungle, or, may be, confronted by a swollen

---

* Thus a journey of 400 miles may be made with great ease in about five days.—Gilchrist's *Vade Mecum*, 1825.

river. A man has just told us that his bearers once deserted him, and that he had to haul his palkee for four days on a country cart. These are contingencies you must face, and I warn you that Government by public notification hold themselves free of all responsibility for you or for your luggage. You may read the notice up in every post office "that neither Government nor any of their officers are responsible to the traveller for the misfortunes and disappointments which are inseparable from dâk travelling; thus every traveller travels at his own risk, and is liable to the losses and increased expenses incidental to delays and accidents, and Government can in no instance be considered liable to make good any losses whatever."

"When a private gentleman requires bearers to be posted for him, he should be very particular in stating to his correspondent whom he relies upon for assistance—the day, even the hour, on which he proposes to commence his journey; the places he intends to halt at for refreshment, and the time he intends to halt for that purpose. If neglectful of these particulars the hamals may reach their stations several days before they are required, and perhaps put the traveller to a great additional expense. Should the traveller on any occasion wish to halt a day at any place, his stating his intention previously would save the posting of one set. For instance a traveller from Bombay to Poona will meet the first Poona set at Kholapoor, and, supposing that they take him to the top of the ghât to breakfast, they can, having refreshed themselves, take him on in the evening to Wurgaon, or they might come to Karlee to breakfast and run to Wurgaon or Talligaon in the evening. For the extra labour, however, they would be entitled to at least half a rupee each man additional. The hamals at Panwell are under the Collector at Tanna; at Poona they are under the Collector in the city and under the bazaar master in camp, and this applies to Skolapore."

Now for the question of expense. It may be useful for you to read the following, unless money is out of the question. "A set of dâk bearers comprises twelve, and one mussalchee, for which is charged, payable in advance, at the rate of eight annas per mile; but as in many instances, owing to the delay caused by travellers remaining longer on the road than the stipulated time, this sum is found unequal to the expense, a further sum of four annas per mile is required to be paid as a deposit to cover any eventual expense or demurrage caused by delay on the part of the traveller. Should none occur the full amount of the sum deposited is refunded, upon the traveller furnishing a certificate from the deputy postmaster at the place where his journey is finished, that he arrived there without incurring demurrage." And "when it is reported that a traveller comes on demurrage on any part of the road, the adjustment of the amount deposited to cover such expenses will be postponed until the receipt of the bills for the dâk from *all* the postmasters through whose divisions the traveller may have passed." And if you change your mind during these ten days preliminary to your intended starting you will require to pay for it, which is only fair, as "heaven and earth" have been moved by the authorities all along the line on your account. "When dâk has been ordered and circumstances may render it expedient for the traveller to postpone his journey, or to withdraw the bearers entirely, he will of course be held liable for any expense which may have been incurred on his account. The amount paid for the dâk and deposited to cover demurrage will remain unadjusted until reports are received from the General Postmaster upon the line of route upon which the dâk was ordered."

I will give an abstract of what you will require to pay in Bombay for your palkee passage alone. I need not mention that for all meats and drinks and spiritual ordinances you will require to pay cash down on your line of march. I conclude you are not going this journey in *grande tenue*, and will dispense with a butler; but you will require cherry merrys *in numero;* to the bheestie who souses you with a chattie of cold water over your head in the morning, and to fakeers and all the *omnium gatherum* of mendicants who will persecute you and howl you sick until you give them an obolus. You will observe that through the Nizam's dominions the charges are twice as heavy as through other territories, and the reason I assign for this is that all the hamals must come from Hyderabad, and it is the distance that lends enhancement, not enchantment, to the view.

"Had you any companion?" I once asked a man at the end of a very long palanquin journey. "The only companion I had was my pipe," was the reply. So be sure you take plenty of tobacco and manilla cheroots and several pipes, as everything breakable will go to smash ere you reach Calcutta. I advise you also to take a copy of Bunyan's *Pilgrim's Progress* in large type, suitable for schools or for old men whose sight is failing them, as you will meet with Sloughs of Despond and Hills of Evil Council galore, and will find when you get there that Calcutta is not the Celestial City. Moreover, be not tempted by objects of attraction, unless in your immediate purview. Bijapur and Vizianagar are not to be thought of. And any subaltern at some military station a few miles from your line of march, though he be your dearest friend, you must pass by as if he had no existence. Such deviations would put your chain of communication out of gear, and disturb the whole harmony of your arrangements. Hundreds of hamals at fifty different stations are now awaiting you, chewing betel and cleaning their teeth. Not that they object to the detention. Every day's delay is a day's additional pay which you will be required to liquidate.

					Rupees.
Poona range, 259 miles, cost for 12 hamals and musaul at each stage					326
Oil and Muckadum's fees perhaps additional					20
Nizam's Territory, 275 miles, do., would cost					700
Masulipatam Collectorship,		105 miles	,,		33
Rajamundry	,,	100	,,	,,	55
Vizagapatam	,,	122	,,	,,	24
Chicacole	,,	125	,,	,,	31
Cuttack	,,	112	,,	,,	34
Jelassore	,,	126	,,	,,	42
To Tumlook	,,	95	,,	,,	26
Total		1,319 Miles			Rs. 1,291*

I don't think in the whole of India you could take a more uninteresting journey. Half of the halting stations have unpronounceable names, and of half a hundred more the names you have never heard before. There is not one city of great

---

* Postmaster's dâk about R. 1 per mile.—Dr. Gilchrist's *Vade Mecum*, 1825.

and historical renown, neither battlefield nor palace. You have many an ancient river and many a palmy plain, but little else. And when you are done with it, the Duke's Nose at Khandalla and the Temple of Orissa dedicated to Jugannath are about the only objects that will arrest your attention or live in your memory. In Chicacole at Barwa my guide book says "fine whiting here," and at Poonda "fish and oysters," and I am told to "watch the tide," which to one who has seen the Solway or the race horses in the Gulf of Cambay is poor consolation: No, my friend, I would not give the pomphlet of Bandra or the oysters of Jinjeera for all your seas hold between the mouths of the Krishna and the mouths of the great river Mahanadi.

And the Chilka Lake, with its sands knee-deep. Bah! Did not Elphinstone feel there "bilious and ill?" "I walked along the shore at eleven. I found myself still unwell, so I lay down and slept till half-past twelve." Had that sleep ended as it sometimes did there would have been a big gap in the History of India. And here I am reminded by a friend of the late Mr. Joseph Jefferson's experiences, which will apply to 1845 or thereabouts. Some of our readers may recollect that he was long the Father of the Bombay Solicitors, of which fact, on his resuming practice, Chief Justice Westropp reminded him in open Court. He was fifty years on the roll of the Solicitors of the High Court. Mr. Jefferson had been in Ceylon on professional business, and made his way by sea to Madras. It was the height of the monsoon, and his further progress by sea was barred. He applied to the Postmaster to have a palkee dâk laid for Bombay. He was told that it was madness, but the exigencies of business required his presence in Bombay, so what with strong remonstrances and all other legal means the dâk was laid. At first the journey was not so bad as he had anticipated, and became very tolerable as he neared Dharwar. There are some sappy places about Sholapore, but as to how he crossed the Bhima, the Sina, or their numerous tributaries there is no record. The black soil and moorum of Poona would be a caution, so, with firmer footing for his bearers on the tableland of the Dekhan above the Ghauts, from which we can imagine him descending with many a bump, if it was during or soon after a heavy *bursat*, a spectacle would meet his eye fit to appal the stoutest heart. We have all seen it, but under very different circumstances (from the cushioned seat of a first class railway carriage). Campoli Tank almost obliterated as an entity, or converted into a great sea, that in the dusk stretched to the horizon, with long lines of trees which rose above and dotted the surface, marking the track of the great Poona High Road now deep down under water.

How he piloted his way over the labyrinth of muddy dykes, or floundered through the quaking bogs of Tanna and Kalyan, or steered his aerial bark over the plastic gum of Salsette, determined that it should not "serve as paste and cover to his bones," we cannot imagine.

We take it for granted that Mr. Jefferson had been interned in his portable tabernacle, excepting for intervals of sleep and refreshment, for fifteen days. As he emerged from his prison-house and touched the doorstep of his bungalow at Colaba, he must have felt like Noah coming out of the ark after the deluge. That he survived such an ordeal was due to the Providence of God and a robust constitution. It is needless to remind the reader that this was the orthodox mode of locomotion from Sir Thomas Roe to Lord Roberts (for he travelled in this way for several weeks from Allahabad to Peshawar) down to the advent of railways. You ask why the route to Calcutta was not by Nagpore and the Central Provinces? We answer that the road was the old route, and that the Nagpore arrangement was not yet inaugurated. When one remembers how little there was to see it must have been a blessed exchange. A glance at that *brochure de luxe*, the Bombay and Baroda Railway Guide for 1895, makes one bless his stars that he lives not fifty years ago. For what would an India be without Ahmedabad, Jeypore, Agra, Delhi or Benares? These are names that leave everlasting pictures on the mind's retina. When I scan the names of these great historic cities, crowded with so many associations, military and political, and contrast them with the barren and colourless items of the hundred halting stations by this palkee route, I pity the poor traveller whose lot was sent to make the journey *viâ* Masulipatam from Bombay to Bengal in the year of Grace 1845.

IV.

CLUBS.

(1.) A BOMBAY GOLF CLUB IN THE FORTIES.

THIS Club was originally projected in 1841. The following is the list of office bearers and ordinary members brought down to December 7th, 1845.

OFFICE BEARERS.

H. H. Glass, Esq., C.S., Captain.
J. B. Burnes, Esq., M.D., LL D., K.H., Senior Councillor.
J. Smith, Esq., Junior Councillor.
W. W. Cargill, Esq., Treasurer.
George Buist, Esq., LL.D., Secretary.
Rev. George Cook, Chaplain.

The above form the Council of the Club.

Gregor Grant, Esq., Champion.
C. Forbes, Standard Bearer.
T. J. A. Scott, Poet Laureate.

ORDINARY MEMBERS.

Capt. R. Methen.
Capt. J. Reddie.
G. Farie.
W. Smyttan.
R. M. Kein.
J. Wright.
W. F. Hunter.
H. L. Anderson, C.S.
P. W. LeGeyt, C.S.
T. F. Grey.
T. Edmond.
J. Gordon.
D. Blane, C.S.
Lieut. J. Rennie, I.M.
Col. Dunsterville.
Capt. C. Rowley.
H. B. Herrick
A. L. Syers.
R. Burns.
Dugald Bremner.
H. B. Tristram.
Lieut. Fanning, 1st Grenadiers.
Lieut Ta lor, 3rd Regt. N.L.I.
John Stuart, Bank of Bombay.
Capt. Hogg, Sec. to the Commander-in-Chief.
Andrew Glass.
J. Baumbach.
Major Smee.
W. Howard.
Dr. Bremner.
Capt. D. Davidson.
Capt. Swanson.
J. Jamieson.
A. Smart.
A. H. Campbell.
W. Scott.
J. F. Wingate.
R. Brown.
H. L. W. Armstrong.
T. G. Brown.

1842, October 19th.—The London Blackheath Club have resolved that the Captain of the Bombay Golf Club be considered an Honorary Member of the Blackheath Club.

(2.) BOMBAY YACHT CLUB IN 1856.

ESTABLISHED MARCH 3RD, 1846.

The Right Hon. Lord Elphinstone, G.C.H., Patron.
The Hon. Sir William Yardley, Kt., Vice Patron.
Rear-Admiral Sir Henry J. Leeke, K.H., R.N., Commodore.
Spencer Compton, Esq., Vice Commodore.
John Stuart, Esq., Treasurer.
C. Kingcome, Esq., Secretary.

YACHTS.

1st Class.

Water Queen, Lateen.
Cinderella, Lateen.
Challenge, Cutter.
Orient, Cutter.

2nd Class.

Sunbeam, Cutter.

Yachts not *bonâ fide* property, but permitted to sail as yachts of the Club:—

Augusta, Schooner.
Cruiser, Sliding Gunter.
Fox, Lateen.
Shamrock, Sliding Gunter.
Sylvia, Sliding Gunter.
Charlotte, Schooner.
Black Diamond, Lateen.

LIST OF MEMBERS.

Rear-Admiral Sir Henry J. Leeke, K.H., Commodore.
Spencer Compton, Esq., Vice Commodore.

Henry Young, Esq., C.S.
Major H. J. Barr.
Cursetjee Jamsetjee, Esq.
Capt. G. Jenkins, I.N.
J. Stuart, Esq.
Capt. Hamilton, I.N.
T. S. Cowie, Esq.
J. A. Keys, Esq., I.N.
Capt. White.
Dr. Yuill.
W. B. Tristram, Esq.
J. C. Ibbs, Esq.
F. Leggett, Esq.
T. C. Beaumont, Esq.
Capt. E. Evans.
Capt. T. Forman.
Capt. Grainger.
Lieut. R. M. Grieve, I.N.
M. Scott, Esq.
H. E. Leeke, Esq.
Capt. Morris.
Capt. Crockett.
Dr. Ballingall.
C. Kingcome, Esq.
W. H. Barker, Esq., I.N.
Capt. Felix Jones, I.N.
Capt. Gillett.
J. A. Baumbach, Esq.
Capt. Frushard, I.N.
Dr. Reynolds.
The Hon. J. G. Lumsden, C.S.
W. H. G. Dunlop, Esq.
Capt. W. Barker, I.N.
Lieut. H. A. Fraser, I.N.
J. R. Robson, Esq.
Commodore R. Ethersey, I.N.
Gilbert Cowie, Esq.
John Ritchie, Esq.
Capt. R. Hunt.
J. A. Mackenzie, Esq.
Lieut. A. D. Taylor, I.N.
J. Wood, Esq.
H. Scott, Esq.
J. Macfarlane, Esq.
J. Cuvillier, Esq.
John Cassels, Esq.
W. T. Hunter, Esq.
C. J. Davies, Esq., C.S.
J. J. Lowndes, Esq.
Capt. Burke.
Capt. Kempthorne, I.N.

A goodly show of members and yachts also, considering that most of the Bombay yachts were destroyed in the great hurricane of November 1st and 2nd, 1854.

(3.) BYCULLA CLUB, EARLY DAYS.

THE Oriental Club was founded in London in 1824, limited to six hundred members, with the Duke of Wellington as its first President. On July 6th, 1826, "Gregarius" writes to the *Bombay Courier* advocating a club in Bombay on the model of the Oriental. The Bengal Club in Calcutta was projected in March, 1827, and the first dinner recorded of that club took place on July 16th, 1827. A Bombay Club had been established in London in May, 1822, consisting of members of the Services who had retired, which, no doubt, was absorbed in the Oriental. The clubs which, previous to this time, had existed in Bombay had no local habitation. For example, the *Sans Souci* often held its meetings in Cameron's Tavern, a splendid hostelry for its day. Duncan Cameron died in 1822, and I fancy the *Sans Souci*, which has a venerable history, did not long survive him. Then there was the Highland Society, affiliated to the London one. They had no fixed habitation. Their first dinner was at Parell on May 21st, 1822, and was a splendid entertainment, given to the members by Mountstuart Elphinstone. This club had a chequered existence, and lingered on till, I think, 1840, when it died of sheer inanition. The Saint Andrew's dinner had no corporate existence, but consisted of a miscellaneous crowd drawn from the Caledonians and their guests year after year. It is now more honoured in the breach than the observance, and threatens to follow the Highland Host.

The idea of the Byculla Club did not take shape until 1832. On February 1st of that year the *Courier* writes :—"A club has long been considered a desideratum in Bombay, and might be introduced with great ease now that both the other Presidencies have led the way." And on September 5th of the same year the *Courier* begins an article headed in capitals :—

"PROSPECTUS FOR THE ESTABLISHMENT OF A CLUB IN BOMBAY.—The example of Bengal and Madras proves that a general club may be established at all the Indian Presidencies, and supported on a handsome scale at a very moderate expense." Then the writer calculates, from a total of 1,300 belonging to the Services, and the legal and mercantile men, that if 700 joined it at Rs. 70 each, a capital of Rs. 49,000 would result; and then he adds—" Preliminary steps have been taken. We have been requested to state that it has been submitted to the Right Honourable the Governor and the leading members of society at the Presidency, and has met with their cordial approval. In addition to this, three hundred gentlemen in and near Bombay have come forward and offered their support, and a donation, amounting to Rs. 8,000, has already been made. Subscriptions commenced on July 1st, 1832, and the club is expected to open on January 1st, 1833.*

On July 1st, 1833, we meet with this advertisement, which is the first occasion the name is mentioned:—

" BYCULLA CLUB.—The monthly meeting of the committee of the club will take place in the club room on Saturday, the 6th inst., at 10 P.M. A ballot for the admission of candidates will be held the same day at 3 P.M.—Club Room, July 1st, 1833."

The club as a corporate society was no doubt formed between July 1st, 1832, and July 1st, 1833. On February 12th, 1833, a correspondent signing himself "Junglee" asks: "What has become of the club?" We will now endeavour to answer that question from the materials at our disposal. On September 5th, 1832, the reader will see that, so far as the support of the members was concerned, the club was *un fait accompli.* It was the difficulty in securing premises which caused the delay. Various sites were suggested, and buildings already existing were pointed out as suitable for the purpose. Whether it was to be in the Fort or miles away from it, this everlasting question came up, while as yet the promoters had found no resting-place for the soles of their feet; like the dove from Noah's ark, they fluttered about Byculla, Mazagon, and an impregnable position within the walls of the Fort.

---

* Henry Blosse Lynch, 1807–78; master attendant Bombay dockyard, 1849; founder of the Indian Navy Club, once famous for its cuisine and its hospitality to the other Services.—*Dict. Nat. Biog.*

On March 16th a meeting was called of the "Bombay Club"—so it was called here—and William Newnham was requested to take the chair. The committee reported that there was no eligible building in the Fort available. Then the "Grove," Mazagon, was talked about at the meeting, but nothing came of it. An opinion was expressed that it was too far for men whose daily duties led them to the Fort. The rent was Rs. 225, and otherwise it looked a likely place which could be fitted for the purposes of a club. This bungalow, erected one hundred and twenty years ago, and associated for many years with the Ashburners, can still be seen, though some little alteration has been made in it. Less than the rent named was taken for it twenty years ago. It is on the Mount Road, and is approached by a long, straight aveuue, bordered with rows of casuarina trees. It is close adjoining Mazagon Castle, the oldest inhabited part of Bombay in this direction, for Mazagon was a place of strength long before we set foot on the island. Nothing, however, came of the "Grove."

Here we must make a digression, and hark back to 1821. The Byculla Race Stand was built in six months, and was to be opened on January 1st, 1822. It was thus elegantly described in the pages of the *Courier*:—The body of the building in figure is nearly that of a square, and consists of a principal floor supported by a rustic basement, from the north or principal entrance of which is projected a colonnade of the purest Grecian Doric, surmounted by a tastefully constructed iron balustrade, which encompasses the balcony on a level with the principal floor, and with which it immediately communicates by means of a longitudinal range of folding sashes. The Byculla Race Stand contains an assembly room for ladies, forty-eight feet long, twenty-four broad; tint of the walls, maiden's blush; admirably adapted for dinners and balls on a limited scale. It is entered from a commodious landing-place, in the middle having an ante-chamber on each side, which also communicates with the principal apartment. That it was found to be limited is evident from an entry under date February 18th, 1826: "Ball at Race Stand unavoidably abandoned, the limited accommodation of the building being found inadequate for the purpose." A great number of men were members of both clubs, and when at their wits' ends would very likely cast their eye on the Race Stand buildings. Be that as it may, we have evidence sufficient that the Turf Club made over their interest in the Race Stand to the Byculla Club—when, and how, and for what consideration, I know not. But it does not matter.

In the *Courier* of January 25th, 1834, is this notice: "We have been requested to notice that though *the Race Stand has been given up to the Byculla Club*, it will be open as usual during the races to those ladies and gentlemen who wish to see the running." I have italicised what seems to put beyond a doubt that the Race Stand, which still exists as a portion of the Byculla, had been some time previously made over to it. The following advertisement may have had reference to this transference, and may have been one of the "questions of importance" submitted to the meeting: "The New Bombay Turf Club call a meeting of subscribers in the Club Room on the 14th instant, to discuss questions of importance. Bombay, June 6th, 1833." The transference of the Race Stand may be supposed to be one of those questions. If this theory of mine is correct, the Race Stand built in 1821 was the nucleus of the Byculla Club Buildings, and still remains as that place which year after year is graced by the beauty and fashion of Bombay.

The following notices may be interesting to some members, and show that the vexed question of the removal of the club cropped up at intervals during its early years:—

"January 14th, 1837.—Meeting of members of Byculla Club. Entrance donation reduced to Rs. 100; the same received from new members in five monthly instalments of Rs. 20 each."

"January 14th, 1837.—Wanted to rent by the Byculla Club, a large airy house within the Fort. Tenders to be made to the Secretary, at the Club House, till 25th instant."

The *Courier* on January 20th, 1837, remarks: "It is in contemplation to remove the Byculla Club to the Fort. . . . A comprehensive scheme for increasing the number of members may then be appropriately termed the Bombay Club." On January 30th, an adjourned meeting of the Byculla Club was held to take into consideration the feasibility of removing the club into the Fort in Rampart Row or vicinity.

One of the earliest dinners given by the Byculla Club was a magnificent entertainment to Chevalier Ventura, General of the army of Runjeet Singh, at which the Admiral of the Fleet and the Commander of the Forces were present. This was on January 11th, 1839; and on January 1st, 1840, it is noted that Captain Outram was entertained to dinner by the Byculla Club, fifty members being present, and J. Pollard Willoughby, Esq., in the chair. The two leading Government servants at this period were Newnham, Chief Secretary, and Wedderburn, Accountant-General. But two unofficial members of the community were revolving great schemes, and for fifty years afterwards their names were household words.

William Nicol, arriving fresh from the Marine, about 1822, threw down the gauntlet to Fortune by essaying the construction of a Bombay Bank;* and John Skinner,† with a splendid mercantile training in Leghorn, arriving in 1825, distinguished himself by founding the Bombay Chamber of Commerce. It had its beginning on September 22nd, 1836, in a small meeting in a room in the Custom House, when a few men met "to establish a society to be called the Bombay Chamber of Commerce." These two men were instrumental in moulding the commercial destinies of Bombay at this period.

---

* A CARD.—Preparations are now making to establish a bank at this Presidency, the general plan of which is similar to the subscription banks of Great Britain. The capital will be ten lakhs of rupees, divided into 100 shares of Rs. 10,000 each. The objects of the establishment are quite unconnected with the performance of mercantile or agency business, and those gentlemen who may be disposed to become subscribers may have an opportunity of doing so by applying at the office of Mr. William Nicol, in Medows Street, where plans will be shown and every information given.—Bombay, September 7th, 1822.

† John Skinner, late of Leghorn and Gibraltar, and George Adam, late H.E.I.C.S., this day establish themselves in Bombay under the firm of Adam, Skinner and Co., 30, Medows Street, May 12th, 1825.

(4.) BYCULLA CLUB, 1856.

Members of the Managing Committee.

(Elected half-yearly.)

Colonel J. Hale.	Dr. E. T. Downes.
Captain Rivers.	J. Baumbach, Esq.
F. Chapman, Esq.	W. Johnson, Offg. Secy.

Hours for Opening and Closing the House.

The Club House shall be opened for the reception of members at six o'clock in the morning, and closed at twelve o'clock at night, after which hour the lights in the sitting rooms are not to be kept burning.

No supper will be furnished after twelve o'clock. The lights in the Billiard Rooms are not to be kept burning after twelve o'clock at night. No play of any kind shall be allowed on Sunday. Smoking is allowed at half-past eight o'clock from October 1st to March 31st, and at nine o'clock from April 1st to September 30th in the new dining-room.

Rules for the Admission of Guests.

1.—That every member shall be at liberty to entertain one or more guests every evening at the Club, provided he has given notice on the previous day to the Steward of the number of the visitors he is about to introduce.

2.—That every member entertaining a guest at the Club shall be responsible for the supplies furnished to him and for all damages done by him.

3.—No stranger, unless he has dined at the Club, shall be admitted to the Billiard Room, nor will any stranger be allowed to engage the Billiard Table except through his host or some other member of the Club.

4.—It shall be competent for the Committee from time to time to refuse the admission of persons not fitted to be admitted as guests, or who have misconducted themselves as such.

5.—It shall be competent for the Committee from time to time, by a written order to the Steward, to refuse the right of introducing guests to any members in arrears to the Club, or who shall have refused to conform to these rules, or have introduced improper persons, or otherwise have abused the privilege of introducing guests.

6.—A book shall be kept, to be called the Visitors' Book, in which the names of the visitors each day shall be entered, and of the members introducing them, respectively, and the book shall be taken to every member introducing a guest, and such member shall sign his name opposite to that of his guest.

The Managing Committee consider that the rule requiring the previous notice is one which is absolutely necessary to preserve; for, otherwise, the members of the Club may be put to the greatest inconvenience by an unforeseen number of guests coming to share in supplies procured for members only.

The Managing Committee are anxious, however, to press the rule no farther than the necessity which led to its existence requires, and the Steward has accordingly received orders to inform any member introducing a guest without the notice required by Rule 1, whether the guest can be provided with dinner or not, it being understood that the right of a guest so introduced to dine at the Club must be subordinate to all the members present that evening to have their tables in the first instance properly supplied.

From this most important club, which has bulked so big for more than fifty years in Bombay society, let us turn by way of contrast to Bombay's smallest club. Mr. Herbert Compton, not unknown in letters, and a grandson of our distinguished Chief Justice of the same name, when in Bombay lately informed me that towards the end of "the twenties" there existed a club in Bombay which consisted of only four members. It was called "The Deal Table Club," and its presiding genius was Tom Morris, the "John Docherie" of the *Sporting Magazine*. It was founded on good fellowship and a basis of economical notions that suited camping out on shikaring expeditions. Mr. Compton has in his possession an impression of the seal of this old Bombay club, on which are portrayed the inevitable deal table, two spears, and "the mighty boar."

(5.) A MASONIC LEGACY.

A CORRESPONDENT sends us the following extract from the *Masonic Record of Western India* of 1867, in the belief that it may prove interesting to our Masonic readers:—

It will be remembered by our readers that in February last we referred to a sum of money supposed to have been left for Masonic charitable purposes. The following authentic documents containing all the information on the subject have now been placed at our disposal. It is not without great deliberation on the propriety of publishing the testator's singular will that we print it, however it should be borne in mind that the will was dated 1793. Even as an item of Doctors Commons' lore it would tempt an Editor to give it a place among his collectanea; but, as our readers are aware, reports of property available for Masonic interests will always crop up so long as there be some foundation in fact. We think by placing the following papers on record in type, we embalm therein not only the curiosity of a testator's difficulties, as well as that we rescue a subject buried in musty archives, to be available for easy reference whenever the coveted bequest shall again be the object of inquiry.

No. 504 of 1858.

Territorial Department, Finance.

To H. D. Cartwright, Esquire,
Provincial Grand Master of Western India.

SIR,—I am directed by the Right Honourable the Governor in Council to acknowledge the receipt of your letter, dated the 6th instant, and to forward the accompanying copy of a Report by the Accountant-General, No. 85, dated the 8th idem, and of the documents therewith furnished, as containing all the information on his records respecting the bequest to the Masonic Fraternity alluded to by you.—I have the honour to be, &c.,

H. YOUNG,
Chief Secretary to Government.

Bombay Castle, May 31st, 1858.

No. 85 of 1858–59.

Territorial Department, Finance.

I have the honour to submit, for the consideration of his Lordship in Council, copies of the undermentioned letters as containing all the information on my records respecting the bequest to the Masonic Fraternity alluded to. The course to be followed for the recovery of the same is stated in Mr. Standen's letter of the 9th February, 1856.

Letter from Accountant-General to Administrator-General, No. 1765, dated 5th January, 1856.

Letter from L. Acland, Esq., Solicitor, to Accountant-General, of same date.

Letter from Administrator-General, to the Accountant-General, dated 9th February, 1856.

The amount of the estate standing under the head of John McClure is as follows:—

4 per cent. notes in Sicca . .	Rs.	40,900	0	0
4 per cent. Company's . .	„	7,200	0	0
Cash	„	263	9	1

(Signed) E. E. Elliot, Accountant-General.

Bombay, Accountant-General's Office, May 8th, 1858.

No. 1765 of 1855–56.

Territorial Department, Finance.

Estate of John McClure.

To J. H. Standen, Esquire, Administrator-General.

Sir,—I have the honour to transfer to you the accompanying documents relative to a claim on behalf of an alleged descendant of John McClure, to his Estate, which has been transferred to Government under the provisions of Act No. VIII of 1855, and to request that you will favour me with your opinion thereon.—I have the honour to be, etc.

(Signed) E. E. Elliot, Accountant-General.

Bombay, Accountant-General's Office, January 5th, 1856.

Bombay, January 5th, 1856.

SIR,—I am instructed by Mr. Donald McClure, of Glenelg, in the county of Inverness, to apply to you for the funds lately transferred to you by the Administrator-General as the estate of the late John McClure.

The following are the circumstances on which my client rests his claim to the estate in question.

John McClure by his will, dated February 12th, 1793, appointed Messrs. Wedgborough, White, Speak, and Richardson, and the Grand Master of the Lodge No. 1 in Bombay to be his executors, and the will then states as follows :—

"Item having all my slaves and property with me I reckon them the property of my female companion at my decease, but as I am in a land of liberty I don't consider them as slaves but servants.

"Item my ready money I divide into four equal parts as follows :—

"1. To an orphan named William Ross.

"2. To one ditto named James Mallick.

"3. To a female named Elizabeth Fennel, whom should I have children by her they will share equally with the other legatees and herself.

"4. To a child named Margaret by a Malabar other this child is to be allowed interest of half my fortune for her education four years the other half to accumulate for the benefit of the legatees should any of the legatees die that share shall descend to the others so as the longest life take the whole and at the death of all the above legatees the whole shall descend to Bombay Lodge No. 1 for the benefit of Master Masons' illegitimate children and upon the accounts of my death one-tenth of my fortune shall be allotted for that purpose.

"I have remitted home £500 for the benefit of my mother for her natural life.

"Three of the foregoing legatees are with me, and I entrust the education of the other to my Executors and Mr. Samuel Speak who has the care of him for the present."

The Testator made a codicil to his will, dated February 10th, 1795, which was as follows:—

"SIR,—By this deed I appoint you my joint Executor with Mr. John Wedgborough, in case of any accident to me you will act for the benefit of my legatees mentioned in my former will and power including my only son George, born at Palm Islands to share a moiety of my effects whatever they are.

"You will make a demand on the resident of Boure for the contents of the enclosed Bond and recover what is due to me from the new Albion Company."

The above was addressed to Thomas Watkin Court. The Testator died in 1796, and the will was proved by all the Executors except the Grand Master of Lodge No. 1 Bombay. The Codicil was proved at Calcutta by Thomas Watkin Court. The Executors retained the estate in their hands until the death of the survivor which happened in 1831, when administration was taken by the Ecclesiastical Registrar of the Supreme Court, who transferred the property to the Administrator-General, who transferred it to you under the provisions of the recent Act No. VIII. of 1855 regulating the disposition of funds in the hands of the Administrator-General.

From enquiries made of the Grand Lodges of England and Scotland it appears there was no Lodge No. 1 in Bombay in 1793 or in 1796, and if there had been such a Lodge the Master could not have been a Grand Master.

No payments have been made from this since it came into the hands of the Ecclesiastical Registrar in 1831, nor, so far as I know, has any claim been made for the fund.

Donald McClure, my client, is the grandson of a brother of the said John McClure, and as his next of kin has obtained letters of administration *de bonis non* with the will and codicil of John McClure annexed, to be granted to him by the Prerogative Court of the Archbishop of Canterbury, and he claims these funds on the ground that the residuary bequest for the benefit of Master Masons' illegitimate children is void on the grounds of immorality and uncertainty. You will observe that clause 4 of the will makes no disposition of the moiety of the property the interest of which is directed to be applied for the education of the Testator's daughter during a period of four years, the remaining part of the clause referring exclusively to the other moiety.

I apprehend that my client's title to receive this money is sufficiently made out by the letters of administration *de bonis non* which have been granted to him, but for your further satisfaction I send herewith copies of declarations made by Angus Bruce, Norman McLeod, Malcolm McCrae, Donald McClure, and Malcolm Macrae, also of a certificate signed by the Reverend John Macrae, a list of the descendants of Duncan Roy McClure, and of a declaration made by my client, which documents make out my client's claim as next of kin. The originals are with me, and I shall be happy to produce them for your inspection, together with the letters of administration *de bonis non*, with the will and codicil of John McClure annexed, letters of administration to the estate of Donald McClure and Malcolm McClure, the father and grandfather of my client, and a Power of Attorney from my client authorising me to receive the Estate in question.

I am, etc.,
(Signed) LAWFORD ACLAND.

To the Accountant-General.

No. — of 1856.

Estate of John McClure, deceased.

To the Accountant-General, Bombay.

SIR,—With reference to your letter No. 1765 of 1855–56, requesting my opinion as to a claim to the Estate of John McClure put forward on the part of certain parties alleging themselves to be his next of kin, I have the honour to inform you that I think the case is one for the decision of the Supreme Court. I find that many other claims have been made to the Estate at different times and by a great variety of parties, some representing themselves to be next of kin, others to be descendants of legatees under the will. For us to determine which, if any of these claimants have right on their side, would involve, as appears to me, far too grave a responsibility, moreover the legal difficulties of construction in the will are very considerable and such as I think it is for the Supreme Court alone to decide.

I am therefore of opinion that the claim of Mr. Acland's client is not satisfactorily established, and that gentleman should be advised to proceed by Petition to the Supreme Court, under the provisions of Section 52 of Act VIII. of 1855.—I have the honour to be, &c.,

(Signed) JAMES H. STANDEN,
Administrator-General.

Bombay, Administrator-General's Office, February 9th, 1865.

V.

BIOGRAPHICAL.

(1.) ALBUQUERQUE.

THE reader will seek in vain in these Commentaries (*Albuquerque*, in 4 vols., by his son), for an exhibition of Western India at the period when the Portuguese broke ground upon it. Of what were the political divisions at the time in question, or who were the rulers, we absolutely, as far as this book is concerned, know nothing, and for this information must apply to other sources. Except the names of a few towns which dot the littoral, and which the Portuguese conquered, the whole land is enveloped in a cloud of mist, through the rifts of which we catch a glimpse of such shadowy forms as Zamorin, Hadalcai, Balagat, Narsinga, Sheikh Ismail, and Cambay. Yet these names represent the masters of this portion of Asia. Occasionally we catch a glimpse of hosts of swarthy warriors armed with buckler, spear, and bow, emerging from the passes of the Western Ghauts to the plains below, but of the powers that sent them there we have only the faintest indications. Bijapur had already its citadel, or Arkila, and was bulging out its ground plan of magnificent distances. Mahomed Bigarra sat amid the glories of Ahmedabad or Champanir, and Krishna Deva, greatest of its sovereigns, ruled at Vizyanagar on the Tongabudra. Bombay (Maim it is called), or what existed of it, stood at the junction of the two empires which had borne the brunt of war for a century—that is, the land on which her huts were built was the King of Cambay's (Sultan of Ahmedabad), and the men who occupied them were his subjects. Across the harbour all that magnificent scene we now cast our eyes upon from Malabar Hill was the Zamorin's. If we understand the matter aright, the boundary of these two kingdoms was the Bombay Harbour and the Tanna Creek. All north of this inlet belonged to Cambay; all south (Goa excepted) to the Zamorin. We now crave the attention of our readers to the following:— The Commentaries state that the Zamorin offered Chaul (thirty miles from Bombay) to Albuquerque as a site for a fort. In fact, Chaul gave its name to the south side of our harbour down to the end of the seventeenth century (*Bombay Gazetteer*). The Commentaries also state that the King of Cambay offered Maim (Bombay) to Albuquerque for the same purpose. We place our contention before our readers and leave each to settle the question for himself. A few miles here or there in a thousand do not matter much. The facts as they are stated seem to us perfectly conclusive as to the political division of the coast line of Western India in or about 1510.

If we are correct in this, Bombay was Mahomedan, and eyed across the water the Hindoo kingdom of the Zamorin. There is one fact brought into bold relief by the Commentaries of Albuquerque, and it is this—that the Guzerattees held naval supremacy from the Strait of Bab-el-Mandeb and the mouth of the Persian Gulf to Malacca. They were the great carriers all over the Indian Ocean. The Hindoos are not generally credited with being a maritime people; but it is expressly said of those of Goa (1506) "they were a maritime race, and more inured to the hardships of the sea than all other nations, built ships of great burden, and navigated the coasts." And, again, in regard to Ceylon and the Far East—"The Guzerattees understand the navigation of those parts much more thoroughly than any other nation on account of the great commerce they carry on in these places." We accept these statements as we find them, but there is no getting over the fact that, wherever Albuquerque engaged pilots on the coasts of Africa, Arabia, or India, they were Moors, and we are driven to the conclusion that the captains who navigated these ships were Arabs of Hindoostan, while the crews may have been lascars or Hindoos. This much is certain, that on the Asiatic side—say, from Malacca to Calicut, and from Calicut to Jeddah, the bulk of the overland traffic was carried on by the people of Guzerat all through the Middle Ages, whence their cargoes were transhipped on Arab buggalows to Cosseir, and thence by caravan to the Nile, which bore them on its flood to Rosetta.

Here follows a strange story of Albuquerque:—"He was a man of the strictest veracity, and so pure in the justice he administered that the Hindoos and Moors, after his death, whenever they received any affront from the Governors of India, used to go to Goa to his tomb and make offerings of choice flowers and oil for his lamp, praying him to do them justice"—so say the Commentaries. That the Moors placed offerings of flowers and sought justice at the tomb of Albuquerque we do not believe. The Moors were not fools. There was a great deal of human nature in the Moors. You might as soon expect a Covenanter to worship Claverhouse or a Hollander the Duke of Alva. The Moors have never worshipped Albuquerque, nor will they ever do so as long as the Black Stone remains at Mecca or pilgrims make the Haj. If the Moors had bespattered Albuquerque's tomb with mud it would have been much more to their liking. At Cochin, at Cannanore, at Calicut, at Goa he came down upon them like the destroying angel: everywhere his course was written in blood. At every port he touched, from Muscat to Malacca, he cut off their ears and noses and let them go. At Panjim he shut up 150 of them in a mosque and burned them to ashes. At Kishim he gave no quarter, but put men, women, and children to the sword.

He sent fifteen blind kings from Ormuz, so that they and their seed might never have a chance of reigning in these parts for evermore. Some of these ports he could never have reached without the help of Moorish pilots. If I remember right, it was a Moorish pilot who conducted him all the way from Africa to India, kidnapped, no doubt. Another led him to Ormuz, and those waters which no European fleet had ever visited since that of Nearchus. He picked up a third at Bab-el-Mandeb, to guide his prow through the sinuosities and treacherous reefs of the Red Sea. Strange, is it not, that these were the very men whose race he had sworn to exterminate. "Here I am," said Luther, "I can do no otherwise. God help me. Amen." "Albuquerque went straight to his chamber, cast his eyes up to heaven, and besought God to forgive his sins." I wonder whether this sin was among them, but God pity the poor pilots who were forcibly abducted on such an errand and cozened to lay open their maps and plans to the gaze of this great navigator, so that he might plough his way to scenes of guilt and rapine, and the murder of their friends. He rose from his knees with "The Lord is on my side: I will not fear what man can do unto me." These are some of the flowers the Moors might have placed on the tomb of Albuquerque. You see that Albuquerque hated the Mahomedans with a fierce and implacable hatred. I am sure he loathed them to such an extent that he wished they had all one neck that he could at once make an end of them. This feeling was born of the Iberian Peninsula. He detested the Moors in Spain, and as much the Moors out of Spain. This was the pivot upon which his creed revolved, and all else was subordinate to it. And I do not wonder at it, for he must have drank in this hatred with his mother's milk. The Crusaders were dead, but as long as he was alive there was a great Crusader, a Crusader of no half measures, but one as bloody as Richard, determined to solve that question which had worried Europe for centuries by exterminating the hated race, root and branch. For this there was nothing he would not do. He would divert the Nile into the Red Sea and desiccate Egypt. He would capture the body of Mahomed at Medina and exchange it for the Holy Sepulchre.

This was the everlasting question that presented itself to his mind, and which he revolved under the weird shadows of the Peak of Aden, by the palm-fringed islands of Goa, as well as at Ormuz, with its visions of Nearchus. (It was there, I think, that a Moor brought on board a *Life of Alexander*, written in Persian, bound in crimson velvet, and presented it to Albuquerque. In the audacity of his schemes he was quite a match for Alexander.) Here is his solution of the question, for he had quite made up his mind what he should do to effect this stupendous *coup*. He would land 300 horsemen at Yembo, capture the garrisons of Mecca and Medina, and in six weeks disembark with the body of the Prophet before reinforcements could reach his enemies from the grand Soldan of Egypt. He would search out the Soldan's fleet in the Red Sea, and if he did not find it he would go on to Suez and burn it—for him a magnificent conception, the beauty of which consists in its simplicity. But he did not live to carry it out, as he died at the bar of Goa, December 16th, 1515. Such a deed would have changed the face of the world, from Delhi to Vienna, and would have constituted a world-wide revolution. But one thing he did though he left the other undone. He diverted the commerce of the East from the channels in which it had flowed for a thousand years to the Tagus, from the Adriatic and the Bosphorus. By blocking up the Gulf at Ormuz and the Red Sea at Aden, and placing an embargo on Calicut and Malacca, he threw the commerce of the East round the Cape to Lisbon. After Albuquerque's time a deep silence fell on the wharves of Venice. The camel caravans ceased to come from Cossier to Cairo. Indian spices no longer perfumed the painted chambers of Rosetta, and Alexandria was reduced to the white heap of ashes which it remained till the time of Volney. "God help me" he found graven in Latin on some old Crusader's swords which had found their way to Socotra, and no doubt he girded one of them on himself, as we may see in a picture of this grim and bearded warrior of the North. And God helped him, or history is belied. Portugal and India were thence to be riveted together until Portugal ceased to respect herself, and India prepared the way for other invaders.

The reader does not now require to ask why Albuquerque courted and coquetted with the Hindoo sovereigns of Western India. It was to compass his own ends, for whoever were his allies they must fight the Mussulman. This is the key to all his Hindoo alliances, and explains his league with Honore and Cochin, by whose assistance he entered Goa. The biggest Hindoo kingdom in Southern India at this time (it stretched from sea to sea) was Vizyanagar, so Albuquerque speedily enlisted its sympathy and assistance to make war on Bijapur and the other Mussulman Kings of the Dekhan. Western India was about to change owners, and already in the throes of a new birth, and Vizyanagar was nothing loth; for Bijapur, Bedur, Nagar, and Golconda, Muslim sovereignties of the Dekhan, were already on the war-path, and one of them was to raze her empire to the ground. The Hindoo dynasties, in fact, were all quaking with a great fear. Not only here, but in the north, the elements were seething and prognosticating mighty revolutions. The sound of Baber's raids came down the Khyber Pass like the roll of distant thunder. Cabul and Kandahar were at his feet, and in October 1511 Baber was proclaimed King of Samarcand, then one of the richest and most populous cities in the world. Then there was the King of Ormuz. Here is his portrait, as he sits on his throne, and you may read it along with Milton's *Wealth of Ormuz and of Ind*: "He is fifteen years of age, dressed in a petticoat of crimson satin and a cloth girded around him, a golden dagger and a sceptre of gold in his hand, with the head of crystal set in gold." Albuquerque built palaces and churches, coined money and abolished *Sati*, and founded Goa, which has been Portuguese for 380 years, all which redounds to his fame. He encouraged marriages between the Portuguese and the natives. In 1510 there were 450 Portuguese married to native ladies, daughters of the principal men of the land. His views, we are told, were not shared by everybody, for there were men, even then, who looked ahead and had grave doubts on the wisdom of his policy.

"Many disapproved of his permission to the Portuguese to marry natives, and several leading men even wrote to the King of Portugal on the subject" (Commentaries). Albuquerque was a man of grim humour. Somebody asked for tribute to the King of Ormuz after his conquest by the Portuguese. Albuquerque sent him a parcel of cannon-balls, and told him that was the only tribute his King paid on account of states under his mastery. Once when his cash-box was empty a lascar importuned him for his wages. Plucking two hairs from his beard, "Take these hairs of my beard, and go and put them in pawn." At Ormuz he ordered three stone anchors to be taken from the King of Cambay's big ship, the *Meri*, and built them into the foundations of a new fort. His captains sent him a remonstrance, which he put under the portal, henceforth named for ever, "The Doorway of Remonstrance." Some renegades were in the hands of the enemy, who knew full well that if they were given up they would at once be killed. A stipulation was exhorted from him for their lives. Albuquerque signed it. They little knew their man. Once in his power he ordered their right hands and the thumbs of their left hands, and their ears and noses to be cut off, and the hair of their heads and beards torn out. Death would have been preferable. But then, you see, "he kept his word," honourable man. Not like our Richard, who broke his oath at the siege of Acre (1191), when he hanged the 2,700 Turkish hostages. After his death he was immediately shrouded and clothed in habit of Santiago (St. James), buskin, spurs, sword and belt, on his neck a stole, on his head a velvet cap. "Go to now," says St. James the Apostle (not he of Costello), "and howl . . . ye have nourished your hearts as in a day of slaughter." Goa was conquered by Albuquerque on November 25th (St. Catherine's Day), 1510. It was a bloody conquest. No quarter was given. Men and women and children were put to the sword. This was Albuquerque's order, and the blood of 6,000, young and old, ran into that sea which we see to-day fringed with palm trees. This was Albuquerque's "day of slaughter," which rises in judgment against him, not forgetting Ruy Dias, hanged for visiting a Moorish woman, and which Camoens does not neglect to notice in the *Lusiad*.

I take it that Albuquerque was a man of an iron will, and had not much of the milk of human kindness about him, and that he was deaf to the wails of the widow and the orphan—he must have made thousands of them. And yet his appearance was prepossessing. His massive beard, even at sixty-three, came down to his waist, his stature was middle size, his nose long.

The Ambassador of Sheikh Ismail was so much struck with the view he had of him that he requested him to allow a full-length portrait of him to be taken, so that he might carry it to his master in the Arabian desert. Behold the fine arts of 1510! He was reticent to a degree, especially when his captains mutinied, when his King frowned, when the Viceroy, Almeida, who preceded him, gave him the cold shoulder, razed his house to the ground, and immured him in the tower of Cannanore. But when he ascended from the dungeon to the Viceregal throne he again found his tongue. His last words were written to the King of Portugal. "As for the affairs of India, they will speak for themselves and for me." Yes, India can speak for itself, more particularly the Mahomedan portion of it, and "for me" the verdict in 1893 is somewhat different from that of 1515.

His friends inscribed on his tomb, "Let him that excels take the precedence." In his particular line I suppose many have excelled him.

Alexander at Persepolis, Titus at Jerusalem, Alaric at Rome, or coming nearer home, Nadir Shah at Delhi, or Napoleon at Jaffa.

(2.) AQUAVIVA OF SALSETTE.

In the year of our Lord 1583, or about the time when William Shakespeare was philandering with Anne Hathaway, and when Mary Queen of Scots lay a prisoner in Fotheringay, five Jesuit priests were murdered at a place called Coucolim, in the Salsette of Goa. One of them was Rodolph Aquaviva, known in after times as "Akbar's Christian." The reader will note that there are two Salsettes, the one near Bombay, sometimes called the Salsette of Bassein, and the other the Salsette of Goa, which was the scene of the catastrophe to be narrated.

Aquaviva was a son of the Duke of Atri, a town five miles from the Adriatic and about sixty miles south of Ancona. The family of the Emperor Hadrian hailed from this quarter, and the guide-books tell us that the town is situated on the summit of a hill, from which is obtained a splendid view of the surrounding country, with the open sea beyond. The name Aquaviva ("living water") is said to have been originally derived from the streams which gush down the mountains and which add so much to the beauty of the landscape.

The fortunes of the Atri family seemed to culminate when two of Rodolph's brothers became cardinals, and his uncle, Claude Aquaviva, was chosen the fifth general of the Jesuits. This last event took place in 1583, and Claude Aquaviva held that great office for a period of thirty-four years, until his death. D'Alembert says that of all men, during two hundred years, Claude Aquaviva did more than any other to enhance the position and greatness of the Order of Jesus. The Atri family became extinct in 1760. The salient points in the life of Rodolph Aquaviva are that he was born in 1550, joined the Order of Jesus in 1568, and set sail for Goa in 1578; that when Akbar sent to Goa for some Christians to expound their law, he and two other *padres* were deputed to his Court at Fatepur Sikri in 1580; that he remained three years at Akbar's Court, that he returned to Goa in 1583; and finally, in that year, when on a missionary tour in Salsette of Goa, he and four others were attacked and brutally murdered by the pagans at a place called Coucolim. In 1893 he was canonized by the Pope, to the great joy of all his admirers throughout the Roman Catholic world.

When he left Rome in the end of 1577, in taking leave of Gregory XIII., the Pope observed to him that he would have liked to accompany him, just as Dr. Wilson exclaimed, when bidding adieu for the last time to Dr. Livingstone, "Had I been ten years younger I would have gone with you to the sources of the Nile." Travelling was slow in those days. To Leghorn by sea, then to Genoa—wrecked on the voyage—thence to Lisbon, his mile-stones on the way being Carthagena, Murcea, and Toledo. The journey from Rome to Lisbon took him two months.

On March 24th, 1578, he put himself on board the *Santo Gregoiro*. This vessel carried 500 passengers and five priests, and touched at the Cape. After leaving Mozambique her deck was littered with Kaffirs, purchased there. Religious instruction was Aquaviva's ruling passion, and he had ample opportunity for its exercise during the voyage. He arrived in Goa on September 13th, 1578, after nearly a six months' passage.

He remained in Goa until November 17th, 1579, when, on the invitation of the Emperor Akbar to send some men to expound the Christian law to him, he and two other priests set out for Fatepur Sikri. Their journey thither was full of dangers. The sea was swarming with pirates, the land with dacoits. To Damaun and Surat he went by sea, for he, like Linschotten, does not mention Bombay, which evidently had not then scratched its name on Aquaviva's map. At Surat he joined a caravan, *via* Indore to Sikri, seven days before reaching which a cloud of dust announced the arrival of a grand corps, mounted on horses, camels and elephants, which had been sent by Akbar to welcome his guests. He arrived at Sikri February 27th, 1580, having taken more than three months on the journey from Goa. He had been forty-three days *en route* from Surat to Sikri.

It is matter of history beyond all doubt that Akbar gave to the fathers a most hearty welcome, and, short of becoming a Christian himself, did everything he could to make their stay in Fatepur Sikri agreeable. Was it not a great thing to eat the bread and drink the water—Ganges water—of the Great Mogul? Doubtless they were pleased with this—who would not be so? It is human nature. However, it was not all plain sailing. There was a fly in the amber. Akbar had a long arm that reached from Ahmedabad to Afghanistan, but even he could not be everywhere at the same time. So when he uttered, "I'm off to the wars again," the countenances of his visitors fell, for when he was away the lick-spittles who had *salaamed* them down to the ground, and who dwelt in the precincts of the palace, reviled the Christian dogs. The children also vented their doggerel—

> "Nasarani
> Kelb i ani," &c.

Akbar gave permission to his people to embrace Christianity, but he did not wish to proclaim this officially. There were reasons for this. "If I did this I should be no longer Akbar." So he might have ruminated. There was a power behind the throne greater than the throne itself. Had this not been so, Akbar might have been the Constantine of Asia. Aquaviva was not a foolish man, and, if he hoped at all, did not hope overmuch. As early as September 28th, 1580, he wrote these words. They are letters of fire and proclaim him quite the reverse of Noer's estimate in his *Akbar*, where he terms Aquaviva "a visionary." His words are these, written six months only after his arrival in Sikri:—

"The conversion of the King is very uncertain."

These are not the words of a visionary. The conferences at the Ibadat-khana were attended by Aquaviva, who, according to the testimony of Akbar himself, was agile enough to baffle, nay even to demolish, the arguments of his skilful opponents, Moslem and Hindu. Which is the true religion? Oh, Akbar, find out that if you can, and in the end make a god of thyself, to be worshipped and cast aside as the veriest scum. I have no doubt that long ere this Akbar had his face under control.

Under those shaggy eyebrows of his was a region altogether unexplored by the outside world. So, when this monk, pale of face, and spent with frequent prayer and fasting, narrated that a child was born in Bethlehem in a stable, and lay in a manger, and that this child was the Son of God, his countenance remained immobile and impassive before the great mystery. He did not wear his heart on his embroidered sleeve for the Ulemas to peck at. He retired, and in some dim recess of the Palace tried his alchemy on all religions, to weld, if he could, or amalgamate them into one whole, which should be the creation of his genius. Futile enough and pinchbeck at the best.

The reader may wish to know of some of the acts of Aquaviva at Sikri and Agra. Kinglake, in *Eothen*, says: "The Oriental is not a contriving animal." So Aquaviva may be credited with some share of the philanthropic enterprises in Sikri and Agra in Akbar's time. His refusal to accompany Akbar to a *sati* may have influenced that great man in his endeavours to put a stop to the rite. He built at Agra what may be regarded as the first Christian Church in India. Hither came Akbar alone, where he offered prayers and knelt in the fashion of Christians. When Akbar offered him a *khilat* of many thousand crowns, he politely declined it as contrary to his vow of poverty.

Was he the founder of Medical Missions? He built a hospital, *because* "heathen and Moslem in many places are disposed to the acceptance of the Christian religion by the sight of a work of mercy." Such is the contemporary reason for the building.

If Aquaviva was the apostle of water-drinking he would not belie his name. It might be worth while examining what part, if any, he took in the temperance movement, when Akbar opened a shop in Sikri "where wine was to be sold at a fixed price and only for medicinal purposes." From all we know he may have been the Father Mathew of those besotted times. If so, Akbar would join heart and hand with him in this movement, from the mortal dread he had of that curse which eventually descended on his family and tore away from him two of his children by *delirium tremens*. The effigy of the third, Jehangier, as a royal drinker, cup in hand, is preserved on the coins of the period.

In 1582 Murad was ten and Jehangier fourteen years of age. We know that Jehangier's apartments were within earshot of Aquaviva's, for the boy, hearing strange noises proceeding from his room, crept unobserved, and witnessed with horror the spectacle of flagellation.

Akbar gently detained Aquaviva a year after the other *padres* left. I dare say that it was with a heavy heart that Aquaviva set out for Goa, and as the last view of Agra disappeared from his vision I doubt not he heaved a sigh. Did he ever dream of converting Akbar? I wot not. But if he did, no more noble sentiment could animate the human breast, and it would have been a colossal capture for Christendom, before which the triumphs of Loyola and Xavier might well appear insignificant.

To see these three years apparently wasted, to see such a magnificent dream like some superb porcelain vase shattered to pieces, none of us, even the straitest Presbyterian, can refuse him sympathy, and that homage which is always the meed of heroism in the hour of disappointment. In any case his hour of agony was brief, and I gather from his words that some prevenient grace came to his aid, and showed him a loftier ideal (to wit, his own martyrdom) than even the conversion of Akbar. He believed that it had been registered in heaven, that he on earth, by suffering and death, in the footsteps of his Divine Master, should awake to immortality. And so it came to pass that after three years with Akbar, years of sickness of heart, and not without sickness of body, Aquaviva came back to Goa. We can well believe that he still looked on that palm-fringed isle as the goal of all his aspirations, and that he still trod its white and sandy shore believing that God would work out his destiny, to the ultimate good of man, by giving him his dearest wish—the martyr's crown.

He reached Goa from Agra on May, 1583. The circumstances which led up to the catastrophe at Coucolim were deplorable. There were Aquaviva and four young priests, none of them over thirty-five years of age, engaged in the work of planting crosses, and places of Christian worship. One of their party had killed a cow and polluted a Hindu temple with its blood. On approaching the village of Coucolim they found the natives in a ferment, wild and exasperated with this untoward occurrence. That mischief was brewing against the missionaries there seemed little doubt, for, on approaching the gate, a naked yogi rushed out with wild gesticulations and contortions, and made it all too evident that the lives of the party were in imminent danger. However, after his disappearance, a headman came out and reported that, though the village was divided, a welcome would be given them, which, in a measure, lulled their suspicions. He was a traitor. Small time elapsed, a calm before the storm, when the sorcerer again made his appearance with dishevelled hair, and cast sand and dirt in the air in his frenzy and paroxysm, as is usual in the East on such occasions. He was followed by a wild and furious multitude armed with spears, scimitars, clubs and hatchets, and bow and arrow also (very much used then; an ancient picture represents Aquaviva with an arrow in his breast). They soon made short work of the strangers and literally hacked them to pieces, casting their dishonoured remains into a deep well.

The same fate was meted out to a multitude of Christian men and women at Cawnpore, and in both cases a monumental memorial was placed on the spot. Though ten generations intervened between the two massacres, it may be said that in death these martyrs are not divided.

All that a man hath will he give for his life, as we are now (1897) seeing every day in this season of plague and famine. Not so, thought Aquaviva. Thrice he could have saved himself. "Fly!" said an Indian. He spurned the suggestion. "Take this musket," said Gonzalo. "I am not sent to kill, but to save alive," was the reply, and when the circle of death was gathering round him, a native Christian offered him his horse, but all in vain. He did not seek death, but met it with, "Into Thy hands I commend my spirit." At this supreme moment Divine grace came to his aid and showed him a loftier ideal than even the conversion of Akbar. And so, with steady gait and unfaltering tongue, he found himself on the borderland, face to face with his destiny at Coucolim—not craven or despairing, but full of Divine hope, radiant if you will, at the joyful issue out of all his troubles.

The event took place on July 25th, 1583. I gather from the narrative that it was no surprise to Aquaviva, and that his hour of agony was short. Agony! Yes, as far as flesh and blood had the making of it; of ecstasy rather, in following in the steps of his Divine Master. Hints are dropped here and there in his letters and conversations from his earliest years that some measure of grace, vouchsafed on rare occasions to the favourites of God (such was then Presbyterian and Papal belief), had been granted to him, so that the blow when it came was not unexpected.

Goa, we may remind our readers, was then in the acme of its glory, though the Church of Bom Jesus was not yet built. It was the Goa of Linschotten's time (1583), and her people were a proud, licentious race, quick to resent an injury and to punish the doers of it. What the vengeance was I do not know, or how it was executed, for on this point history is silent. I gather from the following facts, and I exclude the miraculous, that it was short, sharp and decisive. "In retaliation for these murders the Viceroy sent Yanez de Figueyrodo, the commander of Rachol, to punish the people of Salsette, which he effected in a most ruthless manner. He made a promiscuous slaughter of the inhabitants, destroyed their dwellings, and levelled to the ground every temple in the neighbourhood. Having discovered the leaders, amongst those who had killed the Friars, he made such horrible examples of them that many of the natives fled in terror from the island. After this, Figueyrodo erected a number of new churches and set up crosses on the summits of all the hills around."—Danvers' *Port in Ind.*, 1894.

Two years after the event, a little chapel, under the name of Notre Dame des Martyrs, was built over the well, and a monumental cross adjacent to it. Within one year after the martyrdom, 1,500 pagans of Salsette were baptised. In 1586–87 five villages requested baptism. During the celebration of mass at Coucolim, a troop of zemindars prostrated themselves before the altar. Salsette counted in 1896, 35,508 converts. Verily, in this instance, the blood of the martyrs was the seed of the Church, though it may have come roughly about.

Many legends have gathered round the martyrs of Salsette.

Ex uno disce omnes. One of the priests had made his escape, and had totally disappeared when the pagans let a bloodhound out of the leash after him. It tracked the fugitive to his doom. The owner of that dog came to no good, and appropriately died a howling maniac. In the same manner, the descendants of the man who pushed the drowning women under the Solway have been pointed out web-footed, and crawling crab-like on the ground. The idea that judgment, following in the wake of crime, should be accompanied by some of its concomitant features stretches, you see, from the Balla Ghaut to the Blednoch. The one thing Aquaviva did not bring away with him from Sikri was the doctrine of toleration—had he done so it might have saved his life. The Ibadat-khana was not the only place where Akbar exhibited toleration; he put it in practice throughout his immense dominions. His Minister, Todar Mall, was a Hindu; he adopted the Parsee Calendar; he put his son Murad under a Christian tutor. Had Aquaviva become the apostle of toleration, *and carried the authorities with him,* he might have saved the Portuguese dominion in Asia. This was not to be. No doubt the methods of the Church seem to us hard and unintelligible; but they were the methods of the age. The belief was almost universal that you could compel men by force and fear to worship God as you dictated. Ancient faiths had been rooted out, and nations compelled to accept new beliefs, by what the Bible emphatically calls "the power of the sword." It seems so strange. Albuquerque *versus* the Moslem was the incarnation of this doctrine. It was not confined to Spanish or Portuguese; Scotland burned Patrick Hamilton. England, by turns, Romanist or Protestant, showed the same intolerant spirit. Whoever had the upper hand showed no mercy. Church or stake—there's your choice. Hence you read on Goa tombstones of one, "Captain of this fortress, who destroyed the pagodas of these territories, 1577." Hence, the killing of the sacred cow, and the pollution of the holy places of the Hindus with its entrails. These were among the meritorious works of the time.

From all such deeds I am bound to say, as far as I know the records, that Aquaviva was totally free. The slaughter of the cow, and the desecration of a holy place with its blood was indefensible, and I am glad Aquaviva had no hand in it. Would Loyola have done it? Or Xavier? I trow not. A greater than he had said: "Behold, I send you forth as sheep among wolves. Be ye therefore wise as serpents and harmless as doves."

Pierre Berna that morning had evidently not read with profit these words of the Great Commission, and had founded his act upon the Commentaries of Albuquerque, and not on the words of Jesus. That Bombay did not burn mosques or pagodas was owing to her being one hundred years nearer our time in the march of civilisation; and that the men here who had the grasp of affairs at the time, notably Aungier, having imbibed in England the principle of free inquiry and private judgment, upheld that principle in the interest of humanity, and put an end to all interference with religious beliefs, "as long as they did not sap the foundation of morality or involve a violation of the eternal and immutable Laws of Right."

When the question of the beatification of Rodolph came before his uncle, the General of the Jesuits, he felt that he was too near a relation to give an impartial decision. The great Bellarmine was appealed to, and affirmed that the martyrs of Salsette were worthy of canonisation. At a congregation held in 1741, under Benedict XIV., to settle this business, Cardinal Bellaga uttered a *bon mot*, or something like it. "If two miracles," said he, "are necessary for beatification, we have already one in the unanimous vote of so numerous a body of Cardinals." This, however, was not enough, for the matter trailed its weary length over another century and a half, until Pope Leo XIII. enrolled him among the Saints. By this time the outside world, except his co-religionists, had completely forgotten, after the lapse of three centuries, that there was an Aquaviva of Salsette. I dare say the impression left by this holy man on Akbar was never effaced. He called him an angel, and so he was, for doing good and hating ill is angel's work.

Akbar wore the image of the Virgin next his heart, if I am not mistaken. You may still see the remnants of a sketch in fresco portraying the Annunciation on the walls of Sikri. When the Emperor heard of his death he was overwhelmed with grief: "Would that I had not let him go!" And years after (it was in 1695), when Jerome Xavier, the nephew of the Apostle, visited Agra, Akbar showed him the Bible, and the picture of the Madonna, which Aquaviva had presented to him, and the *Agnus Dei* which he wore from his neck. Is it only a legend or echo of the martyr's labours that Mary Mackany was the Christian wife of Akbar? And that the last words of Shah Jahan's daughter were, a hundred years later, "Je ne veux sur ma tombe aucun monument. L'herbe modeste recouvrira mieux les restes de l'éphémère Jehanara, la pauvre servante des disciples du Christ, la fille de l'Empereur Shah Jahan"?

The bare facts of Aquaviva's career, his heroism, his devotion, his self-denial and his early and violent death, suffice to constitute an exalted character, and have long attracted and fascinated the attention of that great body of religionists to which he belonged, and Aquaviva's story may still be read with profit by every branch of the Christian Church. He is one of the few Europeans who met and conversed intimately with Akbar, and left a record of the same. Every scrap of his writing, every word of his which has been handed down, his form, his face, his features, his habits, his prayers, his mortifications and his flagellations, are recorded and brought before us. Tradition, legend, and even miracle have gathered round his bones and clothed his august personality, even as the moss clothes the mighty oak, or other monarch of the forest, until the admiration of his panegyrists burst forth into loud acclaim—Aquaviva! Living Water! Springing up into everlasting life!

(3.) KIDD, THE PIRATE.

THE following document has been recently unearthed at Welbeck Abbey by the Royal Commission on Historical Manuscripts.*

Everybody knows "Kidd, the Pirate," and he knew us English when we were struggling for existence in Western India.

---

* *Times of India*, 17th Sept., 1897.

Lord Bellamont was Governor of New York and Massachusetts, and we need not remind the reader that New York then belonged to England. Livingston was presumably the progenitor of that great clan of the name which dominated New York society early in the nineteenth century, and of which Chancellor Livingstone, once Resident at the Court of France, was the most conspicuous member.

The *letter* is dated May 12th, 1701. There is no date to the "*petition*." Kidd was executed on May 23rd, his trial and condemnation having taken place in the interval. There was short shrift in those days. The £100,000, though believed in, was never discovered. £6,472, being the only property of his that Government could lay its hands on, was given by Queen Anne to Greenwich Hospital.

William Kidd to Robert Harley (?).

"May 12th, 1701, Newgate.—The long imprisonment I have undergone, or the trial I am to undergo, are not so great an affliction to me as my not being able to give your Honourable House of Commons such satisfaction as was expected from me. I hope I have not offended against the Law, but if I have it was the fault of the others who knew better and made me the tool of their ambition and avarice, and who now perhaps think it their interest that I should be removed out of the world. I did not seek the Commission I undertook, but was partly cajoled and partly menaced into it by the Lord Bellamont and one Robert Livingston of New York, who was the projector, promoter, and chief manager of that design, and who only can give your House a satisfactory account of all the transactions of my owners. He was the man admitted into their closets, and who received their private instructions, which he kept in his own hands, and who encouraged me in their names to do more than I ever did, and to act without regard to my Commission. I would not exceed my authority and took no other ships than such as had French passes, which I brought with me to New England and relied upon for my justification, but my Lord Bellamont seized upon them together with my cargo, and though he promised to send them into England, yet has he detained part of the effects, kept those passes wholly from me, and has stripped me of all the defence I have to make, which is such barbarous as well as dishonourable usage, as I hope your honourable House will not let an Englishman suffer, how unfortunate soever his circumstances are, but will intercede with his Majesty to defer my trial until I can have those passes, and that Livingston may be brought under your examination and confronted by me.

"I cannot be so unjust to myself as to plead to an indictment till the French passes are restored to me unless I would be accessory to my own destruction, for though I can make proof that the ships I took had such passes, I am advised by counsel that it will little avail me without producing the passes themselves. I was in great consternation when I was before that great assembly, your Honourable House, which, with the disadvantages of a mean capacity, want of education, and a spirit cramped by long confinement, made me incapable of representing my case, and I have, therefore, presumed to send your Honourable a short and true statement of it, which I humbly beg your Honourable's perusal and communication of to the House, if you think it worthy their notice. I humbly crave leave to acquaint your Honour that I was not privy to my being sent for up to your House the second time, nor to the paper lately printed in my name, both which may justly give offence to the House, but I owe the first to a Coffeeman in the Court of Wards, who designed to make a show of me for his profit, and the latter was done by one Newy, a prisoner in Newgate, to get money for his support at the hazard of my safety. The sense of my present condition (being under condemnation), and the thoughts of having been imposed on by such as seek my destruction, thereby to fulfil their ambitious desires, make me incapable of expressing myself in those terms as I ought, therefore do most humbly pray that you will be pleased to represent to the Honourable House of Commons that in my late proceedings in the Indies I have lodged goods and treasure to the value of one hundred thousand pounds, which I desire the Government may have the benefit of. In order thereto I shall desire no manner of liberty, but to be kept prisoner on board such ship as may be appointed for that purpose, and only give the necessary directions, and in case I fail therein I desire no favour but to be forthwith executed according to my sentence. If your Honourable House will please to order a committee to come to me, I doubt not but to give such satisfaction as may obtain mercy, most humbly submitting to the wisdom of your great assembly."

This petition of William Kidd brings to mind the fact that exactly two hundred years ago (1697) this man's name was in the mouth of every English colonist in Western India. "The terror of the merchants of Surat and of the villagers of the coast of Malabar," are Macaulay's words. And no wonder! His name had been heralded as bearing the mandate of leading members of the English Cabinet to destroy and wipe out from the Indian seas the curse of piracy for ever. And, lo and behold, he turns pirate himself, and on such a grand scale that the maritime and commercial world stand aghast! His capture of the *Quedah*, merchant, and a dozen others was followed by reprisals of the Mogul Government of Aurungzebe.

And if the old American ballad be true, all this was done with a show of religion.

"My name is Captain Kidd,
And I sailed, and I sailed.
My name is Captain Kidd
And so wickedly I did
God's laws I did forbid,
As I sailed, as I sailed.
I had the Bible in my hand,
As I sailed, as I sailed,
And I buried it in the sand
As I sailed."

In 1698-9 news leaked out in London; complaints reached Government. Bellamont was asked to arrest Kidd on his arrival. He returned to Boston in July, 1699, when he was put in gaol, and sent to England in the spring of 1700. His crowning act of boldness in this buccaneering crusade was the capture and plunder of an English ship at Rajapore, in 1697.

I think the daring and audacity of this deed is without a parallel. Kidd had only escaped from capture himself at the hands of a united Dutch and English squadron which was acting as convoy to the Pilgrim Fleet from the Red Sea. One would have thought that he would at once, having got out of their clutches, have trimmed his sails to the wind and made for the open sea. Nothing of the kind. He ran in to Rajapore, under the battlements of Jinjheera, boarded an English ship, and with a wild halloo, his motley crew no doubt singing out, "Up and waur them a' Willie," snatched away Bombay property to the value of two lakhs. This was "to beard the lion in his den," for as I take it the Admiral of the Mogul fleet was "at home." Kidd got off scot-free, which was the best or worst of the business, good for Kidd *pro tem.*, and bad for Bombay, as insurance did not protect her against the King's enemies, of whom Kidd was the biggest.

This I say was an act of great daring, for Jinjheera was the strongest droog or seaport in the whole of Western India. Jinjheera had defied the world, at all events defied Sivaji, who was a world in himself, and had battered away at its walls a mile across the water with his big guns for nine successive years, and could not take it. Kidd is described as living on a competence in Boston, America, when in 1695, in an evil hour, Livingston, a man of some importance, got hold of him and introduced him to Lord Bellamont, Governor of New York and New England. The great store-houses of the pirates in Madagascar had been supplied from New York, and William, King of England, had asked Bellamont to do what he could in suppressing the buccaneering business, which looked as if it would drive the English out of India. The English Government, having plenty on its hands, could not commission its ships on this business, but as an alternative Bellamont and four members of the Cabinet, *and* Kidd, subscribed each £1,000, by which means the *Adventure*, galley, of thirty guns, with a crew of 200 Europeans, was fitted out. Men could not be got in London, and she was manned in New York. She finally left Plymouth in May, 1696.

I can scarcely imagine a more exciting life than the pirate's. The land-lubber who delved, wove, or span was the meanest of

God's creatures. So Kidd swings himself into his hammock to dream of the gold of the Indies.

"I'm afloat, I'm afloat
On the wild raging sea,
My bride is my bark,
And my home is the sea.
Up, up with my flag
As it floats on the sea.
I'm afloat, I'm afloat,
And the Rover is free."

Kidd's destination was Madagascar and the mouth of the Red Sea. Being unsuccessful in accomplishing the end he had been sent on, *i.e.*, the destruction of the pirates and their settlements, or from whatever other reason, he made for the coast of India, Cochin and Calicut, and throwing off all trammels, he attacked the ships he had come out to protect, and gave up the *rôle* of privateer! He spared no nationality. All was fish that came to his net, and his appetite grew on what it fed, until gorged with the plunder, as he admits himself, of £100,000 (£250,000 nowadays). In 1697, when Kidd was at Jinjheera, it was the stronghold of Sidi Kassim, the same man who eight years before (1689) had landed at Mazagon 20,000 men, and a ghastly freight of human heads, driving the English, *nolens volens*, to the shelter of their castle walls, and leaving the marks of their bullets on its gates, which remain visible to the present day. Did Kidd know about all this? Of course he did. He had been years on these waters before he had heard the name of Bellamont, knew every inlet, and doubtless the Rajapore and Bassein Creeks were as familiar to him as the Kyles of Bute.* He must have known also that this piratical act was an insult to Aurungzebe, whose Admiral the Sidi was, and a still greater insult to Bombay and the English, whose goods he had stolen. Was Kidd ever in Bombay? asks the reader. I have no doubt he was in some of his former voyages, as he was a veteran sea-dog when Bellamont got hold of him, and though his "logs" have been lost, we are safe in saying that in 1697 he could have made his way to a Punch-house in Dongri Killa, or Moodi Khana, without difficulty. The place where this exploit of

* He was born in Greenock.

Kidd's occurred is recorded "off Rajapore." Rajapore is on the mainland, and twenty-five miles south of Bombay, opposite to which, at about a mile distance, is the fortified Island of Jinjheera. The present Nawab, who is a gentleman, is the ruler of the oldest existing dominion in Western India. The creek, the island, and the surrounding hills make up a picture of rare beauty. Jinjheera looks like a bit cut out of Valetta. It is about a mile broad, and every inch is packed with houses, which rise tier above tier, until, at an altitude of 200 feet, you reach the Ballakilla, where, on a miniature maidan, a huge cannon stretches out its lazy length—presiding genius of the place.

The sea-walls are not of the "rough-and-tumble" kind which round Khenry, but are well built, and at full tide rise forty feet sheer out of the water. You can promenade the whole circumference. The great gateway is something to see—slimy with "glaur" and seaweed, it looms high overhead, and gives you an eerie feeling when you think that many a man here took his last look of the world as he stepped from his tony to his funeral pyre.

Melrose Abbey, Scott says, is best seen by moonlight. What a weird sight Jinjheera must be then! But there is no use thinking about it; though the Dewan was with us, the sun was set, and the guardians refused to break the ancient custom, which is not to allow anyone to enter after sundown. I dare say Kidd saw as much of this place as he wanted. One look would be enough.

"Sir Ralph the Rover sail'd away,
He scoured the sea for many a day,
And now grown rich with plundered store
He steers his course for Scotland's shore."

We cannot give the reader a portrait of Sidi Kassim, otherwise Yakut Khan, the man who was here in Kidd's time, but we can introduce him to his tomb. Here you may sit awhile, or sleep o' night, if you care to rough it on a charpoy, cheek by jowl with his sarcophagus. Here he rests after the hurly-burly of stormy times (1670–1707). Other chiefs also—

"Their bones are dust
And their swords are rust,
And their souls are with the saints, we trust."

The place Khokari is on the mainland, only a mile or two away; and, on a rising ground on the sea margin, among trees, is of uncommon beauty. There is an Arabic inscription on Yakut's tomb; they all remind one of the grand tombs at Rosa, above Ellora. The Koran is recited every Thursday, and the Nawab sees to it that the tombs are all kept in good repair.

Kansa Fort, a small fortified island which guards the Rajpoori Creek, was formerly used for political prisoners, who were executed by being chained to the rocks at low water and the tide allowed to rise gently over them. This would have been Kidd's punishment—had he been taken. There is a splendid passage in Carlyle's *French Revolution* on the state funeral decreed by the French Government to Paul Jones, ending with "six feet in his native kirkyard would have been better," or words like these. Kidd's death and funeral were public enough, and paid for by the State. He was hung in chains after being executed at Tilbury.

These two Scoto-Americans, though the dates of their birth are divided by one hundred years, had much in common, I mean in their passion for distinguished patrons and in the grief and trouble they found on the ocean wave.

The question arises, Is Kidd going to be whitewashed? His latest biographer, Laughton, the eminent naval writer, has these words: "Whatever may have been Kidd's crimes, it is clear that he had not a fair trial, and was found guilty on insufficient evidence."—*Dict. Nat. Biog.*

The East India Company wrote to Surat that they hoped he would be "hung, drawn and quartered." Had he come into, and been caught in Bombay in 1697 he would have been hanged first and tried afterwards. I may add that he was *not* the pirate of whom Byron wrote, "He was the mildest-mannered man that ever scuttled ship or cut a throat."

(4.) STERNE'S ELIZA.*

THE new volume, the fifty-fourth, of the *Dictionary of National Biography* contains an admirable sketch of Sterne, the renowned author of *Tristram Shandy*. I make no apology for introducing the new and interesting matter in it concerning Eliza Draper, for which Mr. Sidney Lee well deserves the thanks of all Bombay readers.

"On this his penultimate visit to London (December, 1766–May, 1767) Sterne occupied new lodgings at 41, Old Bond Street, above a silk-bagwig-maker's. He spent much time at the house of Sir William James, a retired Indian commodore, who lived in fashionable style in Gerrard Street, Soho. He had met James casually in society, and James's wife and little daughter attracted him. In the repeated hospitalities they offered him he took a genuine delight. Visitors from India were often his fellow-guests at James's table, and there, late in December, 1766, Sterne first met Mrs. Eliza (or, more properly, Elizabeth) Draper, a visitor from Bombay, who was to play an important part in what remained of his life.

"She was a daughter of May Sclater (b. 1719), a member of a good west-country family, who had gone out to India in 1736. In India her father married a lady named Whitehill, and apparently settled at Anjengo on the Malabar coast, where Eliza was born on April 5th, 1744. After being educated in England, she reached Bombay on the return voyage on December 27th, 1757, and when little more than fourteen she married, at Bombay, on July 28th, 1758, Daniel Draper, at the time a writer in the East India Company's service, who next year became Secretary to the Government at Bombay.

"Draper was a dull official, fully twenty years his wife's senior. A boy was born in 1759, and a daughter (Elizabeth or Betsy) in October, 1761. In 1765 Mrs. Draper and her husband paid a visit to England with a view to placing their children at school. Draper soon returned alone to his post at Bombay, and left his wife to follow him later.

---

* *Times of India*, April 29th, 1898.

"Mrs. Draper, when Sterne met her, was no more than a coquettish schoolgirl, who had read widely, and aped the ethical theories of the blue-stocking school. She chattered of "the rights of women" in matters of education and marriage. But there was no doubt of the reality of her conviction that a wrong had been done her by yoking her in immature years to a husband of formal manner and illiterate tastes, who rendered conjugal life detestable to her. Sterne was not slow in winning her confidence. The sympathy of a distinguished man of letters flattered her vanity. She knew him as the 'mild, generous, and good Yorick,' and became a whole-hearted 'idolater of his worth.' He opened a correspondence with her in his customary vein, calling her his 'Bramine,' in allusion to her Indian connections. He cursed fate that both were married already, sent her his books, and having had her portrait painted, wore it round his neck. But within a month or two of their first meeting Draper summoned his wife home. Eliza fell ill at the thought of leaving her children and relatives. Sterne assigned her melancholy to the coming separation from him. On April 3rd, 1767, Eliza sailed from Deal for Bombay in the *Earl of Chatham*, East Indiaman. Sterne and she never met again. Her health and spirits recovered on the voyage. New admirers were forthcoming, and most of the impression Sterne had made on her passed away. . . .

"Mrs. Draper, on learning of Sterne's death from Mrs. James, and of his wife's and daughter's distress, collected six hundred rupees herself in their behalf, and induced a friend, Colonel Donald Campbell, to collect an equal sum among his fellow-officers. Campbell brought the money to Miss Sterne, with an introduction from Mrs. Draper, who thought he might prove an eligible suitor. In any case, Mrs. Draper offered to provide for Lydia if she would join her in India. Lydia wrote resenting Mrs. Draper's patronage, and defending her mother's character from the aspersions her father had cast on it. With less excuse she joined her mother in a threat to publish, from copies in their possession, Sterne's letters to Mrs. Draper unless a heavy sum of money was at once remitted to them. Mrs. Draper, violently perturbed, wrote to Becket the bookseller, promising any reasonable recompense if he would secure the letters, in case they were offered for sale, and hand them to Mrs. James. Mrs. Sterne was better than her word, and the letters did not at the time pass out of her hands.

"The later history of Sterne's Eliza was followed with interest by Sterne's admirers. On arriving at Bombay at the end of 1767, she made the best of the situation, and in 1769 removed with her husband to Tellichery, where he had been appointed chief of the factory. She acted as his amanuensis, and was not, despite the death of her son in England, unhappy there. She described the town as the Montpellier of India, and enjoyed the social distinction accorded her by both English settlers and natives (*cf. Magazine of Indian Art*, January, 1891, Vol. IV. No. 33, letter from Mrs. Draper, from Tellichery, April, 1769, edited by Sir George Birdwood). Her main anxiety at Tellichery was due to the malicious conduct of Sterne's wife and daughter in threatening to publish her correspondence with Sterne. Every member of the family, including Sterne himself, whom she now declared to have been tainted with the "vices of injustice, meanness, and folly," became the subject of Mrs. Draper's warm denunciation. In 1771 Draper removed from Tellichery to fill the same post of chief of the factory at Surat. But intrigues at Bombay jeopardised his prospects. He was recalled thither in 1772, and was for a time without remunerative employment. Life in Bombay was increasingly irksome to Mrs. Draper, as a chance of returning to England with a competency grew more remote. On April 15th, 1772, in a long rambling letter to Mrs. James, she defended the attitude she had maintained to Sterne's family, and set forth in elaborate detail her impatience with her husband and Indian society, as well as her views on life and literature. At length, driven to desperation by her renewed antipathy to her husband, she fled, on January 12th, 1773, from his house—called both Marine House and Belvedere House—at Mazagon, which overlooked Bombay Harbour (see her farewell letters in *Times of India*, February 24th, 1894). It is said that she was aided in her escape by Captain Sir John Clark, and let herself down to his ship by a rope from a window. But she denied, in letters to her friends at home, that she compromised herself in any other way. Mrs. Draper's disappearance created a sensation throughout India. Writs were taken out against Clark in the Mayor's Court at Bombay, but he eluded them successfully (David Price, *Memoirs*, 1839). Mrs. Draper retired to the residence of her maternal uncle, Thomas Whitehill, at Rajamundry, eighty miles from Masulipatam, and wrote home with composure of her contentment there, and of her intention to retaliate if Draper proceeded to extremities. A year later she returned to England. There she met Wilkes, William Coombe, and other literary men, and exercised over them some of her old fascination (*cf.* Rogers, *Table Talk*, ed. Dyce, p. 117). Her pride in her relations with Sterne revived, and in 1775—the year in which Sterne's daughter published some of his correspondence without making any reference to her—she authorised the publication, under the title of *Letters of Yorick to Eliza*, of ten letters that Sterne had addressed to her between December, 1766, and April, 1767. The volume was dedicated to Lord Chancellor Apsley by an anonymous editor, who said he had copied the letters, with Eliza's permission, from the originals in her possession. Her replies were not given.

"*Letters from Eliza to Yorick* (1775, printed for the editor), and William Coombe's letters, supposed to have been written by Yorick and Eliza (1779, 2 vols.), were forgeries, some of which were foisted on reprints of the genuine collection. That volume gave Sterne's Eliza a reputation little less universal than Sterne's. But she did not long enjoy the equivocal distinction. Dying at Bristol on August 3rd, 1778, before she had completed her thirty-fifth year, she was buried in the cloisters of the Cathedral there on August 6th. A sculptured monument still stands there to her memory. Eliza's husband, who was the object of much sympathy both in India and England, attained the first place in the Bombay Council, and finally returned to England on October 10th, 1782. His and Eliza's daughter, their only surviving child, married on January 10th, 1785, one Thomas Nevill, Esq. (*Gent. Mag.*, 1785, i. 75). Draper died in St. James's Street in March, 1805.

"Eliza's fame died hard (*cf.* James Douglas, *Bombay and Western India*). L'Abbé Raynal, who met her in India, gave it new vigour when, in the second edition of his *Histoire des*

Indes (1779), he rapturously and at great length apostrophised her in his account of Anjengo, her birthplace. In 1813 James Forbes, in his *Oriental Memoirs* (i. 338–9), wrote of Abbé Raynal's rhapsody of Anjengo that "however insignificant the settlement may be in itself, it will be for ever celebrated as the birthplace of his and Sterne's Eliza, a lady with whom I had the pleasure of being acquainted at Bombay, whose refined taste and elegant accomplishments require no encomium from my pen." A tree at Masulipatam, where she stayed for a time with her uncle Whitehill, was known, until it was swept away in 1864, as "Eliza's Tree"; and the house that she had occupied in Bombay was, until its demolition in 1874, regarded as a literary shrine. A picture of it formed, in 1831, a scene in Burford's famous panorama in London (*cf. Mirror of Literature*, 1831, xviii. 17, with view of house and an apocryphal account of the later life of Sterne's Eliza). . . .

"A letter from Mrs. Draper to her friend Mrs. James, dated Bombay, April 15th, 1772, covering twenty-four folios, is also bound up with the unpublished Journal at the British Museum (Addit. MS. 34527, ff. 47-70). Other unpublished sources for Mrs. Draper's career are thirteen letters from her to members of her father's family, belonging to Lord Basing, who descends from Richard Sclater, a brother of May Sclater, Mrs. Draper's father. The first, dated Bombay, March 13th, 1758, was written before her marriage, and is signed Eliza Sclater; the latest is dated from Rajahmundry, January 20th, 1774. The letter from Mrs. Draper, from Tellichery, in 1769, which was printed in the *Magazine of Indian Art*, is now in the British Museum. Those printed in the *Times of India* in 1894, which are in private hands in Bombay, were communicated by Mr. James Douglas of Bombay."—*Dict. Nat. Biog.*

(5.) STERNE'S ELIZA'S LAST LETTER TO DANIEL DRAPER.

STUDENTS of Sterne will, we believe, look upon the letters which we publish below as a literary "find" of no small interest. They are from the pen of Sterne's Eliza, and relate to an affecting period of her life that has never, we believe before been generally known. They were penned on the eve of her elopement with Sir John Clark, who was here in command of a frigate. Mrs. Leeds, the individual mentioned in the letters, was an European attendant who caused all the mischief between the old Councillor and his wife. She used to put on Mr. Draper's Conjee cap when he took his afternoon nap, and at that time it was said received many attentions and more gold mohurs from him.

I.

Mrs. Eliza Mihill.

My Dear Betty.—This may be the last hour I may have it in my power to write or do anything of use for the benefit of you my faithful servant and dear friend; for in the latter capacity, indeed, I've rather wished ever to consider you, therefore let me dedicate it as properly as the peculiarity of my situation will admit. When Mr. Horsley went to England I consigned some few jewels to him, the amount of which would be about £500 or £600, and which I ever intended for you in case I could not induce Mr. Draper to make you a present exceeding it, and more suited to my wishes. Accept it, my dear woman, as the best token in my power, expressive of my good-will to you. Do not hesitate from any point of delicacy or principle to Mr. Draper. I am as incapable of taking mean pecuniary advantages, as the most moral persons breathing can be. This little fund, by right, is my due; it is what results from the sale of my ornaments, little perquisites due to me as a woman, and which he never would have possessed if I had not received them; nor will they be *his*, if you decline having them—that is the worth of them. Take it then, Betty, without any scruple of conscience. The enclosed is an order on Mr. Horsley for the delivery of it to you. You will, perhaps, see England before me. God bless you, my dear woman! Visit my child sometimes, and speak kindly to her of her mother. My heart is full. The next twenty-four hours will, in all probability, either destine me to the grave or a life of reproach —shocking alternative; but I will endeavour to bear my fate, so as to assure my own heart. I had deserved a better, if chance had not counteracted the good propensities assigned me by nature. God give you health and a peaceable establishment in England, my dear woman. Adieu.

(*Signed*) ELIZA DRAPER.

Bombay, Marine House, January 14th, 1773.

II.

GEO. HORSLEY, ESQ.

DEAR HORSLEY,—If you knew the misery and compunction with which I addressed this to you, you would, in spite of reason and justice, think me entitled to some degree of pity, though I am lost, for ever lost, to every claim which could entitle me to your esteem. This hour is my own, but whether the next may produce my death or distraction, or whatever else, heaven only knows. I dedicate it as one act of just benevolence, by requesting you to pay to Betty Mihill, or her order, the sum of money which may have resulted from the sale of my diamond rings, be it what it will. Adieu, Horsley! God restore you to health, and the enjoyment of yourself.

(*Signed*) ELIZA DRAPER.

January 14, 1773.

III.

DANIEL DRAPER.

If you knew, Draper, with what anguish I accosted you at present, I think, and cannot help thinking it, that the severity of justice should give place to the sentiment of compassion; in a farewell letter—I will not recriminate—I would even be all in fault, if that might serve to alleviate the disgrace inflicted on my husband, by my elopment from him; but, Draper, be candid, I beseech you, as you sometimes can be, when it makes against yourself to be so, and then think if you have not a great deal to reproach yourself for in this late affair—if you can say you have not. I must, I fear, be miserable, as my sole prospect of happiness is derived from the idea that your own consciousness will befriend me in this particular instance; and, if it does, let it operate so as to prevent your pursuing me in a vindictive manner.

I speak in the singular number, because I would not wound you by the mention of a name that I know must be displeasing to you; but, Draper, believe me for once, when I solemnly assure you that it is you only who have driven me to serious extremities. But from the conversation on Monday last he had nothing to hope, or you to fear. Lost to reputation, and all hopes of living with my dearest girl on peaceable or creditable terms, urged by a despair of gaining any one point with you, and resenting, strongly resenting, I own it, your avowed preference of Leeds to myself, I *myself proposed* the scheme of leaving you thus abruptly. Forgive me, Draper, if its accomplishment has excited anguish; but if pride is only wounded by the measure, sacrifice that, I beseech you, to the sentiments of humanity, as indeed you may, and may be amply revenged in the compunction I shall feel to the hour of my death for a conduct that will so utterly disgrace me with all I love, and do not let this confirm the prejudice imbibed by Leeds's tale, as I swear to you *that was false*, though my present mode of acting may rather seem the consequence of it than of a more recent event. Oh! that prejudice had not been deaf to the reasonable requests of a wounded spirit, or that you, Draper, could have read my very soul, as undisguisedly as sensibility and innocence must ever wish to be read! But this is too like recrimination, which I would wish to avoid. I can only say in my justification, Draper, that if you imagine I plume myself on the success of my scheme, you do me great wrong. My heart bleeds for what I suppose may possibly be the sufferings of yours, though too surely had you loved, all this could never have been. My head is too much disturbed to write with any degree of connection. No matter, for if your own mind does not suggest palliatives, all I can say will be of little avail. I go, I know not whither, but I will never be a tax on you, Draper. Indeed, I will not, and do not suspect me of being capable of adding to my portion of infamy. I am not a hardened or depraved creature—I never will be so. The enclosed are the only bills owing that I know of, except about six rupees to Doojee, the shoemaker. I have never meant to load myself with many spoils to your prejudice, but a moderate provision of linon has obliged me to secure part of what is mine, to obviate some very mortifying difficulties. The pearls and silk cloathes are not in the least diminished. Betty's picture, of all the ornaments, is the only one I have ventured to make mine. I presume not to recommend any of the persons to you who were immediately officiating about me; but this I conjure you to believe as strictly true, that not one of them, or any living soul in the Marine House or Mazagon, was at all privy to my scheme, either directly or indirectly, nor do I believe that any one of them had the smallest suspicion of the matter, unless the too evident concern occasioned by my present conflict induced them to think something extraordinary was in agitation. Oh, Draper! a word, a look, sympathetick of regret on Tuesday or Wednesday would have saved me the perilous adventure, and such a portion of remorse as would be sufficient to fill up the longer life. I reiterate my request that vindictive measures may not be pursued. Leave me to my fate, I conjure you, Draper, and in doing this you will leave me to misery inexpressible, for you are not to think that I am either satisfied with myself or my prospects, though the latter are entirely my own seeking. God bless you, may health and prosperity be yours, and happiness too, as I doubt not but it will, if you suffer your resentments to be subdued by the aid of true and reasonable reflections. Do not let the false idea of my triumphing induce you to acts of vengeance, I implore you, Draper, for indeed that can never be, nor am I capable of bearing you the least ill-will, or treating your name or memory with irreverence now that I have released myself from your dominion. Suffer me but to be unmolested, and I will engage to steer through life with some degree of approbation, if not respect. Adieu! again Mr. Draper, and be assured I have told you nothing but the truth, however it may clash with yours and the general opinion.

(*Signed*) ELIZA DRAPER.

(6.) THE PRIVATE LIFE OF WARREN HASTINGS.*

It was reserved for the generation 1840–50 to drink the wine of life in Macaulay's *Essays* and *History of England.* To a young man of that day these writings were a big goblet from which he quaffed the flowing nectar and partook of the intoxication thereof. True or not true, Whig or not Whig, did not matter much, and so it came to pass that his reader sat up all night, wandering over his Field of the Cloth of Gold when he ought to have been in blankets. Macaulay was ostracised by Edinburgh electors, 1847 to 1852. He had seen them but seldom; a bailie reminded him on the hustings of his alliterative "septennial smile of supercilious scorn," which was very cruel. He was "called back." And I can never forget his reappearance. You could have got guineas for a ticket. A few minutes of breathless expectation, and then there emerged from a trap-door behind the platform, pale and emaciated, with scanty grey hair, clad in an olive-green coat, the hero, amid thunders of applause. Again there was silence, and with a faltering voice and tremulous with agitation the words fell from his lips (I give them from memory)—"After five years of separation we meet again in kindness."

Macaulay shows the Governor-General in the fierce light (and it was a fierce light) that beats upon the Viceregal throne. In the *Private Life of Warren Hastings* we come into his immediate presence and become an inmate of his home. We now know that his caligraphy was exquisite, that his wife was supremely beautiful, that he was a very temperate man, that he wrote letters to his wife after he was fifty with all the ardour of five-and-twenty, that in early life he nearly beggared himself by benefactions to his relations, that when he was eighty he offered his services to Government—wanted employment; that in his Indian journeys he rode on horseback, and did not love the palanquin overmuch; that he did the same when he was seventy-four, for many miles on his tour to Scotland; that he

* *The Private Life of Warren Hastings*, by Sir Charles Lawson, Fellow of the University of Madras, &c. London: Swan Sonnenschein & Co.

was over-anxious for a title, and that the Prince Regent parried his solicitation with—"What would you think of a Lord Shakespeare?" That Mrs. Hastings *may* have smoked a *hookah*, that Hastings had *amour propre*, and would not let bygones be bygones with Sheridan, who had denounced him; but turned on his heel and refused to kiss the rod: "Thou art not my friend, and I'm not thine." Warren Hastings was a domestic man and did not keep late hours; if he had done so he would not have lived to eighty-six. Not like him who in the same cycle sang the praises of—

"The wee short hour ayont the twal."

When he dined with Sir Elijah Impey on his return home he sat till twelve. But he was then fifty-three. This was on June 25, 1785, which his diary records, followed the next day by the suggestive entry—"Not well; Mrs. H., headache; breakfasted at ten."

At the age of seventy-four he set out for Scotland. The Edinburgh which Warren Hastings saw in 1806 was not the Edinburgh we see to-day. *The Lay of the Last Minstrel* had just been published (1805), and Jeffrey, Brougham, and other of the young "Giants of Criticism" had launched the *Edinburgh Review*. Madame Hastings, we are sure, in Edinburgh, had no weary hours to wait for the great Proconsul's coming home at night, though the era of whisky-toddy drinking had commenced in the Scotch capital. A dinner given to him by old Indians was at Oman's Hotel, and though there was much conviviality, his diary records—"Left them at half-past eight." Oman's in after years was the *locale* of some of the *Noctes*. I remember well spending an evening with the widow and family of the Ettrick Shepherd, who on one occasion was master of the revels, and I looked at the lines on that pale face (wasn't her sister the mother of General Alexander Cunningham, so lately among us?), delved deep no doubt by long weary waiting o' nights for the sound of James Hogg's heavy footfall on the silent streets of old Edinburgh. A voice at my elbow says, "A bucket of cold water would have served him better," and perhaps a more effective cure, if we may believe the modern novel on the modern woman. But circumstances alter cases.

When Chambers, who afterwards became Chief Justice of Bengal, embarked for Calcutta, he carried a special letter of introduction to Warren Hastings from Dr. Samuel Johnson. This was in 1774. Our readers may remember that when Johnson travelled to the Hebrides he paid a pleasant visit with Boswell, in 1773, to Alexander Macdonald at Kingsburgh and his celebrated wife Flora Macdonald. Hereby hangs a tale which looks very like a kind of Johnsonian marriage in Calcutta. John Macdonald, son of the said Alexander and Flora Macdonald, proceeded to Calcutta in 1781, and, as Major John Macdonald, married Miss Chambers, daughter of the Chief Justice of Bengal. "Men sometimes are masters of their fates," but not always where ladies are concerned; then they are mastered by their mistresses.

The threads of fate are here curiously interwoven in the web of life. Perhaps the initial letter of this marriage was by Johnson's introductory letter itself.* It has been said that when a Governor-General of India receives notice of his appointment, the first thing he does is to look up an atlas. When Hastings was appointed in 1773, Major Rennell's maps of India were not published, and the source of geographical knowledge for that generation lay hid in Guthrie's *Grammar*, whose first edition had appeared in 1770. This was where poor Burns got all his knowledge about the "Gentoos." This book (the 23rd edition, 1819) now lies before us, and it is curious to note that a year after the death of Hastings the tide of public opinion was not altogether in his favour, if we may judge from this sentence (p. 698): "During the administration of Warren Hastings, a new war arose in India, rather in consequence of his ambitious spirit than from that necessity which alone could justify it."

If Warren Hastings saw the India of 1895, how would he

---

* "On returning home he devoted himself to his favourite pursuits, but it is as a writer on military tactics, and man of science, that Colonel Macdonald is especially entitled to our notice. His productions are specially translations from the French, but he produced in 1808 a Treatise on Telegraphic Communication, Naval, Military, and Political; and in 1816 a Telegraphic Dictionary, extending to 150,000 words, phrases, and sentences. During the latter part of his life he resided at Exeter, where he died in 1831, aged seventy-two."—Maunder's *B. Dict.*

be astonished! The grain of mustard seed of his day has grown into the greatest of all trees, and the administration of the Indian Empire attracts the admiration of the world.

Warren Hastings did not think that the whole body of terrestrial wisdom was contained in the Anglo-Saxon Empire. In a minute recommending to the Directors Mr. Gladwin's translation of the *Ayeen Akbery*, he thus unburdens himself of these words of weight: "The original constitution of the Mogul Empire, described under the immediate inspection of its founder, will serve to assist the judgment of the Court of Directors on many points of importance to the first interests of the company. It will show when the measures of their administration approach to the first principles which, perhaps, will be found superior to any that have been built on their ruins, and certainly most easy, as the most familiar to the minds of the people, and when any deviation from them may be likely to counteract or to assimilate with them. Dated Fort William, June 3, 1783." This is a philosophical reflection which redounds to the greatest credit of Warren Hastings, and reminds us that a good deal of India's just government is built upon the foundation of the prophets and apostles of its own, but specially of Akbar.

Though the witches' cauldron of the Rohilla War has been boiling for many years, and still continues to bubble over, we cannot resist the temptation of throwing a trifle into the pot. There is a lurid light about a certain letter* from one present, recording in 1824 what were his impressions of events in 1774, and one can fancy Macaulay may have seen it when writing his essay on Warren Hastings. This, however, is a mere guess. The writer of the letter saw the fort where Fysoolah Khan entrenched himself and finally gave in. It was said that two-thirds of them died of famine and disease, and truly the number of graves and the limbs and offal of dead cattle and horses strewed about were ample proof of the assertion. It was a sight most distressing and sickening. Rohilkund, when our army entered it in 1774, was a garden; in a few years afterwards it was rendered a desert by the Vizier's government.

* *The Rohilla War.* From *Asiatic Journal*, Vol. XVIII, page 276. 1824.

The Rohillas were commanded by Hafiz Khamal Khan. The Vizier brought his head to Colonel Champion. "I well remember the tragic scene . . ." The Vizier's irregulars for many miles continued destroying vast numbers of their brave enemies.

There is much in this book that was never intended to be published, but we are bound to say that nothing crops up to add to the reckoning against Hastings, for even his amatory vapouring letters to his dear Marian lean to virtue's side. When he went to a Presbyterian church in Edinburgh, he says he "heard nothing"; but even Macaulay in Scotland, and in similar circumstances, fifty years after took to reading the eighth chapter of Romans. I like the spirit which dictated the following act. Inglesford Church was rebuilt by him and he inscribed on stone the fact that the original building had been erected by Ethelbald, King of the Mercians, about the year 716. At the foot of the tablet he caused to be engraved the pregnant, notable words from Holy Writ: "For a thousand years in Thy sight are but as yesterday when it is past, and as a watch in the night."—Psl. xc., 4. Hastings' diary in, and *en route* to and from Edinburgh, furnishes nothing for the *gobe-mouches*, and anticipates our age in its telegraphic sententiousness. That he came to grief colliding with some fir trees which lay across the path, and could not get the doctor to bleed him, and a description of the hostelries on the way, is about the sum total of contents. Hastings must have been a strong man, to do 900 miles in a lumbering coach and on horseback when he was 74. How a man's life is taken to pieces by private memoranda and letters we have seen from Carlyle, and now on the eve of Burns's centenary an auto-de-fé is promised us, in which every word is twisted, until even the sentiments in the "Cottar's Saturday Night" are denied as being his own. The grubbers, fortunately, will find their pursuit a waste of time in the *Private Life of Warren Hastings*. Hastings is the greatest instance of Anglo-Indian longevity on record; and he was not what you would call a strong man. "Delicate from childhood," our author writes. Not cradled in ease, not the Sybarite of hill stations, for they were non-existent, not nursed by surgeons-general or specialists, he had as much trouble as has ever fallen to the lot of mortal man. Fever, duel, "the slings and arrows of outrageous fortune," passed over him like water on a duck's back. He had a legion of enemies, and the hate and malice of the greatest statesmen and orators of England, and yet he survived them all, and at eighty-six could look back on his long life as on a landscape, the plains of which were bathed in the sunshine of his genius. The destiny which his labours foreshadowed was not to be in his day. But it came at last:

> "To scatter plenty o'er a smiling land
> And read their history in a nation's eyes."

For Sir Charles Lawson's book we have only words of unqualified approbation. The research, the industry, and the disposition of the materials are beyond all praise. The portraits, embracing every individual in any way associated with Hastings, are exquisitely finished, and the great trial scene a *chef d'œuvre*, while the caricatures will be new to most people. Altogether a most delightful book to read, to study, and to linger over, and of which the author may well be proud.

(7.) WAS NELSON IN BOMBAY?

THE letter which follows finally settles the above question. The present writer, to whom it is addressed, has no property in it. It belongs to the nation—a kind of treasure-trove to be returned to the original owner thereof—and the public are now put in possession of it:—

"Record Office, London, September 8th, 1897.

"Sir,—With reference to your letter of August 18th on the subject of the transfer of Nelson from H.M.S. *Seahorse* to H.M.S. *Dolphin*, which has been referred by the Admiralty to this Department, I am directed to state that it appears from the books of H.M.S. *Seahorse* that this transfer took place on March 15th, 1776, and at this date the *Seahorse* was at Bombay.—I am, Sir, your obedient servant,

R. A. ROBERTS, Pro. Secy."

Little is needed at the present day to attract the attention of the reader towards anything concerning Nelson. His fame is now greater than it ever was before, inasmuch as both writers and readers have multiplied tenfold. From his birth to his death, almost everything connected with the man has been made the subject of discussion. One portion of his life has, by the common consent of his biographers, been avoided, as there was almost nothing known about it. I mean the details of his Indian career. *Ex nihilo nihil fit.*

Curious, is it not, that his Arctic experience in 1773 should present us with his adventures with the bear and walrus, while, in his memoirs, there is not one word on the wild beasts of India? There are none of his letters from India to which we can refer. Nor is there extant a single conversation of his in after years bearing upon the subject, except the adamantine statement: "I visited every port in India, from Bengal to Bussorah." The Admiralty has now made it clear that Bombay was one of those ports. The writers of *Nelson's Life* are not to blame. You cannot make bricks without straw. Nelson was then between fifteen and seventeen (1774–76)—"alike unknowing and unknown." During a considerable portion of this time he was in very bad health, and, no doubt, he would try to forget the disagreeables of his early days in India, and wipe them out of the tablets of his remembrance. People who escape with a whole skin from battle, plague, shipwreck, or from sudden death, are not given to prate much about it. An Indian fever is a dismal recollection, a kind of nightmare which may fairly account for Nelson's reticence.

My own personal connection with the subject has not been slight. It had been the dream of my life to bring Nelson to Bombay, and with Clive and Wellington complete the triumvirate—"the three mighty men" who here laid the foundation of their greatness, and gave an imperishable lustre to the annals of our City. A frantic endeavour, which I made many years ago, was received with a smile of incredulity, when Mr. (now Sir James) Campbell kindly lent me a book named *Travels in Asia and Africa*, by Abraham Parsons, 1808. I there read the following paragraph under date May 12th, 1775, Bushire:—"There arrived and anchored in the road his Majesty's ship *Seahorse*, Captain George Farmer, from Bombay, but last from Muscat." And after reading that passage, as a Scotsman would say, I was "as sure as death" that Nelson was then and there abroad that ship, and that he also had spent a considerable portion of his time in Bombay waters.

The *Seahorse* belonged to Sir Edward Hughes' squadron, which Parsons notices was at anchor in Bombay harbour on February 18th, 1776, and as Nelson was sick, he was transferred from the *Seahorse* to the *Dolphin*, homeward bound. About that time additional strength was given to this speculation. Nor did my faith waver in the years that followed, though the man in the street would occasionally ask me, " Any word of Nelson ? " And there was no reply, but a disposition to curse the *Seahorse* and wish her at the bottom of the sea, and all that belonged to her, as if she had been an ogre of the *Arabian Nights*. At this stage an ingenious friend* said to me, " Why don't you write to Sir Evan MacGregor, K.C.B., Secretary to the Admiralty ? " I did so. The reply which I have given above came by return of post. Thanks is a poor word to Sir Evan, for he will give, I am sure, crores of happiness to every European mortal—man and woman—living in these Eastern parts. Everybody will rejoice in the discovery, as of a new planet added to our firmament. The mice and the bookworms, human and entomological, have been more merciful to the " log " of the *Seahorse* in the Record Office than the white ants of Bombay. The *Seahorse* has perished, but her " log " remains for ever, like the fame and name it enshrines. It is idle to say that this is a valuable letter. It is the first authentic statement that Nelson was in Bombay. Where he came first in sight of India we know not; but we now know where he saw it for the last time.

We may take it for granted that Nelson was in the *Seahorse* during her voyage to the Persian Gulf, and that he was in Bombay both before and after it. Parsons' book becomes Nelson's as far as this voyage is concerned, for he was a passenger from Bushire to Bombay, and unwittingly held the pen which describes what Nelson may have seen and experienced in this eventful voyage. " Bengal to Bussorah "—one can see even in the rotation of Nelson's words the course of his progress; and the sickness, which marred and ended Nelson's Indian

---

* Professor Macmillan, now (1899) Principal of the Elphinstone College.

career, is fully narrated by this most veracious chronicler. Nelson was at Bussorah in the *Seahorse*, or on his own hook. The English agent had retired from Bussorah, and was then at Bushire, and Captain Farmer offered to go to Bussorah to protect English interests. From Parsons' journal it appears, however, that the *Seahorse* remained at anchor in Bushire roads for two months and three days. The Gulf and the Shatt-el-Arab (Tigris and Euphrates united) were full of craft going and coming. The voyage thither took about five days. So we may be sure (there is no doubt about it) that in May or June, 1775, Nelson was on the outskirts of Bussorah. What he saw there we gather from Parsons. It was then beleaguered by 50,000 Persians, and the Turks, maugre visions of famine, were holding out stoutly. The Bussorah which Nelson saw was the ghost of its former self, for in 1773 the plague had devoured 200,000 of its 300,000 inhabitants. Like a conflagration, it burned up everything consumable, and after six months there was not a single case. It came with appalling suddenness, and left, as this visitation of God often does, like a flash of lightning, leaving huge gaps in every family, while many families were totally extinguished. In the Bombay of 1897 we have had our share of plague, but it would appear we have been mercifully dealt with hitherto, when compared with this mighty disaster of 1773.

This great plague, named by the Arabs "Wubba-el-Kebeer," is still a huge landmark in traditional history to all the dwellers in Mesopotamia—not "a blessed word," you may be sure, in those days and in that region of the earth. There is a Scots proverb, "The Scots aye reckon frae an ill hour." Witness Flodden and Culloden. In like manner, with Jew and Arab, all local chronology dates every event from some year either before or after the "Wubba-el-Kebeer." This is the pivot on which all local history has revolved for 120 years.

A graphic incident belongs to this period. A merchant of Bussorah noticed with dismay that letters ceased to come from Bagdad. He despatched a *kossid*, who did not return. Another followed, and he likewise did not return. Bagdad might have been swallowed up, who could tell? Again, a third time, a man who had a charmed life, and had braved death in every form, set out on camel back. He returned—he said he would do so.

Man and camel sank to the earth as he reached the merchant's gate, and exclaimed with a voice barely audible, "God is great." His story was soon told. It was about sunrise on a Friday that he reached the great gates. Everything was as silent as death. No janissary sentry or *boab*, not one call to prayer of Allah by muezzin, from Bagdad's hundred minarets, woke an echo from tomb or caravanserai. He strode blindly forward through deserted streets. Near a cemetery he saw some living skeletons, hanging on life by their eyebrows, and jackals preying on the dead. This was all he saw in Bagdad.

It will be seen that Western India and the shores of the Persian Gulf, about the time of Nelson's arrival, were in a state of extreme agitation. Indeed, on April 4th, 1775, Parsons received news of the siege and capture of Thana, and the death of Mr. Watson, the Company's Superintendent of Marine. There was not much to see from Bushire roads, except the great barrier of rock called the Ladder, or Devil's Staircase, which divides Persia on this side from the outside world. The heat was considerable, 98° in the captain's cabin, which the sun could not penetrate. In sailing down the Gulf, Parsons, and no doubt Nelson, saw on the same day and at the same time Ormuz, Keshim, and Gombroon. If Nelson knew that Baffin, whose name is inscribed on the Arctic circle, was buried in Keshim, it must have had a melancholy interest for him. He would remember his own experience only two years before, when the *Racchorse* was embedded in thick ribs of ice. Baffin was killed at the siege of Ormuz in 1622.

There can scarcely be a doubt but that Nelson's sickness originated in the Persian Gulf. It may have begun in the filthy surroundings of Bussorah, but Muscat bowled him over. When Nelson joined the Navy, his biographer Southey says, "His countenance was florid, and his appearance rather stout and athletic, but when he had been about eighteen months in India (and this exactly tallies with his service in the Persian Gulf), he felt the effects of that climate, so perilous to European constitutions. The disease baffled all powers of medicine; he was reduced almost to a skeleton; the use of his limbs was for some time entirely lost, and the only hope that remained was from a voyage home. Accordingly he was brought home by Captain Pigot, in the *Dolphin*, and, had it not been for the attention and careful kindness of that officer, Nelson would never have lived to reach his native shores."

The following description of the condition of the men on board the *Seahorse*, written by Parsons at Muscat, in August, 1775, gives a graphic account of Nelson's sickly surroundings during the voyage from Muscat to Bombay, in August, 1775:—

"The water we took in at Bushire was brackish, and produced fluxes among our crews, and in conjunction with the excessive heat in coming down the Gulf, so debilitated our men, that it was common to have eight, ten, and some days twelve men, fall down on the deck through excessive weakness. At length the number on the sick list increased to upwards of fifty on board the *Seahorse*, and the remainder were so very weak that, if any hard duty had been required, they would not have been able to have performed it. Few escaped the disaster, *either officer or private man;* happily it did not last long, as each individual, by rest, recovered in three or four days, whilst others in their turn felt the same effects of the excessive heat, which was greatly increased by the continuance of a south wind during the greatest part of the time. Captain Farmer and myself had recourse to sleeping on the bare deck, in the great cabin near the windows, which were always open, it being impossible to suffer a sheet to be suspended between. The captain and nineteen men out of near one hundred and seventy escaped it. Not a man died of those who were attacked. Thermometer in Muscat in the shade 112°."

My belief is that Nelson arrived in Bombay on August 17th, 1775, somewhat of a wreck, and that he did not return to his normal health until he bade adieu to the *Seahorse* in our harbour on March 15th, 1776.

The dreary seven months would be relieved for three weeks, if the *Seahorse* was relegated to convoy a fleet of merchantmen to Surat or Mangalore, to protect them from pirates and the enemies of England. We can even fancy Nelson in church, for he was a religious man. A special portion was reserved for naval men in St. Thomas's. And now solemnised by sickness, and by memories of Burnham Thorpe, for he was a clergyman's son, we can see him hirpling up the passage to the altar, either with or without support, and can hear him at the end of the service uttering *amen* three times in succession, as he did in his solemn invocation before Trafalgar. Like Wycliffe's "Be—it done. Be it done." He will bait man and horse next door at the Parsonage, to which there is a broad arch and stabling, and, within, a cup for the sick lad, and then wobble his way to the Customs bunder, where a jetty boat awaits him.

I do not look for Nelson seeing much of Bombay during this period of enforced idleness; but in April or March, 1775, ere the *Seahorse* started as convoy on her mission to Bushire, he and Troubridge, flushed with health and the buoyancy of youth, would do everything and dare everything. Elephanta and its big beast, a climb up Karanja, with a collation of oysters from the Carnegie of that ilk, who then held sway, would be merely a morning's relaxation. A horse is a vain thing for safety. They thought not so. And now for Mahim. Hurrah!

> "My eyes! how she did pitch
> And wouldn't keep her own to go in no line,
> Though I kept bowsing, bowsing at her bowline,
> But always making lee-way to the ditch
> And yaw'd her head about all sorts of ways.
> The devil sink the craft!
> And wasn't she tremendous slack in stays!"

Helter-skelter through Bazaar Gate, past Dongry, scattering natives, dogs and ducks right and left, on and on to Mahim Woods, where, descrying a Punch House, they shorten sail and at length cast anchor. Some one reads a notice on the gateway "By the Laws of England, the tavern keeper may detain the person of a guest, who eats, or the horse which eats, till payment is made of what they have had. There is an ordinary here every day, beef, mutton, fowls, ducks, fish and greens in season at Re. 1, each person to be allowed one beaker of Punch, and as much country beer as they (*sic*) can drink."

A halloo! And this is the place for us!

And so, wild with excitement, for now other middies have joined them, they eat, drink and tell stories, sing, laugh and drink healths—the "skeely skipper" is not forgotten—ending with "old folks at home," until Morpheus tempts them with a siesta. A great day for India—and as they hand over their passes to the adjutant at Church Gate, after a rollicking ride, they vow they never had such a glorious time of it.

"So off I goes and leaves the inn astarn!"

Nelson must have seen everything in and about Bombay worthy of observation. I can see him in many devious ways and places, the Pinjrapole, the Gruel House, the Burning Ghaut, the Towers of Silence, the Rope Walk and the big Dock, nothing like them out of England. I can see him under the old tamarind tree which still abuts on the Cathedral footpath, and which then to a midday crowd, like wisdom crying in the streets, resounded to the stentorian voice of the auctioneer. I can see him in the new burying-ground of Sonapore, still scanty of graves, but soon enough to be supplied with abundance of tomb and cenotaph. He may have looked at the Naval Department of the Colaba Convalescent Hospital, but I am not aware that he was ever an inmate of it.

We come now to that passage in his life which is without date or locality, when in the blackness of despair he would have thrown himself overboard, had not a good angel arrested him and pointed the way to heaven. Southey, and he himself, place it in the period of his great Indian sickness.

"I felt impressed," said he, "with a feeling that I should never rise in my profession. My mind was staggered with a view of the difficulties I had to surmount, and the little interest I possessed. I could discover no means of reaching the object of my ambition. After a long and gloomy reverie, in which I almost wished myself overboard, a sudden glow of patriotism was kindled within me, and presented my king and country as my patron."

"Well, then," I exclaimed, "I will be a hero, and, confiding in Providence, I will brave every danger."

He often said that at that moment a radiant orb was suspended before him, which urged him onward to renown. That this great revulsion from despair to ecstasy took place on board the *Seahorse* as she lay in Bombay harbour I have not the slightest doubt. The sickness, developed at Muscat, made him its prey for months together, and it was little short of a miracle that his bones did not hansel the new burying-ground of Sonapore.

We now come to the last scene of all which ends this strange, eventful history. Cæsar and his fortunes are to be carried in the *Seahorse* no more.

Behold then Nelson (*ætat.* 17) on the deck of the *Dolphin*, on March 15th, 1776, taking his last view of India. Muscat you have seen has done its work, and he hauls himself, or is hauled up the companion from his bunk on deck, supported by a crutch or friendly arm, for he has lost the use of his limbs. He turns his bleary eyes harbourwise, and drinks in every salient point. There he stands like Ajax, praying for light. Every object is cast upon his vision in dim perspective. The Lighthouse on Old Woman's Island; the Moormen's Tombs; the great palm trees on the Brab Bastion of the Castle; Mark House, white against the sky; Belvedere, which once sheltered the beautiful and luckless Eliza; Gibbet Island, where, before or after this, the Malay murderers of his brother (?) were hung in chains.*

The curtain drops on that amphitheatre of hills so familiar to us all, Karnala, Karanja, Bowmelang, Queen of the Mahratta's Throne, Matheran, and. all sink for him for ever into oblivion.

"A thousand suns shall shine on thee,
A thousand moons will quiver,
But not by thee my steps shall be
For ever and for ever."

He may have seen Commodore Watson, in his splendid uniform as Superintendent of the Bombay Marine, and, it is said he applied for that office "once on a time" when it was vacant. But this is a minor matter. What I wish to impress on the reader is that Nelson when in India was not always a cripple, that his mind was not a perfect blank, that he was not always sleeping when his eyes were shut.

On that memorable day, when it was decided whether the French or the English should be masters of India—it was

* The story is in the *Life of Sir James Mackintosh.* No brother of Nelson's was murdered. See *Nineteenth Century*, Nov. 1897. It may have been a relative.

twenty-three years after this—he knew three things, the germs of which he may have caught up during his Indian apprenticeship, which were likely to occur in the event of his defeat:—

1. That the Masters of the Gulf of Suez could easily run down an expedition to India.

2. That the rich province of Guzerat would afford by reason of food and forage, an ample basis for military operations, and

3. That Bombay would be the first object of attack.

As soon as the Battle of the Nile was decided, though he thought at the time his skull was fractured, almost the first thing he did was to write a letter to the Governor of Bombay.

But amid his sufferings and exertions, Nelson could not yet think of all the consequences of his victory; and that no advantage from it might be lost, he despatched an officer overland to India with letters to the Governor of Bombay, informing him of the arrival of the French in Egypt, the total destruction of their Fleet, and the consequent preservation of India from any attempt against it on the part of this formidable armament. "He knew that Bombay," he said, "was their first object if they could get there, and he trusted that Almighty God would overthrow in Egypt these pests of the human race. Bonaparte had never had to contend with an English officer, and he would endeavour to make him respect us." This despatch he sent on his own responsibility, with letters of credit on the East India Company, addressed to the British Consuls, Vice-Consuls and merchants on the route. "If he had done wrong," he wrote, "he hoped the bills would be paid, and he would repay the Company, for, as an Englishman, he should be proud that it had been in his power to put our settlements on their guard."

"The information which by this means reached India was of great importance. Orders had just been received for defensive preparations on a scale proportionate to the apprehended danger, and the extraordinary expenses which otherwise would have been increased were thus prevented."—Southey's *Life of Nelson.*

(8.) A FORGOTTEN TRIAL.

I WROTE some ten years ago of Robert Henshaw that very little was known about him. The Advocates' Library in Edinburgh has now enabled me to modify or explain away this statement.* His trial in 1805 was a big event, but has now descended to complete oblivion. In *Mackintosh's Life* (2nd Edn., 1836) it is alluded to. No names are given. Considering the effluxion of time, however, and as all the parties concerned and their immediate descendants have disappeared from the face of the earth, there can be no reason now for withholding its details from the public. It was the considerations which were painfully forced upon Sir James Mackintosh in the course of this trial which turned his attention to the nature and constitution of the Courts of India, and induced him, in 1807, to state his views, the justice of many of which has been recognised by their final adoption, more particularly in the establishment of our own High Court in 1824, which gives to the trial an importance far above any that it might otherwise possess.

The trial took place on November 5th, 6th, 7th and 8th, 1805, and the circumstances which led up to it were these. There had been a partial failure of the rains in 1802 and a total failure in 1803. As soon as the gravity of the situation was realised the Bombay Government prohibited the export of grain. They also imported rice to the value of £600,000, and encouraged the merchants to import £400,000 more. It was estimated that this action saved the lives of 100,000 people. The awful pictures of the famine were never effaced from the memories of those who saw them. Robert Henshaw, who had the complete confidence of Government and the public, was chosen to superintend, as Customs Master, the whole business of food supplies, and it was for the issuing of "permits" for a consideration, and the clandestine export of grain, that he was tried before a Grand Jury in the Recorder's Court of Bombay, Sir James Mackintosh being then Recorder. The prosecuting counsel had never before experienced such a fatiguing case—"an infinity of anxiety

* *Trial of Robert Henshaw at Bombay*, 1805: Edin. 1807.

and fatigue greater, I will venture to say, than has ever fallen to the lot of any counsel in any country."

In this great emergency Robert Henshaw held, as Customs Master, the most lucrative office next to the Governorship, for his legitimate earnings were over Rs. 6,000 a month, besides a percentage on grain, which yielded him a lump sum of about a lakh of rupees. Whoever needed any increase to his income, it was not Henshaw. The vulgar mind would think that he was "rich beyond the dreams of avarice." So thought the outside public as they saw him pass in a cloud of glory in his alderman's purple palanquin, wielding the export and import trade of Bombay, and holding the destiny of her merchants in the hollow of his hand. Little knows the outside public. Henshaw's affairs were embarrassed, and early in 1804, eighteen months before this trial, he had consulted Charles Forbes about them. How his embarrassment came about it is needless to inquire. A man in a position like his is bound to spend a great deal of money, though he be neither ostentatious, extravagant, nor careless of his affairs. The reader does not require to be told that if any or all of these had existed the Public Prosecutor would have made the most of it, even if he had been engaged in gambling speculations, the hell-fire that has consumed so many. But the reader requires to be told that he (Henshaw), "a worthy liberal man," found himself in a Bombay the like of which had never been seen before and has never been seen since. In 1804, out of a population of 150,000 in the island of Bombay, 25,834 bodies were burnt or buried, and I ask any one who is an adept in the arithmetic of mortuary returns if it is possible to estimate the amount of misery and woe expressed by this fact. It is beyond all computation. That he, the most popular man of his time, in common parlance "everybody's body and worst friend to himself," should have sauntered unconcerned amid these scenes of disease and death, not screened off by the bulwarks and entrenchments of modern civilisation, until he crossed the boundary line which divides the just from the generous, is out of the question. Bombay was then an open sepulchre, into which descended Henshaw's money and, alas! his reputation. And I have nothing but pity and commiseration for the man; indignation is out of the dictionary.

Though all tradition and written record of these events have passed away, you may still, after the lapse of ninety years, read on a lofty structure abutting on what used to be Bombay Green, the name of "Henshaw's Buildings."

By throwing aside the dining tables of the Great Western Hotel, you may easily, in imagination, with a very little upholstery reconstruct the bench, the bar, and the jury box. The Recorder's Court in its outside aspect, as you may see in *Qui Hi* (1816), was very much the same building as you see it now. You have only to look at the portrait of Sir James Mackintosh, taken two years before, when he was thirty-eight, by Sir Thomas Lawrence, for an exact presentment of the Recorder. James Morley (Morley Hall, Colaba), the Sheriff, a barrister of great weight, sits on the Judge's left. I presume the Mayor and Aldermen did not, for obvious reasons, exercise their privilege of sitting beside the Judge on this melancholy occasion. The Company's Solicitor and Counsel for the Crown (whom we now call Advocate-General) was Stewart Moncrief Threipland, says Mackintosh after the trial, "flourishing here as he deserves." His name first appears as a barrister in Bombay in 1802. The names of the jurymen are given below.* All the jurors wear wigs, are in their best blue coats with brass buttons and knee-breeches, a fine costume which puts to shame the feeble and flabby trousers of these degenerate days, which knickerbockers are doing something to redeem. The place is stuffy enough. There will be loud complaints about it after this *cause célèbre*. Our friend Duncan Cameron, of the Bombay Tavern, whose stumpy figure appears in *The Master of Qui Hi*, does all he can to assuage the thirst of the impatient jurors.

Looking around I can see Luke Ashburner, the Foreman,

* Special Jurymen :—Luke Ashburner, Esq., Foreman; John Elphinstone, Accountant-General; Captain Samuel Landon, City of London, East Indiaman; Thomas White, Esq., Hon. Co.'s Civil Service; John Leckie, Esq., Agent for Victualling His Majesty's Squadron; Thomas Malcolm, Esq., Agent for Victualling His Majesty's Squadron; William Kidd, Esq., 1st Officer, City of London; Mr. James Borthwick, Assistant Accountant-General's Office; Mr. Roger Francis Hereford, Watchmaker; Mr. William Denniston, Assistant, His Majesty's Naval Storekeeper: Captain William Webster, Merchant Service; Mr. James Benjamin Wallace, Clerk in Accountant-General's Office.

and the other members of the Grand Jury craning their necks, when Threipland, in a strong Scotch accent, drags from some reluctant witness the story of a string of pearls which was a long time destined to adorn the neck of Lady Mackintosh, and, as morsel after morsel is elicited (for the more unwilling the witness is to continue the evidence the more desirous are they to hear), Abbaji turns pale and then green, and divulges the whole story. They have heard whispers of this before, but the name of Mrs. Nisbet (Nisbet Lane and Mrs. Nisbet's Chapel), the wealthy widow, is mentioned as a friend of the Judge and a suitable go-between to present the necklace to his Lordship. It raises something like a suppressed titter, and gives zest to the entertainment, by co-mingling the element of the social with the dry-as-dust of the law. Sir James at this stage falls back in his chair with a heavy sigh, and the Royal Arms, in gold and scarlet, gleam overhead. Where there is standing room I wot there is no lack of visitors. Charles Forbes, William Erskine the calm, and Richards the talkative, General Waddington also, with his lovely daughter, who became Mrs. Hough, you may easily fancy looking in.

The prisoner at the bar was in deep mourning when he received his sentence, so runs the record. By a strange irony of fate, Robert Henshaw had just reached the culminating point of a most successful career. On or about March 13th, 1804, he, an Alderman of the city, who had served the Company since 1704, was chosen chairman of the great meeting in honour of Arthur Wellesley. But more than this, as we learn from a friend (Sir John Jardine) to whom we are much indebted for the fact, on April 16th of the same year, 1804, he had held a meeting at his own office, and laid a scheme before it, which was adopted, for the Bombay Civil Fund. An annual dinner was proposed, and Mr. Warden suggested that another of the Trustees should write a song for the occasion. Another song will be sung before the year is out. Moreover, in this very business of the famine, the cause of all his present mischief (bad enough in all conscience), it was he who, so early as September 10th, 1803, first prognosticated "an inevitable famine." Not long thereafter one hundred corpses were found lying, some of them at their own doors, in the Khandalla villages on the Ghauts. Verily, the famine was sore in the land.

It was 1 o'clock on the morning of November 7th, when Mackintosh—so late were the hours—descended the stairs of the Court and again breathed the open air. He was just about setting foot on his dennet, when his eye caught a glimpse of something which loomed on the opposite side of the street, a tall figure with its back to the Dockyard, in Oriental costume, black like a silhouette with its clean-cut edges against the sky, an eye also gleaming in the dark like that of a wild beast or some avenging fury, and the figure cursed the Court and Dewan and all belonging to it with a fierce and a bitter curse.

In view of this apparition, or whatever it was, Mackintosh, regarding his life, could only order his coachman to drive on. He passed Government House, then the abode of Jonathan Duncan *; it was as silent as death. A single *buttee* gave a flickering light where that "ancient" slept the sleep of the just. The theatre was closed. Not so the Bombay Tavern, with its twinkling lights and sounds of uproarious mirth from Bobbery Hunt, or something of that kind. He passed the tamarind tree,† which you may still see, under which for generations dead men's effects and property of all kinds were sold by auction. The stench was awful from the Bombay Green—you might have cut it with a knife. Musk rats ran squeaking up the gulleys, and the owls screeched from the gloomy precincts of the Parsonage.

On the Green he could dimly observe the white rafters of a rendezvous for the ladies, which had been hastily run up in view of a hostile visit of the combined fleet. He then emerged from Church Gate Street, where you may be sure the sentries were all alive, and even the adjutant awake and saw that the gates were opened and closed behind the judge, making to the carriage a profound obeisance as it rumbled across the draw-bridge. Far and wide over the esplanade, like a crimson curtain, a lurid glare overspread the hemisphere, filling the

* Now the Imperial Bank of Persia.

† On the footpath round the Cathedral. Mr. (now Sir) James M. Campbell, Collector of Bombay, has kindly pointed it out to me.

lungs with acrid smoke, and the sputtering sparks and "fiery spume" from the sandalwood shot high into the air, showed indubitably that they were from burning bodies on Back Bay and in the region of Sonapore. Famine feeds the fire. For there is no want of bodies nowadays. Even Padre Burrows'* Godown (the burying-ground) claims its uncomplaining tenants by the score. Speeding on his course he passed the Pawan Chakki, of gruesome duel memories; passed the Windmill also, the great sails of which were flapping idly in the midnight wind; passed the new jail at Omerkhadi, spick and span. Who is to be its first inmate? Ah! who can answer that question? He then passed the Dongari outskirts, whose nocturnal orgies are portrayed by Rowlandson, the caricaturist, in *Qui Hi*.† Drunken men staggering about—

> "So 'mid the gloomy mansions where they dwell
> The lost souls walk the flaming streets of hell."

It was amid such cogitations as these that he bowled over the mud heaps on Parell Road, which, though now perfectly dry, sometimes ran four feet deep with water during the monsoon; cantered up the avenue of mango trees; and, finally, more dead than alive, with broken body and exhausted mind, tumbled out at the portals of Parell.

I now come to the *pros* and *cons* of Henshaw's case, and I do not quarrel with the verdict of the jury, nor the penalty inflicted upon him. Had I been a young Scotsman in Forbes's or Bruce's counting-house in 1805, the case would have been very different, for in my country at that period any contraband traffic or infraction of Customs Law was viewed as a very lenient offence, and grave elders who "took the book" (family worship) and administered the Communion were said to be mixed up with it. But two blacks don't make a white. And then, O reader and writer, bethink thyself, this man was the head of the Customs, and placed there for its defence and protection. I do not trouble you with the Act 33 of George III., but the Customs

---

* Burrows' Lane, on the way to the cemetery at Dabul, still called by this name after Padre Burrows.—*Times of India*, May 14th, 1896.

† *The Grand Master*, or *Adventures of Qui Hi in Hindostan*. London: Thomas Tegg & Co., 1816.

Master's oath which he took on entering the office was explicit enough, "that I will not take, or receive, any present, gratuity, or advantage whatsoever; so help me God." This was the damning spot that the judge could not, should not, and did not, get over. But the jury! they kicked and jibbed, and nearly broke the traces that bound them to the judgment seat. I read that "the Court adjourned on the morning of the 7th at one o'clock, the jury were then given into the charge of a sworn officer, and retired to an apartment provided by the Sheriff for their accommodation." The jury withdrew at 9.30 A.M. the same day, and at 11.30 returned with a verdict of "Guilty, but not to the extent charged in the information." Sent back, and returned in half an hour. Returned with same verdict, and sent back a third time, having been enclosed till six o'clock of the following evening, the 8th! The jury took thirty-two mortal hours to make up their mind.

The explanation of all this is simple enough. The jury were part of the Bombay community, and were anxious to get him off; but the judge was inexorable. Henshaw did not live in Bombay and its neighbourhood for forty years and spend the money he did without ingratiating himself with the European colony. And from all that we know, up to this time he deserved his popularity. The testimonies of Members of Council and other witnesses in Court * establish the fact that he was not only a man of mark, but, as one who had known him for thirty years described him, "a worthy, good, liberal gentleman," and, indeed, the dogged reluctance of the jury to bring in a verdict of guilty conspicuously manifests the same sentiment.†

Everybody had a kindly feeling for Henshaw—pity and commiseration for one brought so low, rather than indignation. It has never been hinted that there was any Pharisaism about him, like one or two London evil-doers of later years. The real criminals were the parasites who begged, borrowed, or plundered him of his money, the wretches who ate his bread for naught,

---

* *i.e.* Lewis Corcoran, Member of Council.

† Henshaw being in Goa in 1774, was the first to announce the arrival of a Portuguese expedition for the recovery of Salsette. The Bombay Government at once took the hint and captured Salsette.—*Bombay Gazetteer History.*

and the soakers who drank his wine, and praised his liberality when it was great, and turned aloof from the fallen man when his days were dark ; or rather, I should say, that devil in human shape, Abbaji, who, like the trailing serpent, suggested the evil to Mrs. Henshaw, that by the sale of "permits" he could get rid of his indebtedness in an easy and comfortable way.

The judge thus alluded to the story of the pearl necklace. "Messrs. Humphreys and Stevens, Attorneys of the Court, have sworn that Abbaji held some communication with them on the subject of presenting a pearl necklace to myself. I hope that I shall always be able to contemplate such things with the same calm indifference and contempt which I now feel, and that I never shall be obliged or have an inclination to view them in so serious a light as to inspire indignation. I am a member, though a most humble member, of that body of magistrates among whom purity in the administration of justice has for ages ceased to be a distinction. A melancholy and memorable exception from this high praise, indeed, occurred in the instance of one of the greatest and best, except for this single stain, one of the best men that ever lived. The Lord Chancellor Bacon, with all his splendid acquirements, and habits which seem repugnant to such meanness, in which respect I may again be called upon to remind you of his fall, stooped on one occasion to this degrading vice, but having lamented over this one blot in the long succession of British judges, I may hope that the purity of the illustrious train which followed, impressed from early youth upon my mind, will not be forgotten as an object of imitation in my riper years. I may hope without presumption that—

'Some spark of their celestial fire,'

will

'Meanest of their sons inspire.'"

Mackintosh dismissed the jury to their solitude with these words, "I shall only further express my confidence that you will do justice between the public and the defendant, or, in the simple and venerable language in which our ancestors have described the duty of a juror, will well and truly try, and true deliverance make, between our Sovereign Lord the King and

Robert Henshaw, and a true verdict give according to the evidence." His summing-up lasted eight hours, and was delivered in a slightly nasal voice, with which the Court became familiar.

Mackintosh could not, and did not, forget his duty, though the whole world of social Bombay was against him. What he suffered by his action in this weighty case we are not left to guess: "I was treated in the grossest manner, there was no liberal public to support me, and no firm Government to frown down indecent reflections on the administration of justice." So he wished himself anywhere out of this Bombay world, even as Governor of Botany Bay! "I am most serious," says he. So he lost no time in placing the Ghauts between him and Bombay, and did not return to it until early in January, 1806.

The final verdict of the jury was "Guilty on the ninth count of the information," which imputes to Robert Henshaw the receipt of Rs. 17,840, or £2,230, as a gift or present from Manore Rowjee. The news spread like wildfire, and was received with universal consternation, and was that evening discussed wherever men were clustered together, in the Bombay Tavern over their madeira, at the Promenade on the Ramparts, at the Bunder Head, at the Royal Bastion and Scandal Point, in the lordly mansions of Mázagon and the lonely shanties of European dwellers in the Mahim Woods, in cadjan huts of the natives, and, above all, next day in the Customs House itself, whose Master had been tried for extortion and found guilty. Henshaw came up to receive his sentence on November 15th, one week after the trial ended. Mackintosh had no brother Judge to consult with, and society was stunned by the event. How many bottles of wine and arrack were consumed, and how many hubble-bubbles smoked I know not. This I know, that when the Judge rose the Court was crowded, and you could hear a pin fall:—"In execution of the 62nd Statute, the Court doth, therefore, order and adjudge that you, Robert Henshaw, do pay a fine of Rs. 17,840, being the amount of the presents found by the Jury to have been received by you, and that you be imprisoned till you make payment of the same."

The blow fell in the Court upon the unfortunate man amid

the friends who had accompanied him, and after a few moments of profound silence—we quote from the record—the old man in his weeds of woe uttered these touching words: "My children will have it mingled in the tale of degradation which will be told against their father," &c. He found sufficient security and was forthwith discharged. If Henshaw's trial gave us the High Court, it was a blessing in disguise, and we need not regret it; and something may be forgiven to the author of the Bombay Civil Fund. Robert Henshaw died at Bath in 1826, aged eighty-two.

> "Be kind to my remains, and oh! defend
> Against your judgment your departed friend."

(9.) SIR BARTLE FRERE.

I THINK it will be generally agreed that any time during the last twenty years, in the Western Presidency, when in company or in the society of people who were intimate with its history, the name of Sir Bartle Frere was mentioned, a very high position was assigned to him. "Next to Mountstuart Elphinstone" was the general award. With that dictum I am in thorough agreement. There is no doubt that he is head and shoulders over any other ruler in Western India of this century. The biographer has had an uncommonly hard task of it; first and foremost because he had never seen the man; and secondly, as we presume, because he had never been in India; and thirdly, because of difficulties as to the inception of a biography, on which, for obvious reasons, we do not enter. These difficulties he has been able to surmount, by the assistance of Lady Frere and her daughters and a legion of friends over the world, while all Sir Bartle's letters and diaries, minutes, manuscript and printed, literally in thousands, have been placed at his disposal, to which may be added the reminiscences of many devoted friends who had been associated with him at one time or another. For four years Mr. Martineau has worked incessantly and with a will. If any man thinks little of this biography let him go and write a better one.

It is the only life of Frere we shall likely have, and we are thankful. Portions of the book will interest some more than others. The India for Indians and the Africa for Africanders—peace be to them. Ah that Africa! Many of us could dispense with it altogether here, and wish Frere had put it on one side, like Elphinstone and Viceroyalty.

Providence threw down the gauntlet and Frere picked it up, and strode on, hero that he was, to meet the giants in the way. We follow him reluctantly. It is a new country of kraals and laagers and velts, everything is strange, the one thing that is not strange is Frere—he is the same man such as he was in Poona, in Calcutta, in Satara, in Shckarpore. To readers like us the ground is not inviting—it is like leaving the gardens of Damascus for the rough quarries of the desert and the rougher voices of angry men. To accept a destiny like this was heroism of the noblest kind, and he went through it, hard and grinding as it was, to the bitter end. He fought a good fight, he finished his course, and kept the faith. To exchange India for Africa was to exchange Hesperides for Styx and Acheron. To Frere it must have been singing the Lord's song in a strange land.

Frere arrived in Bombay during the monsoon of 1834, having come across from Mocha in a buggalow. At the Byculla banquet in 1867, Mr. Scoble gave an amusing account of his appearance on arrival. "Thanks to Lady Frere, who had converted the 'loafer'-looking individual into the Governor of Bombay."

Ten years after, in 1844, he gives the best description of the vans from Cairo to Suez, which we have seen. A Parsee told him they were "licensed to carry four *stouts* or six *thins*."

His brother William, a C. S., was here before him—a jolly man, which could scarcely be said of Sir Bartle, and very popular. Lived at the "Parsonage," and also at "Altamont." He was a good Samaritan; he took Anderson, the author of *Western India*, into his house, and saw that he was well tended and nursed until his death. Frere, as we all know, became private secretary to the Governor, Sir George Arthur, and married his daughter, who became Lady Frere.

Two secretaries—Mr. Erskine and Mr. Brown—had previously done likewise, and carried off respectively a daughter of the then Governor. It would be easier to recount what Frere could not do than what he did. That at nineteen he scolded his way through Egypt in Arabic, that he addressed in durbar the sirdars of the Dekhan in Mahratta, that he and a companion brought in one day four lions in a cart; this was in Kathiawar in 1839. That he killed a tiger with a pistol, and followed up a wounded lion on foot.

He it was who first introduced (1849–50) municipalities into India, and in 1854 postage-stamps into Sind, a couple of years before they were adopted throughout India, and commenced that system of canal irrigation so beneficial to Sind; and it was he, let it never be forgotten, who in 1857 ordered Outram to bring back to India his troops as fast as possible. In 1858 he suggested the name of Empress of India, eighteen years before the proclamation; in the same year advocated Quetta as an outpost. He it was who in 1860, at his breakfast table in Chowringhee, took a young and unknown man by the hand, who became Sir William Mackinnon, the founder of the British India Steam Navigation Company. There are three scenes in Sir Bartle Frere's life which remain indelibly stamped on the memory. The first was the durbar in the town hall of Bombay (1866), where occurs a vacant space. The Imaum of Muscat and his turbaned followers strode in sandalled majesty towards the daïs, where Frere stood, pale and erect, to receive them. The second was giving his arm to Mrs. Hough, one of the ancients of the earth, and leading the way with her to the drawing-room at Parell; and the third was when he drove in august procession along Rampart Row with the heir to the throne. This was in 1875, when his star was in the ascendant and shone out in unclouded brilliancy. There was no more talk then of Parell as the Land of Promise, no more stories of washing hands with invisible soap.

The portion of the book devoted to the Prince of Wales's visit to India we consider very meagre, and will disappoint all who took part in the grand ceremonies of the Royal progress. This was the culmination of Sir Bartle's career, and deserved a fuller narration.

Sind is well done, and perhaps the most satisfactory portion of the biography. Perhaps also to Frere himself these ten years were the most pleasing and agreeable part of his life. He was there unhampered by trammels, and able to carry out the schemes he originated for the benefit of the great Province. Sind liked him and he liked Sind.

It would be a fine subject for a picture. Frere and Charles Napier in that old bungalow at Clifton we knew so well, where there was no sound but that of the waves of the Indian Ocean as they dashed eternally on the beach. Some native, when he saw the tower of Karachi Church slowly rising as it was being built, said to Frere, "The English mean to stop here." So we have, and the Khan of Kelat no longer eats uncooked cauliflower and unboiled peas.

There are some excellent tit-bits here and there. Thus after Lawrence's speech at Glasgow, recommending teaching Christianity in Government Schools, Canning writes, November 1st, 1860, "Really Sir John Lawrence ought to be shut up and Edwards have his head shaved. The latter is exactly what Mahomet would have been if born at Clapham instead of Mecca." And this from Sir George Clark, May 17th, 1860, "Government writers in the *Friend of India* have already cost us forty millions sterling."

He was much against Masterly Inactivity, a phrase we think coined by Sir James Mackintosh, but much used after the *Edinburgh Review* article in 1867.

And this from Dr. Hewlett expresses what was at the time the feeling of the majority :—

"Many hopes are expressed, many prayers are uttered, that Sir Bartle Frere may be Governor-General yet. Truly that would be a happy day for India."

For the young soldier and civilian he looked for other things than passing examinations merely. "It is really of more consequence to the natives that he should be good in the cricket field and on horseback, popular with servants and the poor, and the champion of bullied fags, that he should have a mother who taught him to say his prayers, and sisters who helped her to give him reverence for womankind and respect for weakness, than that he should be first to take a double-first at Oxford."—*Letter to Lord Goderich*, 1858.

"Why talk of irrigation? If you had seen men's bones as

I have, lying unburied by the roadside, and on entering a village had found it untenanted by a living person, you would understand why."

Here is a pregnant sentence. Something of the same kind exists in Orme, and it is a declaration that ought never to be forgotten:—"Success is one of the native tests of right, and as long as we are visibly able to command them they will obey us, and no longer"; or again, "The wisdom of such men as Mountstuart Elphinstone is never obsolete."

Here he quotes as against recluses like Sir William Macnaghten:—"I often think that a few dozen of champagne might have averted the Kabul disaster."

"A puppy dog in Bond Street or Fleet Street; it is bigger and stronger than any elephant in Africa." This in reference to people who framed indictments against him. And once for all, on September 22nd, 1879, in letters of fire:—"But unless my countrymen are much changed, they will some day do me justice. I shall not leave a name to be permanently dishonoured." So say we all of us. His wish has been fulfilled. His statue in Bombay and on the banks of the Thames and the banks of the Indus have done honour to the illustrious dead. The men for whom Frere had an unbounded admiration, and to whose confidence he was admitted, were all men of the most distinguished courage, masterful if you will—but of laconic character. We have only Sir Charles Napier, Outram, Jacob and Dighton Probyn. These men were faithful unto death.

For a man who has never been in India, Mr. Martineau falls into few, if any, errors. He says: "To take a walk with exercise and refreshment, which under ordinary circumstances is an Englishman's unfailing resource, is practically impossible in India." The Gauls laughed at the Roman soldiers and thought they were mad, walking up and down. And in India all the year round, with few exceptions, one may take a morning's walk and nobody laughs—even from Clifton to Karachi.

The book is very interesting, specially to those of us who have been some time in Western India, and names start up in quick succession—resurrection of the dead, and literally of the living too—Arthur Crawford, Dr. Hewlett, J. M. Maclean, Sir James Ferguson, Miss Mary Carpenter, Miss Prescott, and many others. One name is conspicuous by its absence. Dr. Wilson was one of Bartle Frere's dearest and oldest friends, for when he arrived in the country he carried a letter of introduction to him. Each esteemed the other. The Prince of Wales delegated to Frere the melancholy duty of conveying his deepest sympathy to the dying man. And as Dr. Wilson had human nature in him, it pleased him—this royal act. In 1869 Sir Bartle Frere sent to the present writer a letter, which I cannot lay my hands on, in which he stated his unstinted admiration of the man, and of the work which this great missionary had carried on for a period of forty years in Western India, and I am sure I am right when I say that he placed him the highest he had ever known of any man in his own special vocation.

Here are two portraits of Frere at different periods: 1851, *ætat.* 36 :—

He was then in full physical vigour. Six feet in height he was strong and active, but slender and well proportioned. His face, youthful looking for his age, was thin, with clearly cut regular features, aquiline nose, and light brown hair. A moustache shaded his mouth, which was full of expression. His eyes were hazel, deeply set under dark eyebrows, and very keen and steadfast in their gaze. He had a clear, soft voice, and spoke slowly and deliberately. But the great charm of his presence lay in the expression of his open countenance and sweet and ready smile, in the frank and dignified simplicity, and the invariable kindness and courtesy of his manner, in his absolute self-forgetfulness and ready sympathy.

1879. He was now in his sixty-fourth year. Age had whitened his hair, but it had as yet little enfeebled him, and it had dimmed none of the brightness of his keen steadfast eye, weakened nothing of the expression of intelligence, firm will, and calm, genial frankness written in his countenance. His face though worn was comparatively little changed, but years of ceaseless mental strain, and especially the wearing anxiety of the last eighteen months, had cast over the delicately-cut features a still greater refinement and a graver expression.

Personally Elphinstone and Frere were not unlike, and except Frere's moustache and some minor features, the pen-and-ink portraits of our author which we give are good for either. Both were tall and neither of them robust, both were fond of warriors "and the stern joy which warriors feel in foemen worthy of their steel." Both were fond of the natives, promoters of education, friends of missions, and both were men of deep and unostentatious piety. Both were ardent sportsmen, both were men of gentle birth and cultured ease, and both lived and died for India.

"To him high office was never a source of wealth," is said of Frere. The words are remarkable. Buist delineates Elphinstone as follows :—"When excited, his whole countenance lighted up with a glow of warmth, his bright eye gleamed out, and his thin lips, becoming compressed, showed, though placid, he was far from inanimate, though usually tranquil how easily he could be awakened into energy and fire," which will do for Frere, who beneath a velvet glove sometimes discovered a. hand of steel. Hyperion curls, the reader may leave with Elphinstone.

"Look here upon this picture, and on this;
The counterfeit presentment of two brothers,
See what a grace was sealed on this brow;
Hyperion's curls; the front of Jove himself;
An eye like Mars to threaten and command;
A station like the herald Mercury,
Now lighted on a heaven-kissing hill;
A combination and a form indeed,
Where every god did seem to set his seal
To give the world assurance of a man."

Regarding the old Bank of Bombay and Frere's connection therewith, it becomes me to speak with bated breath. We were all sinners in those days, and let him that is without sin cast the first stone. "Evil be thou my good," we all say now, as we cast our eyes over the palatial buildings, constructed on what was once called Frere Town Why was the name given up, which we would not have had without the Bombay mania? Let the earth lie light on Frere. If men with the most brilliant gifts and the highest mercantile education went astray to doom, surely Frere, the Civilian, may be let alone. He at all events did not touch the unclean thing, tarnish his hands with filthy lucre, or barter away his responsibilities for promotion-money. Did he delay informing Sir John Lawrence of the condition of the Bank? A general belief. What then? Frere was altogether outside the magic circle, knew only such things as were told to him, until the storm came and the winds blew, and beat upon the house and it fell, and great was the fall thereof.

There is a story, and we believe that W. W. Cargill was the first man to inform Sir John Lawrence of the hopeless condition of the Bombay Bank. It was at Simla Sir John inquired during dinner "How is the Bombay Bank?" Cargill shook his head. After dinner he told him all. Had the Oracle spoken months before it would have been all the same Nothing could have saved the bank but a continuance of the American War, and we may be thankful that it did not continue, or we would now be living under an oligarchy of plutocrats. Poor Cargill, with all his wisdom, died in Paris last year. Strange, isn't it, that he whose name appears as Interim Secretary in an advertisement of the bank's inception in 1839 should be fluttering like the stormy petrel over the doomed ship as she was going to pieces in the year 1865?

Frere, however tardy he may have been in gauging the crisis and despatching minutes thereon to his superiors, held out a beacon light on October 22nd, 1864, of "Breakers ahead," and this, be it remembered, months before it was realised by even a few. Sir Charles Wood as late as February 17th, 1865, continuing to write:—"In regard to all the schemes for investing your plethora of capital, there is nothing for it but to let them have their swing." *Let them have their swing.* This shows the little Frere had to do in the making of the mania.

In the margin of the Blue-Book where MacLeod Innes spoke of "supineness and inaction," are written these words in Frere's handwriting in pencil:—"I only know that when the bank was first in trouble the Governor had scarce a white hair in his head, and that when he left Bombay he had few brown ones." People at the time, and since, wonder that Bombay was so fatuous. But they forget that the men of Bombay in 1864–65 were not amenable to reason. They thought that a new era had dawned upon the world. Did not the Chairman of the Bank at its annual meeting say that "Banking was only in its infancy!" As if the lessons of political economy and financial experience were of no account, and were all to make way and disappear before the new order of things.*

As for Premchund, he is held in this book to have caused much of the mischief. There is this to be said, that he was wanting in the training and education of his European *confrères*. To whom much is given, of him much shall be required. In the short time he was in possession of money, say two and a half years, he gave away thirty lakhs for benevolent purposes. MacLeod Innes, one of the Royal Commission, mentioned on leaving the country that he was not so black as he was painted.

(10.) THE MEN OF BOMBAY IN 1837.

THE population of the Island of Bombay in 1837 was about 250,000. There are only 221 names of Europeans in the Bombay Directory of 1838. The passage out overland of a first-class passenger from London was £125. There was not a single bungalow inhabited by a European on Malabar Hill. One European policeman was stationed at the Point. The view of the harbour from it was a complete forest of masts; two or three tiny steam-boats were nowhere. There were no cotton mills. No water was yet introduced from outside, and no gas. The first cargo of ice arrived from Boston on October 1st, 1836, and soda-water had been introduced in March, 1835. Lucifer matches came about 1838. Among shop-keepers John Treacher, auctioneers Bennett and Co., horse-dealers Abdul Raman, are the only names I can recognise. Postage was enormous; *i.e.*, 15 annas for under a tola to Calcutta. Many merchants clubbed together, wrote on the thinnest paper, and sending

---

* £1,889,933 of the paid-up capital was lost.—*Dict. Nat. Biog.* *Frere.*

their letters under one cover somewhat lessened the exaction. Postage to England under one tola was Re. 1. Inland postage in England or India had to be added.

The town was fortified, and no buildings were allowed within a radius of 1,000 yards. Men dined in white jackets and smoked their hookas afterwards. The standard drinks were beer and brandy *pawnee*. John Fleming told me that even when he arrived a dozen years after, champagne was never seen except at birth or marriage rejoicings (an exception would be made on the night of the day in which the accession of Queen Victoria was proclaimed).

A number of people were drowned every year in crossing Colaba Ferry, but that frightful nuisance is going to be put an end to, as Grant has gone in for a substantial causeway.

Sir Robert Grant

was Governor of Bombay 1835 to 1838. Parell, in Sir Bartle Frere's days, was called "The Land of Promise," and in Grant's time "Chancery," because you could get no reply. Daniel Wilson, the Bishop of Calcutta, who knew the family well, thus alluded to Grant's habit of delay. It was at the laying of the foundation-stone of the Grant Medical College in 1843. He spoke as follows: "He delayed cases too much, in order to take time to weigh every possible circumstance that could sway his judgment, and discover the means of least hurting the feelings of those whose request he was compelled to decline." Sir Robert Grant was more than a person, he was an individual, and the *beau ideal* of a religious Governor—one of the Clapham School that gave such a galaxy of philanthropists to the world. And he was no bigot, for when after a long struggle the political emancipation of the Jews was becoming an accomplished fact it was he who moved a resolution on the subject which Macaulay was content to second. Grant's speech made a great impression, and I think Mackintosh said it was one of the best speeches he ever listened to. He wrote hymns, and good ones too, and the man who writes a good hymn is no ordinary man. Poetry was in the family, for Lord Glenelg, his brother, wrote the Prize Poem on "The Restoration of Learning in the East." The following extract reads appropriately on the eve of the Queen's Diamond Jubilee :—

> "Yes, it shall come. E'en now my eyes behold
> In distant view the wish'd-for age of gold,
> Lo o'er the shadowy days that roll between
> A wandering gleam foretells the ascending scene!
> Oh doom'd victorious from thy wounds to rise
> *Dejected India*, lift thy downcast eyes
> And mark the hour whose faithful steps for thee
> Through Time's pressed ranks bring on the *Jubilee!*"

His father, Charles Grant, was a celebrated man in his day in all Indian affairs. Born the day after Culloden, and in the vicinity of the battle-field, he rose to be thrice Chairman of the East India Company. Sir Robert Grant, his son, has many memorials in Bombay, such as Grant Buildings, Grant Road, and Grant Medical College.

The Army.

In 1837 the following regiments were quartered in Bombay City :—The 6th Regiment of Foot, Warwickshire, facings blue lace, gold; Her Majesty's 40th Regiment, 2nd Somersetshire, facings white lace, gold; Regiment of Artillery, 1st Troop, Beni Boo Ali, Headquarters, Bombay, jacket blue, facings red lace, gold; Corps of Engineers, jacket red, facings blue velvet lace, gold; the 4th or Queen's Own Regiment of Light Dragoons is at Kirkee, coat scarlet, facings light yellow lace, gold; the Queen's Royal Regiment of Foot is at Belgaum, facings blue lace, gold; the Royal Tiger at Poona, facings white lace, gold; Bombay Light Cavalry—Light Wing, Rajkote, Left Wing, Hursole, jacket French grey, facings white; Bombay Light Cavalry at Deesa, jacket French grey, facings white; Regiment of European Infantry at Poona, facings white. There were twenty-six native regiments quartered at various stations over all the Bombay Presidency. Their facings were various—white, sky blue, black, buff, deep buff, light buff, yellow, pale yellow, dark green, etc. The whole of these troops were under the command of his Excellency General Sir John Keane, K.C.B., who at a later date was to sit down before the Fort of Ghaznee with great resolutions, which he was able to carry out. Captain C. Birdwood, 3rd N.I., is Fort Adjutant of the Garrison of Assirghur. The story of his two sons, Mr. H. M. Birdwood, C.S.I., and Sir George Birdwood, is suggested by that honoured name, but need not be further touched upon here.

MERCHANTS.

John Skinner was *facile princeps* among the merchants. You may see his picture in the Chamber of Commerce—a portrait large as life. He was cut short by cholera in Calcutta in the year 1844. His brother, Charles Binnie Skinner, is here also. He survived John fifty years. No man as chairman has equalled him in popularity until we come down to Sir Frank Forbes Adam. The Chamber was established on September 23rd, 1836. Mr. Skinner was its first chairman. F. M. Brownrigg is chairman for 1837, and Harry George Gordon, deputy, a name long conspicuous afterwards in the banking and mercantile world. The chairman's firm, Brownrigg, was of great importance for many years after this; and of a partner in it, and one of the committee of the Chamber in 1848, William Seton Brown, the following recent notice of his death from the *Scotsman* may be of interest:—

"We regret to announce the death, in Norfolk Square, London, of Mr. William Seton Brown, the founder of the Convalescent Hospital at Corstorphine, which was built entirely at his expense and transferred in free gift to the Royal Infirmary. Mr. Brown was born, we believe, in the neighbourhood of Prestonpans, but came to Edinburgh very early in life, and was educated at the High School here. He went to India about fifty years ago, and was for some time in business at Bombay. But on the opening of the trade to China about 1850 he removed to Shanghai, where he seems to have been very successful as a merchant; and on his return to this country he resided chiefly in London or its neighbourhood. Mr. Brown was a son of the late Dr. William Brown, long well known as the secretary of the Scottish Missionary Society, and grandson of John Brown, of Haddington, the well-known commentator on the Bible. Though widely and actively benevolent, he was modest and retiring in his habits, and seldom made himself prominent in any public movements. In addition to the Convalescent Home at Corstorphine, the little village of Cockenzie, in his native parish, was indebted to him for a handsome and well-equipped public school, which, we understand, has done much good service among the fishers' children in that quarter."

David Sassoon was in 1837 in the very prime of life, say about forty-five. His place of business and dwelling-place were in Tamarind Lane, No. 9, where he was busy laying the foundations of the future greatness of his family. A quiet unpretending man in Eastern dress, he comes out like Isaac at eventide, making his way by Church Gate, as I have no doubt he did, to witness the spectacle of the Queen's Accession Proclamation on the esplanade. The China trade does not monopolise him, for you may find him on some quiet evening with Dr. Wilson. These two men had an unbounded admiration of each other, which in Dr. Wilson's own words commenced with Mr. Sassoon's arrival in 1832. Premchund Roychund does not scruple to affirm that "Dr. Wilson was the best man that ever was in Bombay." I suppose the reason why he was so much thought of by men of all religions was that his expositions of their beliefs were always conducted with temperance and discernment.

W. S. Lindsay, author of a monumental work on *The History of Shipping,* was hereabouts at this period. He says himself:—

"In 1838 the author was a young man in command of the *Olive Branch,* a barque of 400 tons, and sailed along the whole of this coast, frequently following the route which Nearchus had taken, and sometimes obliged to anchor on account of the intricacy of the navigation, as Nearchus had done over-night. He can, therefore, confirm the accuracy of Heeren's condensed description of the voyage in its difficulties and dangers, and can testify to the abundance of the dates which formed a portion of the author's return cargo to Bombay, and also he may add to the 'robbers' by whom he was attacked, conveying from an inland town in the vicinity of Bushire some treasure which was destined for his ship."

W. S. Lindsay began his life work in the Liverpool Docks, was the architect of his fortune, and wore his honours meekly, and I have great pleasure in placing him among the first Bombay merchants of 1837.

I may remind the reader that there was neither a bank nor an exchange broker in Bombay in 1837. R. W. Crawford, of Remington and Company, is a foremost Bombay man of 1837. In after years he was long member for the City of London and Governor of the Bank of England. Head and shoulders above all the people, as I remember him, tall and stately, a massive figure, with white hair; he wore white stockings and buckles on his shoes. John Smith, of William Nicol and Company, is a young and rising man. As the saying is, he is "all there." In his prime he is to become one of the greatest pioneers of railway enterprise in Western India. His widow, of great wealth, married the celebrated Dr. Duckworth.

None of the young lions of 1864 have yet put in an appearance. Ah, my friends, these Back Bay days became Black Bay days. The ugly marks are still drilled deep in clouds and sorrow in many a heart—plague of greater proportions than the Bubonic. Montaigne says of this last that it is "short, stupid, and without pain." This was long and lingering, for men were stretched on a hot gridiron that awakened, and kept in tension, the most acute sensibilities of their nature. Sir Bartle Frere found his hair turned grey even in the process of looking at it. He was in 1837 Assistant to the Revenue Commissioner, but his Governmental days are far ahead, and he may now drink tea under the Duke's tree at Nagar, or breast the swelling and dark waters of the Bhima in peace and quietness. Some of the natives, who became conspicuous in after years, were no doubt in this year of Grace 1837 all alive, making mud-pies, playing *Eki-Beki*, or working mischief while gaining knowledge at Mr. Boswell's school. Premchund Roychund was no doubt in swaddling clothes, and had not obtained his first brokerage from W. W. Cargill. There is no indication yet of such dom-daniels as the mighty Arab Haji Ismail Haji Hubib, or Goculdas Tejpal, who has written his name on a large hospital, or of that Cama (Byramjee Hormusjee), who rose in 1865 to such colossal proportions, or of those two brothers, great by riches and hereditary descent, who dispensed the princely hospitalities of Lowji Castle. I mean Byramjee and Ardaseer Hormusjee, or of Byramjee Jejeebhoy, who astonished Bombay with his house, the old Sudder Adowlut at Mazagon, all in gold and colours. It was the old Tarala of Sir James Mackintosh. The two houses of Forbes and Company and Ritchie Steuart and Company of 1837 are the only English firms which have come down to us in 1897. Every other name, as far as I can see, has disappeared.

THE CIVIL SERVICE.

Among civilians, John Wedderburn was one of the most distinguished. Dr. Wilson knew him well, and I have heard him say in the Town Hall that in finance he was considered to have no superior in Western India. John Pollard Willoughby arrests the attention as the bosom friend of Outram. To Outram, Bombay was a dark and lonesome place without Willoughby. They were a kind of David and Jonathan. Then there were the two Freres, William and Bartle. William came first, and Bartle in 1833. I have always heard William spoken of as the favourite, a genial man, and not cold-blooded. It was at his house, Malabar Hill, in 1857, that the most faithful historian of Western India died. I mean the Rev. Phili Anderson, only 42—and to have done so much! Sir George Birdwood has repeatedly said to me that his book on Western India and his papers in the *Bombay Quarterly Review* ought to be republished. It is refreshing to meet with two men among the civilians of 1837 who are still alive (1899). Hugh Malet was appointed in 1829. He discovered Matheran. The other is Robert Keith Pringle, now 96, who was appointed in 1821 and retired in 1851 after distinguished service. Or has the last died very recently?* Any way, he is in the India Office List for 1897. Samuel H. Mansfield, whose nephew is now his Excellency the Governor of Bombay, was Assistant Collector at Poona in 1837. A contemporary of Sir Bartle Frere, Jonathan Duncan Inverarity, is Assistant Collector at Ahmednugger; that name, by whomsoever worn, has been a household word in Bombay for sixty years. Henry Edward Goldsmid was also assistant in Nagar, great in Revenue Survey. A wail of grief went up when he died in Cairo, and many anecdotes and pleasant traditions still exist of this eminent civilian in the Bombay Presidency. Lestock Robert Reid, appointed as far back as 1816, had gone to the Cape for his health. Quite a Nestor in after years, and chairman of *the* Oriental Bank, the progenitor of many able men and fair women—

> "Strong in himself and children stands
> The first among his peers."

William H. Hart, after whom Hart Point at Matheran is named, was also of this time.

---

* Died, I think, in 1897.

The Church.

The Venerable Thomas Carr, D.D., is at present Archdeacon, as Bombay was made a bishopric only in this same year. You may see his recumbent image at full length, graven on marble, in the Cathedral.

Rev. Henry Jeffreys, A.M., is Senior Chaplain, and has been here since 1818, a man of wonderful verve. His caustic and witty sayings lived a generation after him. A great temperance advocate, he did much good among the seamen and many others. For thirty years his robust constitution withstood every epidemic in Bombay, and yet, strange to say, he had no sooner arrived home in England than he was seized with cholera and died, I think, in 1848. The Rev. Kew Fletcher, A.M., is Chaplain at Byculla in 1837. I saw him in his parsonage near the Baboola Tank in 1865. He was then a venerable and much respected man, and in a year long gone by had lost his young wife, a Miss Jewsbury, whose sister was a faithful companion and helpmeet of Mrs. Thomas Carlyle. The house was covered with creepers and greenery, which is all I can recollect of it.

Drs. Cook and Stevenson are the ministers of the Scotch Church. Captain C. D. Mylne, the father of that most worthy and distinguished prelate, Bishop Mylne, who is still among us (1897), has not reported himself in 1837. Time enough. There is no hurry. His name and that of Mrs. Mylne in a very few years will be in every good work. There was another active philanthropist in Bombay in 1837, the Rev. Robert Nisbet. You all know Mrs. Nisbet's School. It has done a great deal of good, and I am certain that its supporters will not allow the plague to snuff it out.* Mr. Nisbet gave me his company in Egypt for a few days, I think in 1851, on his way out to India, where this big brawny man had laboured some twenty years. I took him to St. Mark's Tomb, and on leaving it he uttered these words: "Of all, over the world, who have been reading St. Mark's Gospel on this Sunday morning, we alone have visited his tomb."

Nathaniel Spencer is undoubtedly one of Bombay's worthies.

---

* It no longer exists (1897).

You will find him now Assistant in the Secretariat, where he will soon be a Secretary. He is "a stoop" in St. Andrew's Kirk, cheerful and buoyant to the last, and the progenitor of a family that has done good service to the city. I heard him remark outside to a group of Scottish orphans, old and young, and when he was of a great age: "If any of you gentlemen would like a game of leap-frog I am ready to give him a back."

Charles Morehead, M.D., Surgeon to the Right Hon. the Governor, and in medical charge of the Byculla Schools, afterwards Principal of Grant Medical College, must be mentioned. His father was a school-fellow of Mountstuart Elphinstone, and became Dean of Edinburgh, and his published sermons were so popular that Charles accidentally in Poona, in 1831, heard one of them preached by the Chaplain there. This was preaching by proxy, the preacher not knowing that the son of the author was a listener, though he knew afterwards. A brother of Charles was twice acting Governor of Madras.

The youngest and one of the most notable individuals of our day was born in the Marine Lines, the last of which we saw the other day, and of which Norman Macleod said when he was here in 1867 that he had seen such pictures of wigwams in books of African travel. There was a child, "yea, Lord, and a man-child," born in 1831, and that child is now (1897) Dean of Canterbury, a most able speaker and writer, as is known to everybody. His father, the Rev. C. R. Farrar, and Mrs. Farrar were, in 1837, Agents of the Church Missionary Society. He and Dr. Wilson some years previously made a long philanthropic excursion of 400 miles through Khandeish. Though, as is natural, the Dean has but a dim remembrance of Bombay, Dr. Wilson used to mention that he had often dandled the child on his knees. Dean Farrar is thus the youngest of our Bombay men of 1837.

The Law.

Sir Herbert Compton, Chief Justice, to his eternal credit, rose from the lowest rung of the ladder—from common soldier, man before the mast, or an equally humble position. He was succeeded by Sir Erskine Perry, who had a better start, for his father, Perry of the *Morning Chronicle*, the greatest journalist of his time, died worth £130,000. The money was put into a bank. The Bank broke, and so Erskine was obliged to come to India, where honours were heaped upon him, and more when he returned to England. The names associated with him are almost historical. His father married a sister of the great Porson, and his wife, a Bonaparte, died and was buried at Byculla in 1841. He is later than our *anno domini*, but we give him a place as a man of the period. William Howard in 1837 is a barrister, became Advocate-General, and died in 1862 in an English hunting-field. The encomium passed on him at his death was: "The Bombay Bar never had a superior to William Howard."

The Marine.

Sir Charles Malcolm, Rear-Admiral, was Superintendent of the Port, that office which was so long and so well filled by Sir Henry Morland in our day. An outcry that he gave contracts to his brother's firm, Shotton Malcolm and Co., may have been "fudge," as Sir Charles was not likely to peril his position by anything of the kind. Malcolm was an elder in St. Andrew's Kirk in 1837, just as John Skinner was Trustee of St. Thomas's. Malcolm's wife died in Bombay and was buried in the Scotch Kirkyard. The oldest member of the Indian Navy in 1837 was Captain Grant. He had been captured in 1820 by outlaws in Kathiawar, and kept in durance for three months with great suffering, never having his boots off for several weeks, the effect of which he felt for fifty years. I once spent a day with him on a friend's moor, when too young to shoot or even carry the bag. I can only recollect his sandy hair, freckled face, and genial jokes. I only knew him then as the laird of Barholm, Kirkcudbrightshire. Had I known what I know now, I should most certainly have dubbed him the "*Lion of the Gir.*"

Two Botanists.

John Graham, author of "Catalogue of Plants in Bombay and Vicinity," is here. You will find him at the General Post Office, where he is Deputy Postmaster-General. Destined to an early death in 1839 at Khandala, his monument is visible there to all railway travellers who choose to look out for it. I had thought that Jacquemont came under this date, but I see that he died in 1832 in Marine Lines, I think in the bungalow of William Nicol. I was present at the exhumation of his remains in 1881. There was very little to recover, and the French Government had anticipated this by sending out in a warship a beautiful little polished rosewood child's coffin. The loose sand was riddled through a sieve, and the bones of Jacquemont, or what remained of them, were decently transferred to the coffin, and it to a hearse with four horses at the gate of the Sonapore Cemetery. I presume the coffin was destined for the Paris Pantheon. Before the coffin left, a wreath of *Jacquemontia* was placed reverently on all that remained of this distinguished botanist and traveller. It was Mrs. Martin Wood who did this graceful and appropriate act of devotion, an act never done before, and never to be done again under like circumstances. Maneckjee Cursetjee, the late well-known judge, was at both funerals, that of 1832 and that of 1881.

THE PRESS.

Thomas Holcroft, son of the blind traveller, was in Bombay about this period. The following letter of introduction, written to Dr. Buist, the eminent editor of our *Times* for eighteen years, has not been seen by many people during this generation :—

"Chelsea, September 30th, 1839.

My Dear Sir,—Mr. Thomas Holcroft, whom I have known for a long time, and can recommend, a man of perfect integrity and respectability, is about proceeding to Bombay on some editorial speculation, which is to bring him, in more than one sense, into your neighbourhood. He is very desirous of being introduced to you, and to be related in friendly neighbourhood, as the case may be found to admit. Pray receive him on this recommendation. Try him a little. You will find him, I think, a man whose qualities will stand wear, not worse than they look at first sight, but better. With many kind remembrances and regards I remain,

Yours very sincerely,
THOMAS CARLYLE."

Conclusion.

In closing this chapter I ask myself, What can I see of 1837? I can see Outram, chafing at his state of subordination; I can see Governor Grant bursting into a flood of tears at some action of his Government, or when his motives are misconstrued by an undiscerning public. I can see Sam Mansfield of an evening at whist—it is long whist—carrying everything before him. I can hear Dr. Wolff in the Town Hall, and the words *Haleb ma fecsh* ("Aleppo is not," or "There is no Aleppo") still ring in my ears. The message had been carried by a mounted courier flying from the plague, who met him on his way to that city. I can see Captain John H. Wilson, who has made seven voyages to Suez in the *Hugh Lindsay.* A lonely man is he of the Indian Navy, and he is about to retire. Well for him he does not know what is before him, for no honour or reward shall ever reach him from the East India Company, albeit he has opened the way of our overland mail and steam navigation to Suez. I can see John Wilson ("Don't call me the Reverend") at midnight, snatching an hour of troubled sleep from Sanskrit, Prakrit, and other mysteries, with his faithful Dhunjeebhoy not far off—"Faithful found among the faithless, faithful only he" (I saw him hale and hearty on June 7th, 1897, walking on the Victoria Road). Once awake, the Doctor is keen to demolish absurdities in men and things. I see him again at midday at the porch of his doorway, his eye beaming a welcome, bowing with courtly demeanour as the great Jejeebhoy, the Parsee magnate, steps from his carriage. And as the sun dips like a ball of fire into the Arabian Sea I catch sight of him in the Fort, in the classic region of Tamarind Lane, on the house-top, discussing Moses and the Prophets with David Sassoon, each no doubt worthy to have held—

> "by Solomon's own invitation,
> A torch at the Great Temple's dedication."

(11.) PEOPLE WHOM INDIA HAS FORGOTTEN.

Garcia d'Orta—Elihu Yale—Hon. Sir John Gayer—Rev. Richd. Cobbe—John Cleland—Hector Macneil—W. B. Hockley—Sir T. E. Perry—R. Orton—J. J. Waterston—Lola Montez—Robt. Brown—A. M. Kavanagh.

No history can be final. New material is perpetually cropping up to superadd, modify, or supplant that which has gone before, and this is as true of Indian history as of any other. Macaulay had scarcely been dead when new accounts of Clive and Hastings were laid before the public. Gibbon seems like the Pyramids. Successive generations scratch their names on his monumental work and pass on. The industry and inquisitiveness with which men now search out documentary and archæological evidence render all this a foregone conclusion. And even were there nothing of this kind going on, the judgment of men on the same events alters in different generations. Lord Lawrence seems to hold his own pretty well, though there is an occasional squeak against him. Everywhere there is a strong disposition to question the judgment of our predecessors. Moreover, of the amount of information daily accumulating there is no doubt that a great deal is new, and now made available for the first time. Take, for example, the *Dictionary of National Biography*, of which more than half a hundred volumes have been published. In these, without any exaggeration it may be said, a new world has been laid open to the reading public. The massive books which contain the reports of the Royal Commission on Historical Manuscripts are also a mine of great wealth. From these (not forgetting the *Bombay Gazetteer*) and other sources the following slight sketches have been compiled.

Garcia d'Orta, Friend of Camoens.

In 1538, ten years after its acquisition by the Portuguese, Bombay was rented in perpetuity to Garcia d'Orta, a physician and professor of Lisbon, who lived in India from 1534 to 1572. Garcia paid a yearly quit rent of about £85 (1,432½ pardaos). In his work called "Conversations on Drugs," written in 1563,

Garcia mentions the island under the name of Bombaim and Mombaim. He also notes that his tenant Simao Toscano sent him mangoes from a tree that yielded twice a year.—*Bombay Gazetteer*, Vol. XXVI., Part 3, page 256.

"In Colaba Mrs. Hough's famous mango tree fruits twice yearly, at Christmas, as well as in the usual season of mangoes (May). The explanation most certainly must be that when it was about five years old, it received a serious injury at Christmastide, and at once flowered, and so fell into the habit of flowering and fruiting at Christmas."—G. Birdwood (Sir George) in *Bombay Saturday Review*, July 28, 1866.

Dr. d'Orta is interesting to Anglo-Indians. Not only was he owner of the ground where Bombay now stands, but he printed the first book, "Dialogues on Simples and Drugs," etc., issued from the press of India (*Impresso em Goa per Johanes de Emdem, X de Abril de* 1563 *annos*). An Italian translation appeared in Venice in 1597.—Burton's *Camoens—the Lyrics*, 389.

"Early in 1567 the kindly Viceroy gave the poet Camoens another lucrative employment. He became *Alcaide mor* (High Bailiff or Governor), *Provador dos defuntos* and *Vedor das obras* (Inspector of Public Works) at the wealthy factory of Chaul. But he never had the talent of success . . . He began to cry like a child for home. The idea of dying in India became intolerable; his spirit was broken. Sixteen years of wayfare and warfare in his gorgeous tropical exile had done their work."—*Camoens, His Life and his Lusiads: a Commentary by Richard Burton*, Vol. 1, page 26.

Burton sent from Goa to the *Times of India* in 1841 the first stanzas he translated from *Lusiads*. The following, recommending Dr. Garcia d'Orta to Viceroy Count of Redondo, and translated by Sir Richard Burton, is from the last of his Lyrics :—

I.

"That sole and single sample
Of hero daring, godlike bravery,
Which merited, in temple
Of Fame eternal sempiternal day,
Great son of Tethys, who for years full ten
Scourged the miserable Trojan men.

II.

No less of glory gained
For herbs and medicinal policy,
As dextrous and long trained
In prowest exercise of soldiery;
This wise the hands that death to many gave,
Gave life to many, strong to slay and save.

III.

Nor disregarded aught
That fere and doughty youth no fear could tame;
Of arts to mortals taught,
By beardless Phœbus for the languid frame;
And if a dreadful Hector could he kill,
Eke deadliest wounds were healed by his skill.

IV.

He with such art was dight
By his half-human Master wise and old,
Whence grew so strong his sprite,
In virtue, science, counsels manifold,
That well knew Telephus, wounded by his steel,
The hand that harmed was the hand to heal.

V.

Thus you, O excellent
And most illustrious County! Heaven's own gage
Given us to represent
For present ages past heroic age,
In whom transmewed your forebear's memories,
Honours and glories to new life arise.

VI.

Albe your thoughts be bent
On warfare busied, with hard campaign,
Or with sanguinolent
Taproban or Achem who haunts the Main,
Or with our hidden foe, Cambayan fere;
Who each and every quakes your name to hear.

VII.

Yet aid that olden love
Learned Achilles held in high repute;
Look! That becomes you more
To see how fruiteth in your days the fruit
Set by that Hortulan (Orta) life to show
New herbs and simples herbalists unknow.

VIII.

Look on your Viceroy years
An Hortulan produceth many an herb
Thro' fields the Hindoo ears
Which e'en those witches, of their wits superb
Medea and magic Circe ne'er saw,
However learned the twain in Magian law.

IX.

And see how heavy fraught
Wi' years and burthen of experience lore,
An old man science-taught
By Muses haunting learned Ganges-shore
In Podalirius subtle Sylvan spell
Chiron (Achilles' master) doth excel.

X.

The same implores with stress,
Your aid his valued volume, not voluminous
May see the light of press,
And rain on physic radiance new and luminous,
And sweet secrets to our ken betray
Hid from all Antients of the classic day.

XI.

Thus may you not deny
One who your kindly aura would secure;.
For an your name soar high
In bloody warfare with the Turk and Moor,
And one that aideth man with Death to fight
And with the hero Greeks your name be hight."

Camoens, the national poet of Portugal, was Inspector of Public Works at Chaul. This place is twenty miles from Bombay, and even in the absence of Shepherd's steamers the distance would constitute no barrier to the prosecution of the friendship of the two men. Is it an idle conjecture—is it not the nearest approach to a certainty—that the Governor of Chaul and the Lord of Bombay—for Garcia acknowledged no master but his feudal superior of Portugal—is it not, I say, more than probable that Camoens and Garcia once on a time, hand in hand, or arm in arm, sauntered through shady groves in Mazagon to drink inspiration from fruit and flower, or through some vista catch the glory of the everlasting hills?

Elihu Yale, Governor of Madras, 1687–92, Educationist.

Yale University is a name authorised by law, and is one of the four principal Universities of the United States. Founded in 1701, it received the name of its benefactor in 1718. It has been the *alma mater* of a great many distinguished men, among others of Calhoun, Fenimore Cooper, Dwight, Jonathan Edwards, Dana, and Silliman. It has seventy professors and 1,500 students. It is stated by Alexander Hamilton that Yale hanged his butler for leaving his service without giving him notice; but I have no doubt this is a skipper's yarn. We find in the *Indian Gazetteer* that, being a Welshman, he probably gave the Fort of St. David's its name. The epitaph on Yale's tombstone states that he was born in America, but he must have had Welsh proclivities, having been buried in Wales. He lies buried in the churchyard of Wrexham, North Wales, ten miles from Hawarden. His tomb in front of the church door is inscribed with the lines:—

> "Born in America, in Europe bred,
> In Africa travelled and in Asia wed;
> Where long he lived and thrived, in London dead,
> Much good, some ill he did, so hope all's even,
> And that his soul through mercy's gone to heaven."

The tooth of Time had almost effaced the quaint lines when a party of Yalensians visited the church a few years ago, and, seeing the state of things, caused the lettering to be re-cut. The church itself is more than five centuries old, and the curfew is rung by its bell every evening.

The Honourable Sir John Gayer.

Sir John Gayer was Governor of Bombay, and assumed charge of office May 17th, 1694, making it over November, 1704. Under Gayer, Waite, and Aislabie, that is from 1694 to 1715, Bombay Governors held the title of General. During the last three years (1701 to 1704) of his nominal command Gayer was in confinement at Surat. In 1711 he made his will in Bombay Castle. He left £5,000 for the benefit of young ministers of the same principles as Richard Baxter. Nonconformists might do well to inquire what has become of this benefaction. Sir John Gayer was a nephew of the Sir John Gayer who was Lord Mayor of London in 1646, a remarkable man, who had travelled a great deal, and, for aught we know, may have been in India. When he was in Africa a lion passed without injuring him. For this deliverance he founded "The Lion Sermon," which is still preached annually in London.

REV. RICHARD COBBE.

He had the merit of raising the subscriptions for, and seeing to the completion of, the Bombay Church in 1715. He was suspended in 1719, and went home, but took with him some Zend manuscripts, an inspection of which first fired the zeal of Anquetil Du Perron, who laid the foundation of Zoroastrian scholarship.

In 1766, fifty-two years after he had been appointed Chaplain, he published the only account of the building of the Church (now the Bombay Cathedral). His son was Chaplain to Admiral Watson in 1757, and was much esteemed. We believe that a son of the latter was long Political Agent at Moorshedabad, and again, in the fourth generation, General Cobbe, who retired from the Bengal Army somewhere about 1877, continued this most interesting genealogical succession.

JOHN CLELAND, 1707-1787, DESPERADO.

Cleland, Portuguese Secretary, Overseer of the Oarts, Collector of the Pension, arrived in India October 1st, 1729. —*Forrest's Selections.*

He is said by Allibone to have been the son of Colonel Cleland, *i.e.*, Will Honeycomb of the Spectator's Club. From records in the *Bombay Gazetteer*, I find that on October 4th, 1734, John Cleland was required to take the oath of fidelity to the East India Company. *Bombay Consultation* of November 1st, 1735, has the following :—

"The correspondence with the country Governments growing very large and proving a great trouble to the President, and the present Secretary for the Portuguese affairs being infirm, a proper person is wanted for this branch. —Mr. John Cleland being well versed in the Portuguese language and otherwise well qualified for the post is accordingly placed in that office."

In 1736 he was in the service of the East India Company at Bombay. He left Bombay in a destitute condition, somewhat hurriedly, and for unknown reasons connected with a quarrel he had with members of Council there. For many years he wandered in obscurity over the cities of Europe.

An infamous book was published in 17—. It is said he received £10 for it, the publishers making £10,000 by the sale thereof. For some service, secret or otherwise, he received from Lord Granville a pension of £100 a year. It is stated that "Grose's Travels," 1750–64, in two volumes, which deal mostly with the Bombay Presidency, were written out by him from notes received from Grose. It may interest the reader to learn that John Henry Grose, the Bombay Civilian, was a brother of the celebrated antiquarian Captain Francis Grose, immortalised by Burns.

HECTOR MACNEIL, POET.

(Born 1746. Died 1818.)

Macneil was, I believe, a purser in the Navy. In the last naval engagement between Sir Edward Hughes and Suffrein, Macneil was on board the *Gibraltar*. He made his mark on the Cave Temples of Western India, in letters to the *Archæologia*, Vol. VIII., 1787, dated 1783, no doubt the year he was wandering about our shores. An unexpected change in the administration at home blasted all the author's fair prospects in India. He cultivated the muses on a little oatmeal, and his declining days were passed happily near Edinburgh (Roslin), his birthplace. A friend had given him a pension of £100 a year. His fame rests on two songs—*Come under my Plaidie*, and *Mary o' Castlecary*. *Will and Jean* is a short poem on the evils of strong drink. He was a contemporary of Burns, though born thirteen years before, and his poems are in the Scotch dialect. There are many allusions to his Indian peregrinations, of which the following scraps selected at random may be taken as examples:—

"Involved in tumults wild uproar,
And dropped on India's burning shore."

And again, showing how far he travelled :—

"Pleased with the fancy, swift I sped,
Wild with the project in my head
  I ranged half India o'er.
From West to East, from isle to isle,
To India's shore and sultry soil,
'Mid tumult, battle, care, and toil
  I following flew,
Aye smoothed the past, and waked the smile
  To prospects new.
When warfare ceas'd its wild uproar,
To Elephanta's far-famed shore,
I led ye, ardent, to explore
  Wi' panting heart
Her idol monuments o' yore
  And sculptur'd art.
Sweet flew the hours (the toil your boast)
On smiling Salsette's cave wrought coast,
Though Hope was tint and a' was cross'd,
  Not dread alarms
Ye felt, fond fool! In wonder lost
  And Nature's charms.
Whether at midnoon, panting laid,
You woo'd coy zephyr's transient aid
Under the banyan's pillar'd shade,
  On plain or hill,
Or plantain green that rustling play'd
  Across the rill,
Or 'neath the tamarind's sheltering gloom
Drank coolness wafted in perfume."

The last six lines, I dare say, will appeal to the heart of the jungle-wallah. They are from *The Scottish Muse* of Macneil. The "plantain rustling play'd" and "the tamarind's sheltering gloom" are true to life.

Lord Byron wrote: "Macneil's poems are deservedly popular."

William Browne Hockley, C.S., Novelist.

The particulars of this man's life have only been recently rescued from oblivion. When Sir Bartle Frere edited *Pandurang Hari* in 1872 he knew very little about the author. When Frere joined the service in 1824 all he could learn was that Hockley served under the Commissioners in the Dekhan and in the

Judge's Court at Broach, that he was given to practical jokes, and fell under a cloud. William Browne Hockley was born November 9th, 1792, and went to Haileybury January 19th, 1812. He proceeded to Bombay May 9th, 1813, and was dismissed from the Judgeship in September, 1821. In June, 1823, he was tried for bribery and corruption at Bombay, and acquitted by the jury after a speech by his lawyer lasting more than four hours. My notes state that the trial for bribery and corruption before a Grand Jury was in the Recorder's Court in June, 1822, that the trial lasted several days, and the Recorder's speech took nine hours in delivery. He was defended by Mr. Ayrton, father of the late Commissioner of Public Works in Mr. Gladstone's Government. He was finally dismissed with a pension of £150 a year, March 17th, 1824. He then disappeared from view, and died August 22nd, 1860. This appears to be all that is known about him. *Pandurang Hari* was first published in London in 1826, when the author was in India. In the *Dictionary of National Biography*, under "Cyrus Redding," it is stated that he edited *Pandurang Hari*, writing up the rough notes sent to him by the author from India. As the work appears to be homogeneous throughout, it is more than likely that he only revised the proofsheets. *Pandurang Hari* is a novel that displays with wonderful accuracy the condition of the people question in the Dekhan before the English took possession of the country. All grumblers at the state of things as they are ought to read this book, and thank God they live under a better *régime*. But this is one of the things they won't do. Sir Bartle Frere thought it a faithful picture, and as he lived so near the times which Hockley depicted, and was so long identified with the Dekhan, his judgment may be accepted as final and beyond the reach of cavil. Hockley wrote also the *Zenana*, advertised after 1826 and republished and edited by Lord Stanley of Alderley in 1874. It consists of a series of stories, full of wit, and dealing with the manners and customs of Western India in the olden time.

Hockley wrote *Pandurang Hari* in India and the *Zenana* in England, and one can see in the latter the marks of English surroundings. Another work by the same author, *The Vizier's Son*, which may be found in the British Museum, we have not seen.

Sir Thomas Erskine Perry, Statesman.

(Chief Justice of Bombay, 1847–52.)

He was a son of James Perry, of the *Morning Chronicle*, who died (1821) worth £130,000, a notable man in his day. Erskine was born in 1806, and lost the greater part of his fortune by a bank failure in 1840. He came to Bombay as one of the judges in 1841. After his mother's death his father married a sister of the celebrated Porson. Porson lived with the elder Perry before and after the marriage. When Sir Erskine Perry left Bombay in 1852, a sum of £5,000 was subscribed, which at his request was utilised by founding the Perry Professorship of Law. On his return to England he entered Parliament in 1854, and advocated the abolition of the East India Company, protested against the annexation of Oudh, and advocated the policy of admitting the natives to official posts. He died in 1882. His first wife, a niece of Madame Jerome Bonaparte, died at Byculla, October 12th, 1841.

He had a brother who was British Consul at Venice, and a sister who married Sir Thomas Frederick Elliot, K.C.M.G. She soothed the last years of Miss Berry. These particulars are taken from his memoir in the *Dictionary of National Biography.*

Reginald Orton, 1810–62, Political Reformer.

He was born at Surat and educated near Richmond, in Yorkshire. He was apprenticed to his father, James Orton, Inspector-General of Hospitals, Bombay, 1825–30, made a member of the College of Surgeons, 1833, and practised afterwards in Sunderland.

The *Dictionary of National Biography* says :—"Although only locally conspicuous in his lifetime, he brought about by his energy changes which affected the whole empire."

He got the duty on glass and windows repealed, and he attacked the house duty, which, mainly by his exertions, was ultimately abolished. Allibone states that he was the author of a book published in London, being an essay on *Epidemic Cholera in India.*

J. J. Waterston, Man of Science.

About a year ago the Hon. Mr. W. R. Macdonell directed my attention to this Bombay man. "It appears that in 1851 he read a paper on *Molecules* at a meeting of the British Association. Some years before, towards the end of 'the forties,' he sent a very remarkable paper on the same subject to the Royal Society, which remained buried in the archives of the Society until Lord Rayleigh unearthed it in 1892, and found that Waterston had anticipated modern science by discovering several important laws relating to the molecular constitution of matter."

Mr. Macdonell followed up his valuable communication with the statements—

1. "His paper to the Royal Society was read March 5th, 1846, and committed to the archives.
2. "He contributed a paper to the British Association of 1851.
3. "Do. to the *Philosophical Magazine*, 1858.
4. "His paper of 1846 was reprinted (though I have not been able to verify the reference) in 1892 in the *Philosophical Transactions*, with an introduction by Lord Rayleigh."

Mr. Waterston was Nautical Instructor at Butcher's Island in Bombay Harbour. He was elected a member of the Royal Asiatic Society of Bombay in 1849. In 1856 he is marked "absent in Europe," and does not appear on the roll afterwards.

Lola Montez.

Her real name was Marie Dolores Rosana Gilbert, and she was born in Limerick in 1818. Her father died at Dinapore, 1825. Mrs. Gilbert married a Captain Craigie. In 1826 Marie was sent to Montrose to Captain Craigie's relations. She was educated at Paris and at Bath, from which place in 1837 she ran off with and married a Captain James, coming to India, and returning to England in 1842.

In 1847 she captivated the old King of Bavaria, and the events which followed are matters of history, and are well known to many of my readers. In 1849 she married George Trafford Heald, just of age.

In 1853 she married P. P. Hull of California. In 1857 she lectured in England and Scotland. In 1859 while in New York she met Mrs. Buchanan, wife of the well-known florist, whom she had known in Montrose, and who was engaged in visiting the outcasts of the city. She died in a Sanitary Asylum at Astoria, New York, on January 17th, 1861. These particulars are taken from the *Dictionary of National Biography.* I heard one of her lectures in 1857, "On Beautiful Women." She was tall and had black hair, a pleasing but faded expression, and a fine figure, and giggled a good deal in the course of her lecture.

ROBERT BROWN, 1822–63, PHILANTHROPIST.

He was a prominent Bombay philanthropist from 1845 to 1856, a partner of Ewart, Lyon & Co., a pronounced Christian, and he devoted his life to the rescue of fallen men and women, the education of the ignorant, and helping the destitute; he was a friend to seamen, orphans, and the sick, and a constant worker whenever his help was needed. He was six feet seven inches high, which gained him the sobriquet of *Lang Broon.* Impervious to all the blandishments of the fair sex, he lived and died a bachelor. Dr. Wilson of Bombay is only once mentioned in his memoirs. His meeting with Outram at Satara is merely noted. The fact that Brown was of the Scotch Establishment, and Wilson of the Free Church, may have led them into diverse ways of doing good, though neither of them was bigoted or intolerant. Though Brown was a pronounced Christian, like Havelock, Phayre, Edwards, and Henry Lawrence, like them he made many friends outside of the sphere to which he devoted his life; and hard-headed business men, such as A. H. Campbell and Robert Ryrie, heads of great houses, have testified, and are still happily alive to testify, their admiration of his unique character. Two of his maxims were, "Pray for others more than for yourself," and "not slothful in business, fervent in spirit, serving the Lord." When in Syria, he ventured into forbidden ground and was stoned out of the Mosque of Omar. The wonder is that he was not killed. I have no doubt that his want of care, while on his many travelling expeditions, in drenching rains, and sleeping in wet clothes, shortened his life.

ARTHUR MACMOROUGH KAVANAGH, 1831–1889.

He was born with only the rudiments of arms and legs, but by indomitable resolution and perseverance he triumphed over his physical defects.

He represented Wexford in Parliament, 1866 to 1868, and Co. Carlow from 1868 to 1880. It was an interesting spectacle to see him regularly wheeled into the House of Commons, where he spoke seldom, but with great weight. He and a brother, after travelling through Syria, Asia Minor, and Persia, arrived in Bombay on January 5th, 1851. In December his brother left for Australia, but died on the voyage, leaving his brother in India. Arthur found himself in want of money, and maintained himself by carrying despatches in the Aurangabad district. He afterwards obtained a post in the Survey Department of the Poona district, but returned to Ireland in 1853, and succeeded to the family estates on the death of his brother Charles in that year. In India he had some experience of tiger hunting, in which he acquitted himself brilliantly. He rode to hounds, was an expert angler, and continued to shoot, and shoot well, and was an enthusiastic and experienced yachtsman. He was also a fair amateur draughtsman and painter.

(12.) A BOMBAY OBITUARY.

SOME MEN AND WOMEN OF MARK.

1810, Nov. 10.—Ardaseer Dady died.

1815, Nov., Calcutta.—Mrs. Knox, aged 74 (? 84). She is the end of those who survived the horrid scene of the Black Hole of 1756. At the time 24 years of age, the wife of a Dr. Knox, and *enceinte.* A notice appears under 1801. The last of the survivors of the Black Hole, June, 1756. Her husband, mother, and sister perished in prison. "April (1803), met at Calcutta the grandmother of Lord Liverpool, the only remaining survivor of the Black Hole tragedy."—*Arthur Wellesley's Conversations.*

1815.—General Kenneth Macpherson, who fought at Culloden. Had a house near Tanna in Salsette.

1817.—Died in Calcutta, John Anastasius, a Greek merchant.

1817, March 21.—In her 20th year, in England, Miss Caroline Carnac, daughter of the late James Rivett Carnac, Member of Council, Bombay.

1818, May 9.—Mr. George Dick, oldest Civil Servant in India; officiated as Governor in succession to Sir R. Abercrombie.

1819, Jan. 16.—News of the death at Perth of Dr. Keir—Arthur Wellesley's doctor.

1819, March 27.—Lady King, wife of Rear-Admiral King; brought on shore from the *Minden*, and buried in St. Thomas's Church.

1819, July 24.—Major-General William Stafford Waddington deceased (Mrs. Hough's father).

1819, Aug. 1.—At Aix-la-Chapelle, James Forbes, author of *Oriental Memoirs.*

1819, Sept. 4.—Sir Alexander Anstruther, of Balcaskie, Recorder in succession to Mackintosh, died in Isle of France on July 16, aged 50.

1819, Oct. 2.—Hugh George Macklin, late Advocate-General, died on Wednesday, aged 48. "Of brilliant genius and exalted talents."

1819, Oct. 29.—Mrs. Rose Nisbett, 75; one of the oldest and most respectable inhabitants of Bombay.

1820, Dec. 11.—Constantine Shaw, a Greek merchant, died at Dacca, aged 96.

1821, May 20.—Colonel Charles Barton Barr, 49. A hero of Kirkee. H.E. and Commander-in-Chief at funeral.

1821, Aug. 31.—Jamsetjee Bomanjee Wadia, 67, master builder. On Aug. 30 he wrote a letter to Government, apprehensive of leaving his family in distress, applied for a grant of land, which was given him at the last moment.

1821, Oct. 5.—Claudius James Rich died at Shiraz. His wife, a daughter of Sir James Mackintosh, was companion of his solitude for fourteen years.

1821, Nov. 20.—At Ispahan, Dr. Jukes, on a special mission

to the Court of Persia. Had accompanied Sir Harford Jones and Malcolm to Persia.

1821, Dec. 1.—Sir William Evans, Recorder, died about this time.

1821, Dec. 30.—At Poona, Adolphus Pope, late Sheriff and Editor *Bombay Gazette*.

1822, June 26.—Nicholas Wade, Senior Chaplain, aged 56, interred in the chancel of St. Thomas's, where he had been Chaplain nearly thirty-one years. Died of apoplexy.

1822, June 24.—James Ollyetts Woodhouse, Advocate-General, 53.

1822, July 1.—Duncan Cameron, 56.

1823.—News of the death of Sir Evan Nepean.

1823, Jan. 1.—Sunkersett Baboolsett, 82, Chief of Goldsmiths; widely known.

1823, June 7.—Stephen Babington, died June 22. Monument in Cathedral. Subscriptions. £1,925.

1823, Aug. 2.—Emma, wife of W. Newnham, 24 on July 29. Buried in St. Thomas's Church. "Her body is deposited in the dust, but her soul, we trust, through the merits of the Redeemer, is ascended to God Who gave it."

1824, July 16.—At Paris, Charles Magniac, late of Canton.

1825, July 22.—Colonel Thomas Alexander Cowper, engineer and architect of Town Hall, aged 45.

1825, Sep. 29.—At Poona, Lieutenant-Colonel Commandant George Bridges Bellasis, thirty years' service. "In the midst of the preparations for our approaching gaieties, Death has deprived us of Colonel Bellasis, the life and soul of every party." "The fresh-piled mound remains—and this Marks the last resting-place of Bellasis."

1826, June 25.—Colonel Staunton, of Corygaum, at Cape of Good Hope.

1826, July 27.—Anne, wife of Major-General Wilson, commanding the Presidency; buried in St. Thomas's Church.

1826, Dec. 20.—At Colaba, Captain Seely, Author of *Wonders of Ellora*.

1827, April 18.—At Bath, Robert Henshaw, C.S., 82.

1827, Dec. 22.—Lately, at a village between Alexandria and Cairo, Henry Salt, Consul-General in Egypt.

1828, June 1.—At his residence in Nesbit Lane, Limjee Cowasjee, in his 46th year.

1828, June 23.—Richard Orlando Bridgman, cholera. Advocate-General.

1828, Aug. 18.—Sir Edward West, 45, died this day at Poona. Sir John Malcolm attended his funeral.

1828.—On Aug. 20, the Lord Bishop of Calcutta, at sea.

1828, Oct. 13.—Sir Charles Harcourt Chambers, 39.

1828, Oct. 15.—Lady West died.

1828, Oct. 18.—Sir Charles Harcourt Chambers, acting Chief Justice, 39. Buried in St. Thomas's.

1829, May 19.—At Belmont, Kent, aged 83, the Right Hon. Lord Harris, G.C.B., General in His Majesty's Army, Colonel of the 73rd Foot, and Governor of Dumbarton Castle, and conqueror of Seringapatam. Will sworn under £90,000. Mourning ring as a memorial to his descendants (his daughter, wife of Mr. Lushington, Governor of Madras) "in the hope they may at odd times bring their grandfather to memory, and recollect that, under Providence, he imputes his rise from nothing to his affluent fortune, to his economy and willing privation from self-indulgence through a long life."

1829, Oct. 9.—James Joseph Sparrow, 49, Member of Council.

1829, Nov. 24.—Frederick Rigston, Attorney-at-Law, 47.

1829, Nov. 25.—At Bombay, John Hector Cherry, Collector of the Northern Council, of fever. He was the son of one who occupied one of the highest posts in this Presidency.

1829, Dec. 24.—Of cholera, Sir William Seymour.

1830, Sept. 25.—Rev. James Gray, at Bhooj.

1830, Nov. 25.—Sir James Dewar died.

1831, Jan. 18.—Sir T. S. Beckwith died of malarial fever on Jan. 15. Late Governor and Commander-in-Chief of Bombay. A monument to be erected where he is buried at Mahableshwur.

1831, May 29.—Died on his way to the Neilgherries, Henry Petrie Saunders, on May 2.

1831, June 9.—At Surat, Lieutenant-Colonel Chas. Whitehill.

1831, July.—Turner, Lord Bishop of Calcutta, 45.

1831, Aug. 30.—John Hayes, Commander Indian Navy, died on his passage to New South Wales.

1831, Sept. 6, at Belgaum.—Gen. Kennedy, C.B., born 1762, resided nearly 50 years in India.

1832.—Dec. 7, at Bombay, Victor Jacquemont.

1833.—Order from Bombay Castle, Jan. 1833. Interment within a church, 600 rupees to chaplain; in ground surrounding church, 300 rupees.

1834.—On Sept. 6, James Morléy, advocate.

1835, Jan. 28.—Robert Cotton Money, C.S., died at Sholapore. Papers eulogistic.

1835, Aug. 23.—At Breach House, Lady Malcolm.

1836, June 25.—Aratoon Isaac Aganoor, 76.

1836, Sept. 13.—Motichund Amichund.

1837, Jan. 17.—Jehangier Nusserwanji Wadia.

1838, July 11.—At London, William Shotton, formerly of Bombay.

1838, Nov. 16.—Robert Cutlar Ferguson, M.P., at Paris.

1839, May 28.—W. K. Ewart, formerly of Bombay, killed at Calcutta by a fall from his horse.

1839, June 1.—John Graham, Post-master at Khandala, on 28th ult., from exposure to the sun. "The Botanist."

1839, July 20.—At Emden, Sir Pultney Malcolm, 71.

1839, Nov. 30.—Rear-Admiral Maitland. Died out on a cruise from dysentery. Buried in St. Thomas's Church.

1839, Dec. 26.—Ragojee Angria, died without heirs.

1840, March 30.—William M. Calmont, late editor of *Bombay Gazette*, died of cholera.

1840, Aug. 19.—Thomas Daniell the painter, 91.

1840, Oct. 27.—Charles Edward Stewart, C.S. Son of John Stewart of Belladrum.

1848.—Sir John Peter Grant died at sea.

1849, Nov. 29.—Edward Parsons, assistant Cardwell Parsons and Co.

1850, March 2.—Capt. T. J. Newbold died at Mahableshwur.

1852, Jan. 18.—John Vaupell, Chief Translator and Interpreter High Court, died, 57.

1852, Feb. 29.—At The Cliffe, Malabar Hill, eldest son of Dr. and Mrs. Smyttan, 2.

1852, May.—William Erskine, at Bonn.

1852, June 3.—Col. Mignon, 58. Drowned in a nullah returning from Singhur. His horse ran into Poona before him. Body found several miles down stream.

1853, Oct. 10.—News of Mrs. Arthur Malet and child, ayah and crew being drowned at Bancoot. Night dark; hour 7 P.M., Mr. Malet saved by a kind of miracle.

1854, Aug. 5.—Mr. Green, Acting Principal Elphinstone College, died. "Greatest master of European thought in this country."

1854, Oct. 31.—Lord Frederick Fitzclarence, son of William IV., died at Poorendhur. Unexpected, though sick for some time.

1854, Nov. 10.—Lord Frederick's body laid out in Bombay Castle. His charger (said) is shot. All officers to appear in the new ground at Dockyard at 4.30 P.M. to do honour to the remains on Monday 13. Gazette in black border. No leaden coffin procurable.

1856, March 10.—Two European gents drowned while bathing at Colaba.

1857, Dec. 14.—At W. E. Frere's Bungalow, Malabar Hill, Rev. Philip Anderson; was buried at Colaba, 42.

1858, March 6.—At New York, Alexander Gordon Fraser, father of the Principal of Elphinstone College, descended from Simon, Lord Lovat.

1859, April 15.—At 2 A.M. on this Friday morning, Sir Jamsetjee Jejeebhoy; born July, 1783. Personal and real property 85 lakhs.

1859, May 23.—Manackje Nusserwanje Petit. Many eulogies on him.

1859, June 14.—Mr. Mawson, Editor of *Gazette.*

1859, July 23.—Lady Arnould died, on Malabar Hill.

1859, July 28.—Francis Leggett, Deputy Sheriff.

1859, Aug. 29.—R. S. Campbell, of Ritchie Stewart and Co., died at Poona, 26th inst., 28.

1859, Sept. 10.—Geo. Entwistle, merchant, Karachi.

1859, Nov. 19.—Rev. Joseph Taylor, 68, at his son-in-law's bungalow, Col. Birchwood's, Breach Candy.

1860, April 6.—Manson murdered in South Mahratta Country, buried at Girgaum.

1860, April 20.—John Craig, Joint Editor *Bombay Times and Standard*, dead.

1860, July 31.—On July 26 died a pauper in the General Hospital, Bombay: John Elley, late station-master, Byculla. His grandfather died in 1835, General Sir John Elley, Col. of 17th Lancers, and was buried in St. George's Chapel, Windsor.

1860, Aug. 13.—Sir Henry Ward, Governor of Madras, died of cholera.

1860, Aug. 21.—Lord Elphinstone's death announced.

1860, Sept. 21.—Mr. Spooner's two daughters went out on a fishing excursion without sufficient protection from the sun. One since dead from sunstroke. Mr. Spooner, Commissioner of Customs.

1860, Oct. 1.—Died in Calcutta this evening, Dr. Buist, a few minutes after his arrival from Allahabad. Bombay journalist 20 years.

1860, Nov. 3.—Nowrojee Jamsetjee Wadia, 85, Head of Parsee Community. Bore his severe worldly afflictions with exemplary patience. Succeeded his father, Jamsetjee Bomanjee in 1822. Retired in 1844 on a pension.

1860, Dec. 7.—F. J. M'Kenzie, Clerk Insolvent Court, at Byculla Club, yesterday.

1861, July 13.—W. T. Turquand, C.S., shot himself in Poona, 23 years' service.

1861, Aug. 16.—Rev. Mr. Green, interred in Cathedral Compound.

1861, Nov. 18.—Lady Canning died in Calcutta, of jungle fever.

1862, Jan. 28.—William Howard, late Advocate-General and Chairman Mercantile Bank, killed in hunting-field in England.

1862.—William Howard, from 1836 to 1854 most conspicuous in Bombay. "The Bombay Bar never had a superior to William Howard."

1863.—Stephen Hislop, Missionary and Geologist, drowned at Nagpur.

1865, Aug. 5.—Juganath Sunkersett, 63.

1865, Sept. 2.—Justice Kinloch Forbes died at Poona.

1867, June 15.—W. H. Crawford died at Matheran.

1867, Nov. 20.—Goculdass Tezpal.

1868, April 18.—Capt. John Wellington Young, Indian Navy, dead.

1877, Feb.—Capt. Henry, Superintendent P. & O. Co., greatly respected, killed by a carriage accident at Mazagon.

1850.—The *Calcutta Review*, in an article on Sir James Mackintosh, says: "Of those who enjoyed the privilege of mixing in his circle at Parell, there remain now none in Bombay."

VI.

HISTORICAL.

(1.) HERODOTUS IN MESOPOTAMIA.

HERODOTUS was born B.C. 484. He was never in India, but he was not far from it, for he came to Babylon, Susa and Ecbatana. Of Susa Strabo writes that, if a lizard at midday attempts to cross the street, it is baked at half the distance. Herodotus does not notice the heat. When he came to Egypt he was between thirty and forty years of age, a comparatively young man, but Herodotus is always young, "like the high leaves upon the holly tree." There was no Alexandria then. You can still see a few objects, however, the works of man, which arrested his attention: the Pyramids and the Obelisk at Heliopolis, and you can reconstruct in your imagination the Tower of Perseus on the promontory of Canopus, since immortalised as Aboukir. In Egypt he notices musquito nets, and that the Egyptians "gather in the fruits of the earth with less labour than any other people."

When he crossed the Euphrates he notes a greater wonder, that by "the Providence of God wheat in Babylon, and no where else, grew spontaneously." It is something to hear the Providence of God appealed to. Had it been Pliny, in a so-called more enlightened age, it would have been "the occultation of the Brood star Virgilius." He knew then that the wheat plant was indigenous to the plains of Chaldea, whence it spread all over the world. But he did not know, what we know now, that to Babylonia more than to Egypt we owe the art and learning of the Greeks.

This was the cradle of the human race, and in Herodotus's

time, streams of zodiacal light shot up to the zenith from the plains of Shinar, long after night had descended on the Garden of God. Though he calls the Persian Gulf the Red Sea, he knew exactly where he was in the map of the then known world; knew that the Gulf and the Atlantic, beyond the Pillar Hercules, were one sea, and that it was not, like the Caspian, a mere *mare clausum*. This seems a small matter, but it means that he knew that Africa was circumnavigable 1,800 years before the Portuguese came on the scene. Strabo reasons hastily, from the fact that the Indus gave its name to India, that all its peoples spoke one language. Herodotus writes that many languages were spoken in India. The relation of India to Persia is a complicated piece of History. Esarhaddon knew nothing of India, or Sennacherib, B.C. 701, for both of them invaded some portions of Media "the names even of which their fathers had never heard of," and it is not likely they ever heard of India. Afghanistan, Baluchistan, and the Gedrosian sands presented an impregnable barrier in those days. Herodotus himself had never heard of the Ganges. Cyrus, during thirteen years, B.C. 542-29, overran the mountainous regions between the Caspian and the Indus, and subdued them, and he died of his wounds not far from the Upper Indus. It seems certain that the whole regions contiguous, and on both sides of the Indus and the Punjab were annexed, for without this last the Indian satrapy never could have yielded the revenue it did to Darius (B.C. 516). It was more than a million sterling of our money annually—and supplied greater wealth to his coffers than any other of his two dozen satrapies, enriched the empire to a great extent, and is believed to have been the means of introducing a gold currency to its circulation. More than this, it supplied the empire with the sinews of war, with men as well as money. The Sacae came from the Pamir, or region about Kashgar and Yarkand. They would dare everything, and do everything, except conquer the Greeks. Horse and foot, at Marathon, at Platea under Mardonius, and at Arbela, the Indians fought next to the immortals, and when Xerxes' troops crossed the Hellespont, the white cotton dresses of the Indians from south of the Paropamisus waved in contrast with the red kilts of the Mede and Persian, and the leopard skins of the Ethiopian. They fought with bows and arrows of cane, and great numbers of Indians accompanied their dogs of war.

The wild statements of Herodotus are an admission that he knew next to nothing of India, while sculptures of the elephant only begin to show themselves in the last days of Persepolis after the Macedonian conquest. A parcel of gold coins, pretending to be Babylonian or Assyrian, probably of Alexander, I forget which, found their way from the Persian Gulf a year or two ago—splendid coins—some of them twice the size of a five sovereign piece. A neophyte could have detected the fraud. The experts in London said "the elephant" was fatal, and so they were consigned to the melting pot. The dies must have cost a good deal, but not a tithe of the cost the maker was entitled to. He should have had his wages for his work. Egypt and Assyria must have had an early trade with India, but which was first in the race it is difficult to determine. This commerce is older than the records of profane or sacred history. Rawlinson (to whom I am deeply indebted) says that the route by the Euphrates and Tigris, and the Persian Gulf, with the alternative of caravan, is the shortest and easiest, and that the Red Sea is inferior and circuitous, *quoad* the Ancient world. How comes it, then, that you find cinnamon, which grows nowhere else than in Ceylon and Malabar, as old as the holy oil of Sinai, say 1,456 years B.C.? It must have come by the Red Sea. The centre of Darius's Indian satrapy was the North West. In Thibet and Nepaul, no doubt, were the mines or rivers out of which came his gold dust, and it needs no witch of Eziongeber to inform us that 500 years before Darius, Solomon drew his gold from the same auriferous source, and shipped it at Sopara, leaving Guzerat to furnish its quota of apes and peacocks. Why did ancient India build her houses and temples of wood? Egypt built stone, and Assyria brick and stone; hence their monumental and pictorial history; and hence the baldness of prehistoric India. Asoka, about B.C. 250, seems to have taken heart of grace, being the first to exclaim like Job, "O that my words were engraven with an iron pen on the rock for ever." And he did it, as a dozen inscriptions at Girnar and elsewhere testify. But they are of yesterday compared with Babylon or Abu-simbel.

I suppose that we may take it for granted that human sacrifices, at the time we write of, were not unknown in Britain. Strabo lets in a stream of daylight on this subject. The scene is on the Scilly Islands, one of them now a perfect paradise of narcissi and other floral trophies, and where Druidical circles still attract the stranger: "The Druids wore black cloaks, were clad in tunics reaching to the feet, girt about the breasts, walking with staves, thus resembling the Furies we see in tragical representations." At the laying of the foundation of some hill-fort or public building it was not uncommon, in Western India, to build a maiden in the wall for luck; we could name several which were consecrated or desecrated in this wise. It is Herodotus who now writes: "The Persians on their march into Greece sacrificed at Ennea Hodoi, on the Strymon, nine youths and nine maidens of the country, by burning them alive." The following reads like a page from the Mogul Empire in India: "The Caunians and Lycians, finding resistance impossible, shut themselves up within the walls of their cities Caunus and Kanthus, set them on fire, burned their wives, children, slaves and valuables, and sallying forth, sword in hand, were all slain." I call this *Johur,* and as ghastly significant as anything accounted of in Raisin, Chandore, or Chitore.

Belshazzar's Feast and the Fall of Babylon have exercised the imagination of many a poet and painter, and criticism stands abashed at the glowing narrative. It may serve, however, to strengthen a wavering faith in Holy Writ, that Herodotus is explicit enough on the feasting and dancing on that memorable night. The city, he says, was taken at both extremities, some time before it was known at the great royal rendezvous. The statement of Herodotus that the destruction of Sennacherib's army was due to field mice is a rude awakening to our preconceived notions, and looks askance at poet's pen and painter's brush, though it detracts nothing from Him whose name is the Almighty. It is a sharp descent, however, as one would say, from the wing of an archangel to one of the smallest of God's living creatures. The means are different, but the end is the same. The nibbling of mice may have been as effective as the breath of an archangel. "Look at me and learn to reverence the gods" was the inscription which Herodotus tells us was placed on a statue, with a mouse in its open palm, erected at Memphis, supposed to commemorate the event, and we can only repeat the dictum—

> "Where reason fails with all her powers,
> There faith prevails and love adores."

The version of Herodotus presupposes, I imagine, that the mice must have devoured the food of the army before they attacked their thongs, bucklers, and bowstrings. In Greek, mouse and rat are the same word; in Latin, the rat of Egypt, *Mus Egyptius.* In 1879, millions of rats invaded the Dekhan and destroyed the crops over a thousand square miles.

A glance at Nebuchadnezzar, who built the Hanging Gardens, must suffice. He was the same man who lost his reason for seven years. Herodotus is silent on this, but Berosus fills up the gap; and both, I think, are silent on Daniel's being Viceroy during that period when he was under a cloud. His disease is named *lycanthropy.* In his last years his intellect was perfectly unclouded, and he died B.C. 561, in the eighty-fourth year of his age, having reigned forty-four years.

At the risk of having Charles Lamb's lines thrown at me —"May the Babylonian curse straight confound my stammering verse"—I am sorely tempted to append the beginning of a poem which nearly gained the prize in one of the English Universities. There is little humour in Chaldea except in the "Chaldee Manuscript," which is a modern *jeu d'esprit,* so we gladly avail of it:—

> "When Nebuchadnezzar went out to grass
> With the horned cattle and roaring ass,
> He said, when he tasted the unwonted food,
> 'It may be wholesome, but it is not good!'"

The Indian dogs mentioned by Herodotus were much employed by the Assyrians and Persians in the serious business of war. The mastiff now, or lately, bred by the Bhoteas, in the uplands of Thibet—which, as I understand, is larger than any other mastiff, a magnificent animal, tremendously fierce, strong, and noisy—may be the animal. The breed was kept up by successive importations, and four considerable towns in the plains were appointed to find food for the dogs, and in consequence were exempted from all taxation. This was under Cyrus, and indicates how numerous they were. There were so many in the army of Xerxes when it crossed the Hellespont, that no one could mention the number of them. They are represented on the sculptures with spiked collars. Strabo tells a story, that when Alexander was in India he saw a dog, most likely of the same breed, attack a bull, and could not be loosened from its hold until some time after its leg was cut off.

When Shakespeare makes Antony say, "Cry havoc, and let slip the dogs of war," it has been remarked that he uses no figure of speech. The breed was altered so little that Darwin, on seeing a picture of one from the tomb of Esarhaddon, B.C. 640, said of it, "an undoubted mastiff." True to their hereditary instinct and to their great prototype Nimrod, the Assyrian, Babylonian and Persian were "mighty hunters." The signet of Darius Hystaspes displays him combating with a lion from his chariot. The sculptures are full of the chase. They went for big game. In one we see a lion with an arrow shot right through its body, the barb appearing on the opposite side. There must have been "giants in those days." In another, we see the king of beasts leaping in mid-air, and receiving his death wound from the javelin of a king of men. The progress of an army on its march to Babylon is stopped, so that the monarch may settle accounts with the wild bulls at the foot of Zagros. There is no want of pluck. A Persian descends from his horse, and the wild boar is done to death. Asshur-bani-pal (like Outram and his tiger) spears a lion on foot, or, from a coracle in reedy stream, rouses him from his lair with the yell of Indian dogs. The wild ass is not safe in the deserts of Mesopotamia, and is run down by relays of fleet horses, as is still done in the Run of Cutch, or caught with the lasso, as in use on the Pampas of South America. Stalking and the arrow deal death to the wild sheep among the rocks of Paropamisus. The bags are Brobdingnagian. One record mentions fifty wild bulls on the banks of the Euphrates; another, the capture of twenty ostriches in the Desert of Gobi. During his lifetime the monarch just named slew 350 lions and 257 wild cattle. The same thing took place in our Mogul Empire. Sher Shah is *the* Lion-Knight, *par excellence*, for he slew one with his own hand. And Akbar will stop his army as soon as he hears good *kubber*. He, too, alights from his horse and challenges the tiger to mortal combat; and the wild ass of Jessalmir flees from him in vain. All along his great road, from Sikri to Ajmere, I see his *Kos Minars* decked with trophies of the chase. His *Kamargha*, or *battue*, beats the record. It is five *kos* on each side and encloses 15,000 wild animals. Everybody has a shot. When the Angel of the Darker Drink once reconnoitred Jehangier, he thus cast up his accounts:—A parallel to Asshur-bani-pal. "From the age of twelve to fifty, I killed 28,532 wild animals, of which 17,168, including 86 tigers, 889 *nillgaos*, 90 wild boars and 36 wild buffaloes fell by my own hand, and at fifty six I shot a tiger frcm the saddle." He died happy—that is so far as *shikar* is concerned.

Persia furnishes traditions of the chase down through the Sassanidae. "Bairam that great hunter," of whom Omar Khayyám sings, was otherwise called *Goor*, from chasing the wild ass to the last days of the empire, when hundreds of animals were driven into an enclosure and slaughtered. The crown of Persia was once cast into a tiger's den, where two aspirants were told to "take it who can." We have high authority for the assertion that a good shikari makes a good soldier. When decay of physical courage and prowess creeps into the nation's vitals, and when you cease to find men willing and able to wage war with wild beasts, look out. There were few lion hunts, I should think, in the last days of Babylon or Persepolis, and I cannot at present remember Aurungzebe killing anything bigger than a hare. The ancient Persian took kindly to his drink, and carried it with discretion. Hence the Babylonian's love of walking sticks for support. The cup of Babylon was a golden cup, but it was full of trembling. The Persian was proud of the quantity he could drink, for he made himself a hero, thereby, drunkenness being an institution and intoxication a duty. To be sober was not respectable, so the King of Persia—and we may add to this title from the Bible, "Ethiopia and India"—once a year, at the feast of Mithras, was bound to get drunk.

"Fill high the cup with Samian wine."

Samos was theirs, but Shiraz was nearer, and its golden nectar abounded in Persepolis. The decree in the Book of Esther, that any one could drink as he liked, must have been a mighty relief for sober people. Standing on Indian ground, we have nothing to boast of, and anything from this quarter would be Satan reproving sin. We also have had men mighty in strong drink. Baber and Sher Shah were of that ilk, but Baber broke all his golden drinking vessels and poured the contents of his wine-cellars on the earth; and his resolution must have been sincere, for he built a well and an almshouse on the spot. Jehangier also made resolutions, but, like many of us, broke them. They were like the morning cloud or the early dew. He was a drunkard to the last; in fact, gloried in it, as you may see in the gold coin so prized by numismatists, where he is represented with the wine cup at his lips.

Talking of Shiraz leads one to Malcolm's gift to Sir Walter Scott of a cask of Shiraz wine. Malcolm asked him about it at Abbotsford, when it was discovered that the butler had used it for Xeres, a faint resemblance between sherry and Shiraz. Sir Walter Scott only knew whisky, and in moderation, though he sometimes complains of a headache in the morning.

The Egyptian monarch had only one wife; but it was different in the Persian monarchy, where one among many may have held sway for the time being. Few women in Persia were allowed to appear prominently, or, like Noor Jehan in India, act a conspicuous part. No woman, except Semiramis, appears on the sculptures of Nineveh or Babylon, and their names are never mentioned in inscriptions. Their seclusion was rigid. A married woman could not see her own father or brother, and all representation of the female form was strictly forbidden.

The litters in which the ladies of the second monarchy were carried were closed, like those of the Muslims of the present day, to conceal their charms from the vulgar. One can understand Vashti's repugnance to come from behind the purdah. "The Assyrians allowed their women to make a most rare and occasional appearance; in Babylon it was less rigid." In the last days of the Sassanian Kings, as you may see on the marble slabs of Kermanshah, the ladies of the court, at grand spectacles, sit unveiled and flaunt their charms to the public gaze. You remember Chand Bibi, the noble Queen, veiled her face when she fought on the battlements of Nagar. But the veiling of women is of great antiquity, and has prevailed since Rebekah alighted from her camel, or Medea appeared in public with Jason in the days of the Golden Fleece. Darius Hystaspes transported from the Libyan Barke to the Bactriana Cyrene, the Baraki, nowadays existing (according to Mr. Bellew, *Asiatic Review*, October, 1891) as a sept of 30,000 families round about Cabul. If this statement should be confirmed it would be nothing wonderful. Herodotus says "they gave then the name of Barce to this village, which was still inhabited in my time, in the Bactrian territory."

The tyrants of these times had no scruple in transplanting peoples. The bulk of the inhabitants of Miletus, in Asia Minor, were transported into Inner Asia and settled on the Persian Gulf. The creaking of the water-wheel or the cooing of the pigeon from some palm grove becomes dreadfully monotonous to a stranger, and the soul yearns for woods and hills. I heard Kossuth, after he had come out of prison, say, in unforgettable words: "It is long since I have seen a mountain, and it was at the foot of a mountain that I was born." Such, no doubt, was the feeling of Amyitis, Queen of Babylon, a Princess of Media, a hilly country. It is a beautiful story. She pined for the woods and torrents of her native land, and the king built the Hanging Gardens as a solatium. Jew or Gentile, it is all the same. We cannot all be Ruskins, but every one of us has some spark of this fire of heaven. Yes, at the time of that great upheaval which has been named the Christian Era, Strabo dilates on the beauty of the Alban Hills, the villas of Tusculum, gorgeous as Persian palaces, nestling amid gentle and undulating slopes down to Rome and the sea. The feeling may be dormant, but it may be cultivated in every man. Do you think that Isaac, when he went out to meditate at even-tide, was merely gazing at vacuity, and not at the sunset behind the Euphrates? If he had been in any such stupid abstraction, he would never have seen Rebekah. Or can you conceive that the Almighty put the mountains round about Jerusalem for no other purpose than to serve as a girdle of chalk and limestone? Or, deeper still, we may reverently ask the question: Did Apocalyptic vision reflect the pure water, clear as crystal, of some Asia Minor earthly landscape, and transmute it into the glories of Paradise?

(2.) THE MACEDONIAN INVASION.

> "Why, man, he doth bestride the narrow world
> Like a Colossus, and we petty men
> Walk under his huge legs and peep about."—*Julius Cæsar.*

WE are told that Alexander the Great had a tinge of red in his face and breast, bronzed no doubt like our frontier warriors by summer sun and winter storm. He had an eagle eye, and the turn of his head, which leaned to one side, must have given him an arch or knowing look. He was swift of foot, and in his teens exceedingly agile—could alight from, or mount his chariot at full speed. On the march he would exercise himself by shooting or darting the javelin. None excelled him in horsemanship, and Bucephalus, whose "neck was clothed with thunder," became at once amenable to him, as much by the law of kindness as by the management of bit and bridle. Like Darius, he had his combat with a lion engraved on his signet ring, and sometimes he wore a lion's skin. He could trudge through the slime, and clamber up the sludgy banks of the Indus with the enemy in his teeth, or scale the stony pathways over the limestone of Anti-Libanus, until almost every man of his party fell out from exhaustion. He read much in Asia, and had supplies of books sent him from Greece. Homer was his idol. Above all, he knew what to do and how to do it. On that brown and sandy spot where he planted Alexandria, he began at the beginning. He made the wells first, whereat his soldiers slaked their thirst, and built the city afterwards. He alone discerned the commodiousness of its harbour, and it was he alone who made this half-way house to India. On his coins is deeply engraven his likeness—massive, intellectual, and full of energy. He could be fierce enough when roused. No man who had seen him thus ever forgot his aspect. Cassander, who had been with him in India, and had good reason to remember him, "fierce as ten furies," on a day, long years after, when all Greece owned his supremacy, had a cold shiver as he came accidentally in sight of a statue of Alexander. Yet he could be at times kind and gentle. He threw his own robe over the dead Darius, and wept at the grave of Cyrus, and he was full of inconsistencies. When tormented with thirst, he could pass a cup of cold water from himself to a comrade who had borne the brunt and stour of battle; he could sell thousands into slavery, to ruthless and barbarian masters, or deliver a whole city, men, women and children, to the sword. On his return to Susa from India, he feasted nine thousand of his friends, gave each of them a golden cup, and paid his soldiers' debts to the amount, in our money, of two millions sterling. Was this the plunder of India? What did India gain by the Macedonian Invasion? We cannot answer these questions. He could be magnanimous in a way. He restored his dominions to Porus, that is, made him his lieutenant; he was chivalrous to the ladies of Darius! "Tell him," said the dying monarch, "the gods will reward Alexander for his humanity to my mother, wife and children."

It is difficult to believe that this is the same man who had no hesitation in running through the body, with a dagger, his own friend Clitus, who had saved his life at Granicus. What availed his remorse? It could not bring the dead man back to life again. He said once that he knew that he was not a god, from two things—sleep and lust. But, like Akbar, he had a strong hankering after divinity, with this difference—that Akbar was put out of the conceit of his godship as soon as he saw the inscription on a new coin of *Akbar Akbar* instead of Allah Akbar. This put an end to his deification, by converting the sublime into the ridiculous. Not so Alexander. In his coins, the Indian treasure-trove of yesterday, he survives in all the glory of Jupiter with his eagle and the thunderbolt. He asked a Brahmin in India how a man might become a god, and was answered wisely,—"by doing what is impossible for man to do."

It must be confessed that the man who was taught by Aristotle, painted by Apelles, denounced by Demosthenes, and who afterwards conquered the world, had some temptation to self-apotheosis. I suppose that after the priests of Ammon called him the son of Jupiter, he thought it was all right, and posed as a god among the barbarians. But among the Greeks he required to be more cautious, and when he got drunk, as he sometimes did, and could not walk round the table, his divinity was in danger and rocked uneasily on its pedestal. Some of the aborigines of India chaff their gods with impunity. Clitus tried it once: "Son of Jupiter as you *are!*" but the dagger of Alexander left him no time for repentance. From his birth, every source of divination had been appealed to, and the priests of every religion had been subsidised, from the Magi of Ephesus to the Gymnosophists of India. He had consulted every oracle by which heaven could be propitiated, Delphi in Greece, and Jupiter Ammon at the Libyan Fountains of the Sun. He had sacrificed at every altar, to Pallas Athene at Troy, and most impiously to Jehovah in the Temple of Jerusalem. For his blasphemous assumption of divine honours—for he even courted adoration—he was most justly deprived of the courage of an ordinary mortal, so that he who aimed at being a god became at length less than a man, a beast rather, like his own Bucephalus frightened at its own shadow, before it had been reined in by the hand of its master. In his last days he had sold himself, body and soul, to the wizard and the sorcerer. He had lost the knack of converting bad omens into good. The fates were against him, or, rather, his mind was out of gear.

The Thugs are reported to have been the most superstitious people in India, and the Gypsies the most superstitious out of it, and he was worse than either. You may depend upon it, the red tint went out of his cheek when he saw the first white hare, the first lizard that dropped from the roof, or heard the first owl which screeched from the gloomy fortress of Oxyartes. The Chaldean priests warned him not to enter Babylon, and he remained some time on the outskirts of the city.* So he takes his pleasures sadly in coracle of skin or felucca of cedar, sailing "wearily up and down the Euphrates almost under the shadow of the Temple of Belus," courting the evening breeze to fan his fevered brow. For him the chase has lost all its charm, for what does he now care for lion by reedy stream, or deer in dusky desert? Plutarch tells us that "in Babylon the ground is of so fiery a quality, that the grains of barley often leap up, and are thrown out as if the violent heat gave a pulsation to the earth." In other words, Nature shimmers, the stars come out, and with them the shadow of the grim hero, who is not to be conquered, even by an Alexander.

"I will see you in a little in Babylon." You remember Saul, and how his gloomy and distempered mind and utter prostration of all his powers led him to make a last appeal to the Witch of Endor: the story also of Brutus in his tent at Abydos, when his lamp was dimly burning and the spectre muttered "Thou shalt see me at Philippi." Alexander also had his evil genius in an Indian gymnosophist from the plains of the Punjab. A poor wretch, Calanus by name, from Lahore or thereabouts, had been persuaded to leave his home against the laws of his religion, and accompany Alexander, and swell the triumph of his train on his return to Persia. He, falling sick by the way, and believing that his end was nearing, resolved on self-immolation. He thereupon offered prayers to heaven, poured forth libations, cut off his hair, and heaving it on the faggots, with a steady step ascended the funeral pyre, muttering these cabalistic words within hearing of the bystanders: "I shall see the king in a little at Babylon." They were words of doom.

A similar act of self-destruction took place at Athens in the days of Augustus; and strangers, long afterwards, were shown "The Indian's Tomb" on the banks of the Ilissus. Plutarch tells us that Calanus owed his name to *Cale*, "which is the Indian form of salutation." The Sanskrit कल्याणम्

* Because many ravens were seen when Alexander entered Babylon they were thought to presage his death.—(Sir Thos. Browne's Works. (Bohn.) Vol. 2, p. 80.)

(*Kalyâram*) means "Good Luck." * *Cale*, apparently a word tossed into Europe in the *débris* of the Macedonian Invasion, may have been the solitary specimen of the Sanskrit language (proper names excepted) existing in Europe for a thousand years, and for the existence of which we are indebted to Plutarch. It remains in a kind of way in this year of grace 1892. I am told by those who ought to know, that when any bargain is closed in Guzerat or the Dekhan, say on cotton or other market, a favourite form of expression by buyer or seller is "Kalyan O" ("May good luck come to you.") The town of Kalyan, "a fortunate city," may be as old as Alexander. Tughlak (A.D. 1312–18) wished to change its name to Islamabad, but his intentions could not be carried out. The city had a good name and retained it. Calanus perished in the flames; but the name exists when Taxiles and Patala are no more. Like some Alpine flora, rélic of the glacial period, picked up on Ben Lawers, or a daisy in Calcutta, this fragrant flower—culled by Macedonian hands, I ween, on Punjab plain—survives to us a memorial of the great cataclysm of B.C. 326.

Alexander was great as an explorer, and much increased the bounds of geographical knowledge. A mere list of the places he visited would, even in 1892, startle some members of the Geographical Society. How, with Nearchus' voyage before him, Strabo should have boasted of what he did, and leave Alexander out of his calculations, is incredible. Burton used playfully to remark, when Livingstone's praises were sounded in his ears, "Oh, but he was never in the Brazils." So Strabo and Herodotus were never on the Himalayas. Alexander had seen the Iron Gates, grazed his camel on the Oasis of Siwah, and rode Bucephalus down the Khyber Pass; you need not conjure up the ghosts of such small men as Mahmud, Genghis, or Tamerlane. He, too, had been at Balkh and Samarkand. You may follow him from the pebbly banks of the Danube to the erratic Oxus, and on the brow of Olivet catch a glimpse of him, as he descries the white-robed priests emerging from Jerusalem—not the Jerusalem of railway and telegraph, but Jerusalem still unstained by the blood of Herod

* I owe this to Professor Peterson, who died August, 1899, much regretted.

or the sack of Titus; and you may trace every milestone of his course, until he "had utterly overthrown the greatest empire in the world." And when he draws breath at Babylon, "the oldest seat of earthly empire," to receive the homage of the nations, we know of nothing in history to compare with him except it be Napoleon after Austerlitz. He had entered all the capitals of the Continent in triumph, and was preparing to make of Paris another Babylon, the metropolis of the world. And he, too, "at last led to his bed the daughter of its proudest sovereign," when events took place which baffled all his pretensions, and put an end for ever to his boundless ambition. What Alexander's feelings were on entering upon the new life and strange scenes in India we have no means of knowing. Would that he had written them down in the charming manner of Baber: "Passed the Hindoo Kush; rode all night. The appearance of the stars showed I was in a southern climate. On reaching the top of a hill, Canopus appeared below, far to the south." And then a wild burst of joy, which finds vent in poesy: "On descending from Kabul, all at once I saw a new world of vegetables, plants, trees, wild animals—all different."

I have no doubt that these were some of the new things which opened up to the eye of Alexander, sitting down in the shadow of a neem tree and sucking a melon; in the region of the Khalsa—its bazaars; its new temples and its new gods; its marriage processions redolent of champak and cocoanut; its burning bodies with the perfume of sandalwood: the same unchanging scenes which pass before the eye of the last stranger who descends from the unchanging mountains. His march in India has been described as that of a drunken, revelling army. *Indiæ per quam temulento comminabundus incessit agmine.* This is from "Livy's pictured page," and in the sledge-hammer fashion of the potential Latin tongue. Alexander was once temperate, but Persia, and specially his four months in Persepolis, ruined him. His culminating point of inebriation occurred when he rushed out and set fire to the palace of Xerxes.

> "Thäis led the way
> To light him to his prey;
> And, like another Helen, fired another Troy!"

A splendid beacon light to warn people where they ought not to go is this man, who, Arnold tells us, "planted the civilisation and language of Greece from the shores of the Ægean to the banks of the Indus, from the Caspian to the Cataracts of the Nile." And at what a cost! On his last, greatest, and final triumphal procession into Babylon fell a dark shadow, for there were people who remembered that he had entered India with 130,000 foot and 15,000 horse. He did not bring back one-fourth of the number. No pen has recorded the horrors of the Gedrosian Desert. The bones of his soldiers bleached on Baluchistan, or lay "scattered on the Alpine mountains cold." But long before his decease, drink and delirium had done their work, "marching home."

Sometimes, in the deserts of Sind, when lanes between milk bush and camel thorn were choked with dying and dead; when midnight came on, and the wind sweeping across the desert from beyond the dismal Hala Mountains moaned in low gusts, or whistled through the crevices of his scarlet pavilion; when a tent peg would burst from its moorings, and the wick in the olive oil would sputter and blow about; when darkness wrapped Alexander in its mantle: at some such eerie moment I marvel not that the ghastly spectre of Clitus or Parmenio should put in an appearance, or the poor bath boy he smeared all over with petroleum, a blaze of fire, or some of the 2,000 he hanged on Tyrian shore. It was in drink he killed his great general, Clitus; and it was in drink he ruined Aristotle's kinsman, Callisthenes.

At the orgies which followed the death of Calanus, Alexander offered a crown of gold to the man who drank the most; and the victor died in three days thereafter, followed quickly in ghastly succession by forty-one of the competitors. And in Babylon, writes Plutarch, the day after he had given Nearchus a sumptuous treat, in going to his bath, Medius invited him to take part in a carousal, and he could not deny him. How many tragedies have come after these words "he could not deny him," from the weakest man in the modern, up to the greatest man of the ancient, world. But read further: "There he drank all that night and the next day, until at last he found a fever coming upon him, and in the violence of his thirst he took a draught of wine which threw him into a frenzy, and—he died."

Some years ago, a traveller was met by the common observation that all the great roads which span the valleys and pierce the mountains of the South of Europe were the work of either Napoleon or the Romans. This is more than can be said of Alexander and the Greeks in India. But two cities, Candahar and Secunderabad, bear his name (Mahaffy), and half a dozen Alexandrias may be found in Asia. In the Middle Ages, everything incomprehensible by the European traveller in India was relegated to the Greeks. Coryat calls the iron pillar at Delhi "the brazen column of Alexander," and Linschotten thinks he was the maker of Elephanta. You may easily find a counterpart to Alexander and the priests of Egypt in Bonaparte's confabulations with the Ulemas of Arabia and the monks of Mount Sinai.

Josephus tells us that when Alexander was in Jerusalem, someone brought him the Book of Daniel, and pointed out the passage where he says the Greeks would destroy the Persian Empire, whereat Alexander was exceeding glad. A similar incident occurred to Napoleon. Someone pointed out to the Emperor the theory of Edward Irving that he was one of the living creatures of the Book of Revelations, with the same result. It was well for him that he did not read the same author's *Babylon Foredoomed of God*, for therein he describes Bonaparte as a prince of the blood royal of the infernal regions. In fact, he uses a stronger word.

Long before he entered India, he had doffed the Grecian, and donned a cross between the Persian and Median, costume. He wore a white robe and a Persian girdle, and he exacted from his subjects the servile prostrations of an Oriental despot. Europe was left behind, and he courted the manners of Asia. All his wives were ladies of Asia: Barsine was of Damascus, and had Persian blood in her veins; Roxana was a Bactrian princess; and Statira, tall and stately as the cedar of Lebanon, was a daughter of Darius. His victories of Granicus, of Issus, of Arbela, and over Porus, were all in Asia. The bulk of his life, the greater part of his manhood, was spent in Asia.

For ten years he was seldom out of it; and in Asia he found a grave, leaving—

> "A name at which the world grew pale,
> To point a moral and adorn a tale."

(3.) STRABO ON EGYPT AND INDIA.

UPON the whole, if Strabo were not such a captious critic, I should like him better than Pliny. Pliny is later in the day, and had seventy years more of the world's history to come and go upon, and, of course, made the whole field of animated Nature all his own. But each of these authors diverges from his special vocation. Pliny is glad of an occasion to dart away from Natural History to History proper, and Strabo strays from his Geography to wander over the fields of Time and Space. Nothing comes wrong to him. He will map the earth's surface, known and unknown, and like Le Verrier discovering the planet Neptune, give you a continent, because America *ought* to be where it is. But he goes farther than this: "If the extent of the Atlantic Ocean were not an obstacle we might sail from Iberia to India." Undoubtedly, if you sail far enough you will come to it. At all events Columbus shared this belief, for his dying words were, "I, a native of Genoa, in the distant west, discovered the Continent and Isles of India." But to come nearer home, he will tell you that the Red Sea once came up to the Bitter Lakes, which Oxford has at length arrived at as the only satisfactory clue to an explanation of the *locale* of the Exodus. Talk of the level of the two seas elicited by Robert Stephenson—it is all here in a nutshell. Then there is the Lake system in modern Africa of Livingstone and Burton, which he saw through a glass darkly—but he saw it. And in breadth of view he is far ahead of Pliny, both on his own gods and other people's gods, and considerably more companionable in this, that he has divested himself of much of the vulgar superstition of the times, and of which Pliny was such a laboured exponent. This is apparent in many instances. If some trifle bothers him, he slyly remarks that he will require to consult the oracle of Jupiter Ammon! I believe that all faith had well-nigh disappeared from the

Roman world, for he tells us that women are the only supporters of the festal worship of the gods. It was a period of profound peace—

> "No war or battle sound
> Was heard the world around,"

and men were asking, "Watchman, what of the night?" as if all religion had come to an end. And Strabo's remark looks very like it: "For scarcely is there a man living by himself who pays any attention to such matters."

Strabo, no doubt, had read the Septuagint, and is as fair to Jew and Gentile as a Roman could be, for he admits that Moses did justly, and worshipped God with sincerity, and that the Jews were right-minded persons; and he believes the tradition that the cities of the plain were blasted by the curse of God. He must have chuckled over the reply of the Indian sophist to Alexander, or he would not have recorded it. "He himself did not deserve a gift from one who was satisfied with nothing. Neither did he fear his threats, for as long as he lived India would supply him with food, and when he died he should be translated to a better and a finer existence." Worthy of Stoic or stubborn old Roman.

The magnitude of Indian commerce bulks big in his hands. Whence, he says, comes the opulence of Alexandria? It is from the costly products of India and the double duties (import and export) levied thereon; one hundred and twenty vessels sail every season from Myus Hormus (Cossier or thereabouts); and you have only to look at the bustle of the Mareotic Harbour by canal, to satisfy yourself that it far exceeds the sea-borne commerce of the city with the Mediterranean.

He writes of what he saw, for the great traveller landed in Egypt B.C. 24, in the reign of Augustus. Already Egypt was old; the Pyramids hoary with antiquity, the palaces of Memphis a heap of ruins, mud huts littered the courts of Thebes, the Oracle of Jupiter Ammon dumb and deserted, Heliopolis—like Ellora in our day—a refuge for charlatans and wandering outcasts. But some things there existed which Strabo saw that have now disappeared, such as the Pharos, the Labyrinth, Meroe and the Canopic mouth of the Nile, of which you cannot even trace where it flowed into the sea. Pompey's Pillar, the first object which now cuts the sky line as the stranger gazes landwards, had not then been removed to its present site. And, strange to say, neither Strabo nor Herodotus notes the Sphinx. Whence this reticence? Had the sand covered it up? What renders this visit so interesting is that Strabo arrived in Alexandria only six years after the deaths of Antony and Cleopatra. As everything is being whittled nowadays down to fable and romance, it is refreshing to find this great tragedy among the verities of history. He confirms the accepted version of the story, with the alternative of a poisonous ointment in the case of Cleopatra. You remember this passage in Tennyson's *Dream of Fair Women*, when they were all in their glory:—

> "We drank the Libyan sun to sleep and lit
> Lamps which out-burned Canopus. O my life
> In Egypt! O the dalliance and the wit,
> The flattery and the strife."

Strabo accompanied Ælius Gallus to Syene on the borders of Ethiopia. Human nature is the same in all ages, so we may readily imagine much pleasant converse by moonlight nights on the placid bosom of the Nile, with no sound but the murmur of the water and the flapping of the great lateen sail. This means Egypt, Arabia of necessity, and that phantom of the night, India, dimly discerned through a thick veil which Strabo was endeavouring to rend asunder. Then comes, as always, the great divide. The two friends part, never to meet again—most likely. Strabo returns to Italia, to fame, fortune, and a long life.

Gallus is appointed by Augustus to command an expedition to conquer Arabia; plunges into it with ten thousand men, and emerges twelve months thereafter with a few followers, the bulk of his army having perished by famine and pestilence; and in two short summers from the date of these moonlight siestas, meets degradation and death. No blame to him that he did not conquer Arabia. Treason had done its worst. That geographical research, of which Strabo was a pioneer, was sorely a-wanting. Over such a holocaust is written—"Died by the visitation of God," when it ought to be—"Died by the ignorance of man." But we need not moralise; we do as the Romans do, and more than once have fallen into the same trap. It must be already patent to the reader that the date of Strabo's arrival in Egypt was one of the most interesting periods in the history of mankind. He was an exceptionally lucky man for his age—for any age. If Mr. Froude were now to accompany the Viceroy over the newly acquired Province of Burma, there would be something like it, for his friend and companion, Ælius Gallus, was Prefect or Governor of Egypt. But this does not represent the whole matter. Strabo was a young man of thirty, an age when man is most susceptible of impressions from the outer world, and came brimful of associations. And there was this difference; here in India the fight was for an outlying province of the Empire, there the dispute was for the mastery of the world. Alexandria was then in all her glory, the mart of nations. The crowds which he saw had, only six years before, listened with bated breath to the news of the deaths of Antony and Cleopatra:—

> "A queen with swarthy cheeks and bold black eyes."

As Strabo paced those brown sandy mounds outside the Canopic Gate, he could observe the stones of Cæsar's camp which sheltered Augustus. No age or country has perhaps ever witnessed such a display of historical fireworks, for it has fascinated the minds of dramatists, painters, sculptors and writers of history for well-nigh two thousand years. You may see even in the latest magazine (October, 1891) a picture of Cleopatra. His long sojourn in Egypt seems to have been without alloy. "The Alexandrines pass their summers very pleasantly."

This is the whole record of Kamseen, wind, dust, flies, mosquitoes and scarabæi. He is the only traveller who finds nothing disagreeable. Neither the dogs—those night howlers—nor the braying of camels gave him the least annoyance. Boils and blains are beneath his notice. He compares the city to Ravenna, which, amid marshes, is kept purified by the flowing of water. A great deal of this was owing, no doubt, to the distinguished auspices under which he arrived, and the society of his august companion. He calls Ceylon the Cinnamon country, and the "island of the Egyptian exiles," the mere mention of which raises the ghost of Arabi. All such names, and there are many of them, adumbrate the deep gloom which, in the early days of navigation, followed the venturer through the "Gate of Tears," past the "Cape of the Banished Man," into unknown seas. In regard to India, he explains the difficulties of his position. The reason why India was so little known to the ancient world is not far to find. Very few went to it, and almost none came out of it. He says those who had gone were "ignorant persons who were not qualified to give an account of it."

And again, "Calanus (who burned himself at Antioch) accompanied Alexander beyond the boundaries of India, contrary to the usual custom," and "from one place in India, and from one King only, Pandion or Porus, presents and embassies were sent to Augustus Cæsar. With the ambassadors came the Indian gymnosophist, who committed himself to the flames at Athens." These were, without doubt, the first natives of India seen in any civilised portion of Europe. Pliny, seventy years later, accentuates the Indian's aversion to foreign travel. "The Indians were in manner the only men of all others who never went out of their own country." As we all know, this dread of Kala Pani still survives, fortified by the terrors of religion.

He holds the writers on India very cheap. "Generally speaking, the men who hitherto have written on the affairs of India were a set of liars. Deinarchus holds the first place in the list, Megasthenes comes next; while Onesicritus and Nearchus, with others of the same class, manage to stammer out a few words of truth." This is strong language. But all historians are as dust in the balance compared with Homer. Even Herodotus is a vendor of fables.

> "High o'er the rest the mighty Homer shone;
> Eternal adamant composed his throne."

On his own qualifications as a geographer he is equally clear: "Of all the writers on geography, not one can be mentioned who has travelled over a wider extent of the countries described than we have. Some may have gone farther to the west, but then they have never been so far east as we have; again, others may have been further east, but not so far west, and the same with respect to north and south."

Strabo *in* Egypt, you will thus see, is a much more fascinating subject than Strabo *on* India, and much more for him than for us, for Egypt to the men of his age was the cradle of religion, philosophy, science, art and history. When he passed the Pharos and stepped ashore from the deep harbour, he drank of this elixir, which for him was the nectar of the gods. And he has written *con amore* of all he saw and heard. You can see that his heart is in his work. As he jostled through the crowds and entered the museum, or sat himself down in some quiet corner and shady place of the library, at a time when outside the heat was ablaze, it must have been with a heavy heart and a wrench that he pulled himself away from Egypt to India. Through the Gate of Tears he passed from the known to the unknown. But what a change! Sandracottus for Sesostris, Porus for Pharaoh, Taxila and Taprobane for Thebes and Memphis, Patalene for the Delta, and a parcel of industrious but lying chroniclers for the august names of Homer and Herodotus. If this is history and travel, what is to become of us. With dogged resolution, however, he sat down to evoke order out of the chaos of perversity, fable and imposture, which, like a dense and impervious jungle, surrounded the whole subject. Clearly he was in the best of all places for noting the results of geographical research. So, with stylus and compasses in hand, the cartography of the known world in many sections lying before him, he brings his scrutinising ken to bear upon this India of ours—one of the waste places of the earth.

Searching out manuscripts of voyages and travels, the accumulations of 200 years, from the days of Ptolemy Philadelphus, noting, comparing, collating, separating the chaff from the wheat, and orally gathering to himself the views of the most eminent men of the day, he must have had his head and his hands fuller of India than any mortal of that generation. This is what he makes of it, and we purposely avoid all comment on his observations on religion and the castes of India. Our business is with lighter wares, as we are simply skimming on the surface. People who imagine that the India of these olden times was merely a lotus garden, where it was "always afternoon," are very much mistaken. The bulk of mankind had their duties to perform. Rivers and their banks, tanks and canals, required perpetual looking after to see that each received its fair allowance of water. The land required to be measured, ploughed, sown and reaped, houses repaired or rebuiit. There was the collection of taxes, which implied a Government and fiscal administration; the superintendence of guilds—workers in brass, leather, wood and carpentry, mines and forests. The organisation of their cities seems to anticipate the municipal exigencies of the present day, for they had a registrar of births and deaths, road surveyors, who placed pillars every ten stadia to indicate the way; so that, after all, Akbar's *kos minars* were not such a very new idea. Superintendents of weights and measures, markets and exchange, and regulation of the sales of produce in its season. A body of men was appointed to receive and entertain strangers, assign lodgings, observe their mode of life, and escort them out of the country on their departure; if they fell sick, nurse them, and if they died, look after their effects for the behoof of those concerned.

Whoever discovered a new poison was put to death, unless he could provide an antidote for the same. This argues a judicial administration. He says, further, that the people have no respect for old age, except with wisdom; that they were frugal, and had very few thefts in a camp of 100,000; never drank wine, had few law suits, left their house and property unguarded, ate alone, dressed in white muslin (? well-to-do people); while the rich, accompanied by men carrying umbrellas, wore dresses worked with gold and precious stones, and flowered robes, for they indulged in ornament. He says also that slavery was unknown, and that truth and virtue were respected, and, he adds, "everything was attended to which may improve the looks." This characteristic has come down. Many a domestic, whose face is in no ways beautiful, rejoices in a piece of broken looking-glass, and on idle days ogles and grins on his face by the hour, with the intensest gusto.

Occasionally a hamal in the middle of a street, of all places in the world to hold a mirror up to nature, is nearly bowled over and within an inch of paying a life for a look, while in the indulgence of this fascinating pursuit. Strabo says that India is a highly civilised country. Their boast was a proud one, which we give in his own words: "No army was ever sent out of India by the Indians, and no foreign army had ever invaded or conquered it." He grapples with the orography, the river system and the seasons of India. That the Ganges and the Indus are the greatest rivers, and that their annual rise is owing to the melting of snows, that it rains incessantly for three months, that there are in the year two crops, that rice is sown in beds and stands in water in an enclosure, that the harvest is in the (Italian) winter, that wool grows on trees, and reeds yield honey—all which is above criticism. He who runs may read. He does not mention the Narbudda, on which was Barygaza, the Broach of these latter days.

Our old friend Captain Wood would not have discovered the source of the Oxus, had he anticipated all the hubbub about it. Pamir, "Roof of the World," means Caucasus in Strabo, to which he holds on most tenaciously, like the Indian dogs which he describes, and will not let go. He says "The Oxus is navigable with ease, and large quantities of Indian merchandise are conveyed by it to the Caspian and thence to the Euxine." This is the way our Indian trade is to go in the remote future, for all the Russians must be reading Strabo. His account of the banyan tree is the first given by any European of authority. The elephant, and the methods of its capture, the crocodile of the Indus, the lion and the tiger, attract much of his attention. Twenty thousand people die (1890) of snake bite annually. The number must have been enormous in ancient times, for the war that has been incessantly waged upon them for twenty centuries in Europe and in Asia must have thinned their numbers, particularly in Europe. Pliny gives a list of about one hundred cures for snake bite, and these antidotes were evidently in great demand. Strabo saw in Egypt a snake brought out of India, nearly nine cubits and a span, which does not appear very wonderful. The small snakes, he says, which coil themselves up in tents, vessels, and hedges are more to be dreaded. There was abundance of snake charmers who professed to cure those that were bitten. The monkeys do not attack men, but will roll down stones on those who disturb them. The Macedonians came upon several hundreds of them on an eminence in line, and were prepared to give them battle! But the days of Huniman were then evidently over, and nothing more came of it.

The name of Asoka does not appear in his Indian book, and it is curious to note the absence of all reference to the great reservoirs and the places of pilgrimage—striking features, we presume, of those ancient times.

There was much to be seen in Strabo's time that is seen now, and I am bound to believe that the same dignified courtesy was as conspicuous then as in the days of modern durbars. Some of the great highways of the earth have remained unchanged. When the Proconsul of our days starts for the East, he bids adieu to Europe at Brindisi as of yore, and follows on the Suez Canal some tracks at least of the ancient canal of Sesostris. Should he call at Malta he will still find "the island whence come the little dogs called Maltese." He will still see fights between the mongoose and the snake, the sacred crocodiles, the rafts on jars floating on the Nile, the boatmen who run down the cataracts, and the Bedouins who run up the Pyramids for his amusement, and at his destination night will still be made hideous by the infernal din of tom-toms.

"The first time the Vettones (Europe or Asia, all the same) came to a Roman camp, and saw certain of the officers walking up and down for the mere pleasure of walking, they supposed that they were mad, and offered to show them the way to their camp." This is admirable, and one of the things B.C. 24 which has remained for the amusement of the Proconsul, or any other man, of A.D. 1891.

(4.) OSTIA TO OZEIN, A.D. 68.*

I WAS in Rome in Nero's time; but, being suspected as a friend of the new religion, it was considered advisable that I should leave the country. I wish you to know that

* Although the writer of this paper is aware that the spirit of modern scepticism has not spared the venerable tradition of St. Thomas's Martyrdom in India, he clings to the old story, and even transgresses its limits, by taking the Apostle to Barygaza (Broach). If St. Thomas came to India, it is as likely he landed there as anywhere else.—J. D.

I did not flee from justice—quite the reverse. I fled from injustice and cruelty, and would have faced them to the death, had not the conviction forced itself upon me, that I should serve the cause I had espoused a great deal better by absenting myself from those scenes of judicial murder, where so many of my friends had perished.

It was not I who was the criminal, but the Emperor of Rome; I did not fly to escape death. The turning point in my career was the day I saw Paulus decapitated. I dare say you know the place outside the gates of Rome, by the tomb of Cestius, on the way to Ostia. That was my way. I never afterwards entered the city, but fled to that seaport, as the nearest way of escape from a land accursed by God and all good men. It was a bleak winter day; Soracte was white with snow; and you may believe me that the leaving of Rome was a bitter draught, and it was with a heavy heart that, sitting down on the wayside, I took a last lingering look of the apex of the Capitol as it faded away to a mere speck on the distant horizon.

I had enormous difficulty in obtaining a license for Egypt, but, once secured, I lost no time in availing myself of it, and I at once embarked for that country. The die was cast, and I was not long in bidding adieu to Portus Romanus. Our voyage was the old story, Parthenope and Virgil's tomb. Then came Pompeii and Herculaneum, their white houses gleaming in the sun in all their glory among the vineyards of Vesuvius, unconscious of the destruction that was so soon to come upon them. Then followed Sicily, Calabria and Rhegium. Aetna kept us company for days. We had a quick voyage, for, in one week after leaving Mesinum, we saw the white waves break on Pharos Isle and the cliffs which embattle Cæsar's Camp at Alexandria. Had I not been in possession of the Emperor's permit I should not have been allowed to land. As it was, I was detained several days in the harbour of Eunostus, where I amused myself fishing for red mullet, watching dreamily the nautilus with miniature sail gliding over the blue waters, or observing the strings of camels emerging from the yellow western desert, and disappearing amid the green palm groves which then surrounded the Necropolis. Separated by a strip of land lay Mareotis, like a white sheet, dazzling to the eye in the bright sunlight, stretching away to an apparently illimitable extent, and dotted with myriads of sailing craft, big and little.

I did not like Egypt. It is a dirty country. The dead dogs and camels which lay about the streets, and the legions of flies which battened on their carcasses, left me little pleasure in observing the glories of the Ptolemies and the architecture with which they had covered this corner of the brown and sandy desert of Africa. Besides, I did not come out to Egypt to study antiquities or architecture, so the hippodrome, museum, gymnasium, tower, temple and theatre had no attraction for me. Some one asked me to go and see some ruins. No, I said, we have plenty of ruins in Rome: life and liberty are in ruins. Another pointed to Heliopolis. Had Plato survived and been there himself, I would not have troubled him. I had a greater master than he.

On landing I had immediately communicated my design to the Prefect of Egypt, which was to proceed to the Erythrean Sea and countries beyond. Nero had a long arm, and I wanted to be beyond the reach of it. I learned that a galley was likely to leave Berenice, on the Red Sea, for the south, in about two months.

Strange to say, my request was granted. It had been rumoured that I belonged to the new religion, and the Prefect was glad to get quit of me, and have me out of the way. That religion, however, had already found its way to the museum, and was destined to shatter in pieces its accumulated learning of ages. I lost no time in quitting Alexandria; so, tossing myself and my belongings into a *dahabia*, or great, lumbering Nile boat, and threading our way through a canal crowded with shipping, in a day or two I found myself on the broad bosom of the Nile. Whoever has seen only the Tiber will meet with a surprise in the Nile, which the natives call "Sea of the Nile"; and so it is. The Etesian winds soon filled our one great sail and wafted us up that mighty river, past the Pyramids, which I saw from the deck, past the ruins of Memphis, on and on for a whole moon, until we were almost within hail of Thebes. It was a tedious voyage; the bean fields were a mass of flowers, and the fragrance was more exquisite than all the perfumes of Arabia. At length we arrived at Coptos, that great emporium of Araby and Ind. Here we bade adieu to the Nile, and, after waiting a week for the starting of the caravan, prepared for crossing the desert of the Thebaid, which divided us from Berenice and the Red Sea. I had never been on a camel before, or travelled in the desert. But, O Lord, the earth is full of thy wonders. What sunsets! It was a new heaven and a new earth. Sometimes by day we saw cities which vanished like a dream, and at night the moon lightened up an enchanted world with its silver radiance.

I had not long to wait at Berenice, for a stout two-masted ship, built of Indian teak, lay in the offing. I now bade adieu to the big lateen sail of Egypt, and, committing myself to the tender mercies of the Arab sailors, was soon under weigh for Mouza (Mocha). We anchored every night in some bay or creek. I never saw a more desolate or God-forsaken looking country than that which fringes the coast of Arabia-Felix—hills, with razor-like edges, as bare of grass as the Appian Way in August, with islands belching forth fire and flame, as if the Lord still thundered from Sinai and Horeb, which, indeed, were not far from us. Here the genius of Desolation seems to have taken up its abode. The very names of the places are full of lamentation, mourning, and woe, and press with a heavy burden on the spirits: "The Straits of Burial," "The Gate of Tears," "The Gate of Affliction," "The White Man's Grave," "The Harbour of Death," are some of them.

If I told you all I have seen of the Red Sea I am sure you would not believe me. The Erythrean is the chameleon of all the seas. It is sometimes green, sometimes leaden-coloured, like the Great Sea when the Khamsin comes hot and sultry from the desert; sometimes of a silver sheen, it lies in great sheets, a dead level and calm without a ripple, a molten looking-glass, blinding and dazzling to behold. Sometimes it is as yellow as the saffron of Soli, sometimes as black as the Gulf of Tarentum before a thunderstorm—"a dark and stormy water," or again blue as Galilee nestling among its oleanders. I have seen it as red as blood, and once, only once, I saw a sight that made me quake. For days this sea had been coated with an oily-looking scum. It stank horribly, like a Stygian bog. It had neither sound nor motion. A storm arose, and I was awoke at midnight, and, staggering over ropes and piles of broken wood, I reached the hinder part of the ship, and there I saw a sight that I can never forget—"a sea of glass, mingled with fire!" For lo, and behold a sea, far as the eye could reach, as white as milk, with waves crested with fire, breaking upon an unknown shore, while Orion paled his ineffectual fires and drifted lazily across the midnight sky. The Lord was abroad, as He is, indeed, everywhere. But I had almost forgotten; once it rained sand. Sand covered the ship inches deep, and once we were entangled in a sea of pumice stone—scoria and *débris*, vomited forth by burning mountains on the surrounding waters, through which for miles we ploughed sluggishly our weary way. We were two moons on our voyage from Berenice to Mouza, and every bird we saw was of the same colour as the sand of the desert.

At Mouza I made another change of craft, and took my passage in a two-masted *bagala* of 500 tons, substantially built, with a horse's head on the prow, after the fashion of Gades. She was bound for Aden, Barygaza and Craganore, and had a crew of forty Arab sailors. Strange to say, there was not a Jew, Egyptian, Persian or Indian among them; whether prejudice, politics or religion was the cause, I know not; but the Arab did not avoid distant voyages, and procured ships, albeit no timber grew on his shores. He is lord of the sea, as he is also lord of the land. Our skipper was a Phœnician, one of that race who, from the time of Solomon and Hiram King of Tyre, have ploughed the mighty deep from Albion to Taprobane—a man well tanned by sun and storm, gnarled and knotted like the oak on his native hills. I saw him throw a coin into the sea for luck when we were leaving; and, when one of our sailors died and was being put overboard, he put a coin into his turban to pay his shot, he said, in the next world; this was all he disbursed from Mouza to Barygaza. He gabbled many languages, could read none of them, and took his bearings every night by the star Canopus.

Besides our crew, we had hired a company of Greek mercenaries, archers, and men accustomed to the use of both bow and javelin; otherwise our lives and property would have been at the mercy of the pirates who infest the Indian seas we were about to traverse. For, besides our cargo, of which I shall speak presently, we had treasure on board to pay for what we intended to bring back with us—ingots and coins, with Cæsar's image and superscription stamped thereon, all carefully packed and soldered in strong boxes, bound together with clamps of iron.

We drew much water, for we were heavily laden. Our dead weight was tin, lead, and brass, with sundry articles of Greek metal-work and cinnabar. We had 100 casks of the wines of Italy and Asia Minor for the King of Guzerat, bales of the fine linen of Egypt for the Zamorin, antimony for tinging the eyes, and coral from the depths of the Ælanitic Gulf. Incense, spices, and gums from Edom spread a delicious odour all round the ship. And there were two white asses from Nubia; their food was beans and chopped straw; each was attended by a Negro sais, and they were destined for one of the magnates of Sorath.

For our daily provender, for two hundred souls, we had the wheat and lentils of Egypt. The sound of the grinding of the hand-mills never ceased, day or night. We had dried fish of unsavoury odour, and a plentiful supply of that best gift of heaven, the blessed water of the Nile. You may be sure we did not forget to bring with us the leeks, the onions, and the garlic of Egypt. But I had almost forgotten to say we had on board a number of slaves, destined for the harem of the King of Ozein, him who sways the sceptre of Maharashtra. The skipper called them "live lumber." There was no slavery in India before our people touched it. That accursed thing came in with the Romans. So was it with piracy. The seas were silent before our time; so, when you had no commerce, you had no capture. As soon as you cover the sea with your sails every creek in India will swarm with the pirates. O my God, are these the blessings we carry to new countries? Where is the peace and good will to men left by my Divine Master?

The oaths and curses which were launched at these poor wretches as they lay half-naked, huddled together on a pallet of palm leaves, drenched with sea water—for at times we shipped heavy seas—burned into my soul, and left a wound never to be closed in this world. I had no need to be told whence they came, or what country they hailed from. The diverse features which Nature stamps on the faces of men were as familiar to me as my own sandals or turban amid that seething mass of wretchedness and woe. The almond eye of the Arab, the oval face of the Copt, the fairer skin of the Abyssinian, the Ethiop, which carried me back to the time of Moses. They came from regions far remote. One had been kidnapped in Sabea; and, strange to say, we had two Greek slaves from the so-called land of deathless liberty. One had been captured by a human bloodhound as she strolled beyond the Greek quarter of Memphis. Their keeper was a Greek, a beast—for I cannot call him a man.

One of the white slaves sickened and died the day before we reached that volcanic cinder-basket—Aden. We were becalmed, and the heat was awful, worse than when you are groping in the silver mines of Laurium, or in the bowels of the earth among the marble of Carara. I could learn very little about her. She had come with the tin men from the Cassiterides, those islands that are lashed by the mighty waves of the Iberian Ocean. No one knew her language, and she only at intervals muttered *hame, hame* (or hiem, hiem), which no one could understand, except as her last expression of bitterest anguish. She lies buried at the foot of King Solomon's Tanks. A few drops of water trickle from a cranny in the building, which, watering the soil, may one day produce green leaves. The face of that girl haunts me even now, and I shall never cease to hear her moans.

Here was beauty greater than that of all the Fulvias and Flavias of Imperial Rome, saved only by death from the tyranny of ruthless and barbarian masters, or from becoming the plaything of caprice of some petty Oriental despot. It was the month of May when I stood ankle deep in the dust and ashes of Aden. It was then I thought of Italy, and saw, in vision, the crops on the Campagna ripening towards harvest, and the great white oxen ploughing in the happy Tuscan valleys, and yearned to live over again those days when, in Judean fields, my Master read lessons from the rose of Sharon and the lily of the valley.

But these scenes are no longer for me, and I am on the

boundless ocean, and behind me, on a howling wilderness, the sun sets, like a ball of fire, leaving me to night and new stars. One evening after we left Aden, as I lay asleep on deck, I was suddenly awoke by the cry of an Arab sailor (on the outlook) of "*Moussoon*, aho"; and there, sure enough, on the south-west rose a big black cloud that soon over-canopied everything. Then came the straining of cordage, the creaking of timbers, and the rattling of chains; and the wind howled, and the sea rose tumultuously, and the rain fell in sheets, the lightning flashed and the thunder bellowed, all over the ocean. It was indeed the monsoon of Hippalus, which met us as an enemy, but became our friend, for next morning we were able to spread our sails to the wind, and our bark flew through the turbulent element like a bird, as it drove us on to India.

O thou Arabian Sea, that has fondled so many on thy bosom, I love thee well. Not boisterous with Boreas as Magnum Mare, not vexed with frost and fog as Adria or Thracian Bosphorus, not petulant like Pontus or Ægean, but calm and consistent even in thy great wrath, when thy waves are hurled with each revolving season on Socotra or Arabian shore.

"You will be in India to-morrow," said the skipper to me, one morning. "God be praised," said I, "if no mischief befall us."

According to his calculation we were now about one hundred miles from the pirate coast, when a strange craft hove in sight next day, and gave us chase and caught us up. They came so near that we were able to pour a shower of arrows upon them with deadly effect, heaving some stink-pots upon their heads, which spluttered with mortal fire, and made them dance about like so many devils. They were the Sanganians, black as night, and, having dozens of rowers sweating at their oars, they soon disappeared and we saw no more of them. Without our archers we should certainly have been made a prey unto their teeth and bloody cruelty, doomed to die, or told off in gangs to cut out caves in the rocks of Karli, or Kanheri, in the far away Dekhan.

There are two ways in which you can tell you are near India long before you see it. The first is that the sea becomes yellow and muddy. This is the manner of Egypt and the Nile. Here also a great river falls into the sea below Barygaza. It is two miles wide and rises in the Caucasus. Then the sea is full of snakes. The water is alive with them, black and yellow, with white bellies, seething like a boiling pot, and tumbling up the briny yeast in wild confusion.

But now for a sight of land; and, as we gazed vacantly over the waste of waters, simultaneously a king's pilot-boat signalled us to heave to; for you must know that the navigation to Barygaza is so difficult, by reason of shoals, that the king has established a fleet of pilot-boats to reconnoitre all in-coming vessels, and for this purpose they scour the sea as far as Syrastrene. The king does not do this for nothing, but takes toll on this account from every ship that enters his dominions, and if a pilot loses the ship he loses his head. A dense mist covered the shore line as we approached it. Suddenly the curtain lifted, and India appeared. Not the India of my dreams, I ween, but an India of sludge and oyster rocks and mud banks, a dreary, low-lying expanse of coast, where the bittern, on one leg, stands sentinel on an empire of desolation, and a flight of cranes hurtles in the sky, filling the air with harsh dissonance.

I had often asked myself what became of the men who set out from Greece and Egypt for India and never returned. The ghastly evidence lay before me. The shore was strewn with wrecks. Dotted here and there, settling down in the mud, was many a once gallant bark from far off Colzium or Myushormus, monument and grave alike of some storm-tossed mariner from the Isles of Greece.

I dare say you may have seen the ribs of a camel sticking up in the desert. In the clear, crisp morning air they bulk big, and cast black shadows athwart the stony wilderness. The camel is the ship of the desert, and the ship is the camel of the sea. O my God, this is not the India I came in search of. But be of good cheer—"Blessed are they who have not seen and yet have believed."

Hungry, thirsty and faint, I staggered with weary limbs across unsteady planks from the ship into Barygaza. A voice came: "Be of good cheer. Thy soul is vexed with the dried fish of Hydramaut, but beeves and sheep are plentiful in

Barygaza." So I was an hungered, and I did eat, and I sat myself down, like Jonah under his gourd, beneath the shadow of a great cactus. And I prayed and wept, wept and prayed again for the city. O India, thou hast deceived thyself. I fell asleep, and when I rose I was refreshed. A stranger met me, and I said unto him: "Pray, of what religion art thou?" And he said unto me: "Come and see." So I went forth in the strength of my great Master.

Thousands of every race were hurrying to the temples of the gods—not the gods of Greece or Egypt. They had never heard of them, nor the true God. To gain eternal salvation men died by fire, by water, by the hook, and by the car; and women burned themselves with their husbands. But a new religion, with yellow robe and begging bowl, was jostling the gods of India from their seats, and giving passports to man for this world and the world to come. Thousands of men were hewing out their temples from the living rock; and, as one idol after another was portrayed or carved on the walls, the multitudes would burst into cries of the wildest enthusiasm, as if heaven itself had made what their own hands had created.

The stranger then took me over Barygaza. The town is full of crimps and sailors, and her dharamsalas are filled with half the scum of the Eastern world and other abominations. I take my stand at early dawn in their bazaar. I am surrounded with crates of the porcelain ware of China, bales of coarse cotton cloth from Tagara, Gangetic muslins and silk from Serica, that will bring its weight in gold at the gates of Rome, or packed in sandal-wood boxes, furnish robes for some Cleopatra.

What we brought with us lies in motley confusion, to be converted into money, or bartered for the products of the country; but, as a rule, everything exported to Egypt is paid for in bullion or specie. The Romans have plenty of money, and never grudge payment of any thing when they want it. Most of the commodities of India go into little bulk and stand expensive land or water carriage. I see cowrie shells passing from hand to hand, coins of Menander, the *débris* of Bactrian mints from the first Arsacid downwards; golden pieces, hammered out in the shadow of Kylas, and hoondies of the shroffs written with a reed in strange characters from right to left.

From the water-gate ascend a never-ending string of coolies, bearing on their heads the pomegranates, the mangoes, and luxurious fruits of the East; and I remembered the words of Cyrus, that countries which produce delicious fruits rear feeble and delicate men. Yea, true it is, and of verity. The porters of Ostia, or Hierapolis, can carry burdens far beyond the power of India. I heard much of Ozein. Everybody was talking about it. There is only one city in the world praised in Barygaza, and that city is Ozein. Everything that comes by sea goes to Ozein—the tin of Britain, the wines of Cyprus, the silver of Laurium, the alabaster of Thebes, the cinnamon of Ceylon, and the frankincense of Arabia. It was a beautiful city, well watered and glittering with streams, like Damascus. Its towers and temples were seen from afar, its meadows were green with verdure which fattened innumerable kine. What Rome is to Italy, Ozein is to Maharashtra.

Need I tell you of the country outside Barygaza? Rice covers the lagoons, and tree-wool the breezy slopes or higher ground, bread for the food of man and raiment to put on; a green country, after Aden and Arabia. But the wonder of wonders was the tides. At Ostia the Tyrrhenian Sea, and that of Hierapolis itself, measures five feet from the highest to the lowest. Here the tide sometimes rises thirty feet, rushing up the shoals with the speed of a racehorse, a foaming avalanche of water filling the air with a roar like thunder. And the people? The Chinaman is here with his pigtail; and he from Taprobane, with woman's locks, selling pearls; naked ascetics also, smeared with ashes, with their hair coiled on high after the fashion of a turban.

And as for the beasts and birds of this region, they are all in the Book of Job. The lion is there; the bison and wild ass of the desert, with the salt land as his dwelling place; the peacock, with its goodly wings, and the ostrich that scorneth the horse and his rider. "Stranger," I said again, "what is thy religion?" When he answered that he was a Christian, I fell on his neck and kissed him.

Salaam, and *Domine dirige nos.* I gave him a piece of

papyrus, of sacred interest, on which, in indelible ink, I wrote these words which I had received from my blessed Master:—

"Blessed are they who have not seen and yet have believed," my watchword, my talisman, and my guerdon for India; words which will carry me through all suffering, and enable me to face death, if need be, on those mighty plains which lie between Malabar and Coromandel. My name is Thomas, and I am called "The Apostle of the Indies."

(5.) INDIAN NOTES ON PLINY.

"Like the Bible, the *Iliad*, Herodotus and Marco Polo."—*Sir George Birdwood.*

People often wonder where Milton got his Indian fig-tree (banyan) which he plants in the Garden of God. "In Malabar or Dekhan spreads her arms." Pliny's words may have been borrowed from Strabo, who must have been indebted to the soldiers of Alexander. The two great vegetable wonders of India—the plantain and the banyan—in their confused reports had figured as one. Let us read the account given of the wonderful tree in the bulky folios of Philemon Holland's translation of Pliny.* "The leaves of this tree are very broad, made in the form of an Amazonian or Turkish target. A most pleasant and delectable sight, whether a man come neare and look into it, or stand afarre off, so fair and pleasant an arbour it is, all greene and framed archwise, in just compasse." The banana leaves rival in size the Amazonian shields we see in a frieze in the Capitol, but in shape resemble more the shields of the Zulus. Pliny's imagery of arch, mother and daughters, have all been transmuted by the genius of Milton into the purest gold. Not less is he indebted for that sublime passage on the Genius of England, its eye undazzled, like the eagle's, at the midday beam. How quaintly Pliny gives the myth: "If she see any of them to winke or

---

* *The Historie of the World*, commonly called the Natural Historie of C. Plinius Secundus, translated into English by Philemon Holland, Doctor in Physics, and printed in London, by Adam Islip, in the year 1601.

their eyes to water at the rayes of the sunne, she turns it, with the head forward out of the nest as a bastard and not right, strikes them with her winges and forces them to look full against the sun's beams." Here, again, Milton is the alchemist. Carlyle was very fond of illustrating stupidity by the ostrich with its head in a hole. Pliny may have been the inventor of the conceit: "The veriest fool as they be of all others, for as high as the rest of their bodies is, yet if they thrust their head and neck once into any shrub or bush, and get it hidden, they think then that they are safe enough, and that no man seeth them."

Pliny, we think, must have seen the Old Testament, or how should he call the Dead Sea "that accursed lake"? He knew, at all events, of Moses—"Magicians which took their first foundation from Moses." Elsewhere he says, "since the Deluge," which is not much here or there, as the Greeks, and *ergo* the Romans, had this landmark of their own. One thing is clear, he hated the Jews: "A nation above all others noted for contempt and mockery of the gods;" which I do not wonder at, after all they had suffered at the hands of the Romans—sack of Jerusalem included (A.D. 70), which, when Pliny wrote, was only "the other day." As far as I have seen he does not in this book condescend to mention the Christians. Jew or Christian—perhaps, like his accomplished friend, Gallio the Proconsul, he "cared for none of these things." Pliny may have witnessed the stoning of St. Paul; but whether he did so or no, the fact remains that he was born before our Lord died, and lived during the time the greater part of the New Testament was written. There must have been sayings or expressions—common enough parallel passages. Here are two: "A thing ordinarily seen—that in our own country we are least regarded"; and "Are the clouds red about the sun as he goes down, you shall have a fair day the morrow after," the counterparts of which are in the New Testament, as I take it, the proverbial philosophy of the time. This may be useful to some poor staggerer at the grave of Lazarus: "Alabaster, a white stone out of which boxes and pots are made to receive sweet perfumes and ointments." The mines were at Thebes, and are still unexhausted. I do not think he had Esau's mess of pottage in his eye when he wrote, "Eating lentils maketh men mild and patient." It would have been a formidable illustration for the contention. You remember the Lord Bishop of Calcutta preached nearly an hour from the text, "Ye have need of patience"; the patience he spoke about, however, did not come of "eating lentils." Curious enough it is to note that the builders of the Temple of Diana at Ephesus chose cedar for the timber work, 400 years after Solomon had made the same selection. The wooden man—4,000 years old—in the Cairo Museum is of the same material. Am I right—was the algum, imported by Solomon from India, teak? Some of the teak in the roof of Karli Caves must be 1,500 years old. Note also that the temple at Cyzicum had neither nail nor pin in its timber work, and that all lame or unsound beasts were excluded in sacrifice from the Roman and the Jewish ritual.

A notable verse in Scripture is, "I am the Rose of Sharon and the Lily of the Valley." Pliny holds that the rose is the first of all flowers, and the lily only second thereunto, an estimate which may hold good until the end of time. The Israelites remembered the leeks and the onions and the garlic of Egypt, and Pliny does not forget these vegetables, for which that country is and has been always famous. Old age may find a new comfort in the interpretation, all unconscious as it is of Solomon's, "The almond tree shall flourish," when it reads Pliny's dictum, "The almond is most fertile when it is old."

When he speaks of where Jerusalem "stood," he authenticates the date of his own history, written soon after its destruction; and when he describes Jerusalem as the greatest city, not only in Jewry but in Asia, he makes it appear larger than it is generally understood to have been. When Pliny wrote, the "balm of Gilead" still scented the morning air. And he is very explicit. "It can abide no place but Jewry; and not all Jewry, but only about Jericho." The story goes that the Queen of Sheba brought a specimen of it and gave it to Solomon, and he put it in his garden there. But I have read, and can confirm, that every vestige of it has disappeared.

He is better still on Jericho—as the name denotes, "City of Palm Trees." Our readers are aware that there are very few palm trees in Syria. But here they are at this day (1891). Pliny stands midway between Joshua's times and ours (3,300 years), the same then as now. Phœnicia got its name from the palm, and it is the symbol on its earliest coinage, and overshadows "Judæa Capta" on the coin of Vespasian, since it was—

> "Trodden down by all in turn,
> Pagan, Frank, and Tartar."

Pliny's Cœle-Syria is almost a blank; Damascus little; Baalbek nothing. And yet the three great hewn stones, when laid in position, 230 feet in length, must have been there. Hadrian's columns came after, and no work of mortal man is so imposing, not even the Acropolis, at a distance.

But why did he not notice this great centre of the worship of Astarte-Ashtaroth and its Temple of Heliopolis? For the same reason, perhaps, that Herodotus takes no notice of the Sphinx, the greatest wonder of Egypt. It was a god, and *sub silentio*, for it was not lawful for man to utter.

I had almost forgotten Soli of Cilicia, a seaport, a pleasant place, even now, to spend an idle day, with its amphitheatre not quite so large as Arles or Verona. It has given the word "solecism" to the English language. From Pliny's account it must have been a kind of Grasse. It exported crocuses to Alexandria, and saffron ointment to Rome, and Paul quoted Aratus, "one of your own poets" (born here), to the men of Athens. But I must cross over to Egypt. Pliny mentions that Alexander the Great went to consult the oracle of Jupiter Ammon. The temple is on the Oasis of Siwah, some sixty miles west of Alexandria, and forty miles inland, in the Libyan Desert. Brown in the last century, and St. John in this, have seen it. I knew him well, his donkey also, who "ate with the family," and carried his master on that memorable expedition. The fountains of the sun are there, and some gigantic ruins to attest its former grandeur. Alexander used to swear by Jupiter Ammon; so did Sir Charles Napier. He mentions that the flowers in Egypt have no scent, and that cherries will not grow in Egypt, which is true enough; that the Egyptian priests wore cotton raiment, that Cleopatra's sails were purple, that the best amaranth comes from Alexandria, and that the favourite dates were from Thebes and Arabia, possibly from Mount Sinai, and they still rank high.

He omits Egyptian wine, noticed in Horace. Curious enough, a promontory in Lake Mareotis is the site also of the present vineyards which supplied the Mareotic wine. You remember Lesseps, at the opening of the Suez Canal, presented a bottle of Egyptian wine to the Empress Eugenie. Pliny says that "wine is the only drink that giveth strength within and fortifieth the vital power." But no man will swear by this if he reads his chapter on drunkenness among the Romans, and of the drunkards who have the audacity to say that they, of all men, are the only ones who enjoy themselves. Of the wine of Pompeii, which some of us have tried, he says, "If a man drink thereof overnight, he shall be sure not to have his head in good tune until noon the morrow after." There now lies in the museum next to the Hotel Diomede an object-lesson dug out of the ruins, which appeals to the passers-by—a drunkard naked, resting on his elbows on a pallet of straw, and has been transfixed into stone by the sculptor. His wife, her face in shadow, like that of Grief on the tomb of Canova, bends over him, and with a hand pressing on each side of his temples, endeavours to alleviate his agony, while an amphora, bottom upwards, which is suggestive, completes the group.

The India of Pliny's time is a dark, dim, and distant region on which Pliny's light is as darkness. He calls Herodotus "the Prince of Lyars." Had he done for India one hundredth part of that which Herodotus did for Egypt, we would have been thankful. But Herodotus had been in Egypt, about which the information obtainable was very large, and Pliny had not been in India, the knowledge of which in his time was exceedingly small. So the verities were against him. No man then living in Europe could have done much more. Why did he not let it alone, instead of groping blindfold among what he himself admits were "the monstrous and fabulous reports that go of India"? But what could he know of India? He saw its drugs, its spices, and its diamonds. India, to the Roman of his days, was the land of silks and precious stones, beryl, turquoise, agate and sardonyx, ivory and ebony. He saw also its Calicut pepper, upon which the East India

Company began its trade fifteen centuries later. He knew that cotton was produced there, and he had seen millet (jowari), the seed of which had been brought out of India, growing in the Campagna seven feet high, and he adds that some of the chaplets which crowned their heroes came out of India. He never seems to think that there was a civilisation in India, though drugs require ages of experience and wisdom in their selection, and diamonds great art and skill in the cutting and polishing thereof. When this was exhausted he fell back on the confused reports of the soldiers of Alexander—very confused, for Arrian was not yet born, and Ptolemy was not born; consequently, the Periplus unwritten. Hence the locusts three feet long, and the ants which dug out the gold, and all the swarm of "Gorgons, Chimæras, Furies, and their snakes;" and yet gold coins in his age were being produced beyond the Indus, and silver coins at Supara on the Arabian Sea, that would not disgrace the mints of Rome. For there were in India in Pliny's time great cities, and when he died under the slopes and by the fumes of Mount Vesuvius, Barygaza, from the broad bosom of the Nerbudda, was already wafting her commercial argosies north, south, east, and west. Uujain, Kanouge, Moultan and Delhi (with another name thereabouts) dominated these respective regions. Tagara, from her eyrie on Dowlatabad, held the key of the Dekhan, and the sound of the mason's mallet resounded from the storied arches of Karli. You may depend upon it, India was not a land only of Gymnosophists, or even of Buddhists seeking Nirvana. Then, as now, thousands of artisans earned their livelihood by the sweat of their brow, and the ryot laboured in his field "from morn to dewy eve"; there were marriages, processions, fairs, mighty crowds of men and women jostling, fasting, praying, and darkening the spacious highways which led to the five holy places of India.

The history of the world, to the Englishman, centres in Britain, and to it we now turn our attention. We were not the men we thought we were. Pliny draws aside the curtain, and here are our ancestors in all their hideous deformity—at all events, as they appeared to the Roman of A.D. 76. "Woad, with the juice whereof the women of Britain, as well the married wives as the young maidens their daughters, anoint their bodies all over, resembling the colour of Moors and Ethiopians, in which manner at some solemn feasts and sacrifices to go all naked." O Pliny! You do not mean it or believe it! Elsewhere he says: "The British murder men in sacrifice to please their gods;" and again, "Magic holds great sway in Britain." "Physician, heal thyself." This is Pliny, who would not plant a scallion without consulting the stars, or the occultation of his favourite, whatever it may be we know not—"the occultation of the Brood Star Virgiliæ."

However, we have some redeeming qualities, like a certain person not so black as he is painted, for he tells us "the British oysters are the best in all the world." We do not need Pliny to tell us this. Moreover, Julius Cæsar dedicated a breastplate of English pearls in the Temple of Venus. He tells us that Britain has lead and tin in abundance, that amber trickles down the trees, and that the natives knew the use of marle in agriculture. He does not condescend to notice the Scots, and with reason, if Gibbon tells the truth, that the Romans fled in terror from a country of lakes and blue mists, and naked savages scuttling along the hills.

> "A foe from abroad or a tyrant at home
> Could never thy ardour restrain;
> The invisible bands of Imperial Rome
> Essayed thy proud spirit in vain."

But this is not the 30th of November. Pliny tells us of a race of creatures which live upon smells—I mean perfumes aromatic—for anything else decimates the tribe. Rome with its *cloaca maxima* must have been their charnel-house. This is against a modern theory that all perfumes of every description are injurious.

"After long drought, after it beginneth to rain, the earth will send up a vapour and exhalation so heavenly and divine as no perfume is comparable to it"—what Solomon calls "the smell of Lebanon." We had a long drought in India this year before the rains came. At many a hill station after a first shower the languid denizen, as he stepped out in a glint of sunshine, must have sniffed up an exquisite perfume, and revelled in it as much as did the nose wiseacres of Pliny.

> "Why comes this fragrance on the summer breeze,
> The blended tribute of ten thousand flowers?"

The blended tribute of ten thousand flowers? The answer of scientific men is that the perfume of all the flowers now dead and buried has been stored up in the earth, and bursts forth after the pattering of the first shower.

There is a story told in one of the American books, published by David Douglas, how the author came to England for the express purpose of hearing the nightingale. It was late in the spring, and he only managed it by the merest chance, by staying out all night in some solitary part of the South of England. He was happy, packed up his traps and set off at once for America. Had he gone to the Riviera in May, he would have fallen on his feet. Passing through a dense forest at midnight, and in bright moonlight, I never heard such exquisite melody. The woods were perfectly vocal. Pliny when he went to Spain may have passed this way and had a similar experience. This is what he writes:—"Nightingales sing fifteen days. There is not a pipe or instrument in the world, devised with all the art and cunning of man, so exquisitely as possibly might be, that can afford more musique than this pretie bird doth, out of that little throat of her's."

Pliny's Rome of 1,300,000 inhabitants and its forty Triumphal Arches was not the Rome we see nowadays. She was then in a blaze of glory (or what the world calls glory), Mistress of the World, and rioting on the plunder of 100 provinces. Neither was it the Rome of the Republic, when frugality, self-denial, and valour were conspicuous virtues. It was then the wedding ring was of iron, and that the motto for dinner was "one dish and no more," and that the gods were as well pleased with the offering of a little cake with salt thereon as with the slaughter of 100 oxen. It was then that Cincinnatus, driving the plough, and covered with mud and dust, was offered the Dictatorship. The question has been asked if men in Greece and Rome had statues during their lifetime, and Pliny answers it. The winners at the Olympian Games had them,

Julius Cæsar and Varro, also Suffelia, a lady, "for that she had frankly conferred on the people of Rome a piece of meadow ground lying under (*sic*) the Tiber, which was her own free land."

(6.) INDIAN NOTES ON THE CRUSADES.

WHAT do the Crusades teach us about India? They tell us that "Indian linen was well-known in Egypt at the time of Saint Louis' Expedition (1250). William of Tyre speaks of the Indian traffic across the Isthmus of Suez. Saladin's forces were drawn (so he says) from all Asia, from the Tigris, and as far as India, and in his letter to Frederick Barbarossa he styles himself "Lord of the Land of India and its Dependencies." And elsewhere that he carried his sovereignty to "the centre of India Citerior," where-ever that may be. Saladin was a Kurd, born on the Tigris, and he died at Damascus in 1192, aged 57. I suppose his lordship over India was a figure of speech, even as Barbarossa claimed the "two Ethiopias" (Red Sea and the Persian Gulf).

We are all interested in the Old Man of the Mountain whose successors are with us in Bombay. When Saint Louis was in Acre he received an Ambassador from the Old Man of the Mountain with the extraordinary present of his shirt, with this explanation: "Our Lord informs you that as the shirt is worn nearest the body, he sends you his shirt, a symbol that you are the King for whom he has the greatest affection. A gold ring also with his name engraven on it with which he espouses you. Also an elephant of crystal set in amber with a border of gold." It is also added that when the box which contained these presents was opened a splendid perfume filled the room. The Ambassador left, and returned in fifteen days, so this Old Man of the Mountain must have had his dwelling-place somewhere up in the Lebanon.

The explanation of this is that there were three Dais or Priors of the Chief of the Hashisheen, whose place was Alamut in Persia. One of them had Syria, who (everything in these days being fair in love and in war) slew Count Raymond of Tripoli and Conrad of Montserrat during the Crusades. It was the Prior of this region no doubt who made love to Saint Louis.

It is a curious circumstance that no Scotsman is mentioned in either Richard of Devizes' Account of the third Crusade (1189) or in Joinville's Account of the Crusade of Saint Louis (1247). Probably there were some Scotsmen among the 12,000 Northmen, said to be Danes and Frisons, who arrived in 1189 at Acre, "men inured by labour to the rigours of the North, large limbs, invincible minds, and devout fervour for the faith." Typical Scotsmen! When Acre was taken (1193) hardly one hundred survived. Under 1192, Richard says York abounds in Scots, "vile and faithless men, or rather rascals." Du Cange remarks: "There is scarcely a kingdom where great numbers of Scots are not to be found." Probably an explanation of the absence of Scotsmen among the Crusaders may be found in Sir Walter Scott's writings.

Richard says that the "Natives of Syria were astonished at the English, who devoured three times the bread and one hundred-fold more wine than the Gentiles." Elsewhere he adds: "Fresh eels without wine are bad for digestion"—also A.D. 1191.

The army remained outside the walls of Joppa and refreshed themselves with abundance of fruits, figs, grapes, pomegranates, and citrons produced by the country round." There is no mention of oranges, so we may conclude that the famous orange groves of Joppa, now the admiration of every tourist, were not then in existence.

I am afraid the Crusades did not always create honour and chivalry. What about the 2,700 hostages of the Turkish army whom Richard ordered to be hanged at Acre? And hanged they were, "as they deserved to be in the sight of God and man" is the record. And this is prefaced by these memorable words: "Crossed the River of Acre in the name of the Lord." I read that at Acre the English beheaded all Saladin's messengers except one man; that our women dragged the Turks by the hair of the head and beheaded them; that at Messina the victors carried off their noblest women; that in 1192 Richard, against the clearest treaty stipulations, attacked a caravan travelling from Egypt to Damascus, captured 4,700 camels and slew 1,700 Turks of whom it is recorded "a boy might have killed ten of them."

The Crusaders defended themselves by the convenient doctrine that "it was right that art should overreach art, and that the treachery of the tyrant should be deceived by its own example." Was not this Clive's doctrine on the Nuncomar business? So I do not wonder that after this the Saracens put their sick prisoners to death in the galleys, and threw their bodies into the sea, dragged the dying pilgrim from his litter and made an end of him, or that the Crusaders met with French and Syrian slaves working in the streets of Jerusalem.

Here is an innocent relation:

"Our men caught a fisherman with Greek fire sadly mangled, and then decapitated him."

"Two of the Turkish ships from Alexandria dashed on the rocks; most of the men on board perished, amid the shouts and laughter of the Christians, who beheaded some of them who were cast on shore by the fury of the waves." Not very Christian conduct, I think.

"Found twenty Saracens sowing barley and took them prisoners to Askelon." This does not look chivalrous. If we wish to see conspicuous instances of chivalry we must go to the Saracens. "When the Christians were in Jerusalem several Turks came to Saladin to kill them and take vengeance, but he would not allow them." "The Saracens took off my coat of mail, and from pity seeing me so very ill, they flung over me one of my own scarlet coverlets lined with miniver, which my lady mother had given me, bade me be comforted, that he would give me something to drink that would cure me in two days. This he did, and I was soon well."

Chivalry and the Crusades go together, so we are often told. The besiegers are in want of earth, and a woman throws her body in to fill up the gap. It would have been chivalry in a man to prevent her and to take her place. During a siege at Ontala, in Rajasthan, in Jehangier's time an elephant refused to push at a spiked gate, when a Rajpoot Chief placed his body between it and the gate, when the elephant at once broke it open and passed in over the body of the Chief. There are more instances of genuine chivalry in Tod's *Rajasthan* than in all the books of the Crusades I have read. Louis leaps into the sea at Damietta and advances sword in hand to encounter the enemy on shore. Richard leaps into the sea at Joppa and his hosts follow him through the waves. Did not our meanest soldiers do the same at Aboukir?

Richard came to a valley and, looking up, in the distance he beheld Jerusalem, the only glimpse he ever got of it. There was not much chivalry in this. He had just pierced one of the enemy and cast him dying from his horse.

The Bishop of Salisbury, in his interview with Saladin, gave forth some words of ancient chivalry, and did not forget that he was an Englishman. "In short, my Lord, in my humble opinion, if any man hating your Majesty's sins were to bring your virtues into comparison with those of King Richard, and were to take both of you together, there would not be two other men in the world that could compete with you."

"Saladin replied that he had such an exalted opinion of King Richard's honour, magnanimity, and general excellence that he would rather lose his dominions to him than to any other king, always supposing he was to lose his dominions at all."

No one who had not been in the East could have written the following:—

"Sir Geoffrey de Sergines defended the king as a faithful servant does the cup of his master from flies." (Joinville.)

Or this exquisite simile:

"The Turks are like the fly, which, if you drive it away will go, but when you cease, it will return; as long as you pursue it, it will fly, but it reappears the moment you desist." (Richard of Devizes.)

If the Crusades quickened religious life it was certainly not among the Crusaders.

1190.—"At Cæsarea the Archbishop of Canterbury, when he saw the army given to drinking, women, and dice, prayed he might be released of this life, and in fifteen days died of fever."

1250.—Louis on his passage home bewailed the death of his brother, the Count d'Artois, and asked what had become of his other brother, Count d'Anjou. He found him playing at dice, and flung the dice and tables into the sea, and all the money that lay on the tables after them.

Piety was at a discount even among the Templars. Joinville gave three hundred and sixty livres to the Master to keep for him. When he some time afterwards asked for his money, the Master said he did not know him, and did not owe him anything. "You seem to insinuate that our brotherhood are all thieves."

"In future I will not trouble these monks with the keeping of my cash," is Joinville's comment.

What society was in Rome we may gather from the following:—

1254.—On leaving Acre the Legate told Joinville "I am much concerned and grieved at my heart that I should be forced to quit such good and religious companions to return among such a set of wretches as the Court of Rome consists of."

Saladin's name was Joseph. Some of us know Joseph's Well in Cairo, perhaps the deepest artificial well in the world. The average globe-trotter mistakes the name for Joseph the Patriarch. It was, however, one of the great works constructed by Yusef Saladin. His parents were not noble, but he was not of obscure or plebeian birth. When he served under Nuradin, Sultan of Damascus, a curious circumstance took place. He set out on a visit to Edfrid of Tours, the illustrious Prince of Palestine, and was there mantled, and after the manner of the Franks received from him the belt of knighthood. Once, at Easter, he saw in the Church of the Sepulchre the Holy Fire, but was convinced it was a fraud.

Richard, we read, was never overwhelmed with adversity. He was tall of stature, graceful in figure, his hair between red and auburn, his limbs were straight and flexible, his arms rather long (a great endowment all over the East, and elsewhere —witness Rob Roy), and not to be matched for wielding the sword or striking with it, and his long legs suited to the rest of his frame, while his appearance was commanding, and his manners and habits suitable.

Joinville writes of St. Louis: "I assure you I never saw so

handsome a man under arms. He was taller than any of his troop by the shoulders; and his helmet, which was gilded, was handsomely placed on his head, and he bore a German sword in his hand.

"The good King performed that day the most gallant deeds that I ever saw in any battle. It is said that had it not been for his personal exertions, his whole army would have been destroyed.

"His mother taught him to believe in God, and to love and fear Him in his youth; and he has ever since that time lived a virtuous and holy life.

"He was so weakened by the Crusade that on his return he could not support the weight of his armour, nor remain long on horseback. I was once forced to carry him in my arms."

These are the "three mighty men of the Crusades." Richard the Lion resembled Akbar and Jehangier in this, that he did not allow the operations of war to interfere with the pleasures of the chase. If Baber hunted rhinoceros on his way to Lahore (1526), and Akbar elephants on his way to Mandu (1618), Richard did not scorn pig-sticking in Palestine (1192). On one occasion he met with a huge wild boar. Richard was on horseback; his lance broke, when Richard foiled the charge of the boar by jumping over his back. Returning to his bristly foe, brandishing his sword, he polished him off with the same weapon. At Joppa he often went out hawking.

Albert of Aix records that at Antiochetta, Duke Godfrey was once so severely wounded by a bear that he took several months to recover.

Close to Cæsarea was the "River of Crocodiles." Two soldiers were devoured by them. "That ancient river—the River Kishon," is now, we believe, the only habitat of this beast in Syria.

Men kept close to their religions in those days, and did not trouble themselves with the authorship of the last chapters of Deuteronomy. Louis was of opinion that no one, however learned and acute a theologian he might be, ought to dispute with the Jews. "Some of our men denied the faith. I told the Admiral I did not believe them."

Saladin had declared that a Christian was never known to be a good Pagan, nor a good Saracen a Christian. His doctrine was evidently that of Akbar: "Your religion is good for you, my religion is good for me"; or that of Yusef Adil Khan, of Bijapur (1502): "My faith for myself, your faith for yourself."

Saint Louis, as one would expect, nailed his colours to the mast, when offered his life by recanting. He was to take an oath, that if he broke his word, he was to spit upon the cross and trample it under foot. The King refused, and said he would rather die a Christian than live under the anger of God, His blessed Mother, and the Saints.

The tourist of to-day may visit Messina, Malta, and Rhodes without a passing thought on the Crusades. Yet these were once the bulwarks of Christendom. Sunrise or afterglow on the Nile no longer awakens memories of Damietta and Rosetta, or the heroism of Saint Louis.

The tourist may indeed sleep in Ramleh and Jaffa, or bivouac at Tiberias, without a single reminder of them. Even at the Holy Sepulchre, where he is shown by the monks the sword and spurs of Godfrey, the interest is momentary, for a greater than he dominates the Holy Land and the Holy Sepulchre. It is on the field of Hattim, the Flodden of the Crusaders, where all the Templars bit the dust; or in Jerusalem wreathed in snow, amid cold and ice, that you begin to realise the sufferings of the Crusaders; or on a wild night, when your tent is blown down, and amid torrents of rain and peals of thunder your outlook is the Sea of Galilee, streaked with flashes of the lightning of heaven, that you drink in the memory of the Crusades—morion, hauberk, and glittering spear, of the 100,000 that broke in a great wave on the shores of Syria, and 14,000 of the Crusaders were sold into slavery; or spending a day in Saladin's great Castle of Banias (Subeibeh), on the high road to Damascus. There, alone, after a toilsome climb, first among the stunted oaks of Basan, then among rocks that bristle like Edur or the crags of Torna, you reach an eyrie, where from gigantic masonry you can look far and wide over the Syrian Plain: it is there you first drink in memories of Richard and Saladin, and the clashing of the swords that shook the world.

(7.) MAHRATTA BALLADS, AND OTHERS.*

THERE are two kinds of ballads. First, there are those which were sung or recited by the minstrels themselves in barons' halls in Europe, or around camp fires or *Kuthas* in the old Dekhan days in the land we live in. These are the genuine article. Such is *Chevy Chace*, eulogised by Addison, and which Ben Jonson said he would rather have written than all his works. The second are imitations—such as Macaulay's *Lays*, or Scott's *Lay of the Last Minstrel*, works of great genius—of what might, could, or should have been the ballads at the time and place laid under contribution, which may be termed literary ballads. Such genuine remains as exist of the first kind are the greatest of literary treasures, for you may annex Homer if you like as the first and greatest ballad-singer. In all lands, and among all peoples, a good ballad is the life blood of a nation, whose spirit it bodies forth, refines, purifies, exalts it; lifts it out of itself; animates to devotion in love and heroism and war. The ballad, pure and simple, is national, patriotic, provincial if you will; and it is the people's property and heirloom, and belongs to the men and women of that nation whose feelings it represents, for they alone can sound its depths and enter "into the spirit thereof." Hence, in some such words Fletcher of Saltoun said, "Let me make the songs of a nation, and let who will make its laws." I suppose that every country in Europe has been ransacked and its ballads translated and imitated. Lockhart's *Spanish Ballads*, once in great request, have been followed by those of every country from the White Sea to Cape Matapan. Of all kinds of translation (and the remark applies in some degree to the imitation), I should consider that of ballad poetry the most difficult. The translator must think as the ballad-monger, and for the time being heave himself among the tumults and episodes that gave them birth, and dare, fight and love as the men and women of the time fought and loved. Try your hand

* *Ballads of the Mahrattas.* By Harry Arbuthnot Acworth, H.M. Indian Civil Service. London: Longmans, Green and Co., 1894.

at the reverse operation, by translating *Chevy Chace* into Màhratta and reciting it before a Dekhani audience. "I never heard this old song that I found not my heart more moved than with a trumpet," said Sir Philip Sidney. *Chevy Chace* on the Moti Mula, I fear, would be a voice crying in the wilderness, no more than the bleating of a sheep borne and carried away by the wind. The old Scotch crusader, wandering into the camp of the Moslem, heard a woman's voice lilting "Oh, Bothwell bank, thou bloomest fair." He was touched to the heart. It would have fallen flat on Raymond of Toulouse, or Godfrey de Bouillon. It is at best a borrowed interest that you and I can have in the wars of the Calmuck or the loves of the Troubadour. And yet there are few countries (I make bold to say that there are none in Asia) that offer such a home for ballad poetry as the Dekhan. For what are the elements of which the ballads of all countries consist? Courage, chivalry, and courtesy. And did they not exist in the country before a single Englishman had planted his foot on the soil thereof? The land is full of castles and brimful of romance. No captive of our nation was ever worried to death, no mine sprung upon us, as on the Hooghly or at Kabul. In all my wanderings over the Dekhan, I have never come across a dungeon in which one Englishman was the worse for the wear; but I have read of our delegates being tenderly kept during war and restored to their families when peace was concluded. I have read of a mailed and dusky Mahratta bending over the body of a dead warrior from the Caledonian hills, and on the bleak uplands of Indryana revive that memory of Otterburn: "He took the dead man by the hand." Of Stewart of Karli, I have often wondered what became of the ballad sung in his honour long years after his death in 1778. I can read in *Panipat* the overwhelming catastrophe of Flodden, when—

> "The flowers of the forest were a' weed awa'."

The man who executed the son of Sivaji at Tulapore was Aurungzebe. There you have jealousy cruel as the grave, while love strong as death comes out in Aurungzebe's daughter, and her affectionate care of the dead man's little son, a captive of war in the sack of Raighur. There is an instance in the

Jacobite wars of a combatant in each army making over to the other the care of the family to him who should survive. The same, I think, took place just before the Battle of Kirkee, between Ford and Moro Dixit. Now all these are splendid subjects for the literary ballad, and the Raighur incident was worthily commemorated in the *Pioneer* some years ago.

Assaye, by John Leyden, is a splendid specimen of the literary ballad :—

"But when we first encounter'd man to man,
Such odds came never on
Against Greece at Marathon,
When they shook the Persian throne
'Mid the old barbaric pomp of Ispahan."
(1803.)

Even from such a trifle as the snatch with which the groom outside Tanna Jail beguiled the time while he awaited the escape of Trimbukji, Heber could extract the golden grain :—

"Behind the bush, the bowmen hide
The horse beneath the tree,
Where shall I find a knight will ride
The jungle paths with me?
There are five and fifty coursers there,
And four and fifty men;
When the fifty-fifth shall mount his steed
The Deccan thrives again."
(1826.)

It might have been a stratagem on the Scottish Border, so complete a similarity of character and incident does a resemblance of habit and circumstances produce among mankind.

And it would be difficult to exceed in beauty this, from *The Old Pindarry*, by Sir Alfred Lyall, 1889 :—

"My father was an Afghan and came from Kandahar,
He rode with Nawab Amir Khan in the old Mahratta war;
From the Deccan to the Himalay five hundred of our clan
They ask no leave from prince or chief as they swept through Hindostan.
Then the streak of the pearly dawn—the flash of a sentinel's gun,
The gallop and glint of horsemen, who wheeled in the level sun,
The shots in the clear still morning, the white smoke's eddying wreath—
Is this the same land that I live in, the dull dank air that I breathe?"

The Song of Sivaji (1894), Levett-Yeats, has good lines:—

"I have lifted my lance point up to heaven
And sworn an oath to the sky,
I have prayed to the sign of the Serpent God
That stands by the river of Wai;
And the Guru his sacred hands hath laid,
With a muttered spell, on my long straight blade."

And the last lines—

"In a moon we stall
Our Dekhani steeds in the Taj Mahal."

These are snatches from the finest literary ballads relating to India that recur to our memory at the moment. Burns, who had an intense admiration of Scottish ballads, pinned his faith to that masterpiece *Tullochgorum.* It points a moral useful enough in India in 1895:—

"Let Whig and Tory all agree,
Whig and Tory, Whig and Tory,
Whig and Tory all agree,
To drop their whig-ma-leerie.
Let Whig and Tory all agree
To spend the night in mirth and glee,
And cheerful sing alang wi' me,
The Reel of Tullochgorum."

From this you will see that *Tullochgorum* is a reel, but it is a ballad also. The name is claimed by the greatest of the Grants. I suppose the name of Field-Marshal Sir Patrick Grant is a household word in many quarters in the North-West. *Ætat.* 90, hale and hearty, the writer vouches for the incident. In the autumn of 1894 he was the honoured guest of Lady S—— at G—— Castle. The workmen thereabouts, much exercised as to who this prehistoric individual could be, as they saw him walking about, a wag allayed their curiosity by telling them he was the Shah of Persia. On hearing this incident told after dinner he exclaimed:—"By George, I'm a much better man than the Shah of Persia. I'm Grant of Tullochgorum." An excellent translation into Latin was given some years ago of *Roy's Wife of Aldivalloch,* by Dr. Lindsay Alexander, one of the Bible Revisers at Westminster. This little nonsense began,

"Rubor uxor Aldivalloch." The late Professor Blackie some few years back, when in Cairo, recited to a group of wandering Arabs the original with mighty fervour. The Sheikhs stroked their beards, for to them it could only be "sound and fury, signifying nothing."

The Mahratta ballads are ten in number.* Sivaji is of 1,327 lines, Holkar's Raid sixty-two, and the subjects of them are the most renowned events in Mahratta history. The importance of Sivaji as the consolidator of this dominion and the idol of his nation is verified in the fact that one-half of their contents describe Sivaji's murder of Afzal Khan, and his general's capture of Singhur. Panipat, Holkar's Raid and the Battle of Kirkee are other subjects dealt with. These ballads cannot fail to interest all Anglo-Indian readers, specially those whose ears are attuned to the place-names of the Dekhan, and have made themselves familiar with such localities as are immortalised in its history. The ballads must have been translated with great care and close application, and could not have been written unless the translator was deeply imbued with the subject, had prepared himself for the work by a long course of study, and many peregrinations among the peoples and the places which are the localities of the ballads, and had furnished his mind with Mahratta history from its commencement to its close. The manners and customs of the people, their eating and drinking, dice-playing and other amusement, the worship of their gods, their art of war, siege and escalade, dash and enthusiasm as they scoured the country on their barbs, attack and defence, and how cheaply human life was held, the interior of their houses, from Raja's palace to Koonbie's hut, their dress, gear of men and horses, their weapons of war, their talk among themselves, and their talk fights with their opponents, all pass before us. The Mahratta was a bloody and deceitful man, as was our own ancestor some centuries ago, and the "raw head and bloody bones" are as much in evidence here as, say, in the Scotland of the Middle Ages. In the Mahratta ballad of Tanaji Maloosre the popular belief that a large lizard, or iguana, pulled up a rope behind it, which enabled the

* Ayton's Scottish Ballads are 130, in two small volumes.

assailants to escalade the bastions of Singhur, is worked up in the narrative. The reader is incredulous, like the audience at Malcolm's dinner party hearing for the first time of the horses of the Dekhan eating sheep's head. London is at present full of performing horses, bears, goats, dogs and monkeys. Even ants and fleas are beckoned by their keeper and come at his call. So what standard of education a Dekhani lizard might reach under skilful and persistent tuition it is hard to say. We believe every word of it. No myth is this faithful batrachian.

"There are more things in heaven and earth, Horatio, than are dreamed in your philosophy." If Omar Khayyám makes—

> "The lion and the lizard keep
> Their court where Jamshid gloried and drank deep,"

there can be no reason why the lizard should not be the first to enter Singhur, the Lion's Den—

> "Coil'd in a box his lizard lies,
> Oft tried and prov'd in like emprise;
> The docile beast was brought, her head
> Was deck'd with pearls and pigments red.
> The chief before her bent and pray'd,
> Now as before, to give him aid:
> A chain of iron strong was bound
> And firmly clamped her midst around;
> Her master bade her mount, and she
> His hest obeyed right dexterously."

One of the greatest difficulties in the way of the translator of Mahratta ballads, we have come to think, are their proper names, which to Northern ears do not lend themselves readily to the flow of English versification or the exigencies of rhythm, and still less of rhyme. Mahableshwur does not strike us as a word of "linked sweetness long drawn out." Burr and Elphinstone seem to defy all prosody; while from Gungaram and Trimbukji, to ears untuned to Dekhani or Konkani symphonies, it must be difficult to snatch a strophe or steal a sentiment. The reply, of course, is that sweet sounds are the patrimony of no country; and that Scotland itself is full of names which vex the soul and harass the measure of even a Scotch poet. Corrievreckan, Auchtermuchty, Tobermory, seem formidable enough. When Burns met with such amorphous names he hesitated for a moment, threw himself into the breach, and coupled Ecclefechan (Carlyle's birth-place) with "laigh ane," or transmogrified by his plastic art Edinburgh into Edina, and Kirkcudbright into "Whiskey Jean"!

I have no doubt that many people will turn aside from the dryasdust of Indian historians to the spirited lines of our author, which, though not always on a level with the majestic simplicity of the ancient ballad, yet——. But a voice from the Editor, and perhaps the translator himself of the Mahratta Ballads, might warn us in the words—

> "I have done the State some service, and they know it;
> No more of that."

We have only room for one more passage. Here are the lines in which the capture of Singhur, the Lion's Den, is announced:—

> "They heard their war-cry thunder'd loud,
> They charged in one resistless crowd,
> O'erwhelmed, confused, and swept along,
> Like driftwood when the stream is strong,
> The Pathans fell, were crushed and died,
> And lost beneath the rushing tide.
> On pour the host in conquering might,
> Tear down the Mogul's ensign white,
> And o'er the fortress of their foes
> Their monarch's orange standard rose;
> And now the cannons' thunder loud
> Peal'd o'er the plain the conquest proud;
> Five times they spoke in flame and smoke,
> And Raj-ghur's distant towers awoke;
> 'Singhur is ours!' proclaimed the king,
> And bid ten guns his answer ring."

To the rest of this volume we direct the reader's attention.

(8.) BROCKEN AND OTHER SPECTRES.

"We saw the glory of Buddha from the edge of the precipice, a circular rainbow on the clouds below, and our shadow in the midst, which the pious pilgrim, kneeling on the edge with outstretched arms, takes to be Puhsien, riding upon his elephant as he came from India."—*A Summer Trip to Chinese Tibet.* Alicia Bewicke Little, in *Cornhill Magazine*, February, 1899.

THE only records of the appearance of the Brocken Spectre in India are, as far as I know—

Matheran, Bombay Presidency, 1865.
Hurrychunderghur, Bombay Presidency, May 9th, 11th and 12th, 1829.
Singhur, Bombay Presidency, May 5th, 1852.
Adam's Peak, Ceylon, February 21st, 1886.

This apparition has been, as everybody knows, seen in the Hartz, Switzerland, Scotland (notably on Ben Nevis and Ben Lomond and on Ben More in 1894), and in countries as far separate as China, the Nevada, and the Loffoden Islands; while Tyndall, Huxley, Scoresby, and about thirty others have recorded their observations on what may still be regarded as a somewhat rare phenomenon.

On May 6th, 1893, at 7 A.M., while I was standing at the end of Louisa Point, on the hill station of Matheran, near Bombay, 2,600 feet above sea-level, the companion who accompanied me suddenly called my attention to something he had seen, and looking round in the direction to which he pointed, I saw a white cloud with the semblance of a human being sketched upon it.

"What's that?" I said, to which question the reply came, "That's yourself."

I took off my hat to the figure, which act of courtesy was returned by the spectre with marvellous celerity.

My friend now came nearer, when there were two of us in perspective. Neither of us was flattered. It was evidently a first rough copy of "dark grey men." We did not hold the mirror up to Nature; Nature held the mirror up to us. This was only her 'prentice hand. Had we waited, a *chef d'œuvre* might have been the result. But beholding what manner of men we were in this glass, we speedily went our way. I was perfectly satisfied that it was my shadow I had seen; but I had not trudged many paces homeward, when I came to the conclusion that the vision I had seen was none other than the weird "Spectre of the Brocken."

I was fortified in this belief by the recollection that about thirty years ago Dr. J. Y. Smith recorded that he had seen such a spectre, himself on horseback, of colossal proportions, crawling along the slope of the opposite hill, not very far from the place where I had witnessed the same phenomenon. At the time of our visit half a gale was blowing, and though it was quite clear of mist on the coign of vantage we had been occupying, a dense fog hung over the plains and in the valley below. The fogs on the Dekhani hills are the usual precursors of the monsoon, and they came up on the Western Ghauts, in 1893, much earlier than usual. The great heat on the plains condenses, and ascends in the form of mist. On this morning the gorge which lay beneath us, between Louisa Point and Prabhul Hill, was chock-full of mist—a perfect sea of vapour driving up in billowy masses, fighting with wind and sun, while across the gulf, as if at the nether end of an Arctic Fiord, the basaltic peak, with which Prabhul is buttressed, stood out in bold relief as black as night.

In these spectral displays the figures are sometimes colossal and sometimes of natural size. Sometimes the halo encircles the head only of the individual or group of figures. The circle which we saw was apparently about twelve feet in diameter, and the figures projected on its disc about eight feet high, as if on the slide of a magic lantern; or gigantic silhouettes of dark-grey, leaden-coloured, somewhat blurred and smudged at the edges, and apparently as near to us as if we had been looking at a big picture in the Royal Academy. Since my return from these hills I have been making inquiries regarding my aerial visitant. I learned first of all that he was a rare creature You could scarcely call him a "familiar spirit," though his evolution was from ourselves. When the Ettrick Shepherd came in sight of a similar manifestation, he instinctively bowed to him as he would to a distinguished stranger.

"I arose and made him a most graceful bow, which he returned at the same moment—but such a bow for awkwardness I never saw! It was as if the Tron steeple had bowed to me."

Like Burns's Devil, he affects lonely places, precipices, and dizzy crags; but he is unlike the demon in this respect, that he hates the darkness, and everything he does is in broad daylight. He only does what you do yourself, and is not amenable to any power on earth, for neither science nor incantation can produce him.

Given certain circumstances, you can produce him by giving him yourself, and obliterate him by your departure. Bow to your *alter ego*—that's all right; but shaking hands means death.

A Moravian missionary (January, 1889) tells us what the Buddhists do on the hill Ngo Mei, China: "The people there call this spectre the living Buddha, and many in their frenzy throw themselves down the precipice into his arms, hoping to attain Nirvana." The Brocken, the highest of the Hartz mountains in Hanover, has no vested interest in him, or the Righi, Matterhorn, Wetterhorn, Snowdon, Skye, Devon, and thirty other places from Adam's Peak to the Polar regions.

Though the spectre has been seen more than once by the same person, it has never been beheld, as far as I can gather, in exactly the same place by the same individual. Adolphus Trollope, who died at the age of eighty-three, was a great traveller, and always on the outlook for it, but only saw it once. Another ascended the Brocken thirty times before he was rewarded. I suppose the spectre, goaded by his importunity and worn out of all patience, had pity on him, and also upon the present writer, after thirty years scrambling up the peaks and passes of the Western Ghauts. A sun-picture himself, I am doubtful of the spectre being a subject for photography. Those who see him are not likely to be carrying a camera. At all events, you must "first catch your hare." The picture (*Encyc. Britan.*, 9th Ed.) of one seen by Sawyer in 1877 is an exact counterpart of the one seen by us, with this difference, that ours had a perfect halo—elliptical—around him, of prismatic colours, instead of the wobbly and irregular cincture we have in this big book.

I am asked if anyone has ever seen a perfectly circular rainbow, and am answered by the same unimpeachable authority, that when seen from the mast of a ship, or from the top of a mountain, and beneath you, rainbows are always circular.

The Brocken is 3,300 feet high, and from the earliest authentic history has been regarded as the seat of the marvellous and the chosen home of the spectre. Amid huge blocks of granite you have the sorcerer's chair, the sorcerer's altar, the magic well, and an anemone, called the sorcerer's flower.

When Henry Irving takes you, in that great masterpiece of *Faust*, to the Walpurgis Dance, the scene is laid in the Brocken, where precipices are convenient:—

> "Firmly seize
> The old projections of the ribbed rock,
> Else it will blow you down into the chasm
> Yawning below us like a sepulchre."

Sir Walter Scott does not seem to have made use of this harmless but robust wraith. His imagination transcends it in *Marmion*:—

> "A royal city; tower and spire
> Reddened the midnight sky with fire,
> And shouting crews her navy bore
> Triumphant to the victor's shore."

It was perhaps a mirage, like Josephus's "chariots full of armed men, which traversed the clouds" when Titus besieged Jerusalem, or like John Knox's "battles arrayed, two armies being seen in the firmament by men of judgment and credit," or as Milton hath it—

> "War appears
> Waged in the troubled sky, and armies rush
> To battle in the clouds."

Sir David Brewster, in 1832, addressed to Scott a letter giving him a full account of the Brocken and other manifestations. Did it come too late? Scott died in 1832. Or did

Brewster, by his skilful analysis of the creature reducing it to its original elements, throw it outside the pale of romance, and capture the spectre in the interests of science? "These spectres," he says, "are mere shadows of the observer, projected on dense vapour or thin fleecy clouds, which have the power of reflecting much light. They are seen most frequently at sunrise, because it is at that time the vapours and clouds necessary for their production are most likely to be generated, and they can only be seen when the sun is throwing her rays horizontally, because the shadow of the observer would be thrown either up in the air or down upon the ground."

Another authority gives the usual concomitants:—

"The observer in bright sunshine, the shadow on fog blown up from below; wind strong, with a sharp drop on the ground in front."*

All these conditions were present in May, 1893, and no other ingredients are necessary. But, even had you the sun in one hand and the clouds and winds in the other, you would brew in vain, and could not produce a Brocken Spectre from the broth in your Witches' Cauldron. Nature always keeps some secret to herself to defy the ingenuity of man, and the concatenation of circumstances, necessary to produce this spectre, has yet to be discovered.

Indeed, the elements are far from prodigal in exhibitions of this sort, and the scientific seeker stands a poor chance; for almost in every instance in which it has been witnessed it has been by the accident of an accident. What is often denied to the philosopher or the meteorologist is vouchsafed to the poor wayfarer—hewer of wood or drawer of water—crawling along some solitary hillside on a misty and disagreeable morning, and is retained in the memory for a lifetime.

For anything we know to the contrary, this spectre in the early ages of the world may have given birth to the Hindoo deities on the "Abode of Snow," or have peopled Olympus with the gods of Greece, for it is the nature of man to place

* Henry Thorpe on Brocken Spectres.

the dwelling-place of his god on a high mountain. But there is room for any amount of speculation here. Is this spectre "the dread mother" of Girnar, that mysterious gnome of the Kalka peak, which conveys the traveller to his doom? Were not the *jinns* of the Arabian Desert humanlike and of enormous size? The bow rested on Ararat, and it is still the *jinn's* abode according to the *vulgus*, and Elphinstone relates that the Afghans in the solitude of their mountains localize a creature which they represent as a gigantic and frightful spectre. Even the spectres of Ossianic heroes may be nothing but fantastic images thrown upon mountain fogs in the Land of the Mist. You may even if you like take the Ghost of Romulus seen by Julius Procolus, for he, too, is among the Alban Hills. The figure is colossal, wears a Roman toga, and is in the open air. As he himself is decked in the same robe, can you doubt that it is his own shadow which he sees of exaggerated proportions?

I am convinced that one-tenth of the appearances of the so-called Spectre of the Brocken has never been reported, and that among the aborigines of every country its manifestation was followed by the deepest awe and silence on the part of the beholder. Least said, soonest mended. Of such luckless individual the old Scotch poet would say—

> "He gapit wide
> But naething spak'."

And I have no doubt this is the reason that we have no record of its existence until within a hundred years of our own time. The Seer buried the secret in his bosom, and it descended with him to the tomb.

Crosses are more difficult of explanation. The cross of Constantine which he saw on his march against Maxentius (A.D. 313) led to his conversion to Christianity, and, incidentally, to that of the Eastern Empire. The cross of Albuquerque was the omen which led the Portuguese to their dominion in India.

Robertson of Brighton was great on sunsets, and the spectral phenomena of the skies, and I note that in April, 1852, a perfect cross was seen by him in the heavens at Brighton. And another Robertson, he of Irvine, whose praise is now in all the Northern churches, must be mentioned; his *tour de force* as poet and orator was "the rainbow round the throne," and his words thereon were a perfect coruscation of genius. Whymper's vision is the saddest of all. "We frequently looked, but in vain, for traces of our unfortunate companions. When, lo! a mighty arch appeared rising above the Lyskamm high in the sky. Pale, colourless, and noiseless, but perfectly sharp and defined, except where it was lost in the clouds, this unearthly apparition seemed like a vision from another world; and almost appalled we watched with amazement the gradual development of two vast crosses, one on either side. . . . But our movements had no effect upon it."*

As to the two great visions of past history, that of Constantine and Albuquerque, either of these two "heroes of the nations" had only to stretch out his arms in presence of the spectre, and a shadowy colossal cross would be the result. Each would see his own shadow converted into the symbol of the faith. The Brighton cross may belong to the same category. Whymper's defies solution on our hypothesis, for he says expressly, "Our movements had no effect upon it."

May not the rainbow which has so often been seen to surround this so-called spectre be the origin of the nimbus in painting and sculpture—a symbol of power and authority, supernatural or divine? Some wanderer in ages long before the Christian era, we will suppose, caught sight of the spectre encircled by a prismatic halo, and so it travels down through all the ages, as in Sakya Muni graven on stone under the Buddhi Tree, in a Greek Divinity, in a Roman Emperor deceased, in Byzantine Painting, in Renaissance and Holy Family. Nay, even Akbar has his portrait taken with the divine aureola round his head, as if to symbolize his title to deification or apotheosis.

---

* *Scrambles Among the Alps in the Years* 1860–69. By Edward Whymper: London, 1871.

I have seen an island-city, with domes and minarets, make its appearance at midday in the centre of Lake Mareotis; a sheet of water with waves breaking on the shore in the deserts of Sindh where water there was none; phantom ships in the sky over the Bitter Lakes; a P. and O. steamer stopped in the grey of the morning in the Red Sea by the appearance of an enchanted island fringed with palms, as in Fata Morgana, and I fancy every Eastern traveller has similar experiences.